Structural Equation Modeling
With AMOS
Basic Concepts, Applications, and Programming

Multivariate Applications Book Series

The Multivariate Applications book series was developed to encourage the use of rigorous methodology in the study of meaningful scientific issues, and to describe the applications in easy to understand language. The series is sponsored by the Society of Multivariate Experimental Psychology, and welcomes methodological applications from a variety of disciplines, such as psychology, public health, sociology, education, and business. Books can be single authored, multiple authored, or edited. The ideal book for this series would take on one of several approaches: demonstrate the application of a variety of multivariate methods to a single, major area of research; describe a methodological procedure or framework that could be applied to a variety of research areas; or present a variety of perspectives on a controversial topic of interest to applied researchers.

There are currently six books in the series:

- *What if There Were No Significance Tests?*, co-edited by Lisa L. Harlow, Stanley A. Mulaik, and James H. Steiger (1997).
- *Structural Equation Modeling With LISREL, PRELIS, and SIMPLIS: Basic Concepts, Applications, and Programming*, by Barbara M. Byrne (1998).
- *Multivariate Applications Is Substance Use Research: New Methods for New Questions*, co- edited by Jennifer S. Rose, Laurie Chassin, Clark C. Presson, and Steven J. Sherman (2000).
- *Item Response Theory for Psychologists*, co-authored by Susan Embretson and Steve Reise (2000).
- *Structural Equation Modeling With AMOS: Basic Concepts, Applications, and Programming*, by Barbara M. Byrne (2001).
- *Modeling Intraindividual Variability With Repeated Measures Data: Methods and Applications*, co-edited by D. S. Moskowitz and Scott L. Hershberger (2001).

Interested persons should contact the editor, Lisa Harlow, at the University of Rhode Island, Department of Psychology, 10 Chafee Road, Suite 8, Kingston, RI 02881-0808; Phone: (401) 874-4242; Fax: (401) 874-2157; or e-mail: LHarlow@uri.edu. Information may also be obtained from one of the editorial board members: Leona Aiken (Arizona State University), Gwyneth Boodoo (Educational Testing Service), Barbara M. Byrne (University of Ottawa), Scott Maxwell (University of Notre Dame), David Rindskopf (City University of New York), or Steve West (Arizona State University).

Structural Equation Modeling
With AMOS
Basic Concepts, Applications, and Programming

Barbara M. Byrne
University of Ottawa

LAWRENCE ERLBAUM ASSOCIATES, PUBLISHERS

2001   MAHWAH, NEW JERSEY   LONDON

Lawrence Erlbaum Associates, Inc., Publishers
10 Industrial Avenue
Mahwah, New Jersey 07430

Cover design by Kathryn Houghtaling-Lacey

C 1 A Y P G
    8 9 3
  < B >

Library of Congress Cataloging-in-Publication Data

Byrne, Barbara M.
    Structural equation modeling with AMOS : basic concepts, applications, and programming / Barbara M. Byrne.
      p.   cm. — (Multivariate applications book series)
    Includes bibliographical references and index.
    ISBN 0-8058-3322-6
    I. Title. II. Series.

  QA278 .B96 2000
  519.5′35—dc21

                                 00-058753

Printed in the United States of America
10   9

Contents

Note: All data may be accessed from the LEA website (www.erlbaum.com)

Preface

❡

The intent of this book is to illustrate the ease with which various features of the AMOS 4.0 program can be implemented in addressing research questions that lend themselves to structural equation modeling (SEM). Specifically, the purposes are threefold: (a) to present a nonmathematical introduction to basic concepts associated with SEM, (b) to demonstrate basic applications of SEM using the AMOS 4.0 program, and (c) to highlight particular features of AMOS 4.0 that address important caveats related to SEM analyses.

This book is intended *neither* as a text on the topic of SEM, *nor* as a comprehensive review of the many statistical and graphical functions available in the AMOS 4.0 program. Rather, the aim is to provide a practical guide to SEM using the AMOS approach. As such, the reader is walked through a diversity of SEM applications that include: analysis of both factor analytic and full latent variable models, implementation of the maximum likelihood approach to bootstrapping, and imputation of missing values using a *direct*, rather than the more commonly used *indirect* approach. Accompanying these applications, throughout the book, are fully illustrated examples of a plethora of graphical features made available by the program. Ideally, this volume serves best as a companion book to the AMOS 4.0 user's guide (Arbuckle & Wothke, 1999), as well as to any statistics textbook devoted to the topic of SEM.

The book is divided into four major parts; Part I comprises two introductory chapters. In chapter 1, I introduce the fundamental concepts underlying the SEM methodology. Chapter 2 focuses solely on the AMOS 4.0 program. Here, I detail the key elements associated with the two substantially different interfaces available to users: a graphical interface (AMOS Graphics) by which models are specified directly from a path diagram, and an equation-based interface (AMOS Basic) by which models are specified via equation statements in a format that resembles the traditional input file orientation.

Part II is devoted to applications involving single-group analyses; these include two first-order confirmatory factor analytic (CFA) models, one second-order CFA model, and one full latent variable model. The first-order CFA applications demonstrate testing for the validity of the theoretical structure of a construct (chap. 3) and the factorial structure of a measuring instrument (chap. 4). The second-order CFA model bears on the factorial structure of a measuring instrument (chap. 5). The final single-group application tests for the validity of an empirically derived causal structure (chap. 6).

In Part III, I present applications related to multigroup analyses. Specifically I show you how to test for measurement and structural invariance related to a measuring instrument (chap. 7), a theoretical construct (chap. 8), and a causal structure (chap. 10). Working from a somewhat different perspective, in chapter 9, I outline the basic concepts associated with latent means structures and demonstrate how to test for their invariance across groups.

Part IV comprises the final two chapters of the book and addresses critically important issues associated with SEM: the problem of nonnormal data (chap. 11) and the problem of missing data (chap. 12).

In writing a book of this nature, it was essential that I have access to a number of different data sets that lent themselves to various applications. To facilitate this need, all examples presented throughout the book are drawn from my own research; related journal references are cited for readers who may be interested in a more detailed discussion of theoretical frameworks, aspects of the methodology, and substantive issues and findings. In summary, each application in the book is accompanied by the following:

- a statement of the hypothesis to be tested
- a schematic representation of the model under study
- a full explanation bearing on related AMOS Graphics input path diagrams
- a full explanation of related AMOS Basic input files. However, because most users will likely use the AMOS graphical approach to structural modeling, only one AMOS Basic input file is described in each of chapters 4 through 10
- a full explanation and interpretation of related AMOS 4.0 text output
- the published reference from which the application was drawn
- illustrated use and function associated with a wide variety of icons and pull-down menus provided by AMOS Graphics for purposes of SEM per se, as well as other important data management tasks
- the sample covariance data matrix on which a particular application was based.

It is important to emphasize that, although all applications are based on data that are of a social/psychological nature, they could just as easily have been based on data representative of the health sciences, leisure studies, marketing, or a multitude of other disciplines; my data, then, serve only as one example of each application. Indeed, I urge you to seek out and examine similar examples as they relate to other subject areas.

Although there are now several SEM texts available, this book distinguishes itself from the rest in a number of ways. *First*, it is the only book to demonstrate, by application to actual data, a wide range of confirmatory factor analytic and latent variable models drawn from published studies, along with a detailed explanation of each input diagram (or file) and text output file. *Second*, it is the first book to incorporate applications based solely on the AMOS 4.0 program and, more specifically, to include example files based on both the AMOS Graphics and AMOS Basic interfaces. *Third*, it is the first SEM introductory book to present example applications involving the bootstrap procedure and the direct estimation of missing data values. *Fourth*, it is the first book to literally "walk" the reader through (a) both the graphical and equation-based AMOS approaches to SEM, (b) model specification, estimation, evaluation, and post hoc modification decisions and processes associated with a variety of applications, and (c) the use of numerous icons, drop-down menus, and diagrammer features associated with the graphical interface of AMOS 4.0. *Fifth*, as far as I am aware, it is the only book to make the actual data on which each application was based, available to the reader. *Finally*, the present book contains the most extensive and current description and explanation of goodness-of-fit indices to date.

Having now written three of these introductory books on the application of SEM with respect to particular programs (Byrne, 1989, 1994c, 1998), I must confess that the writing of the present book was, by far, the most challenging! In weaving together the textual, graphical, and statistical threads that form the fabric of this book, I hope that I have provided my readers with a comprehensive understanding of basic concepts and applications of SEM, as well as with an extensive working knowledge of the AMOS 4.0 program. Achievement of this goal has necessarily meant the concomitant juggling of word processing, "grabber," and statistical programs in order to produce the end result. It has been an incredible editorial journey, but one that has left me feeling truly enriched for having had this wonderful learning experience.

Acknowledgments

As with the writing of each of my other books, there are many people to whom I owe a great deal of thanks. First and foremost, I am truly indebted, in a number of ways, to James Arbuckle, author of the AMOS 4.0 program, for keeping me constantly updated following any revisions to the program, for restructuring all of my data sets into a comma-delimited form, and last, but not least, for his almost instantaneous responses to any queries that I had regarding the program. Fortunately, for me, Jim works around the clock—at least, he always seemed to be on his computer at the other end of the line, no matter what time of day or night (including weekends and holidays!) I sent my e-mail cries for help. Thanks Jim, for always being there whenever I needed answers!

I am grateful to Lisa Harlow for inviting me to tackle the writing of this book for the Multivariate Book Series, and for her continued support throughout the building of its contents. Thanks are due, also, to Werner Wothke for initially providing me with the AMOS program, together with all its related documentation.

I wish also to extend thanks to my two reviewers: Tenko Raykov, for providing me with much clearer and simpler ways of expressing particular statistical concepts; and Jim Arbuckle, for his very thorough reading of the text, the program input files and path diagrams, and described illustrations of particular graphical features of the program. Their comments and suggestions were invaluable to me in the final production of this book.

Of course, once again, I owe a great deal to Larry Erlbaum and his incomparable team of editorial, artistic, and marketing experts. Special thanks are extended to Debra Riegert, Sara Scudder, Art Lizza, Joe Petrowski, and, as always, Larry, without whose encouragement and support this book likely would never have seen the light of day. Indeed, I will never cease to be amazed at the speed with which a lowly manuscript gets transformed into a full-fledged book, complete with all the trimmings, at LEA! Thank you all for another great journalistic experience! Last, but certainly not least, I am truly indebted to my husband, Alex, for his continued support and understanding of the incredible number of hours that my computer and I necessarily spend together on a project of this sort. Based on many years of observation, however, I do believe that he has totally abandoned any attempts to modify my compulsive behavior that (he knows) will inevitably lead me into taking on yet another project of similar dimension.

I

INTRODUCTION

Structural Equation
Models: The Basics

❧

Structural equation modeling (SEM) is a statistical methodology that takes a confirmatory (i.e., hypothesis-testing) approach to the analysis of a structural theory bearing on some phenomenon. Typically, this theory represents "causal" processes that generate observations on multiple variables (Bentler, 1988). The term *structural equation modeling* conveys two important aspects of the procedure: (a) that the causal processes under study are represented by a series of structural (i.e., regression) equations, and (b) that these structural relations can be modeled pictorially to enable a clearer conceptualization of the theory under study. The hypothesized model can then be tested statistically in a simultaneous analysis of the entire system of variables to determine the extent to which it is consistent with the data. If the goodness of fit is adequate, the model argues for the plausibility of postulated relations among variables; if it is inadequate, the tenability of such relations is rejected.

Several aspects of SEM set it apart from the older generation of multivariate procedures (see Fornell, 1982). First, as noted earlier, it takes a confirmatory, rather than an exploratory, approach to the data analysis (although aspects of the latter can be addressed). Furthermore, by demanding that the pattern of intervariable relations be specified a priori, SEM lends itself well to the analysis of data for inferential purposes. By contrast, most other multivariate procedures are essentially descriptive by nature (e.g., exploratory factor analysis), so that hypothesis testing is difficult, if not impossible. Second, although traditional multivariate procedures are incapable of either assessing or correcting for measurement error, SEM provides explicit estimates of these error variance parameters. Indeed, alternative methods (e.g., those rooted in regression, or the general linear model) assume that error(s) in the explanatory (i.e., independent) variables vanishes. Thus, applying those methods when there is error in the explanatory variables is tantamount to ignoring error, which may lead, ultimately, to serious inaccuracies—especially when the errors are sizeable. Such mistakes are avoided when corresponding SEM analyses (in simple terms) are used (T. Raykov, personal communication, March 30, 2000). Third, although data analyses using the former methods are based on observed measurements only, those using SEM procedures can incorporate both unobserved (i.e., latent) and observed variables. Finally, there are no widely and easily applied alternative methods for modeling multivariate relations, or for estimating point and/or interval indirect effects; these important features are available using SEM methodology.

Given these highly desirable characteristics, SEM has become a popular methodology for nonexperimental research, where methods for testing theories are not well developed and ethical considerations make experimental design unfeasible (Bentler, 1980). Structural equation modeling can be utilized very effectively to address numerous research problems involving nonexperimental research; in this book, I illustrate the most common applications (e.g., chaps. 3, 4, 6, 7, 8), as well as some that are less frequently found in the substantive literatures (e.g., chaps. 5, 9, 10, 11, 12). Before showing you how to use the AMOS 4.0 program (Arbuckle, 1999), however, it is essential that I first review key concepts associated with the methodology. We turn now to their brief explanation.

BASIC CONCEPTS

Latent Versus Observed Variables

In the behavioral sciences, researchers are often interested in studying theoretical constructs that cannot be observed directly. These abstract phenomena are termed *latent variables*, or *factors*. Examples of latent variables in psychology are self-concept and motivation; in sociology, powerlessness and anomie; in education, verbal ability and teacher expectancy; and in economics, capitalism and social class.

Because latent variables are not observed directly, it follows that they cannot be measured directly. Thus, the researcher must operationally define the latent variable of interest in terms of behavior believed to represent it. As such, the unobserved variable is linked to one that is observable, thereby making its measurement possible. Assessment of the behavior, then, constitutes the direct measurement of an observed variable, albeit the indirect measurement of an unobserved variable (i.e., the underlying construct). It is important to note that the term *behavior* is used here in the very broadest sense to include scores on a particular measuring instrument. Thus, observation may include, for example, self-report responses to an attitudinal scale, scores on an achievement test, in vivo observation scores representing some physical task or activity, coded responses to interview questions, and the like. These measured scores (i.e., measurements) are termed *observed* or *manifest* variables; within the context of

SEM methodology, they serve as *indicators* of the underlying construct that they are presumed to represent. Given this necessary bridging process between observed variables and unobserved latent variables, it should now be clear why methodologists urge researchers to be circumspect in their selection of assessment measures. Although the choice of psychometrically sound instruments bears importantly on the credibility of all study findings, such selection becomes even more critical when the observed measure is presumed to represent an underlying construct.[1]

Exogenous Versus Endogenous Latent Variables

It is helpful in working with SEM models to distinguish between latent variables that are exogenous and those that are endogenous. *Exogenous* latent variables are synonymous with independent variables; they "cause" fluctuations in the values of other latent variables in the model. Changes in the values of exogenous variables are not explained by the model. Rather, they are considered to be influenced by other factors external to the model. Background variables such as gender, age, and socioeconomic status are examples of such external factors. *Endogenous* latent variables are synonymous with dependent variables and, as such, are influenced by the exogenous variables in the model, either directly or indirectly. Fluctuation in the values of endogenous variables is said to be explained by the model because all latent variables that influence them are included in the model specification.

The Factor Analytic Model

The oldest and best known statistical procedure for investigating relations between sets of observed and latent variables is that of *factor analysis*. In using this approach to data analyses, the researcher examines the covariation among a set of observed variables in order to gather information on their underlying latent constructs (i.e., factors). There are two basic types of factor analyses: exploratory factor analysis (EFA) and confirmatory factor analysis (CFA). We turn now to a brief description of each.

Exploratory factor analysis (EFA) is designed for the situation where links between the observed and latent variables are unknown or uncertain. The analysis thus proceeds in an exploratory mode to determine how and to what extent the observed variables are linked to their underlying factors. Typically, the researcher wishes to identify the minimal number of factors that underlie (or account for) covariation among the observed variables. For example, suppose a researcher develops a new instrument designed to measure five facets of physical self-concept (e.g., Health, Sport Competence, Physical Appearance, Coordination, Body

---

[1]Throughout the remainder of the book, the terms *latent, unobserved*, and *unmeasured* variable are used synonymously to represent a hypothetical construct or factor; the terms *observed, manifest*, and *measured* variable are also used interchangeably.

Strength). Following the formulation of questionnaire items designed to measure these five latent constructs, he or she would then conduct an EFA to determine the extent to which the item measurements (the observed variables) were related to the five latent constructs. In factor analysis, these relations are represented by *factor loadings*. The researcher would hope that items designed to measure health, for example, exhibited high loadings on that factor, and low or negligible loadings on the other four factors. This factor analytic approach is considered to be exploratory in the sense that the researcher has no prior knowledge that the items do, indeed, measure the intended factors. (For texts dealing with EFA, see Comrey, 1992; Gorsuch, 1983; McDonald, 1985; and Mulaik, 1972; for informative articles on EFA, see Fabrigar, Wegener, MacCallum, & Strahan, 1999; MacCallum, Widaman, Zhang, & Hong, 1999; and Wood, Tataryn, & Gorsuch, 1996.)

In contrast to EFA, *confirmatory factor analysis* (CFA) is appropriately used when the researcher has some knowledge of the underlying latent variable structure. Based on knowledge of the theory, empirical research, or both, he or she postulates relations between the observed measures and the underlying factors a priori and then tests this hypothesized structure statistically. For example, based on the example cited earlier, the researcher would argue for the loading of items designed to measure sport competence self-concept on that specific factor, and *not* on the health, physical appearance, coordination, or body strength self-concept dimensions. Accordingly, a priori specification of the CFA model would allow all sport competence self-concept items to be free to load on that factor, but restricted to have zero loadings on the remaining factors. The model would then be evaluated by statistical means to determine the adequacy of its goodness of fit to the sample data. (For more detailed discussions of CFA, see, e.g., Bollen, 1989a, Hayduk, 1987, and Long, 1983a.)

In summary, then, the factor-analytic model (EFA or CFA) focuses solely on how, and the extent to which, the observed variables are linked to their underlying latent factors. More specifically, it is concerned with the extent to which the observed variables are generated by the underlying latent constructs, and thus strengths of the regression paths from the factors to the observed variables (the factor loadings) are of primary interest. Although interfactor relations are also of interest, any regression structure among them is not considered in the factor-analytic model. Because the CFA model focuses solely on the link between factors and their measured variables, within the framework of SEM, it represents what has been termed a *measurement model*.

The Full Latent Variable Model

In contrast to the factor-analytic model, the full latent variable (LV) model allows for the specification of regression structure among the latent variables. That is to say, the researcher can hypothesize the impact of one latent construct on another in the modeling of causal direction. This model is termed "full" (or "complete") because it comprises both a measurement model and a structural model: the measurement model depicting the links between the latent variables and their observed measures (i.e., the CFA model), and the structural model depicting the links among the latent variables themselves.

A full LV model that specifies direction of cause from one direction only is termed a *recursive model*; one that allows for reciprocal or feedback effects is termed a *nonrecursive model*. Only applications of recursive models are considered in the present book.

General Purpose and Process of Statistical Modeling

Statistical models provide an efficient and convenient way of describing the latent structure underlying a set of observed variables. Expressed either diagrammatically, or mathematically via a set of equations, such models explain how the observed and latent variables are related to one another.

Typically, a researcher postulates a statistical model based on his or her knowledge of the related theory, on empirical research in the area of study, or some combination of both. Once the model is specified, the researcher tests its plausibility based on sample data that comprise all observed variables in the model. The primary task in this model-testing procedure is to determine the goodness of fit between the hypothesized model and the sample data. As such, the researcher imposes the structure of the hypothesized model on the sample data, and then tests how well the observed data fit this restricted structure. Because it is highly unlikely that a perfect fit will exist between the observed data and the hypothesized model, there will necessarily be a differential between the two; this differential is termed the *residual*. The model-fitting process can therefore be summarized as follows:

$$Data = Model + Residual$$

where Data represent score measurements related to the observed variables as derived from persons comprising the sample, Model represents the hypothesized structure linking the observed variables to the latent variables, and in some models, linking particular latent variables to one another, and Residual represents the discrepancy between the hypothesized model and the observed data.

In summarizing the general strategic framework for testing structural equation models, Joreskog (1993) distinguished among three scenarios, which he termed *strictly confirmatory (SC)*, *alternative models (AM)*, and *model generating (MG)*. In the first instance (the SC scenario), the researcher postulates a single model based on theory, collects the appropriate data, and then tests the fit of the hypothesized model to the sample data. From the results of this test, the researcher either rejects or fails to reject the model; no further modifications to the model are made. In the AM case, the researcher proposes several alternative (i.e., competing) models, all of which are grounded in theory. Following analysis of a single set of empirical data, he or she selects one model as most appropriate in representing the sample data. Finally, the MG scenario represents the case where the researcher, having postulated and rejected a theoretically derived model on the basis of its poor fit to the sample data, proceeds in an exploratory (rather than confirmatory) fashion to modify and reestimate the model. The primary focus, in this instance, is to locate the source of misfit in the model and to determine a model that better describes the sample data. Joreskog (1993) noted that, although respecification may be either theory or data driven, the ultimate objective is to find a model that is both substantively meaningful and statistically well-fitting. He further posited that despite the fact that "a model is tested in each round, the whole approach is model generating, rather than model testing" (Joreskog, 1993, p. 295).

Of course, even a cursory review of the empirical literature will clearly show the MG situation to be the most common of the three scenarios, and for good reason. Given the many costs associated with the collection of data, it would be a rare researcher indeed who could afford to terminate his or her research on the basis of a rejected hypothesized model! As a consequence, the SC case is not commonly found in practice. Although the AM approach to modeling has also been a relatively uncommon practice, at least two important papers on the topic (e.g., MacCallum, Roznowski, & Necowitz, 1992; MacCallum, Wegener, Uchino, & Fabrigar, 1993) have recently precipitated more activity with respect to this analytic strategy.

Statistical theory related to these model-fitting processes can be found (a) in texts devoted to the topic of SEM (e.g., Bollen, 1989a; Hayduk, 1987; Kline, 1998; Loehlin, 1992; Long, 1983b; Saris & Stronkhurst, 1984; Schumacker & Lomax, 1996), (b) in edited books devoted to the topic (e.g., Bollen & Long, 1993; Hoyle, 1995a; Marcoulides & Schumacker, 1996), and (c) in methodologically oriented journals such as *British Journal of Mathematical and Statistical Psychology*, *Journal of Educational and Behavioral Statistics*, *Multivariate Behavioral Research*, *Psychological Methods*, *Psychometrika*, *Sociological Methodology*, *Sociological Methods & Research*, and *Structural Equation Modeling: A Multidisciplinary Journal*.

THE GENERAL SEM MODEL

Symbol Notation

Structural equation models are schematically portrayed using particular configurations of four geometric symbols—a circle (or ellipse), a square (or rectangle), a single-headed arrow, and a double-headed arrow. By convention, circles (or ellipses) represent unobserved latent factors, squares (or rectangles) represent observed variables, single-headed arrows ($\rightarrow$) represent the impact of one variable on another, and double-headed arrows ($\leftrightarrow$) represent covariances or correlations between pairs of variables. In building a model of a particular structure under study, researchers use these symbols within the framework of four basic configurations, each of which represents an important component in the analytic process. These four configurations, together with their brief description, are as follows:

- Path coefficient for regression of an observed variable onto an unobserved latent variable (or factor).
- Path coefficient for regression of one factor onto another factor.
- Measurement error associated with an observed variable.
- Residual error in the prediction of an unobserved factor.

The Path Diagram

Schematic representations of models are termed *path diagrams* because they provide a visual portrayal of relations which are assumed to hold among the variables under study. Essentially, as you will see later, a path diagram depicting a particular SEM model is actually the graphical equivalent of its mathematical representation whereby a set of equations relates dependent variables to their explanatory variables. As a means of illustrating how the above four symbol configurations may represent a particular causal process, let me now walk you through the simple model shown in Fig. 1.1, which was formulated using AMOS 4.0 (Arbuckle, 1999).

In reviewing the model shown in Fig. 1.1, we see that there are two unobserved latent factors—math self-concept (MSC) and math achievement (MATH)—and five observed variables—three are considered to measure MSC (SDQMSC, API-MSC, SPPCMSC), and two to measure MATH (MATHGR; MATHACH). These five observed variables function as indicators of their respective underlying latent factors.

Associated with each observed variable is an error term (err1–err5), and with the factor being predicted (MATH), a residual term (resid1)[2]; there is an important distinction between the two. Error associated with observed variables represents *measurement error*, which reflects on their adequacy in measuring the related underlying factors (MSC; MATH). Measurement error derives from two sources: random measurement error (in the psychometric sense), and error uniqueness, a term used to describe error variance arising from some characteristic that is considered to be specific (or unique) to a particular indicator variable. Such error often represents *nonrandom* measurement error. *Residual* terms represent error in the prediction of endogenous factors from exogenous factors. For example, the residual term shown in Fig. 1.1 represents error in the prediction of MATH (the endogenous factor) from MSC (the exogenous factor).

---

[2]Residual terms are often referred to as "disturbance terms."

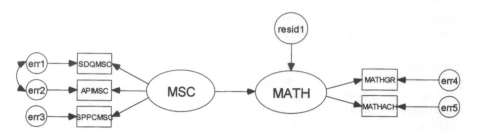

FIG. 1.1.   General structural equation model.

It is worth noting that both measurement and residual error terms, in essence, represent unobserved variables. Thus, it seems perfectly reasonable that, consistent with the representation of factors, they too should be enclosed in circles. For this reason, AMOS path diagrams, unlike those associated with most other SEM programs, model these error variables as circled enclosures by default.[3]

In addition to symbols that represent variables, certain others are used in path diagrams to denote hypothesized processes involving the entire system of variables. In particular, one-way arrows represent structural regression coefficients and thus indicate the impact of one variable on another. In Fig. 1.1, for example, the unidirectional arrow pointing toward the endogenous factor, MATH, implies that the exogenous factor MSC (math self-concept) "causes" math achievement (MATH).[4] Likewise, the three unidirectional arrows leading from MSC to each of the three observed variables (SDQMSC, APIMSC, SPPCMSC), and those leading from MATH to each its indicators, MATHGR and MATHACH, suggest that these score values are each influenced by their respective underlying factors. As such, these path coefficients represent the magnitude of expected change in the observed variables for every change in the related latent variable (or factor). It is important to note that these observed variables typically represent subscale scores (see chap. 7), item scores (see chap. 4), item pairs (see chap. 3), and/or carefully selected item bundles (see chap. 6).

The one-way arrows pointing from the enclosed error terms (err1–err5) indicate the impact of measurement error (random and unique) on the observed variables, and from the residual (resid1), the impact of error in the prediction of MATH. Finally, as noted earlier, curved two-way arrows represent covariances or correlations between pairs of variables. Thus, the bidirectional arrow linking err1 and err2,

---

[3]Of course, this default can be overridden by selecting "Visibility" from the Object Properties dialog box (to be described in chap. 2).

[4]In this book, a *cause* is a direct effect of a variable on another within the context of a complete model. Its magnitude and direction are given by the partial regression coefficient. If the complete model contains all relevant influences on a given dependent variable, its causal precursors are correctly specified. In practice, however, models may omit key predictors, and may be misspecified, so that it may be inadequate as a "causal model" in the philosophical sense.

as shown in Fig. 1.1, implies that measurement error associated with SDQMSC is correlated with that associated with APIMSC.

Structural Equations

As noted in the initial paragraph of this chapter, in addition to lending themselves to pictorial description via a schematic presentation of the causal processes under study, structural equation models can also be represented by a series of regression (i.e., structural) equations. Because (a) regression equations represent the influence of one or more variables on another and (b) this influence, conventionally in SEM, is symbolized by a single-headed arrow pointing from the variable of influence to the variable of interest, we can think of each equation as summarizing the impact of all relevant variables in the model (observed and unobserved) on one specific variable (observed or unobserved). Thus, one relatively simple approach to formulating these equations is to note each variable that has one or more arrows pointing toward it, and then record the summation of all such influences for each of these dependent variables.

To illustrate this translation of regression processes into structural equations, let's turn again to Fig. 1.1. We can see that there are six variables with arrows pointing toward them; five represent observed variables (SDQMSC–SPPCMSC; MATHGR, MATHACH), and one represents an unobserved variable (or factor; MATH). Thus, we know that the regression functions symbolized in the model shown in Fig. 1.1 can be summarized in terms of six separate equationlike representations of linear dependencies as follows:

$$MATH = MSC + resid1$$
$$SDQMSC = MSC + err1$$
$$APIMSC = MSC + err2$$
$$SPPCMSC = MSC + err3$$
$$MATHGR = MATH + err4$$
$$MATHACH = MATH + err5$$

Nonvisible Components of a Model

Although, in principle, there is a one-to-one correspondence between the schematic presentation of a model and its translation into a set of structural equations, it is important to note that neither one of these model representations tells the whole story; some parameters critical to the estimation of the model are not explicitly shown and thus may not be obvious to the novice structural equation modeler. For example, in both the path diagram and the equations just shown, there is no indication that the variances of the exogenous variables are parameters in the model; indeed, such parameters are essential to all structural equation models. Although researchers must be mindful of this inadequacy of path diagrams in building model input files related to other SEM programs, AMOS facilitates the specification process by automatically incorporating the estimation of variances by default for all independent factors.

Likewise, it is equally important to draw your attention to the specified nonexistence of certain parameters in a model. For example, in Fig. 1.1 we detect no curved arrow between err4 and err5, which suggests the lack of covariance between the error terms associated with the observed variables MATHGR and MATHACH. Similarly, there is no hypothesized covariance between MSC and resid1; absence of this path addresses the common, and most often necessary, assumption that the predictor (or exogenous) variable is in no way associated with any error arising from the prediction of the criterion (or endogenous) variable. In the case of both examples cited here, AMOS, once again, makes it easy for the novice structural equation modeler by automatically assuming these specifications to be nonexistent. (These important default assumptions are addressed in chap. 2 where I review the specification of AMOS 4.0 models and input files in detail.)

Basic Composition

The general SEM model can be decomposed into two submodels: a measurement model, and a structural model. The *measurement model* defines relations between the observed and unobserved variables. In other words, it provides the link between scores on a measuring instrument (i.e., the observed indicator variables) and the underlying constructs they are designed to measure (i.e., the unobserved latent variables). The measurement model, then, represents the CFA model described earlier in that it specifies the pattern by which each measure loads on a particular factor. In contrast, the *structural model* defines relations among the unobserved variables. Accordingly, it specifies the manner by which particular latent variables directly or indirectly influence (i.e., "cause") changes in the values of certain other latent variables in the model.

For didactic purposes in clarifying this important aspect of SEM composition, let's now examine Fig. 1.2, in which the same model presented in Fig. 1.1 has been demarcated into measurement and structural components.

Considered separately, the elements modeled within each rectangle in Fig. 1.2 represent two CFA models. The enclosure of the two factors within the ellipse represents a full latent variable model and thus would not be of interest in CFA research. The CFA model to the left of the diagram represents a one-factor model (MSC) measured by three observed variables (SDQMSC–SPPCMSC), whereas the CFA model on the right represents a one-factor model (MATH) measured by two observed variables (MATHGR, MATHACH). In both cases, the regression of the observed variables on each factor and the variances of both the factor and the errors of measurement are of primary interest; the error covariance would be of interest only in analyses related to the CFA model bearing on MSC.

It is perhaps important to note that although both CFA models described in Fig. 1.2 represent first-order factor models, second-order and higher order CFA models

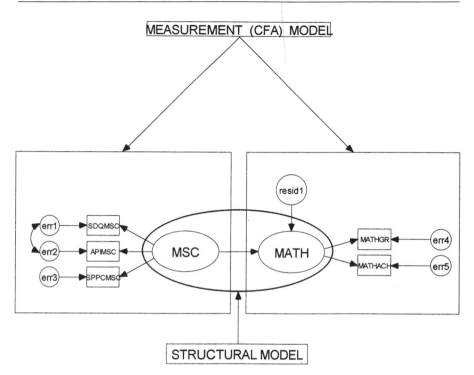

FIG. 1.2.   General structural equation model demarcated into measurement and structural components.

can also be analyzed using AMOS 4.0. Such hierarchical CFA models, however, are less commonly found in the literature (Kerlinger, 1984). Discussion and application of CFA models in the present book are limited to first- and second-order models only. (For a more comprehensive discussion and explanation of first- and second-order CFA models, see Bollen, 1989a, and Kerlinger, 1984.)

The Formulation of Covariance and Mean Structures

The core parameters in structural equation models that focus on the analysis of covariance structures are the regression coefficients, and the variances and covariances of the independent variables; when the focus extends to the analysis of mean structures, the means and intercepts also become central parameters in the model. However, given that sample data comprise observed scores only, there needs to be some internal mechanism whereby the data are transposed into parameters of the model. This task is accomplished via a mathematical model representing the entire system of variables. Such representation systems can and do vary with each SEM computer program. Because adequate explanation of the way in which the AMOS representation system operates demands knowledge of the program's underlying statistical theory, the topic goes beyond the aims and intent of the present volume. Thus, readers interested in a comprehensive explanation of this aspect of the analysis of covariance structures are referred to other texts (Bollen, 1989a; Saris & Stronkhorst, 1984) and monographs (Long, 1983b).

Now that you are familiar with the basic concepts underlying structural equation modeling, let's turn our attention to the specification and analysis of models within the framework of the AMOS 4.0 program. Accordingly, in chapter 2 we examine its basic structure, dual approach to model specification, and output file retrieval, structure, and composition.

CHAPTER

2

The AMOS Program

The purpose of this chapter is to introduce you to the general format of the AMOS program and to its dual approach to the analysis of confirmatory factor analytic and full structural equation models. The name, AMOS, is actually an acronym for "Analysis of Moment Structures" or, in other words, the analysis of mean and covariance structures.

An interesting aspect of AMOS is that, although developed within the Microsoft Windows interface, the program allows you to choose from two completely different modes of model specification. Using one approach, AMOS Graphics, you work directly from a path diagram; using the other, AMOS Basic, you work directly from equation statements. The choice of which AMOS method to use is purely arbitrary and bears solely on how comfortable you feel in working within either a graphical interface or a more traditional programming interface.

Without a doubt, for those of you who enjoy working with draw programs, rest assured that you will love working with AMOS Graphics! All drawing tools have been carefully designed with SEM conventions in mind—and there is a wide array of them from which to choose. With a simple click of either the left or right mouse buttons, you will be amazed at how quickly you can formulate a publication-quality path diagram. On the other hand, for those of you who may feel more at home with specifying your model using an equation format, the AMOS Basic option is very straightforward and easily applied. Indeed, as Arbuckle and Wothke (1999, p. 35) noted in the user's guide, "AMOS Basic can be unbeatable as a workhorse for larger models and batch-oriented estimation results." Furthermore, it allows the user to manipulate and save estimation results. Thus, whenever parameter estimated values are of more interest than the paths themselves, equation mode can be the more efficient interface.

Regardless of which mode of model input you choose, AMOS Graphics or AMOS Basic, all options related to the analyses are available from drop-down menus, and all estimates derived from the analyses can be presented in text or table (i.e., spreadsheet) format. Only AMOS Graphics, however, allows for the estimates to be displayed graphically in a path diagram. Thus, the choice between these two approaches to SEM really boils down to one's preferences regarding the specification of models. In this chapter, I introduce you to the various features of both AMOS Graphics and AMOS Basic by illustrating the formulation of input specification related to three simple models. As with all subsequent chapters in the book, I walk you through the various stages of each featured application. In the interest of space, however, the applications demonstrated in chapters 4 through 12 are structured within the framework of the AMOS Graphics interface. Nonetheless, at the end of each of these chapters, I provide you with (a) the AMOS Basic input file pertinent to one of the models discussed and (b) an explanation of the various components of this file.

Let's turn our attention now to a review of the various components and characteristics of AMOS Graphics and AMOS Basic as they relate to the specification of three basic models: a first-order CFA model (Example 1), a second-order CFA model (Example 2), and a full SEM model (Example 3). We'll begin with AMOS Graphics.

WORKING WITH AMOS GRAPHICS: EXAMPLE 1

AMOS Modeling Tools

AMOS Graphics provides you with all the tools that you will ever need in creating and working with SEM path diagrams. Each tool is represented by an icon (or button) and performs one particular function; as this book goes to press, there are 67 icons from which to choose. A palette displaying 42 of these icons is shown in Fig. 2.1, and a description of each is presented in Table 2.1.

In reviewing Table 2.1, you will note that, although the majority of the icons are associated with individual components of the path diagram (e.g., ⬭ 💹), or with the path diagram as a whole (e.g., 🔲 ; 🔲), others relate either to the data (e.g., 🔲) or to the analyses (e.g., 🔲). Don't worry about trying to remember this smorgasbord of tools, as a simple right click of the mouse will yield a pop-up label that identifies any icon in question. Furthermore, provided that the palette of icons (i.e., the toolbox) is the window that has focus (i.e., its control bar is colored, rather than gray), just holding the mouse pointer stationary over an icon is enough to trigger the pop-up label. Right-clicking then pops up a two-item "What's This/Help" menu.

FIG. 2.1.   Palette of selected drawing tool icons.

These tools have been enhanced substantially from those presented in earlier versions of the program. Indeed, two tools in particular (although they were present in earlier versions of the program)—the Indicator Icon 👯 and the Error Icon 🔲—are worth their weight in gold! Both have reduced, tremendously, the tedium of trying to line up all indicator and error variables in the model in an effort to produce an aesthetically pleasing diagram. As a consequence, it is commonplace to structure a path diagram in just a matter of minutes.

Now that you have had a chance to peruse the working tools of AMOS Graphics, let's move on to their actual use in formulating a path diagram. For your first experience in using AMOS Graphics, we'll reconstruct the hypothesized CFA model shown in Fig. 2.2.

The Hypothesized Model

The CFA structure in Fig. 2.2 comprises four self-concept (SC) factors: academic SC (ASC), social SC (SSC), physical SC (PSC), and emotional SC (ESC). Each SC factor is measured by three observed variables, the reliability of which is influenced by random measurement error, as indicated by the associated error term. Each of these observed variables is regressed onto its respective factor. Finally, the four factors are shown to be intercorrelated.

Initiating AMOS Graphics

To initiate AMOS Graphics, you will need, first, to follow the usual Windows procedure as follows: Start → Programs → AMOS 4.0 → AMOS Graphics. In the most recent version of AMOS 4.0, users now have the option of placing both AMOS Graphics and AMOS Basic on the desktop; each is represented by its own icon. Once you are in AMOS Graphics, click on File, and then select New from the drop-down menu. At this point you will be presented with the screen shown in Fig. 2.3. Although the File drop-down menu is typical of most Windows programs, in the interest of completeness, it is shown here in Fig. 2.4.

Of prime interest in Fig. 2.3 is the blank rectangle to the right of the screen; this space provides for the drawing of your path diagram. Noticeably absent from this

TABLE 2.1
Selected Drawing Tools in AMOS Graphics

Rectangle Icon: Draw observed (measured) variables

Oval Icon: Draw unobserved (latent, unmeasured) variables

Indicator Icon: Draw a latent variable and add one or more indicator variables

Path Icon: Draw regression path

Covariance Icon: Draw covariance

Error Icon: Add error/uniqueness variable to an existing observed variable

Title Icon: Add figure caption to path diagram

Variable List (I) Icon: List variables in the model

Variable List (II) Icon: List variables in the data set

Single Selection Icon: Select one object at a time

Multiple Selection Icon: Select all objects

Multiple Deselection Icon: Deselect all objects

Duplicate Icon: Make multiple copies of selected object(s)

Move Icon: Move selected object(s) to an alternate location

Erase Icon: Delete selected object(s)

Shape Change Icon: Alter shape of selected object(s)

Rotate Icon: Changes orientation of indicator variables

Reflect Icon: Reverses direction of indicator variables

Move Parameters Icon: Move parameter values to alternate location

Scroll Icon: Reposition path diagram on the screen

Touch-up Icon: Enables rearrangement of arrows in path diagram

(Continued)

TABLE 2.1 *(Continued)*

Data File Icon: Select and read data file(s)

Analysis Properties Icon: Requests additional calculations

Calculate Estimates Icon: Calculates default and/or requested estimates

Clipboard Icon: Copies path diagram to Windows clipboard

Text Output Icon: View output in textual format

Table Output Icon: View output in spreadsheet format

Object Properties Icon: Define properties of variables

Drag Properties Icon: Transfer selected properties of an object to one or more target objects

Preserve Symmetry Icon: Maintain proper spacing among selected group of objects

Zoom Select Icon: Magnify selected portion of a path diagram

Zoom-In Icon: Magnify image of path diagram

Zoom-Out Icon: Reduce size of path diagram

Zoom Page Icon: Resize path diagram to fit within AMOS window

Fit-to-Page Icon: Resize path diagram to fit within page boundary

Loupe Icon: Magnify path diagram with a loupe (magnifying glass)

Degrees of Freedom Icon: Display degrees of freedom for a selected model

Link Icon: Link selected objects

Print Icon: Print selected path diagram

Undo (I) Icon: Undo previous change

Undo (II) Icon: Undo previous undo

Redraw Icon: Redraw path diagram on the screen

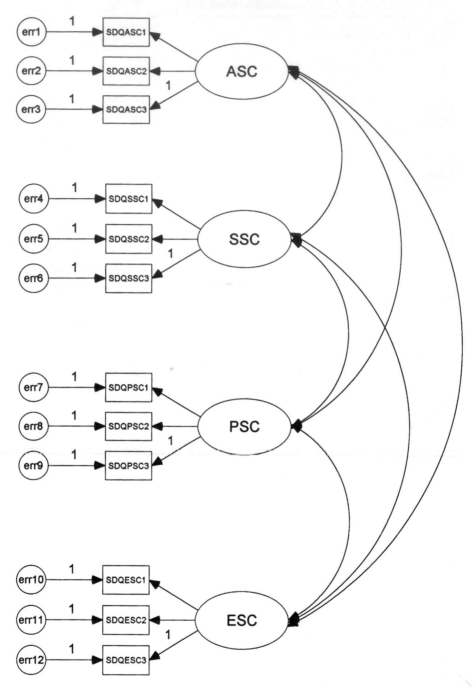

FIG. 2.2. Hypothesized first-order CFA model.

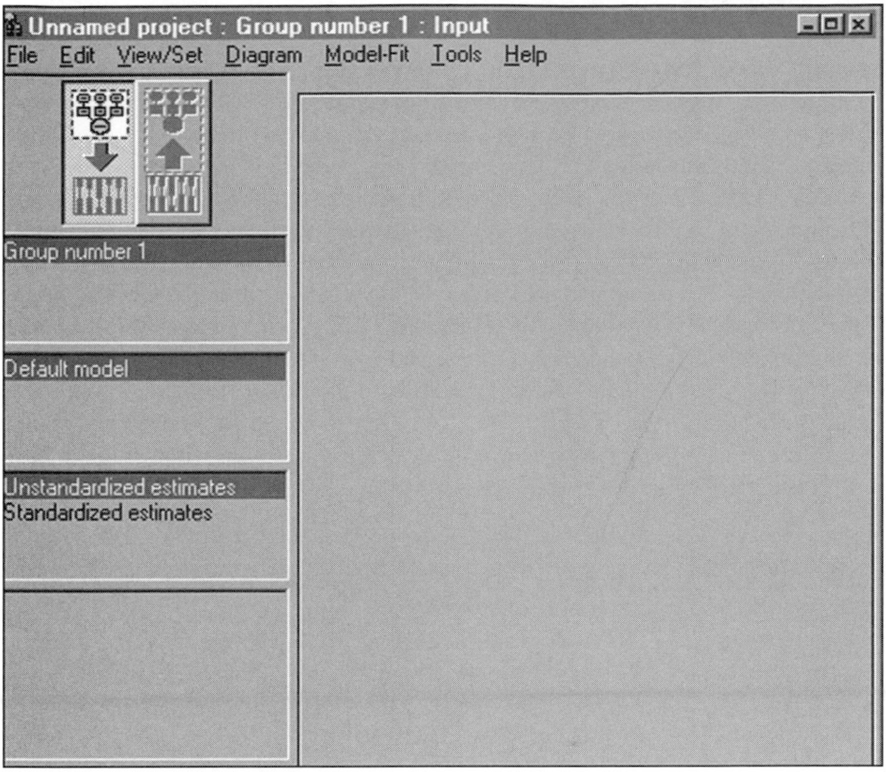

FIG. 2.3.   The opening (empty) screen for AMOS Graphics.

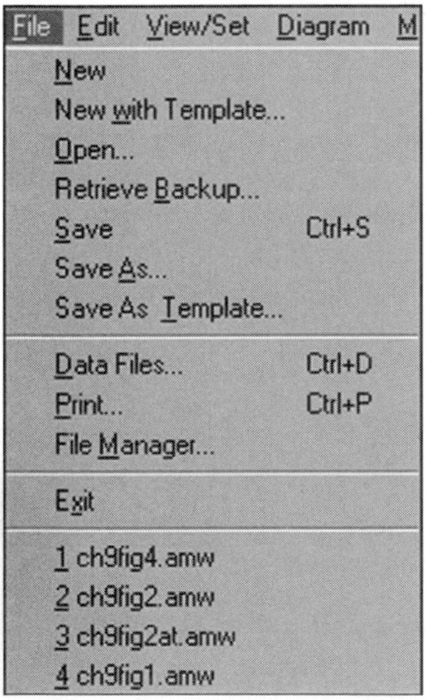

FIG. 2.4.   The AMOS file menu.

captured screen, however, is the palette of tools displayed earlier in this chapter. Because the palette necessarily occupies a portion of the screen, I purposely eliminated it on this occasion to allow for an unobstructed full-screen view. The large highlighted icon in the top left-hand corner of the screen, when activated, presents you with a view of the input path diagram—that is to say, the model specification. The companion icon to the right of the first one allows you to view the output path diagram—in other words, the path diagram complete with the parameter estimates. Of course, given that we have not conducted any analyses at this point, the output icon is not highlighted. Finally, turning to Fig. 2.5, you will see the same empty screen as that shown in Fig. 2.3, but this time with the palette of drawing tools included. Note that although the configuration of icons is the same, the shape and location of the palette is different. This capability to adjust and move the drawing tool palette in AMOS is an excellent feature, as it provides you with complete flexibility in the drawing of a path diagram. These adjustments are made simply by

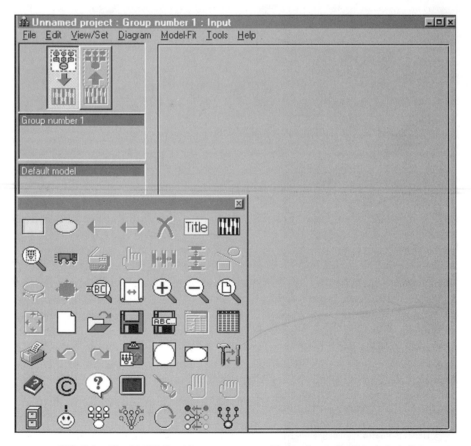

FIG. 2.5.   The AMOS Graphics empty screen with drawing tool palette included.

placing the cursor on any one of the four edges of the palette in a manner that either reduces or increases the size.

Drawing the Path Diagram

Now we're ready to draw our path diagram. The first tool you will want to use is what I call the "million dollar" (indicator) icon (see Table 2.1) because it performs several functions. Click on this icon to activate it and then, with the cursor in the blank drawing space provided, hold down the left mouse button and draw an ellipse; release the mouse button. Figure 2.6 illustrates the completed ellipse shape with the Indicator Icon 🔘 still activated. Of course, you could also have activated the Draw Unobserved Variables Icon 🔘 and achieved the same result.[1]

Now that we have the ellipse representing the first latent factor, the next step is to add the indicator variables. To do so, we click on the Indicator Icon, after which the mouse pointer changes to resemble the Indicator Icon. Now, move the Indicator Icon image to the center of the ellipse and then click on the unobserved variable. In viewing Fig. 2.7, you will see that this action produces a rectangle (representing a single observed variable), an arrow pointing from the latent factor to the observed variable (representing a regression path), and a small circle with an arrow pointing toward the observed variable (representing a measurement error term). Again, you will see that the Indicator Icon, when activated, appears in the center of the ellipse. This occurs, however, only because that's where the mouse pointer is pointing.

However, the hypothesized model (see Fig. 2.2) which we are endeavoring to structure schematically here, shows each of its latent factors to have three, rather than only one, indicator variables. These additional indicators are easily added to the diagram by two simple clicks of the left mouse button while the Indicator Icon is activated. In other words, with this icon activated, each time that the left mouse button is clicked, AMOS Graphics will produce an additional indicator variable, each with its associated error term. Figures 2.8 and 2.9 show the results of having made one and two additional clicks, respectively, to the left mouse button.[2]

In reviewing the hypothesized model again, we note that the three indicator variables for each latent factor are oriented to the left of the ellipse, rather than to the top, as is currently the case in our diagram here. This task is easily accomplished by means of rotation. One very simple way of accomplishing this reorientation is to click the right mouse button while the Indicator Icon is activated. Figure 2.10 illustrates the outcome of this clicking action. As you can see, you are then provided with a variety of options related to your path diagram from which you can choose. At this time, how-

---

[1]Throughout the book, the terms *click* and *drag* are used within the usual Windows framework. As such, *click* means to press and release the mouse button in a single, fairly rapid motion. In contrast, *drag* means to press the mouse button and hold it down while simultaneously moving the mouse.

[2]The 1's that are automatically assigned to selected single arrows by the program relate to the issue of model identification, a topic addressed later in the chapter.

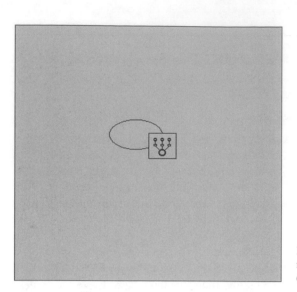

FIG. 2.6. Drawing an ellipse to represent an unobserved latent variable (or factor).

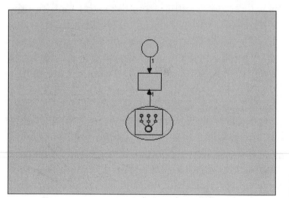

FIG. 2.7. Adding the first error term to the latent factor.

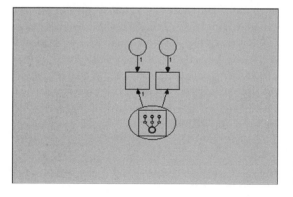

FIG. 2.8. Adding the second error term to the latent factor.

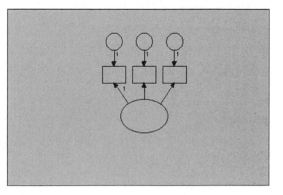

FIG. 2.9. The latent factor with three indicator variables and their associated error terms.

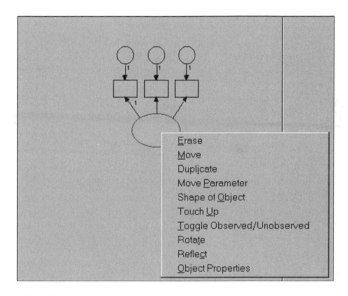

FIG. 2.10.   Pop-up menu activated by click of the right mouse button.

ever, we are only interested in the Rotate option. By moving down the menu and clicking on Rotate with the left mouse button, the indicator variables, in combination, will move 45 degrees clockwise as illustrated in Fig. 2.11; two additional clicks will produce the desired orientation shown in Fig. 2.12. Alternatively, we could have activated the Rotate Icon ⟳ and then clicked on the ellipse to obtain the same effect.

Now that we have one factor structure completed, it becomes a simple task of duplicating this configuration in order to add three additional ones to the model. We can accomplish this task either by clicking the right mouse button and selecting Duplicate, as shown in Fig. 2.13, or by activating the Duplicate Icon 🖫. In either case, each click and drag of the mouse with the left button will generate one

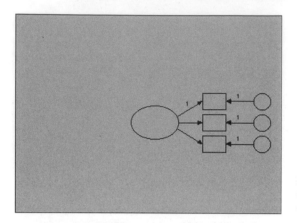

FIG. 2.11.   The latent factor with indicator variables and error terms rotated once.

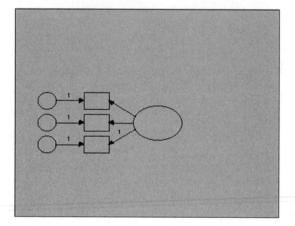

FIG. 2.12.   The reflected latent factor structure shown in Fig. 2.11.

copy of the factor structure. Once you have the number of copies that you need, it is just a matter of dragging each duplicated structure into position. Figure 2.14 illustrates the four factor structures lined up vertically to replicate the hypothesized CFA model. Note the insert of the Move Icon ▦ in this figure; it can be used to make any adjustments in repositioning each of the factor structures, or to move the entire four-factor structure as a unit. To assure that all four factor structures move as a group, you would need to activate the Select All Icon 🖑 and then click on the ellipse with the left mouse button. and drag to the desired position. At this point, you will note that all components of the diagram assume a blue color.[3]

---

[3]Whenever you see that various components in the path diagram are colored blue, this indicates that they are currently selected as a group of objects. As such, they will be treated as one object should you wish to reorient them in any way. In contrast, single parameters, when selected by a point-and-click action, become highlighted in red.

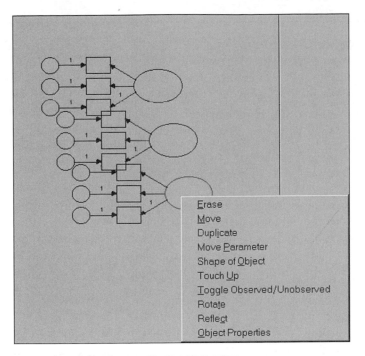

FIG. 2.13. Duplicating the first factor structure.

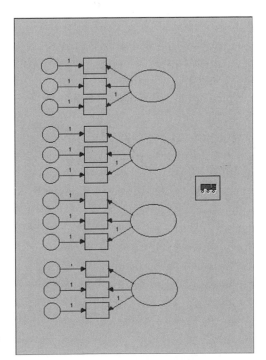

FIG. 2.14. The four factor structures aligned vertically.

Now we need to add the factor covariances to our path diagram. As illustrated in Fig. 2.15, with the addition of the hypothesized covariance between the first and fourth factor, these double-headed arrows are drawn by clicking on the Covariance Icon ↔. Once this button has been activated, you then click on one object (in this case, the first latent factor), and drag the arrow to the second object of interest (in this case, the fourth latent factor). The process is then repeated for each of the remaining specified covariances. Yes, gone are the days of spending endless hours trying to draw multiple arrows that looked at least somewhat similar in their curvature! Thanks to AMOS Graphics, these double-headed arrows are drawn perfectly every single time.

At this point, our path diagram, structurally speaking, is complete; all that is left for us to do is to label each of the variables. If you look back at Fig. 2.13, in which the mouse right-click menu is displayed, you will see a selection termed Object Properties at the bottom of the menu. This is the option you need in order to add text to a path diagram. To initiate this process, point the cursor to the object on which you wish to add text and click with left mouse button. This action identifies the object of interest; the outline of the object is highlighted in blue, indicating that it has been selected for some drawing operation. You then click the right mouse button to activate the menu and select Object Properties. As you can see in Fig. 2.16, the dialog box associated with this selection allows you to choose from a number of options related to the addition of text. For purposes of illustration, I have simply

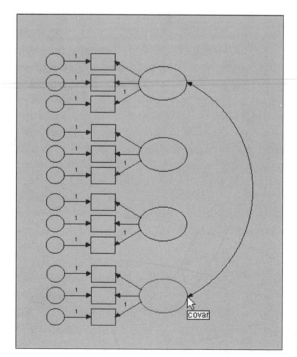

FIG. 2.15.   Drawing the first factor covariance double-headed arrow.

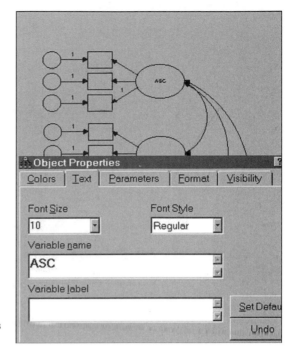

FIG. 2.16. The object properties dialog box.

entered the label for the first latent variable (ASC) and at a font size of 10. All remaining labeling was completed in the same manner. Alternatively, one can display the list of variables in the data and then drag each variable to its respective rectangle.

The path diagram related to our hypothesized CFA model is now complete. However, before leaving AMOS Graphics, I wish to show you the contents of four pull-down menus made available to you on your drawing screen. (For a review of possible menus, see Fig. 2.3.) The first of the four menus shown in Fig. 2.17 relates in some way to path diagrams. In reviewing the Edit and Diagram menus, you will quickly see that they serve as an alternative to the use of the drawing tools, some of which I have just demonstrated in the reconstruction of Fig. 2.2. Thus, for those of you who may prefer to work with pull-down menus, rather than with drawing tool buttons, AMOS Graphics provides you with this option. As its name implies, the View/Set menu allows you to peruse various features associated with the variables and/or parameters in the path diagram. Finally, from the Model-Fit menu, you can calculate estimates (i.e., execute a job), review the degrees of freedom, manipulate groups and/or models, and choose to work with the modeling lab.

By now, you should have a fairly good understanding of how AMOS Graphics works. Of course, because learning comes from doing, you will most assuredly want to practice on your own some of the techniques illustrated here. For those of you who are still uncomfortable working with draw programs, take solace in the fact that I too harbored such fears until I worked with AMOS. Rest assured that

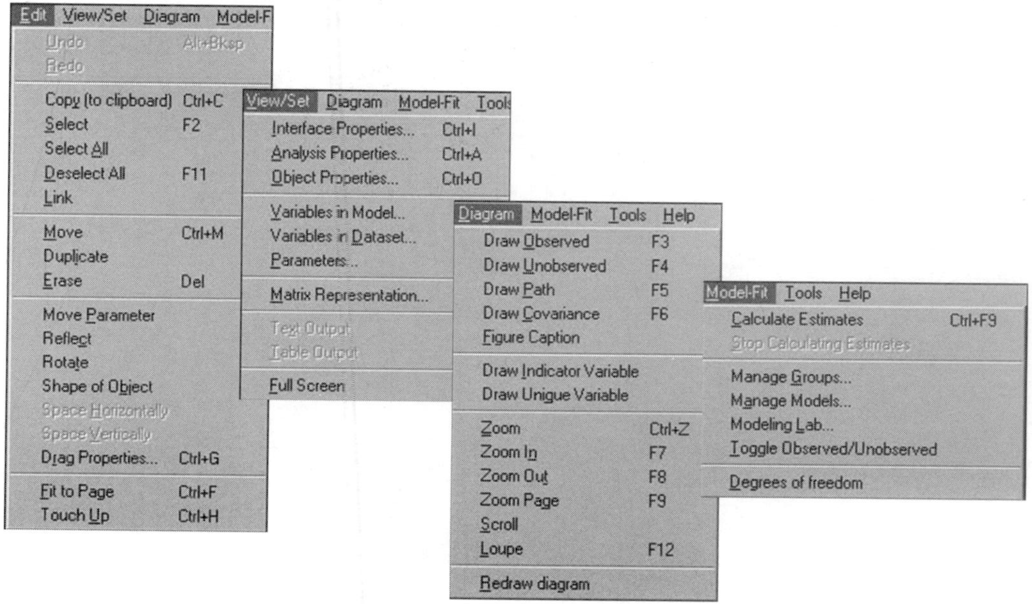

Edit View/Set Diagram Model-F

Undo Alt+Bksp
Redo

Copy (to clipboard) Ctrl+C
Select F2
Select All
Deselect All F11
Link

Move Ctrl+M
Duplicate
Erase Del

Move Parameter
Reflect
Rotate
Shape of Object
Space Horizontally
Space Vertically
Drag Properties... Ctrl+G

Fit to Page Ctrl+F
Touch Up Ctrl+H

View/Set Diagram Model-Fit Tool

Interface Properties... Ctrl+I
Analysis Properties... Ctrl+A
Object Properties... Ctrl+O

Variables in Model...
Variables in Dataset...
Parameters...

Matrix Representation...

Text Output
Table Output

Full Screen

Diagram Model-Fit Tools Help

Draw Observed F3
Draw Unobserved F4
Draw Path F5
Draw Covariance F6
Figure Caption

Draw Indicator Variable
Draw Unique Variable

Zoom Ctrl+Z
Zoom In F7
Zoom Out F8
Zoom Page F9
Scroll
Loupe F12

Redraw diagram

Model-Fit Tools Help

Calculate Estimates Ctrl+F9
Stop Calculating Estimates

Manage Groups...
Manage Models...
Modeling Lab...
Toggle Observed/Unobserved

Degrees of freedom

FIG. 2.17.   Four selected AMOS pull-down menus.

once you have decided to take the plunge into the world of draw programs, you will be amazed at how simple the techniques are, and this is especially true of AMOS Graphics. Now, for a complete change of focus, lets turn our attention to the alternative method of model specification provided by AMOS—AMOS Basic.

WORKING WITH AMOS BASIC: EXAMPLE 1

This approach to model specification, as noted earlier, works within a programming interface. That is to say, in lieu of specifying models via the box, ellipse, and arrow notation that we used with AMOS Graphics, in AMOS Basic, we specify models via sets of equations. To begin working with AMOS Basic, follow the same procedure as you did for AMOS Graphics: Start → Programs → AMOS 4 → AMOS Basic (or click on the AMOS Basic icon on the desktop.) Once you are in AMOS Basic, click on File, and then select New AMOS Engine from the dropdown menu. You will then be presented with the screen shown in Fig. 2.18.

In reviewing this AMOS Basic screen, only explanations related to the four lines in the white portion of the screen are of importance here; they are as follows:

- Sub Main is the command that initiates the AMOS Basic program.
- Dim Sem as New AmosEngine declares sem as an object of type AmosEngine; the term *sem* serves much like a variable name in a program.

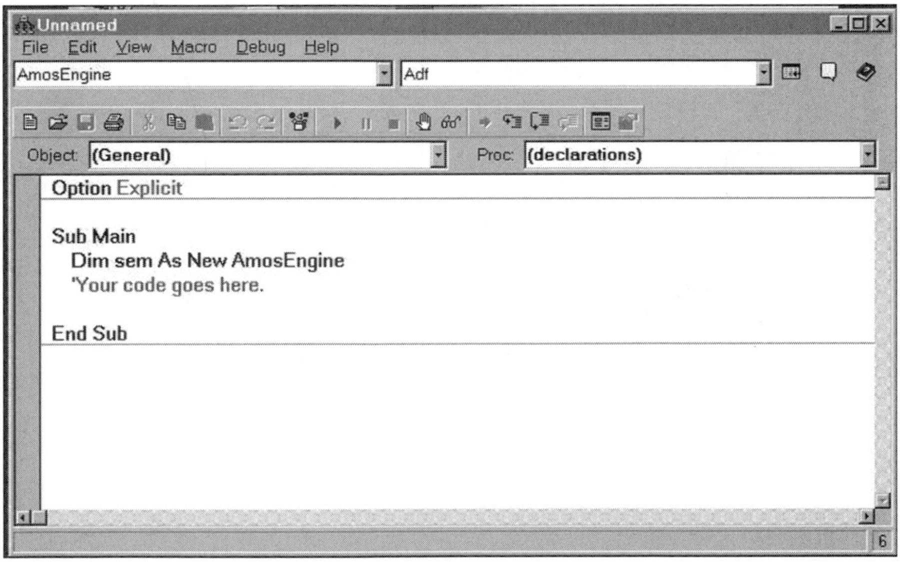

```
Unnamed                                                    _ □ ×
 File  Edit  View  Macro  Debug  Help
 AmosEngine                          ▼  Adf                          ▼  ⊞  ▢  ◈

 ▯ ☞ ▯ ▯  ▯ ▯ ▮  ▯ ▯ ▼  ▶  ‖  ▮  ▯ ◌  ▸ ▯ ▯ ▯  ▯ ▯
 Object: (General)                   ▼   Proc: (declarations)            ▼
   Option Explicit

   Sub Main
     Dim sem As New AmosEngine
     'Your code goes here.

   End Sub




                                                                        6
```

FIG. 2.18.   The AMOS Basic program editor.

- 'Your code goes here. The key here is the single quote. Whenever AMOS Basic encounters a single quote, it treats the quote itself, together with all text to the right of it, as a comment.
- End Sub is the command that terminates the AMOS Basic program.

All equations related to a model are entered between the comment statement and the terminal program command, End Sub. As a means of introducing you to AMOS Basic, we'll once again work from the same CFA model that we used with AMOS Graphics (see Fig. 2.2). In this case, however, our interest focuses on the structuring of the input file that describes the model specification; this file is shown in Table 2.2.

TABLE 2.2
AMOS BASIC Input for Fig. 2.2

Sub Main

Dim Sem as New AmosEngine
'Input File for Figure 2.2'

SEM.BeginGroup "Filename"

    SEM.Structure "SDQASC1 ← ASC"
    SEM.Structure "SDQASC2 ← ASC"
    SEM.Structure "SDQASC3 ← ASC (1)"

    SEM.Structure "SDQSSC1 ← SSC"
    SEM.Structure "SDQSSC2 ← SSC"
    SEM.Structure "SDQSSC3 ← SSC (1)"

    SEM.Structure "SDQPSC1 ← PSC"
    SEM.Structure "SDQPSC2 ← PSC"
    SEM.Structure "SDQPSC3 ← PSC (1)"

    SEM.Structure "SDQESC1 ← ESC"
    SEM.Structure "SDQESC2 ← ESC"
    SEM.Structure "SDQESC3 ← ESC (1)"

    SEM.Structure "SDQASC1 ← err1 (1)"
    SEM.Structure "SDQASC2 ← err2 (1)"
    SEM.Structure "SDQASC3 ← err3 (1)"

    SEM.Structure "SDQSSC1 ← err4 (1)"
    SEM.Structure "SDQSSC2 ← err5 (1)"
    SEM.Structure "SDQSSC3 ← err6 (1)"

    SEM.Structure "SDQPSC1 ← err7 (1)"
    SEM.Structure "SDQPSC2 ← err8 (1)"
    SEM.Structure "SDQPSC3 ← err9 (1)"

    SEM.Structure "SDQESC1 ← err10 (1)"
    SEM.Structure "SDQESC2 ← err11 (1)"
    SEM.Structure "SDQESC3 ← err12 (1)"
End Sub

As you can see from this input file, AMOS makes the writing of equations a very simple task indeed. The program has been constructed in such a way that, in writing each equation, it is simply a matter of reproducing in text that which one sees in the path diagram. In reviewing the equations here, it is easy to see that the first four sets of three equations relate to the factorial structure of the model, while the last four sets relate to the observed indicator variables. Turning to the first equation, for example, we can see that the indicator variable, SDQASC1, is hypothesized as being derived from the latent factor, ASC (i.e., the arrow points toward SDQASC1). Likewise, in the first equation of the observed variables group, we can note that SDQASC1 also derives from the error term, err1. As such, the indicator variable, SDQASC1, may be regarded as a function of both the underlying factor ASC and the associated error term, err1. In other words, although SDQASC1 serves as a measure of the factor ASC, it does so with a certain degree of error; the extent of this error reflects on its reliability as a measure of ASC.

Finally, some mention needs to be made regarding the 1's that appear in parentheses. Recall that, in working with AMOS Graphics, the attachment of an indicator variable to the path diagram automatically produced a 1 on one of any set of paths. In describing the model specifications via equations in AMOS Basic, the same requirement is followed. In the latter case, however, the 1's are enclosed in parentheses. As noted in the previous section on AMOS Graphics, these fixed values relate to the issue of model identification, a topic to which we turn shortly. However, before doing so, it behooves us to first review key parameters to be estimated in SEM models, and then examine model specification defaults associated with AMOS Graphics and AMOS Basic.

AMOS GRAPHICS AND AMOS BASIC: A COMPARISON

Recall from chapter 1 that the key parameters to be estimated in a CFA model are the regression coefficients (i.e., factor loadings), the factor and error variances, and in some models (as is the case with Fig. 2.2) the factor covariances. Given that the latent and observed variables are specified either in the model (in the case of AMOS Graphics) or in the input file (in the case of AMOS Basic), AMOS automatically estimates the factor and error variances for both interfaces. In other words, variances associated with these specified variables are freely estimated by default. However, defaults related to parameter covariances are completely opposite with respect to the two interfaces. AMOS Graphics is governed by the WYSIWYG rule—What You See Is What You Get. In other words, if a covariance path is not included in the path diagram, this parameter will not be estimated (by default); if it is included, its value will be estimated. On the other hand, default rules with respect to AMOS Basic are as follows:

- *Unique latent variables* (e.g., measurement error terms; structural residual terms) are considered to be uncorrelated with each other and with all exogenous variables.
- All *observed exogenous* and *unobserved (latent) exogenous variables* are presumed to be correlated with each other.

These AMOS Basic defaults reflect the conventional assumptions associated with linear regression analysis. For example, in the CFA model displayed in Fig. 2.2, it is assumed that the exogenous (or independent) factors, ASC, SSC, PSC, and ESC are correlated. It is further assumed that the error term associated with each observed variable is independent of all other error terms.

With these default rules of AMOS Basic in mind, let's once again examine the input file in Table 2.2 as it relates to the CFA model in Fig. 2.2. In reviewing this file, we see that all specifications relate solely to the regression (i.e., factor loading) parameters. Specification statements related to the factor variances and those related to the factor covariances are noticeably absent from the input; these parameters, however, will be estimated by default.

One extremely important caveat, in working with structural equation models, is to always tally the number of parameters in the model to be estimated prior to running the analyses. This information is critical to your knowledge of whether or not the model that you are testing is statistically identified. Thus, as a prerequisite to the discussion of identification, let's count the number of parameters to be estimated for the model portrayed in Fig. 2.2. From a review of the figure, we can ascertain that there are 12 regression coefficients (factor loadings), 16 variances— 12 error variances, 4 factor variances—and 6 factor covariances. The 1's assigned to one of each set of regression path parameters represent a fixed value of 1.00; as such, these parameters are not to be estimated. In total, then, there are 30 parameters to be estimated for the CFA model depicted in Fig. 2.2. Let's now turn to a brief discussion of the important concept of model identification.

THE CONCEPT OF MODEL IDENTIFICATION

Model identification is a complex topic that is difficult to explain in nontechnical terms. Although a thorough explanation of the identification principle exceeds the scope of the present book, it is not critical to the reader's understanding and use of the book. Nonetheless, because some insight into the general concept of the identification issue will undoubtedly help you to better understand why, for example, particular parameters are specified as having certain fixed values, I attempt now to give you a brief, nonmathematical explanation of the basic idea underlying this concept. Essentially, I address only the so-called "t-rule," one of several tests associated with identification. I encourage you to consult the following texts for a more comprehensive treatment of the topic: Bollen (1989a), Hayduk (1987), Long

(1983a, 1983b), and Saris and Stronkhorst (1984). I also recommend a very clear and readable description of this topic in a book chapter by MacCallum (1995).

In broad terms, the issue of identification focuses on whether or not there is a unique set of parameters consistent with the data. This question bears directly on the transposition of the variance-covariance matrix of observed variables (the data) into the structural parameters of the model under study. If a unique solution for the values of the structural parameters can be found, the model is considered to be identified. As a consequence, the parameters are considered to be estimable and the model therefore testable. If, on the other hand, a model cannot be identified, it indicates that the parameters are subject to arbitrariness thereby implying that different parameter values define the same model; such being the case, attainment of consistent estimates for all parameters is not possible, and thus the model cannot be evaluated empirically. By way of a simple example, the process would be conceptually akin to trying to determine unique values for X and Y, when the only information you have is that $X + Y = 15$. Generalizing this example to covariance structure analysis, then, the model identification issue focuses on the extent to which a unique set of values can be inferred for the unknown parameters from a given covariance matrix of analyzed variables that is reproduced by the model.

Structural models may be just-identified, overidentified, or underidentified. A *just-identified* model is one in which there is a one-to-one correspondence between the data and the structural parameters. That is to say, the number of data variances and covariances equals the number of parameters to be estimated. However, despite the capability of the model to yield a unique solution for all parameters, the just-identified model is not scientifically interesting because it has no degrees of freedom and therefore can never be rejected. An *overidentified* model is one in which the number of estimable parameters is less than the number of data points (i.e., variances, covariances of the observed variables). This situation results in positive degrees of freedom that allow for rejection of the model, thereby rendering it of scientific use. The aim in SEM, then, is to specify a model such that it meets the criterion of overidentification. Finally, an *underidentified* model is one in which the number of parameters to be estimated exceeds the number of variances and covariances (i.e., data points). As such, the model contains insufficient information (from the input data) for the purpose of attaining a determinate solution of parameter estimation; that is, an infinite number of solutions are possible for an underidentified model.

Reviewing the CFA model in Fig. 2.2, let's now determine how many data points we have to work with (i.e., how much information do we have with respect to our data?). As noted earlier, these constitute the variances and covariances of the observed variables; with p variables, there are $p(p + 1)/2$ such elements. Given that there are 12 observed variables, this means that we have $12(12 + 1)/2 = 78$ data points. Prior to this discussion of identification, we determined a total of 30 unknown parameters. Thus, with 78 data points and 30 parameters to be estimated, we have an overidentified model with 48 degrees of freedom.

It is important to point out, however, that the specification of an overidentified model is a *necessary but not sufficient* condition to resolve the identification problem. Indeed, the imposition of constraints on particular parameters can sometimes be beneficial in helping the researcher to attain an overidentified model. An example of such a constraint is illustrated in chapter 5 with the application of a second-order CFA model.

Linked to the issue of identification is the requirement that every latent variable have its scale determined. This requirement arises because these variables are unobserved and therefore have no definite metric scale; this can be accomplished in one of two ways. The first approach is tied to specification of the measurement model whereby the unmeasured latent variable is mapped onto its related observed indicator variable. This scaling requisite is satisfied by constraining to some non-zero value (typically 1.0), one factor loading parameter in each set of loadings designed to measure the same factor. This constraint holds for both independent and dependent latent variables. In reviewing Fig. 2.2, this means that for one of the three regression paths leading from each SC factor to a set of observed indicators, some fixed value should be specified; this fixed parameter is termed a "reference" variable.[4] With respect to the model in Fig. 2.2, for example, the scale has been established by constraining to a value of 1.0, the third parameter in each set of observed variables. Recall that AMOS Graphics automatically assigned this value when the Indicator Variable Icon was activated and used to add the first indicator variable and its error term to the model. It is important to note, however, that although AMOS Graphics assigned the value of 1 to the lower regression path of each set, this assignment can be changed simply by clicking on the right mouse button and selecting Object Properties from the pop-up menu. (This modification is illustrated with the next example.)

Now that you have a better idea of how the two AMOS interfaces operate, and of the basic notions associated with model identification, we continue on our walk through two additional model specifications. In doing so, we now return to AMOS Graphics.

WORKING WITH AMOS GRAPHICS: EXAMPLE 2

In this second example of model specification, we examine the second-order model displayed in Fig. 2.19.

---

[4]Although the decision as to which parameter to constrain is purely an arbitrary one, the measure having the highest reliability is recommended, if this information is known; the value to which the parameter is constrained is also arbitrary.

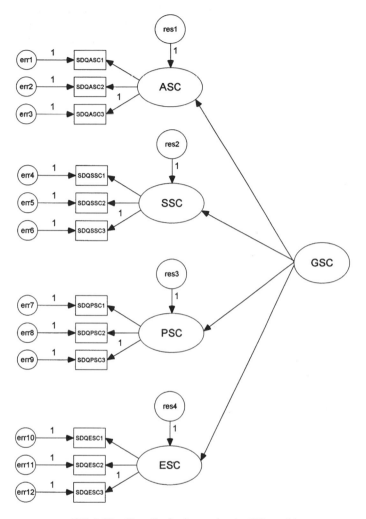

FIG. 2.19.   Hypothesized second-order CFA model.

The Hypothesized Model

In our previous factor-analytic model, we had four factors (ASC, SSC, PSC, ESC) that operated as independent variables; each could be considered to be one level, or one unidirectional arrow away from the observed variables. Such factors are termed *first-order factors*. However, it may be the case that the theory argues for some higher level factor that is considered accountable for the lower order factors. Basically, the number of levels, or unidirectional arrows, that the higher order factor is removed from the observed variables determines whether a factor model is considered to be second-order, third-order, or some higher order; only a second-order model will be examined here.

Although the model schematically portrayed in Fig. 2.19 has essentially the same first-order factor structure as the one shown in Fig. 2.2, it differs in that a higher order general self-concept (GSC) factor is hypothesized as accounting for, or explaining, all variance and covariance related to the first-order factors. As such, general SC is termed the second-order factor. It is important to take particular note of the fact that general SC does not have its own set of measured indicators; rather, it is linked indirectly to those measuring the lower-order factors. Let's now take a closer look at the parameters to be estimated for this second-order model.

I wish to draw your attention to several aspects of the second-order model shown in Fig. 2.19. First, note the presence of single-headed arrows leading from the second-order factor (GSC) to each of the first-order factors (ASC–ESC). These regression paths represent second-order factor loadings, and all are freely estimated. Recall, however, that for reasons linked to the model identification issue, a constraint must be placed either on one of the regression paths, or on the variance of an independent factor; both parameters cannot be estimated simultaneously. Because the impact of general SC on each of the lower order SC factors is of primary interest in second-order CFA models, the variance of the higher order factor is typically constrained to equal 1.0, thereby leaving the second-order factor loadings to be freely estimated.

A second aspect of this second-order model, perhaps requiring amplification, is the initial appearance that the first-order factors operate as both independent and dependent variables. This situation, however, is not so, as variables can serve either as independent, or as dependent variables in a model, but not as both.[5] Because the first-order factors function as dependent variables, it follows that their variances and covariances are no longer estimable parameters in the model; such variation is presumed to be accounted for by the higher order factor. In comparing Figs. 2.2 and 2.19, then, you will note that there are no longer two-headed curved arrows linking the first-order SC factors, thereby indicating that neither their factor covariances nor their variances are to be estimated.

Finally, the prediction of each of the first-order factors from the second-order factor is presumed not to be without error. Thus, a residual error term is associated with each of the lower level factors.

As a first step in determining whether this second-order model is identified, we now sum the number of parameters to be estimated; we have 8 first-order regression coefficients, 4 second-order regression coefficients, 12 measurement error variances, and 4 residual error terms, making a total of 28. Given that there are 78 pieces of information in the sample variance–covariance matrix, we conclude that this model is identified with 50 degrees of freedom.

---

[5]In SEM, once a variable has an arrow pointing at it, thereby targeting it as a dependent variable, it retains this status throughout the analyses.

Before leaving this identification issue, however, a word of caution is in order. With complex models in which there may be more than one level of latent variable structures, it is wise to visually check each level separately for evidence that identification has been attained. For example, although we know from our initial CFA model that the first-order level is identified, it is quite possible that the second-order level may indeed be underidentified. Because the first-order factors function as indicators of (i.e., the input data for) the second-order factor, identification is easy to assess. In the present model, we have four factors, thereby giving us 10 pieces of information from which to formulate the parameters of the higher-order structure. According to the model depicted in Fig. 2.19, we wish to estimate 8 parameters (4 regression paths, 4 residual error variances), thus leaving us with 2 degrees of freedom, and an overidentified model. However, suppose that we only had three first-order factors. We would then be left with a just-identified model as a consequence of trying to estimate 6 parameters from 6 $[3(3 + 1)/2]$ pieces of information. In order for such a model to be tested, additional constraints would need to be imposed (see chap. 5). Finally, let's suppose that there were only two first-order factors; we would then have an underidentified model because there would be only three pieces of information, albeit four parameters to be estimated. Although it might still be possible to test such a model, given further restrictions on the model, the researcher would be better advised to reformulate his or her model in light of this problem (see Rindskopf & Rose, 1988).

Drawing the Path Diagram

Now that we have dispensed with the necessary "heavy stuff," let's move on to creating the second-order model shown in Fig. 2.19, which will serve as the specification input for AMOS Graphics. We can make life easy for ourselves here simply by pulling up our first-order model (see Fig. 2.2). Because the first-order level of our new model will remain the same as that shown in Fig. 2.2, the only thing that needs to be done by way of modification is to remove all the factor covariance arrows. This task, of course, can be accomplished in AMOS in one of two ways: either by activating the Erase Icon $\boxed{\mathsf{X}}$ and clicking on each double arrow, or by placing the cursor on each double arrow and then right-clicking on the mouse which produces the menu shown in Fig. 2.20 (note that the covariance between ASC and SSC has already been deleted); following the latter procedure, you simply select the Erase option. In either case—activating an icon, or right-clicking on the mouse to obtain a menu—AMOS automatically highlights the selected parameter in red.

Having removed all the double-headed arrows representing the factor covariances from the model, our next task is to draw the ellipse representing the higher order factor of GSC. Of course, we do this by activating the Draw Unobserved Variable Icon $\boxed{\bigcirc}$. At this point, your model should resemble the one shown in Fig. 2.21.

Continuing with our path diagram, we now need to add the second-order factor regression paths. We accomplish this task by first activating the Path Icon $\boxed{\leftarrow}$ and

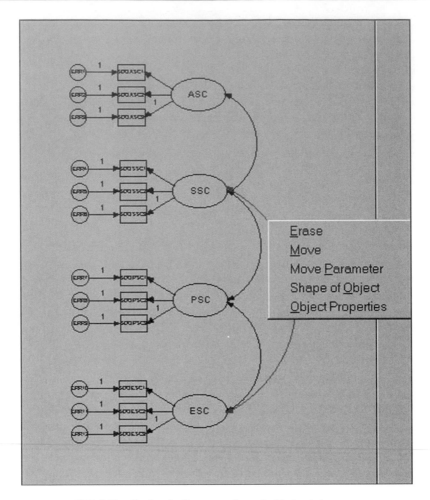

FIG. 2.20.   Erasing the factor covariance double-headed arrows.

then, with the cursor clicked on the central left side of the GSC ellipse, dragging the cursor up to where it touches the central right side of the ASC ellipse. Figure 2.22 illustrates this drawing process with respect to the first path; the process is repeated for each of the other paths.

Because each of the first-order factors is now a dependent variable in the model, we now need to add the residual error term associated with the prediction of each by the higher-order factor of GSC. To do so, we activate the Error Icon 🔲 and then click with the left mouse button on each of the ellipses representing the first-order factors. Figure 2.23 illustrates implementation of the residual error term for ASC. In this instance, only one click was completed thereby leaving the residual error term in its

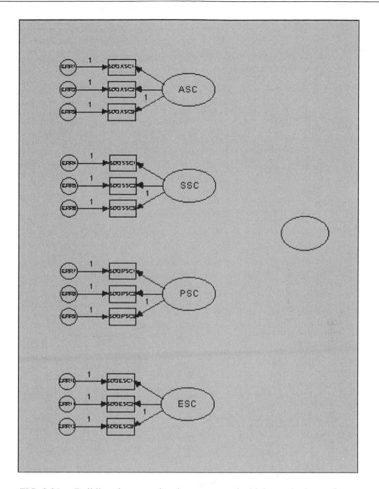

FIG. 2.21.   Building the second-order structure: the higher order latent factor.

current position. However, if we had clicked again with the left mouse button, the error term would have moved 45 degrees clockwise; with each subsequent click, the error term would continue to be moved clockwise in a similar manner.

Our last task for completing our model is to label each of the residual error terms. Recall that this process is accomplished by first placing the cursor on the object of interest (in this case the first residual error term) and then clicking with the right mouse button. This action releases the pop-up menu shown in Fig. 2.24, from which we select "Object Properties". This action subsequently yields the Object Properties box displayed in Fig. 2.25. To label the first error term, we simply add the text, RES1; this process is then repeated for each of the remaining residual error terms.

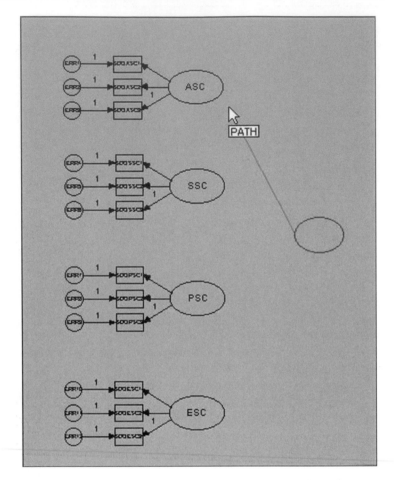

FIG. 2.22.   Building the second-order structure: the regression paths.

With our second-order CFA model completed, let's now turn to AMOS Basic and examine the same specifications in equation form.

WORKING WITH AMOS BASIC: EXAMPLE 2

The Amos input file describing the hypothesized model shown in Fig. 2.19 is presented in Table 2.3.

In reviewing this file, it is important to note several aspects of the program setup that differentiate it from the input file for the first-order CFA model shown in Fig.

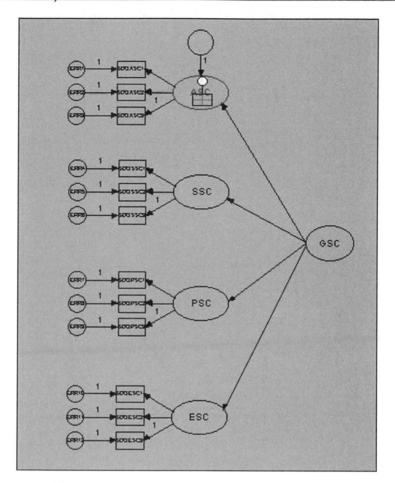

FIG. 2.23.   Building the second-order structure: the residual errors.

2.2. First, you will observe the addition of eight equations that follow the measurement error equations. The first four of these additional equations describe the regression of the first-order factors (ASC, SSC, PSC, ESC) on the second-order factor of GSC, while the last four equations represent the residual error terms associated with the prediction of each first-order factor by the higher-order factor. Second, note the addition of the specification that the variance of GSC is to be fixed at a value of 1.0. Third, recall that, by default, AMOS Basic assumes all independent variables to be correlated. However, given the additional four equations describing the regression paths between the first- and second-order factors, the program no longer makes such assumptions as the status of the first-order factors has now changed to that of dependent variables in the model. As a consequence, the covariances among these factors must be determined by the other parameters in the

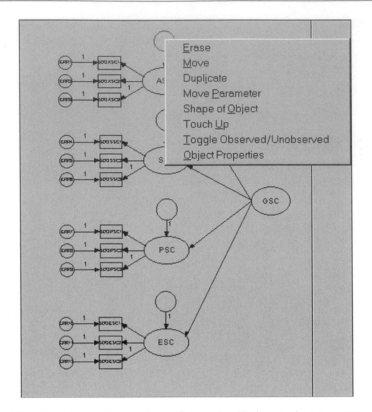

FIG. 2.24.   Labeling the second-order factor and residual errors: the popup menu.

model. As such, it is not possible to explicitly specify them, either as constrained to some fixed value, or as freely estimated parameters. In terms of the AMOS Basic input file, then, this means that no statements related to the first-order factor covariances are included. Finally, note that there are now no fixed values (of 1) associated with any of the second-order regression paths.

Let's now move on to our third and final model. As with the first two examples, we'll return once again to AMOS Graphics.

WORKING WITH AMOS GRAPHICS: EXAMPLE 3

For our last example, we examine a full SEM model. Recall from chapter 1 that, in contrast to a first-order CFA model, which comprises only a measurement compo-nent, and a second-order CFA model for which the higher order level is represent-

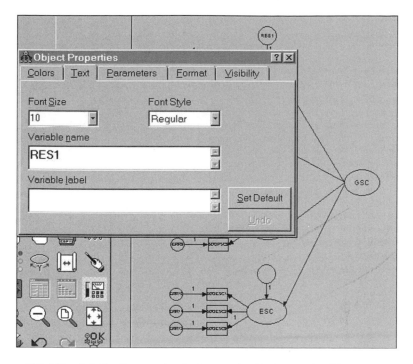

FIG. 2.25. Labeling the second-order factor and residual errors: the object properties dialog box.

ed by a reduced form of a structural model, the full structural equation model encompasses both a measurement and a structural model. Accordingly, the full model embodies a system of variables whereby latent factors are regressed on other factors as dictated by theory, as well as on the appropriate observed measures. In other words, in the full SEM model, certain latent variables are connected by one-way arrows, the directionality of which reflects hypotheses bearing on the causal structure of variables in the model. We turn now to our hypothesized model.

The Hypothesized Model

For a clearer conceptualization of full SEM models, let's examine the relatively simple structure presented in Fig. 2.26. The structural component of this model represents the hypothesis that a child's self-confidence (SCONF) derives from his or her self-perception of overall social competence (SSC; social SC), which, in turn, is influenced by the child's perception of how well he or she gets along with family members (SSCF), as well as with his or her peers at school (SSCS). The measurement component of the model shows each of the SC factors to have three indicator measures, and the self-confidence factor to have two.

TABLE 2.3
AMOS BASIC Input for Fig. 2.19

Sub Main
Dim Sem as new AmosEngine
'Input File for Figure 2.19'

SEM.BeginGroup "Filename"

SEM.Structure "SDQASC1 ← ASC"
SEM.Structure "SDQASC2 ← ASC"
SEM.Structure "SDQASC3 ← ASC (1)"
SEM.Structure "SDQSSC1 ← SSC"
SEM.Structure "SDQSSC2 ← SSC"
SEM.Structure "SDQSSC3 ← SSC (1)"
SEM.Structure "SDQPSC1 ← PSC"
SEM.Structure "SDQPSC2 ← PSC"
SEM.Structure "SDQPSC3 ← PSC (1)"
SEM.Structure "SDQESC1 ← ESC"
SEM.Structure "SDQESC2 ← ESC"
SEM.Structure "SDQESC3 ← ESC (1)"

SEM.Structure "SDQASC1 ← err1 (1)"
SEM.Structure "SDQASC2 ← err2 (1)"
SEM.Structure "SDQASC3 ← err3 (1)"
SEM.Structure "SDQSSC1 ← err4 (1)"
SEM.Structure "SDQSSC2 ← err5 (1)"
SEM.Structure "SDQSSC3 ← err6 (1)"
SEM.Structure "SDQPSC1 ← err7 (1)"
SEM.Structure "SDQPSC2 ← err8 (1)"
SEM.Structure "SDQPSC3 ← err9 (1)"
SEM.Structure "SDQESC1 ← err10 (1)"
SEM.Structure "SDQESC2 ← err11 (1)"
SEM.Structure "SDQESC3 ← err12 (1)"

SEM.Structure "ASC ← GSC"
SEM.Structure "SSC ← GSC"
SEM.Structure "PSC ← GSC"
SEM.Structure "ESC ← GSC"

SEM.Structure "ASC ← res1 (1)"
SEM.Structure "SSC ← res2 (1)"
SEM.Structure "PSC ← res3 (1)"
SEM.Structure "ESC ← res4 (1)"

SEM.Structure "GSC (1)"

End Sub

Turning first to the structural part of the model, we can see that there are four factors; the two independent factors (SSCF, SSCS) are postulated as being correlated with each other, as indicated by the curved two-way arrow joining them, but they are linked to the other two factors by a series of regression paths, as indicated by the unidirectional arrows. Because the factors SSC and SCONF have one-way arrows pointing at them, they are easily identified as dependent variables in the

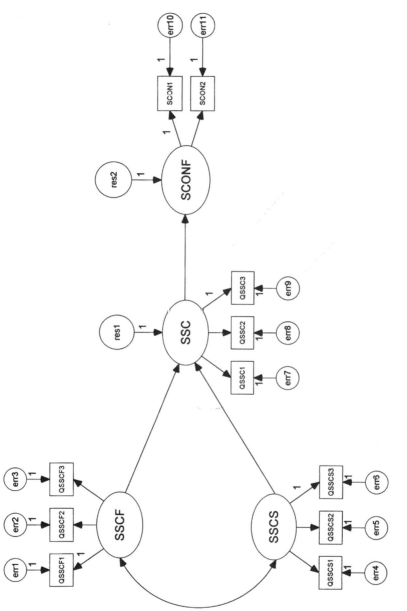

FIG. 2.26.   Hypothesized full structural equation model.

47

model. Residual errors associated with the regression of SSC on both SSCF and SSCS, and the regression of SCONF on SSC, are captured by the disturbance terms RES1 and RES2 , respectively. Finally, because one path from each of the two independent factors (SSCF, SSCS) to their respective indicator variables is fixed to 1.0, their variances can be freely estimated; variances of the dependent variables (SSC; SCONF), however, are not parameters in the model.

By now, you likely feel fairly comfortable in interpreting the measurement portion of the model, so substantial elaboration is not necessary here. As usual, associated with each observed measure is an error term, the variance of which is of interest. (Because the observed measures technically operate as dependent variables in the model, as indicated by the arrows pointing towards them, their variances are not estimated.) Finally, to establish the scale for each unmeasured factor in the model (and for purposes of identification), one parameter in each set of regression paths is fixed to 1.0; recall, however, that path selection for the imposition of this constraint was purely arbitrary.

For this, our last example, let's again determine if we have an identified model. Given that we have 11 observed measures, we know that we have 66 [11(11 + 1)/2] pieces of information from which to derive the parameters of the model. Counting up the unknown parameters in the model, we see that we have 24 parameters to be estimated: 7 measurement regression paths, 3 structural regression paths, 11 error variances, 2 residual error variances, and 1 covariance. We therefore have 42 (66 − 24) degrees of freedom and, as a consequence, an overidentified model.

Drawing the Path Diagram

Given what you now already know about drawing path diagrams within the framework of AMOS Graphics, you likely would encounter no difficulty in reproducing the hypothesized model shown in Fig. 2.26. Therefore, rather than walk you through the entire drawing process related to this model, I take the opportunity here to demonstrate two additional features of the drawing tools that, although not yet illustrated, have been mentioned previously in this chapter. The first of these involves the reorientation of error terms, usually for purposes of improving the appearance of the path diagram. With the residual error terms in the 12 o'clock position, as in Fig. 2.26, we continue to click with the left mouse button until they reach the 10 o'clock position shown in Fig. 2.27. Each click of the mouse results in a 45-degree clockwise move of the residual error term, with eight clicks thus returning us to the 12 o'clock position; the position indicated in Fig. 2.27 resulted from seven clicks of the mouse. Following the reorientation of the two residual error terms, all that remains to be done is to reenter the labels associated with each, provided that these variable names have not been previously entered.

The second feature that I wish to demonstrate is the reorientation of the fixed 1's that the program automatically assigns to the factor loading regression paths.

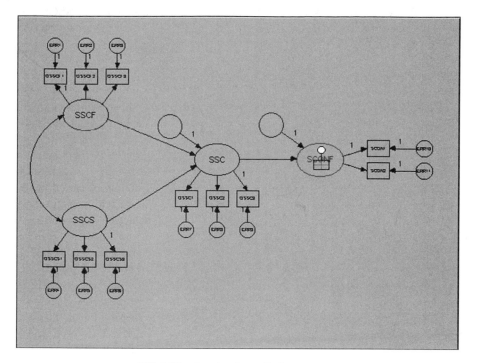

FIG. 2.27.   Rotating the residual error terms.

Turning to Fig. 2.26 again, focus on the SSCS factor in lower left corner of the diagram. Note that the fixed path for this factor has been assigned to the one associated with the prediction of QSSCS3. For purposes of illustration, let's reassign the fixed value of 1 to the first regression path (QSSCS1). This reorientation process is easily accomplished by first clicking on the presently assigned path (QSSCS3) with the right mouse button (the program will then automatically highlight this path in red), and then selecting Object Properties from the pop-up menu. This action will result in the opening of the Object Properties dialog box displayed in Fig. 2.28. Note that the regression weight is listed as 1; to remove this weight, we simply delete the value. We now right-click on the first regression path (QSSCS1) and then select Object Properties. This time, of course, the Object Properties dialog box as shown in Figure 2.29, will indicate no regression weight (the line that you see is actually the cursor); all we need to do is to simply add a value of 1. Implementation of these last two actions yielded the modified originally hypothesized model (Fig. 2.26) schematically portrayed in Fig. 2.30.

In finalizing specification of the full SEM model shown in Fig. 2.26, albeit within the AMOS Basic framework, we return once again to a review of the sets of equations comprising the input file.

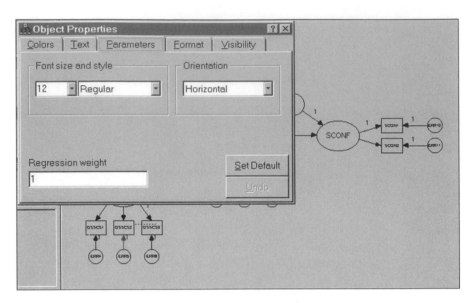

FIG. 2.28.   Reassigning a fixed regression weight: the existing parameter.

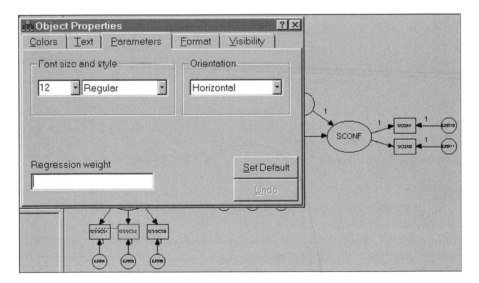

FIG. 2.29.   Reassigning a fixed regression weight: the target parameter.

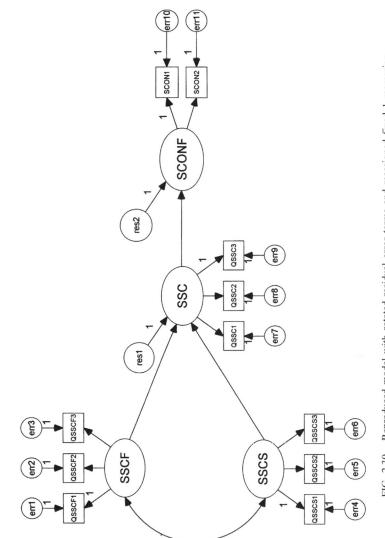

FIG. 2.30. Reproduced model with rotated residual error terms and reassigned fixed 1 regression weight.

WORKING WITH AMOS BASIC:
EXAMPLE 3

As might be expected, the model specification input file related to this model is very straightforward, as will be evident from a review of Table 2.4. Indeed, a cursory comparison between the set of equations shown in Table 2.4 and the path diagram shown in Fig. 2.26 will assure you that (a) all factor regression paths are specified, with one path in each set of indicators per factor being assigned a fixed value of 1.00, and (b) all measurement errors associated with the observed variables, and both residual errors associated with the dependent factors (SSC; SCONF), are

TABLE 2.4
AMOS BASIC Input for Fig. 2.26

Sub Main

Dim Sem as New AmosEngine
'Input File for Figure 2.26'

SEM.BeginGroup "FILENAME"

    SEM.Structure "QSSCF1 ← SSCF (1)"
    SEM.Structure "QSSCF2 ← SSCF"
    SEM.Structure "QSSCF3 ← SSCF"

    SEM.Structure "QSSCS1 ← SSCS"
    SEM.Structure "QSSCS2 ← SSCS"
    SEM.Structure "QSSCS3 ← SSCS (1)"

    SEM.Structure "QSSC1 ← SSC"
    SEM.Structure "QSSC2 ← SSC"
    SEM.Structure "QSSC3 ← SSC (1)"

    SEM.Structure "SCON1 ← SCONF (1)"
    SEM.Structure "SCON2 ← SCONF"

    SEM.Structure "QSSCF1 ← err1 (1)"
    SEM.Structure "QSSCF2 ← err2 (1)"
    SEM.Structure "QSSCF3 ← err3 (1)"

    SEM.Structure "QSSCS1 ← err4 (1)"
    SEM.Structure "QSSCS2 ← err5 (1)"
    SEM.Structure "QSSCS3 ← err6 (1)"

    SEM.Structure "QSSC1 ← err7 (1)"
    SEM.Structure "QSSC2 ← err8 (1)"
    SEM.Structure "QSSC3 ← err9 (1)"

    SEM.Structure "SCON1 ← err10 (1)"
    SEM.Structure "SCON2 ← err11 (1)"

    SEM.Structure "SSC ← res1 (1)"
    SEM.Structure "SCONF ← res2 (1)"
End Sub

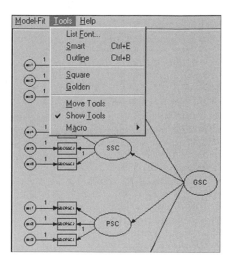

FIG. 2.31.   Tools drop-down menu.

specified, with the regression path of each being assigned a value of 1.00 (i.e., only their variances are of interest). Finally, note that no covariance is specified between the independent factors (SSCF, SSCS); AMOS, by default, automatically presumes these two factors to be correlated.

In this chapter, I have endeavored to show you the dual approaches used by the AMOS program in specifying particular models under study. I hope that I have succeeded in giving you a fairly good idea of the ease by which AMOS makes this process possible. Nonetheless, it is important for me to emphasize that, although I have introduced you to a wide variety of the program's many features in this regard, I certainly have not exhausted the total range of possibilities; to do so would far exceed the intended scope of the present book. As one case in point, I have shown you only 42 of the 67 icons available for use in AMOS Graphics (see Fig. 2.1 and Table 2.1), and I have demonstrated only a subset of this group. However, this fact in itself illustrates the manner by which you are able to tailor AMOS to meet your own specific needs. In this instance, for example, I was able to construct a palette that comprised 42 icons of my choice simply by pulling down the Tool menu (see Fig. 2.31) and selecting the option, Move Tools[6]; the Customize Toolbar box is shown in Fig. 2.32. The white screen to the right of the Toolbar box, under the heading of "Toolbar buttons," lists the icons that are already included on the palette (as shown in Fig. 2.1 and Table 2.1). The white screen on the left, under the heading "Available buttons," lists the functions that can be added to the palette simply by selecting a particular icon and then clicking on the Add → button in the middle of the box. Likewise, an icon can be removed from the palette by clicking on the ← Remove button.

_____

[6]In Figure 2.31, "Show Tools" is shown as checked because the tool palette is in use.

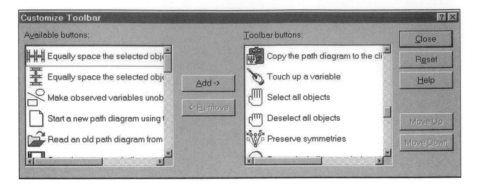

FIG. 2.32.   Customize Toolbar dialog box.

In the *AMOS 4.0 User's Guide*, Arbuckle (p. 7) noted that "no computer program is ever finished as long as people keep using it." To this end, he is continuously updating AMOS in efforts both to keep abreast of new developments in the SEM field, and to modify features in AMOS Graphics that make the drawing and manipulation of path diagrams easier for its users. For this reason, I urge you to use the present book in conjunction with the most recent *AMOS User's Guide* (Arbuckle & Wothke, 1999).

In chapter 1, I introduced you to the basic concepts underlying SEM, and in the present chapter extended this information to include the issue of model identification. Nonetheless, the thrust of chapter 2 was to introduce you to the process of model specification using both AMOS Graphics and AMOS Basic. Now that you are fairly well equipped with a knowledge of the conceptual underpinning of SEM and the basic functioning of the AMOS program, let's move on to the remaining chapters where we explore the analytic processes involved in SEM using AMOS 4.0. We turn now to chapter 3, which features an application bearing on a CFA model.

II

SINGLE-GROUP
ANALYSES

◞◟

Application 1: Testing for the Factorial Validity of a Theoretical Construct (First-Order CFA Model)

Our first application examines a first-order CFA model designed to test the multidimensionality of a theoretical construct. Specifically, this application tests the hypothesis that self-concept (SC), for early adolescents (Grade 7), is a multidimensional construct composed of four factors: general SC (GSC), academic SC (ASC), English SC (ESC), and mathematics SC (MSC). The theoretical underpinning of this hypothesis derives from the hierarchical model of SC proposed by Shavelson, Hubner, and Stanton (1976). The example is taken from a study by Byrne and Worth Gavin (1996) in which four hypotheses related to the Shavelson et al. model were tested for three groups of children: preadolescents (Grade 3), early adolescents (Grade 7), and late adolescents (Grade 11). Only tests bearing on the multidimensional structure of SC, as they relate to Grade 7 children, are relevant to this chapter. This study followed from earlier work in which the same four-factor structure of SC was tested for adolescents (see Byrne & Shavelson, 1986) and was part of a larger study that focused on the structure of social SC (Byrne & Shavelson, 1996). For a more extensive discussion of the substantive issues and the related findings, readers should refer to the original Byrne and Worth Gavin (1996) article.

THE HYPOTHESIZED MODEL

At issue in this first application is the plausibility of a multidimensional SC structure for early adolescents. Although numerous studies have supported the multidimensionality of the construct for Grade 7 children, others have counterargued that SC is less differentiated for children in their preadolescent and early adolescent years (e.g., Harter, 1990). Thus, the argument could be made for a two-factor structure comprising only GSC and ASC. Still others postulate that SC is a unidimensional structure so that all facets of SC are embodied within a single SC construct (GSC). (For a review of the literature related to these issues, see Byrne, 1996.) The task presented to us here is to test the original hypothesis that SC is a four-factor structure comprising a general component (GSC), an academic component (ASC), and two subject-specific components (ESC, MSC), against two alternative hypotheses: (a) that SC is a two-factor structure comprising GSC and ASC, and (b) that SC is a one-factor structure in which there is no distinction between general and academic SCs.

We turn now to an examination and testing of each of these hypotheses.

HYPOTHESIS 1: SELF-CONCEPT IS A FOUR-FACTOR STRUCTURE

The model to be tested in Hypothesis 1 postulates a priori that SC is a four-factor structure composed of general SC (GSC), academic SC (ASC), English SC (ESC), and math SC (MSC); it is presented schematically in Fig. 3.1.

Before any discussion of how we might go about testing this model, let's take a few minutes first to dissect the model and list its component parts as follows:

1. There are four SC factors, as indicated by the four ellipses labeled GSC, ASC, ESC, and MSC.
2. The four factors are intercorrelated, as indicated by the two-headed arrows.
3. There are 16 observed variables, as indicated by the 16 rectangles (SDQ2N01–SDQ2N43); they represent item pairs from the General, Academic, Verbal, and Math SC subscales of the Self Description Questionnaire II (Marsh, 1992a).
4. The observed variables load on the factors in the following pattern: SDQ2N01–SDQ2N37 load on Factor 1; SDQ2N04–SDQ2N40 load on Factor 2; SDQ2N10–SDQ2N46 load on Factor 3; and SDQ2N07–SDQ2N43 load on Factor 4.
5. Each observed variable loads on one and only one factor.
6. Errors of measurement associated with each observed variable (err01–err43) are uncorrelated.

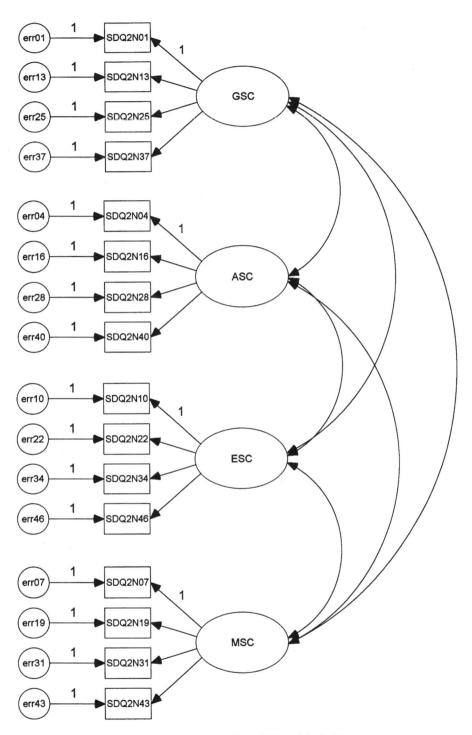

FIG. 3.1. Hypothesized four-factor CFA model of self-concept.

Summarizing these observations, we can now present a more formal description of our hypothesized model. As such, we state that the CFA model presented in Fig. 3.1 hypothesizes a priori that:

1. SC responses can be explained by four factors: GSC, ASC, ESC, and MSC.
2. Each item-pair measure has a nonzero loading on the SC factor that it was designed to measure (termed a *target loading*), and a zero loading on all other factors (termed *nontarget loadings*).
3. The four SC factors, consistent with the theory, are correlated.
4. Error/uniquenesses[1] associated with each measure are uncorrelated.

Another way of conceptualizing the hypothesized model in Fig. 3.1 is within a matrix framework as presented in Table 3.1. Thinking about the model components in this format can be very helpful because it is consistent with the manner by which the results from SEM analyses are commonly reported in program output files. Although AMOS, as well as other Windows-based programs, also provides users with a graphical output, the labeled information is typically limited to the estimated values and their standard errors. The tabular representation of our model in Table 3.1 shows the pattern of parameters to be estimated within the framework of three matrices: the factor loading matrix, the factor variance/covariance matrix, and the error variance/covariance matrix. For purposes of model identification and latent variable scaling (see chap. 2), you will note that the first of each congeneric set of SC measures in the factor loading matrix is set to 1.0^2; all other parameters are either freely estimated (as represented by the dollar [$] sign) or fixed to zero (0.0). In the variance/covariance matrix, all parameters are to be freely estimated. Finally, in the error/uniqueness matrix, only the error variances are estimated; all error covariances are presumed to be zero.

Provided with these two perspectives of the hypothesized model, let's now move on to the actual testing of the model. As described in chapter 2, AMOS provides us with two alternative approaches to model specification—one within a graphical framework using AMOS Graphics, and the other within the more traditional framework of an equation format using AMOS Basic.

We begin by examining the route to model specification, data specification, and the calculation of parameter estimates within the separate frameworks of AMOS Graphics and AMOS Basic. However, because the output for both interfaces is

---

[1]The term *uniqueness* is used here in the factor-analytic sense to mean a composite of random measurement error, and specific measurement error associated with a particular measuring instrument; in cross-sectional studies, the two cannot be separated (Gerbing & Anderson, 1984).

[2]A set of measures is said to be *congeneric* if each measure in the set purports to assess the same construct, except for errors of measurement (Joreskog, 1971a). For example, as indicated in Table 3.1 and Fig. 3.1, SDQ2N01, SDQ2N13, SDQ2N25, and SDQ2N37 all serve as measures of general self-concept (GSC); they therefore represent a congeneric set of indicator variables.

TABLE 3.1

Pattern of Estimated Parameters for Hypothesized Four-Factor Model

Observed Measure	GSC F_1	ASC F_2	ESC F_3	MSC F_4
Factor loading matrix				
SDQ2N01	1.0[a]	0.0	0.0	0.0
SDQ2N13	$[b]	0.0	0.0	0.0
SDQ2N25	$	0.0	0.0	0.0
SDQ2N37	$	0.0	0.0	0.0
SDQ2N04	0.0[c]	1.0	0.0	0.0
SDQ2N16	0.0	$	0.0	0.0
SDQ2N28	0.0	$	0.0	0.0
SDQ2N40	0.0	$	0.0	0.0
SDQ2N10	0.0	0.0	1.0	0.0
SDQ2N22	0.0	0.0	$	0.0
SDQ2N34	0.0	0.0	$	0.0
SDQ2N46	0.0	0.0	$	0.0
SDQ2N07	0.0	0.0	0.0	1.0
SDQ2N19	0.0	0.0	0.0	$
SDQ2N31	0.0	0.0	0.0	$
SDQ2N43	0.0	0.0	0.0	$
Factor variance/covariance matrix				
GSC	$			
ASC	$	$		
ESC	$	$	$	
MSC	$	$	$	$

(Continued)

TABLE 3.1 *(Continued)*

Error variance/covariance matrix

	01	13	25	37	04	16	28	40	10	22	34	46	07	19	31	43
SDQ2N01	$															
SDQ2N13	0.0	$														
SDQ2N25	0.0	0.0	$													
SDQ2N37	0.0	0.0	0.0	$												
SDQ2N04	0.0	0.0	0.0	0.0	$											
SDQ2N16	0.0	0.0	0.0	0.0	0.0	$										
SDQ2N28	0.0	0.0	0.0	0.0	0.0	0.0	$									
SDQ2N40	0.0	0.0	0.0	0.0	0.0	0.0	0.0	$								
SDQ2N10	0.0	0.0	0.0	0.0	0.0	0.0	0.0	0.0	$							
SDQ2N22	0.0	0.0	0.0	0.0	0.0	0.0	0.0	0.0	0.0	$						
SDQ2N34	0.0	0.0	0.0	0.0	0.0	0.0	0.0	0.0	0.0	0.0	$					
SDQ2N46	0.0	0.0	0.0	0.0	0.0	0.0	0.0	0.0	0.0	0.0	0.0	$				
SDQ2N07	0.0	0.0	0.0	0.0	0.0	0.0	0.0	0.0	0.0	0.0	0.0	0.0	$			
SDQ2N19	0.0	0.0	0.0	0.0	0.0	0.0	0.0	0.0	0.0	0.0	0.0	0.0	0.0	$		
SDQ2N31	0.0	0.0	0.0	0.0	0.0	0.0	0.0	0.0	0.0	0.0	0.0	0.0	0.0	0.0	$	
SDQ2N43	0.0	0.0	0.0	0.0	0.0	0.0	0.0	0.0	0.0	0.0	0.0	0.0	0.0	0.0	0.0	$

[a]Parameter fixed to 1.0.
[b]Parameter to be estimated.
[c]Parameter fixed to 0.0.

identical, the two perspectives are not considered separately in the presentation of results. It is important to note once again that, in the interest of space, an elaboration of the AMOS Basic approach to SEM is limited to this chapter only. For all remaining chapters, the AMOS Basic input file, together with any explanatory comments, is included at the end of each chapter.

MODELING WITH AMOS GRAPHICS

Model Specification

The beauty of working with the AMOS Graphics interface is that all we need to do is to provide the program with an hypothesized model; in the present case, we use the one portrayed in Fig. 3.1. Given that I demonstrated most of the commonly used drawing tools, and their application, in chapter 2, there is really no need for me to walk you through the construction of this model here. Likewise, construction of hypothesized models presented throughout the remainder of the book is not detailed. Nonetheless, I take the opportunity, wherever possible, to illustrate a few of the other drawing tools or features of AMOS Graphics not specifically demonstrated earlier. For example, used in combination, two tools that I have found to be invaluable in working on various parts of a model are the Magnification ⊕ and the Scroll ⊞ tools. Click first on the Magnification icon to enlarge the model and then click on the Scroll Icon to move around the entire diagram. The results of these actions are demonstrated in Fig. 3.2. Once you have finished your closeup work, simply click on the Reduction icon ⊖ to return to normal view (you may have to use the Scroll icon to reorient the positioning of your diagram).

Data Specification

Now that we have provided AMOS with the model to be analyzed, we need next to tell the program where to find the data. All data to be used in applications throughout this book have been placed in an AMOS folder called Data Files. To activate this folder, we can either click on the Data File icon ▦, or we can pull down the File menu and select Data Files. Either choice will trigger the Data Files dialog box displayed in Fig. 3.3; it is shown here as it pops up in the forefront of your workspace.

In reviewing the upper section of this dialog box, you see that the program has identified the Group Name as "Group Number 1"; this labeling is default in the analysis of single sample data. The data file to be used for the current analysis is labeled "ASC7INDM.TXT" and the sample size is 265; the 265/265 indicates that 265, of a total sample size of 265, have been selected for inclusion in the analysis. In the lower half of the dialog box, note a button (View Data) that allows you to peruse the data in spreadsheet form should you wish to do so. Once you have

err04
SDQ2N04
err16
SDQ2N16
err28
SDQ2N28
err40
SDQ2N40
ASC
err10
SDQ2N10
err22
SDQ2N22
err34
SDQ2N34
err46
SDQ2N46
ESC
Group number 1
scroll
Title
DF

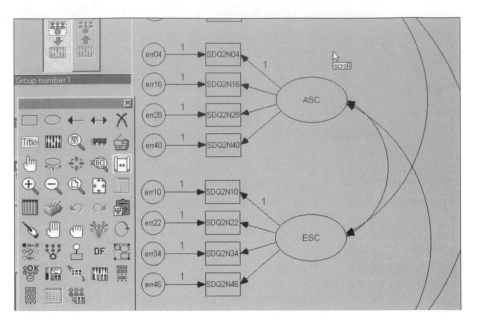

FIG. 3.2. AMOS Graphics: scrolling through magnified version of the hypothesized model.

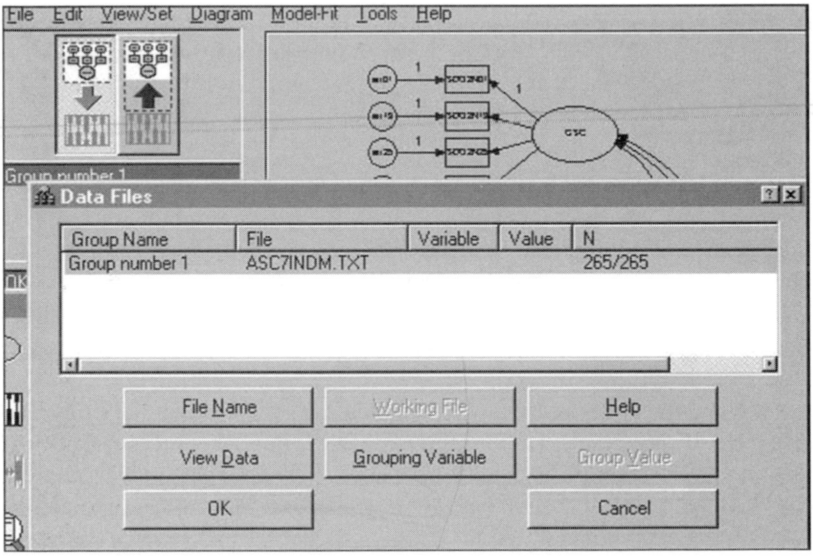

File Edit View/Set Diagram Model-Fit Tools Help
Data Files
Group Name
File
Variable
Value
N
Group number 1
ASC7INDM.TXT
265/265
File Name
Working File
Help
View Data
Grouping Variable
Group Value
OK
Cancel

FIG. 3.3. AMOS Graphics: the Data Files dialog box.

selected the data file that will serve as the working file upon which your hypothesized model is based, you simply click on the OK button.

In the example shown here, the selected data file was already visible in the Data Files dialog box. However, suppose that you wanted to select from a list of several available data sets. To do so, you would click on the File Name button in the Data Files dialog box (see Fig. 3.3). This action would then trigger the Open dialog box shown in Fig. 3.4. Here, you select a data file and then click on the Open button. Once you have opened a file, it becomes the working file and its file name will then appear in the Data Files dialog box, as illustrated in Fig. 3.3.

Before moving on to the parameter estimation section, it is important that I point out some of the requirements of the AMOS program in the use of external data sets. If your data files are in ASCII format (as all of mine were), you will need to restructure them before you are able to conduct any analyses using AMOS. Consistent with SPSS and many other Windows applications, the most recent version of AMOS requires that data be structured in the comma-delimited format. (The semicolon delimiter is used in many European and Asian countries.) Furthermore, in contrast to earlier versions of the program wherein data could be included with a $ Command window, all data must now reside in an external file. (For a more extensive elaboration of acceptable database formats, see Arbuckle & Wothke, 1999.)

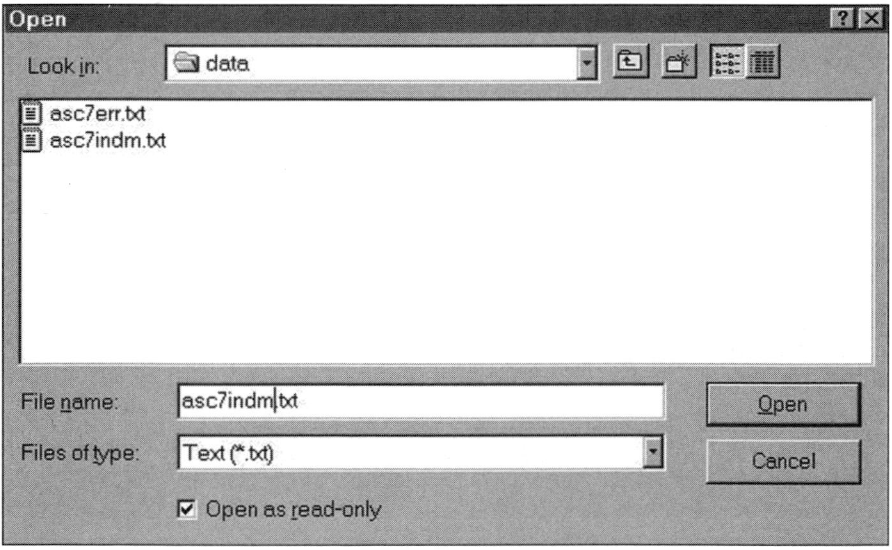

FIG. 3.4.   AMOS Graphics: the Open (Data) dialog box.

Calculation of Estimates

Now that we have specified both the model to be analyzed, and the data file upon which the analyses are to be based, all that is left for us to do is to execute the job; we do so by clicking on the Calculate Estimates icon ▓. (Alternatively, we could have selected Calculate Estimates from the Model-fit drop-down menu.) Having clicked the Calculate Estimates icon, I was presented with the error message shown in Fig. 3.5. Given that SDQ2N28 was, indeed, an observed variable in the model, I reasoned that the problem obviously lay elsewhere in my setup. The question, of course, was where? As it turns out, I had unknowingly made a typographical error in the process of entering variable labels in my reoriented data file; corrected spelling alleviated the problem. I consider it important to point this error out to you as it may save you a great deal of time otherwise spent trying to make sense out of such an error message. The moral of the story here is to always double check your input data before running the analyses!

Once the analyses have been completed, AMOS Graphics allows you to review the results from three entirely different perspectives—graphical, tabular, and textual. In the graphical output, all estimates are presented in the path diagram. These results are obtained by clicking on the View Output Path Diagram icon ▓. Results related to the testing of our hypothesized model are presented in Fig. 3.6.

The full AMOS output can be displayed either in spreadsheet format by clicking on the Table Output icon ▓ or by selecting "Table Output" from the View drop-down menu. Likewise, the output can be displayed in text format by clicking

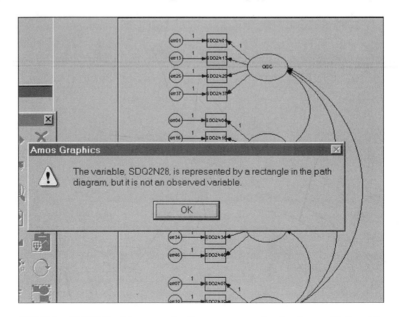

FIG. 3.5.   AMOS Graphics: example of error message related to the specified model.

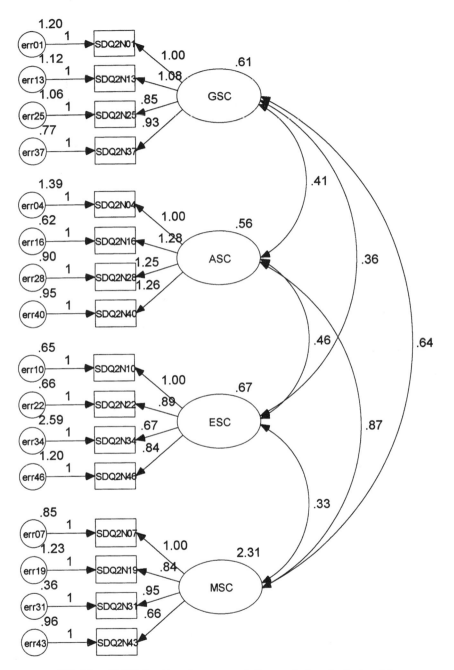

FIG. 3.6. AMOS Graphics: the output path diagram for hypothesized model.

on the Text Output icon ▓, or by making the correct selection from the drop-down menu. As noted earlier, given identical output for both AMOS Graphics and AMOS Basic, all discussion related to the testing of our hypothesized model is presented following the AMOS Basic approach to the analyses. We turn now to this topic.

MODELING WITH AMOS BASIC

Model Specification

As described in chapter 2, program input describing a model, in AMOS Basic, is specified using a series of linear equations. Model specification related to the hypothesized model in Fig. 3.1 is presented in Table 3.2.

In reviewing the input file in Table 3.2, note two commands that were not previously included in the example input files in chapter 2. The first of these (SEM.Text Output) indicates that the preferred output file is that of text. The second command (SEM.Mods 4) requests the computation of modification indices (MIs). The accompanying number 4 indicates that a threshold of 4 is to be used as the cutoff point (i.e., only MIs > 4.00 will be included in the output file).

Turning to the model specification equations, observe that the only specifications provided to the program are linear regression equations related to the observed variables (i.e., the data). The first set of equations (representing the factor loadings) summarizes the influence of each latent factor on its related observed variables; the second set specifies that measurement error is associated with each observed variable. Because only variance related to measurement error is of interest, their regression paths are fixed to 1.0 for purposes of model identification (see chap. 2). Recall that, by default, AMOS Basic assumes all factors to be intercorrelated, all measurement errors to be uncorrelated, and the variance of all independent factors and measurement errors to be estimated. As a consequence of these programmed assumptions, no additional model input is needed.

Data Specification

As was the case with AMOS Graphics, before we can test the model, we must first attach the data. In AMOS Basic, this task is accomplished simply by including the name of the data set in the input file. An important point to note with respect to this input file, however, is that no embedded spaces are allowed in the command lines. For example, "SEM.BeginGroup" cannot be written as "SEM. Begin Group."

Calculation of Estimates

Having specified both the model, and the data to be used in testing the model, via the input file, we are now ready to execute the job. In AMOS Basic, this task is accomplished by clicking on the Start/Resume arrow shown in Fig. 3.7.

TABLE 3.2
AMOS BASIC Input for Hypothesized Four-Factor CFA Model

Sub Main

Dim Sem as New AmosEngine
'Testing for Multidimensionality of SC for Grade 7 Sample'
'1st-order CFA Model'
'Initial Model'

SEM.TextOutput
SEM.Mods 4

SEM.BeginGroup "asc7indm.txt"

    SEM.Structure "SDQ2N01 ← GSC (1)"
    SEM.Structure "SDQ2N13 ← GSC"
    SEM.Structure "SDQ2N25 ← GSC"
    SEM.Structure "SDQ2N37 ← GSC"

    SEM.Structure "SDQ2N04 ← ASC (1)"
    SEM.Structure "SDQ2N16 ← ASC"
    SEM.Structure "SDQ2N28 ← ASC"
    SEM.Structure "SDQ2N40 ← ASC"

    SEM.Structure "SDQ2N10 ← ESC (1)"
    SEM.Structure "SDQ2N22 ← ESC"
    SEM.Structure "SDQ2N34 ← ESC"
    SEM.Structure "SDQ2N46 ← ESC"

    SEM.Structure "SDQ2N07 ← MSC (1)"
    SEM.Structure "SDQ2N19 ← MSC"
    SEM.Structure "SDQ2N31 ← MSC"
    SEM.Structure "SDQ2N43 ← MSC"

    SEM.Structure "SDQ2N01 ← err01 (1)"
    SEM.Structure "SDQ2N13 ← err13 (1)"
    SEM.Structure "SDQ2N25 ← err25 (1)"
    SEM.Structure "SDQ2N37 ← err37 (1)"
    SEM.Structure "SDQ2N04 ← err04 (1)"
    SEM.Structure "SDQ2N16 ← err16 (1)"
    SEM.Structure "SDQ2N28 ← err28 (1)"
    SEM.Structure "SDQ2N40 ← err40 (1)"
    SEM.Structure "SDQ2N10 ← err10 (1)"
    SEM.Structure "SDQ2N22 ← err22 (1)"
    SEM.Structure "SDQ2N34 ← err34 (1)"
    SEM.Structure "SDQ2N46 ← err46 (1)"
    SEM.Structure "SDQ2N07 ← err07 (1)"
    SEM.Structure "SDQ2N19 ← err19 (1)"
    SEM.Structure "SDQ2N31 ← err31 (1)"
    SEM.Structure "SDQ2N43 ← err43 (1)"

End Sub

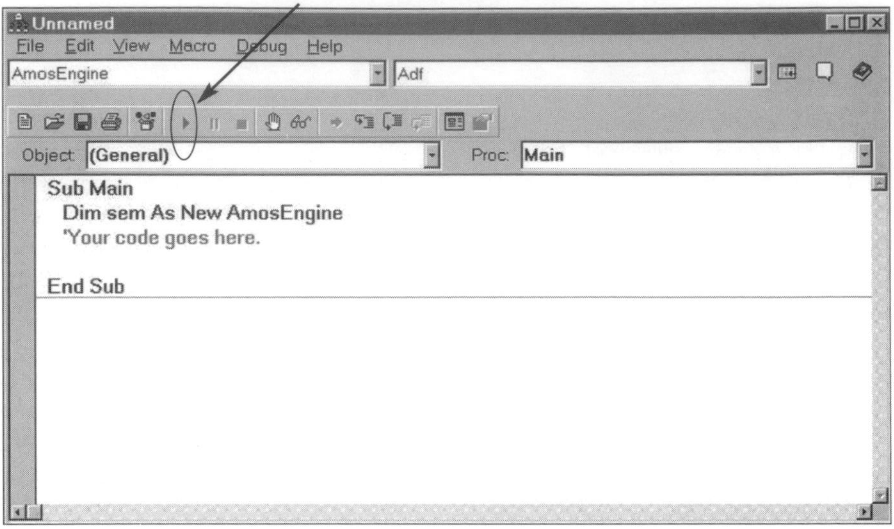

FIG. 3.7.   AMOS Basic: location of the Start/Resume button.

MODELING WITH AMOS:
GRAPHICS AND BASIC

Parameter Estimation

By default, the estimation of parameters will be based on the maximum likelihood (ML) method. However, it is important to note that use of ML estimation assumes that the following conditions have been met: (a) The sample is very large (asymptotic), (b) the distribution of the observed variables is multivariate normal, (c) the hypothesized model is valid (West, Finch, & Curran, 1995), and (d) the scale of the observed variables is continuous. Of these four assumptions underlying the use of ML estimation in SEM analyses, the final one concerning scaling has been the subject of considerable debate over the past few years. Essentially, the controversy evolves around the treatment of ordinally scaled variables as if they were of a continuous scale. A typical example is the situation where the data represent item or subscale scores based on a Likert-type scale, but they are analyzed using either SEM or any traditional statistical techniques (e.g., ANOVA, MANOVA) wherein the assumption is made that the variables are of a continuous scale. Given the prevalence of this practice in the SEM field, I consider it important that you have some understanding of the issues related to this topic. Thus, before proceeding with an examination of our AMOS output, let's digress briefly in order to review some of the major issues and recent literature bearing upon the analysis of categorical data.

The Analysis of Categorical Data

A review of SEM applications over the past 15 years (in the case of psychological research at least) reveals most to be based on Likert-type scaled data with estimation of parameters using ML procedures (see Breckler, 1990). However, given the known limitations associated with available alternative estimation strategies, this common finding is not surprising. Accordingly, the two primary approaches to the analysis of categorical data were developed by Joreskog (1990) and Muthén (1984). Both methodologies use limited information estimators based on Browne's (1984) asymptotic distribution-free (ADF) estimator (Wothke, 1993). Unfortunately, the positive aspects of these categorical variable methodologies are offset by three major restrictions of importance to practical researchers: (a) the need for very large sample sizes, (b) the limited number of observed variables (<25; Bentler & Chou, 1987; Mislevy, 1986), and (c) the very strong assumption that underlying each categorical observed variable is an unobserved latent variable counterpart that has a continuous scale; furthermore, these latent continuous variables are assumed to be multivariate normally distributed (Bentler & Wu, 1995). Because this assumption is extremely strong and may not be appropriate in certain contexts, Bentler and associates (Chou, Bentler, & Satorra, 1991; Hu, Bentler, & Kano, 1992), for example, have argued that it may make more sense to treat the categorical variables as if they were continuous and correct the test statistic, rather than to use a different mode of estimation. Indeed, the Satorra–Bentler scaled statistic (Satorra & Bentler, 1988) can be used to make such a correction. These three impediments have been instrumental in rendering this distribution-free estimation approach of little practical use to most researchers in their analyses of real (as opposed to simulated) data.

In light of these impracticalities, it behooves us to know the risks involved in treating categorical variables as if they were continuous. From a review of Monte Carlo studies that addressed this issue (see Babakus, Ferguson, & Joreskog, 1987; Boomsma, 1982; Muthén & Kaplan, 1985), West and colleagues (1995) reported several important findings. First, Pearson correlation coefficients are higher when computed between two continuous variables than when computed between the same two variables restructured with an ordered categorical scale. However, the greatest attenuation occurs with variables having less than five categories and those exhibiting a high degree of skewness; the latter condition is made worse by variables that are skewed in opposite directions (i.e., one variable positively skewed, the other negatively skewed) (see Bollen & Barb, 1981). Second, when categorical variables approximate a normal distribution, (a) the number of categories has little effect on the χ^2 likelihood ratio test of model fit. Nonetheless, increasing skewness, and particularly differential skewness (variables skewed in opposite directions), leads to increasingly inflated χ^2 values; (b) factor loadings and factor correlations are only modestly underestimated. However, underestimation becomes more critical when there are fewer than three categories, skewness is greater than 1.0, and differential skewness occurs across variables; (c) error variance estimates, more so than other parameters, appear to be most sensitive to the categorical and skewness issues noted in (b); and (d) standard error estimates for all parameters tend to be low, with this result being more so when the distributions are highly and differentially skewed (see also Finch, West, & MacKinnon, 1997).

At the present time, AMOS does not yet offer researchers the option of analyzing data with the categorical nature of the variables taken into account. However, from this cursory discussion, you should now have some understanding of the multiplicity of difficulties involved in structuring a SEM program to incorporate such an option. In this book, therefore, all applications are based on ML estimation, with all data being treated as of a continuous scale. Thus, I consider it important that you be cognizant of two valuable points in support of this strategy. First, maximum likelihood estimation is less problematic when the covariance, rather than the correlation matrix, is analyzed; analysis of the latter can yield incorrect standard error estimates (Joreskog & Sorbom, 1996a). Second, when the number of categories is large, the failure to address the ordinality of the data is likely negligible (Atkinson, 1988; Babakus et al., 1987; Muthén & Kaplan, 1985). Indeed, Bentler and Chou (1987, p. 88) argued that, given normally distributed categorical variables, "continuous methods can be used with little worry when a variable has four or more categories." More recent findings support these earlier contentions and have further shown that the χ^2 statistic is influenced most by the two-category response format and becomes less so as the number of categories increases (Green, Akey, Fleming, Hershberger, & Marquis, 1997).

Let's turn now, then, to the results of our initial test of model fit.

AMOS Text Output: Hypothesized Four-Factor Model

As noted earlier, in reviewing output from either AMOS Graphics or AMOS Basic, one can choose between having the results presented in Table format (i.e., spreadsheet form), or in Text format (i.e., regular text form). Throughout this book, I have chosen to present this information in Text format. To facilitate the presentation and discussion of results in this current chapter, the material is divided into three sections: (a) Model, Parameters, and Estimation Summary, (b) Model Assessment, and (c) Model Misspecification. We turn first to Table 3.3, in which all information related to the job run is summarized.

Model, Parameters, and Estimation Summary

The initial information provided in the AMOS text output file can be invaluable in helping you to resolve any difficulties with the specification of a model. Listed first are all the variables in the model, accompanied by their categorization as either observed or unobserved, and as endogenous or exogenous. Consistent with the path diagram in Fig. 3.1, all the observed variables (i.e., the input data) operate

TABLE 3.3
AMOS Text Output for Hypothesized Four-Factor CFA Model: Parameter and Model Summary

Your model contains the following variables

SDQ2N37	observed	endogenous
SDQ2N25	observed	endogenous
SDQ2N13	observed	endogenous
SDQ2N01	observed	endogenous
SDQ2N40	observed	endogenous
SDQ2N28	observed	endogenous
SDQ2N16	observed	endogenous
SDQ2N04	observed	endogenous
SDQ2N46	observed	endogenous
SDQ2N34	observed	endogenous
SDQ2N22	observed	endogenous
SDQ2N10	observed	endogenous
SDQ2N43	observed	endogenous
SDQ2N31	observed	endogenous
SDQ2N19	observed	endogenous
SDQ2N07	observed	endogenous
GSC	unobserved	exogenous
err37	unobserved	exogenous
err25	unobserved	exogenous
err13	unobserved	exogenous
err01	unobserved	exogenous
ASC	unobserved	exogenous
err40	unobserved	exogenous
err28	unobserved	exogenous
err16	unobserved	exogenous
err04	unobserved	exogenous
ESC	unobserved	exogenous
err46	unobserved	exogenous
err34	unobserved	exogenous
err22	unobserved	exogenous
err10	unobserved	exogenous
MSC	unobserved	exogenous
err43	unobserved	exogenous
err31	unobserved	exogenous
err19	unobserved	exogenous
err07	unobserved	exogenous

```
Number of variables in your model:   36
Number of observed variables:        16
Number of unobserved variables:      20
Number of exogenous variables:       20
Number of endogenous variables:      16
```

Parameter Summary

	Weights	Covariances	Variances	Means	Intercepts	Total
Fixed:	20	0	0	0	0	20
Labeled:	0	0	0	0	0	0
Unlabeled:	12	6	20	0	0	38
Total:	32	6	20	0	0	58

(Continued)

TABLE 3.3 *(Continued)*

Model Summary

The model is recursive.

Sample size: 265

Computation of Degrees of Freedom

                    Number of distinct sample moments: 136
        Number of distinct parameters to be estimated: 38

                              Degrees of freedom: 98

Minimum was achieved

Chi-square =   158.511
Degrees of freedom =   98
Probability level =   0.000

---

as dependent variables in the model; all factors and error terms are unobserved, and operate as independent variables in the model. This information is followed by a summary of the total number of variables in the model, as well as the number in each of the four categories.

The next section focuses on a summary of the parameters in the model. Moving from left to right, we see that there are 32 regression weights, 20 of which are fixed and 12 of which are estimated; the 20 fixed regression weights include the first of each set of 4 factor loadings and the 16 error terms. There are 6 covariances and 20 variances, all of which are estimated. In total, there are 58 parameters, 38 of which are to be estimated. Provided with this summary, it is now easy for you to determine the appropriate number of degrees of freedom and, ultimately, whether or not the model is identified.

The program next provides you with an overall summary of the model to be tested and the data to be used. As such, we see that the hypothesized model is of a recursive type, and that the sample size is 265. Finally, it provides you with the information needed in determining the identification status of the model. As shown, we have 136 pieces of information (i.e., number of distinct sample moments) from which to compute the estimates of the model, and 38 parameters to be estimated, leaving us with 98 degrees of freedom. Recall that the only data we have to work with in SEM are the observed variables; in the present case, we have 16. Based on the formula $p(p + 1)/2$ (see chap. 2), computation of the sample covariance matrix for these data therefore yields 136 sample moments [16(17)/2].

From this information, we can conclude that we have an overidentified model with 98 degrees of freedom.

The last few lines in this section of the AMOS output serve as a summary of the estimation process. We are advised that the Minimum was achieved, thereby assuring us that the estimation process yielded an admissible solution. Finally, to provide you with a quick overview of model fit, the program prints out the chi-square (χ^2) value (158.511), together with its degrees of freedom (98) and probability value (0.000).

Model Assessment

Of primary interest in structural equation modeling is the extent to which an hypothesized model "fits" or, in other words, adequately describes the sample data. Given findings of an inadequate goodness of fit, the next logical step is to detect the source of misfit in the model. Ideally, evaluation of model fit should derive from a variety of perspectives and be based on several criteria that can assess model fit from a diversity of perspectives. In particular, these focus on the adequacy of (a) the parameter estimates and (b) the model as a whole. We turn our attention first to the fit of individual parameters in the model, of which there are three aspects of concern: (a) the feasibility of the parameter estimates, (b) the appropriateness of the standard errors, and (c) the statistical significance of the parameter estimates.

Parameter Estimates

Feasibility of Parameter Estimates. The initial step in assessing the fit of individual parameters in a model is to determine the viability of their estimated values. In particular, parameter estimates should exhibit the correct sign and size, and be consistent with the underlying theory. Any estimates falling outside the admissible range signal a clear indication that either the model is wrong, or the input matrix lacks sufficient information. Examples of parameters exhibiting unreasonable estimates are correlations >1.00, negative variances, and covariance or correlation matrices that are not positive definite.

Appropriateness of Standard Errors. Another indicator of poor model fit is the presence of standard errors that are excessively large or small. For example, if a standard error approaches zero, the test statistic for its related parameter cannot be defined (Bentler, 1995). Likewise, standard errors that are extremely large indicate parameters that cannot be determined (Joreskog & Sorbom, 1989).[3] Because standard errors are influenced by the units of measurement in observed and/or latent variables, as well as the magnitude of the parameter estimate itself, no definitive criterion of "small" and "large" has been established (see Joreskog & Sorbom, 1989).

---

[3]Inaccurate standard errors are commonly found when analyses are based on the correlation matrix (Bollen, 1989a; Boomsma, 1985).

Statistical Significance of Parameter Estimates.   The test statistic here is the critical ratio (c.r.), which represents the parameter estimate divided by its standard error; as such, it operates as a z-statistic in testing that the estimate is statistically different from zero. Based on a level of .05, the test statistic needs to be $>\pm1.96$ before the hypothesis (that the estimate equals 0.0) can be rejected. Nonsignificant parameters, with the exception of error variances, can be considered unimportant to the model; in the interest of scientific parsimony, albeit given an adequate sample size, they should be deleted from the model. On the other hand, it is important to note that nonsignificant parameters can be indicative of a sample size that is too small (Joreskog, personal communication, January 1997).

Let's turn now to this section of the AMOS text output file, which is presented in Table 3.4. It is important to note that, for simplicity, all estimates related to our first hypothesized model are presented only in the unstandardized form; further options are examined in subsequent applications.

As you can readily see, results are presented separately for the factor loadings (listed as regression weights), the covariances (in this case, for factors only), and the variances (in this case, for both factors and measurement errors). The parameter estimation information is very clearly and succinctly presented in the AMOS text output file. Listed to the right of each parameter is its estimated value (column 1), standard error (column 2), and critical ratio (column 3). An examination of this unstandardized solution reveals all estimates to be both reasonable and statistically significant; all standard errors appear also to be in good order.

Model as a Whole

In the text output summary table presented in Table 3.3, we saw that AMOS provided the overall χ^2 value, together with its degrees of freedom and probability value. However, this information is intended only as a quick overview of model fit. Indeed, the program, by default, provides many other fit statistics in its output file. Before turning to this section of the AMOS output, however, it is worthwhile to review four important aspects of fitting hypothesized models; these are: (a) the rationale upon which the model-fitting process is based, (b) the issue of statistical significance, (c) the estimation process, and (d) the goodness-of-fit statistics.

The Model-Fitting Process.   In chapter 1, I presented a general description of this process and noted that the primary task is to determine the goodness of fit between the hypothesized model and the sample data. In other words, the researcher specifies a model and then uses the sample data to test the model.

With a view to helping you to gain a better understanding of the goodness-of-fit statistics presented in the AMOS Output file, let's take a few moments to recast this model-fitting process within a more formalized framework. As such, let S represent the sample covariance matrix (of observed variable scores), Σ (sigma) the population covariance matrix, and θ (theta) a vector that comprises the model parameters.

TABLE 3.4
AMOS Text Output for Hypothesized Four-Factor CFA Model: Parameter Estimates

```
Maximum Likelihood Estimates
----------------------------
```

Regression Weights:

	Estimate	S.E.	C.R.	Label
SDQ2N37 <-------- GSC	0.934	0.131	7.117	
SDQ2N25 <-------- GSC	0.851	0.132	6.443	
SDQ2N13 <-------- GSC	1.083	0.154	7.030	
SDQ2N01 <-------- GSC	1.000			
SDQ2N40 <-------- ASC	1.259	0.157	8.032	
SDQ2N28 <-------- ASC	1.247	0.154	8.082	
SDQ2N16 <-------- ASC	1.279	0.150	8.503	
SDQ2N04 <-------- ASC	1.000			
SDQ2N46 <-------- ESC	0.843	0.117	7.212	
SDQ2N34 <-------- ESC	0.670	0.148	4.530	
SDQ2N22 <-------- ESC	0.889	0.103	8.642	
SDQ2N10 <-------- ESC	1.000			
SDQ2N43 <-------- MSC	0.655	0.049	13.273	
SDQ2N31 <-------- MSC	0.952	0.049	19.479	
SDQ2N19 <-------- MSC	0.841	0.058	14.468	
SDQ2N07 <-------- MSC	1.000			

Covariances:

	Estimate	S.E.	C.R.	Label
ASC <-----------> ESC	0.464	0.078	5.909	
GSC <-----------> ESC	0.355	0.072	4.938	
ASC <-----------> MSC	0.873	0.134	6.507	
GSC <-----------> MSC	0.635	0.118	5.377	
GSC <-----------> ASC	0.415	0.079	5.282	
ESC <-----------> MSC	0.331	0.100	3.303	

Variances:

	Estimate	S.E.	C.R.	Label
GSC	0.613	0.138	4.456	
ASC	0.561	0.126	4.444	
ESC	0.668	0.116	5.738	
MSC	2.307	0.273	8.444	
err37	0.771	0.088	8.804	
err25	1.056	0.107	9.878	
err13	1.119	0.124	9.002	
err01	1.198	0.126	9.519	
err40	0.952	0.095	10.010	
err28	0.896	0.090	9.940	
err16	0.616	0.068	9.003	
err04	1.394	0.128	10.879	
err46	1.201	0.118	10.164	
err34	2.590	0.233	11.107	
err22	0.657	0.075	8.718	
err10	0.653	0.082	7.926	
err43	0.964	0.092	10.454	
err31	0.365	0.065	5.638	
err19	1.228	0.121	10.133	
err07	0.854	0.100	8.535	

Thus, $\Sigma(\theta)$ represents the restricted covariance matrix implied by the model (i.e., the specified structure of the hypothesized model). In SEM, the null hypothesis (H_0) being tested is that the postulated model holds in the population [i.e., $\Sigma = \Sigma(\theta)$]. In contrast to traditional statistical procedures, however, the researcher hopes *not* to reject H_0 (but see MacCallum, Browne, & Sugarawa, 1996, for proposed changes to this hypothesis-testing strategy).

The Issue of Statistical Significance.   As you are no doubt aware, the rationale underlying the practice of statistical significance testing has generated a plethora of criticism over, at least, the past four decades. Indeed, Cohen (1994) noted that, despite Rozeboom's (1960) admonition more than 33 years ago that "the statistical folkways of a more primitive past continue to dominate the local scene" (p. 417), this dubious practice still persists. (For an array of supportive, as well as opposing views with respect to this article, see the *American Psychologist* [1995], *50*, 1098–1103.) In light of this historical bank of criticism, together with the current pressure by methodologists to cease this traditional ritual (see Cohen, 1994; Kirk, 1996; Schmidt, 1996; Thompson, 1996), the Board of Scientific Affairs for the American Psychological Association recently appointed a task force to study the feasibility of phasing out the use of null hypothesis testing procedures, as described in course texts and reported in journal articles. Consequently, the end of statistical significance testing, relative to traditional statistical methods, may soon be a reality.

Statistical significance testing with respect to the analysis of covariance structures, however, is somewhat different in that it is driven by degrees of freedom involving the number of elements in the sample covariance matrix and the number of parameters to be estimated. Nonetheless, it is interesting to note that many of the issues raised with respect to the traditional statistical methods (e.g., practical significance, importance of confidence intervals, importance of replication) have long been addressed in SEM applications. Indeed, it was this very issue of practical "nonsignificance" in model testing that led Bentler and Bonett (1980) to develop one of the first subjective indices of fit (the NFI); their work subsequently spawned the development of numerous additional practical indices of fit, many of which are included in the AMOS output shown later, in Table 3.6. Likewise, the early work of Steiger (1990; Steiger & Lind, 1980) precipitated the call for use of confidence intervals in the reporting of SEM findings (see MacCallum et al., 1996). Finally, the classic paper by Cliff (1983) denouncing the proliferation of post hoc model fitting, and criticizing the apparent lack of concern for the dangers of overfitting models to trivial effects arising from capitalization on chance factors, spirited the development of evaluation indices (Browne & Cudeck, 1989; Cudeck & Browne, 1983), as well as a general call for increased use of cross-validation procedures (see e.g., MacCallum et al., 1992; MacCallum, Roznowski, Mar, & Reith, 1994).

The Estimation Process.   The primary focus of the estimation process, in SEM, is to yield parameter values such that the discrepancy (i.e., residual) between the sample covariance matrix S and the population covariance matrix implied by the model $[\Sigma(\theta)]$ is minimal. This objective is achieved by minimizing a discrepancy function, $F[S, \Sigma(\theta)]$, such that its minimal value $(F_{\min})$ reflects the point in the estimation process where the discrepancy between S and $\Sigma(\theta)$ is least $[S - \Sigma(\theta) =$ minimum]. Taken together, $F_{\min}$ serves as a measure of the extent to which S differs from $\Sigma(\theta)$.

Goodness-of-Fit Statistics.   Let's now turn to the goodness-of-fit statistics that are presented in Table 3.5. This information is taken directly from the AMOS output. For each set of fit statistics, note three rows. The first row, as indicated, focuses on the hypothesized model under test (i.e., Your Model), the second, on the saturated model; and the third, on the independence model. Explanation of the latter two models, I believe, is most easily understood within a comparative framework. As such, think of these three models as representing points on a continuum, with the independence model at one extreme, the saturated model at the other extreme, and the hypothesized model somewhere in between. The independence model is one of complete independence of all variables in the model (i.e., in which all correlations among variables are zero) and is the most restricted. The saturated model, on the other hand, is one in which the number of estimated parameters equals the number of data points (i.e., variances and covariances of the observed variables, as in the case of the just-identified model), and is the least restricted.

For didactic reasons, all goodness-of-fit statistics are provided only for the initially hypothesized model in this first application; hereafter, only a selected group of fit statistics will be reported. We turn now to an examination of each cluster, as they relate to the Hypothesized model only. (Formulas related to each fit statistic can be found in Arbuckle and Wothke, 1999.)

Focusing on the first set of fit statistics, we see the labels NPAR (number of parameters), CMIN (minimum discrepancy), DF (degrees of freedom), P (probability value), and CMIN/DF. The value of 158.511, under CMIN, represents the discrepancy between the unrestricted sample covariance matrix S and the restricted covariance matrix $\Sigma(\theta)$ and, in essence, represents the likelihood ratio test statistic, most commonly expressed as a chi-square (χ^2) statistic. It is important to note that, for the remainder of the book, I refer to CMIN as χ^2. This statistic is equal to $(N - 1)F_{\min}$ (sample size minus 1, multiplied by the minimum fit function) and, in large samples, is distributed as a central χ^2 with degrees of freedom equal to $\frac{1}{2}(p)(p + 1) - t$, where p is the number of observed variables, and t is the number of parameters to be estimated (Bollen, 1989a). In general, $H_0: \Sigma = \Sigma(\theta)$ is equivalent to the hypothesis that $\Sigma - \Sigma(\theta) = 0$; the χ^2 test, then, simultaneously tests the extent to which all residuals in $\Sigma - \Sigma(\theta)$ are zero (Bollen, 1989a). Framed a little differently, the null hypothesis (H_0) postulates that specification of the factor loadings, factor variances/covariances, and error variances for the model under study are valid; the χ^2 test simultaneously tests the extent to which this specification is true. The probability value associated with χ^2 represents the likelihood of obtaining a χ^2 value that exceeds the χ^2 value when H_0 is true. Thus, the higher the prob-

TABLE 3.5
AMOS Text Output for Hypothesized Four-Factor CFA Model: Goodness-of-Fit Statistics

Summary of models

Model	NPAR	CMIN	DF	P	CMIN/DF
Your model	38	158.511	98	0.000	1.617
Saturated model	136	0.000	0		
Independence model	16	1696.728	120	0.000	14.139

Model	RMR	GFI	AGFI	PGFI
Your model	0.103	0.933	0.906	0.672
Saturated model	0.000	1.000		
Independence model	0.628	0.379	0.296	0.334

Model	DELTA1 NFI	RHO1 RFI	DELTA2 IFI	RHO2 TLI	CFI
Your model	0.907	0.886	0.962	0.953	0.962
Saturated model	1.000		1.000		1.000
Independence model	0.000	0.000	0.000	0.000	0.000

Model	PRATIO	PNFI	PCFI
Your model	0.817	0.740	0.785
Saturated model	0.000	0.000	0.000
Independence model	1.000	0.000	0.000

Model	NCP	LO 90	HI 90
Your model	60.511	29.983	98.953
Saturated model	0.000	0.000	0.000
Independence model	1576.728	1447.292	1713.561

Model	FMIN	F0	LO 90	HI 90
Your model	0.600	0.229	0.114	0.375
Saturated model	0.000	0.000	0.000	0.000
Independence model	6.427	5.972	5.482	6.491

Model	RMSEA	LO 90	HI 90	PCLOSE
Your model	0.048	0.034	0.062	0.562
Independence model	0.223	0.214	0.233	0.000

Model	AIC	BCC	BIC	CAIC
Your model	234.511	239.742	475.900	408.541
Saturated model	272.000	290.721	1135.915	894.843
Independence model	1728.728	1730.931	1830.365	1802.004

Model	ECVI	LO 90	HI 90	MECVI
Your model	0.888	0.773	1.034	0.908
Saturated model	1.030	1.030	1.030	1.101
Independence model	6.548	6.058	7.067	6.557

Model	HOELTER .05	HOELTER .01
Your model	204	223
Independence model	23	25

ability associated with χ^2, the closer is the fit between the hypothesized model (under H_0) and the perfect fit (Bollen, 1989a).

The test of our H_0—that SC is a four-factor structure as depicted in Fig. 3.1— yielded a χ^2 value of 158.51, with 98 degrees of freedom and a probability of less than .0001 ($p < .0001$), thereby suggesting that the fit of the data to the hypothesized model is not entirely adequate. Interpreted literally, this test statistic indicates that, given the present data, the hypothesis bearing on SC relations, as summarized in the model, represents an unlikely event (occurring less than one time in a thousand under the null hypothesis) and should be rejected.

However, both the sensitivity of the likelihood ratio test to sample size and its basis on the central χ^2 distribution, which assumes that the model fits perfectly in the population (i.e., that H_0 is correct), have led to problems of fit that are now widely known. Because the χ^2 statistic equals $(N - 1)F_{min}$, this value tends to be substantial when the model does *not* hold and sample size is large (Joreskog & Sorbom, 1993). Yet the analysis of covariance structures is grounded in large sample theory. As such, large samples are critical to the obtaining of precise parameter estimates, as well as to the tenability of asymptotic distributional approximations (MacCallum et al., 1996). Thus, findings of well-fitting hypothesized models, where the χ^2 value approximates the degrees of freedom, have proven to be unrealistic in most SEM empirical research. More common are findings of a large χ^2 relative to degrees of freedom, thereby indicating a need to modify the model in order to better fit the data (Joreskog & Sorbom, 1993). Thus, results related to the test of our hypothesized model are not unexpected. Indeed, given this problematic aspect of the likelihood ratio test, and the fact that postulated models (no matter how good) can only ever fit real world data approximately and never exactly, MacCallum et al. (1996) recently proposed changes to the traditional hypothesis-testing approach in covariance structure modeling. (For an extended discussion of these changes, readers are referred to MacCallum et al., 1996.)

Researchers have addressed the χ^2 limitations by developing goodness-of-fit indexes that take a more pragmatic approach to the evaluation process. Indeed, the past two decades have witnessed a plethora of newly developed fit indexes, as well as unique approaches to the model fitting process (for reviews, see Gerbing & Anderson, 1993; Hu & Bentler, 1995; Marsh, Balla, & McDonald, 1988; Tanaka, 1993). One of the first fit statistics to address this problem was the χ^2/degrees of freedom ratio (Wheaton, Muthén, Alwin, & Summers, 1977), which appears as CMIN/DF and is presented in the first cluster of statistics shown in Table 3.5.[4] For the most part, the remainder of the AMOS output file is devoted to these alternative indexes of fit and, where applicable, to their related confidence intervals. These criteria, commonly referred to as "subjective", "practical", or "ad hoc" indexes of fit, are typically used as adjuncts to the χ^2 statistic.

---

[4]Wheaton (1987) later advocated that this ratio not be used.

Turning now to the next group of statistics, we see the labels, RMR, GFI, AGFI, and PGFI. The root mean square residual (RMR) represents the average residual value derived from the fitting of the variance–covariance matrix for the hypothesized model $\Sigma(\theta)$ to the variance–covariance matrix of the sample data (S). However, because these residuals are relative to the sizes of the observed variances and covariances, they are difficult to interpret. Thus, they are best interpreted in the metric of the correlation matrix (Hu & Bentler, 1995; Joreskog & Sorbom, 1989). The standardized RMR, then, represents the average value across all standardized residuals, and ranges from zero to 1.00; in a well-fitting model this value will be small, say, .05 or less. The value of .103 shown in Table 3.5 represents the unstandardized residual value. Not shown on the output, however, is the standardized RMR value, which is .043 and represents the average discrepancy between the sample observed and hypothesized correlation matrices. It can be interpreted as meaning that the model explains the correlations to within an average error of .043 (see Hu & Bentler, 1995).

The goodness-of-fit index (GFI) is a measure of the relative amount of variance and covariance in S that is jointly explained by Σ. The AGFI differs from the GFI only in the fact that it adjusts for the number of degrees of freedom in the specified model. As such, it also addresses the issue of parsimony by incorporating a penalty for the inclusion of additional parameters. The GFI and AGFI can be classified as absolute indexes of fit because they basically compare the hypothesized model with no model at all (see Hu & Bentler, 1995). Although both indexes range from zero to 1.00, with values close to 1.00 being indicative of good fit, Joreskog and Sorbom (1993) noted that, theoretically, it is possible for them to be negative; Fan, Thompson, and Wang (1999) further cautioned that GFI and AGFI values can be overly influenced by sample size. This, of course, should not occur as it would reflect the fact that the model fits worse than no model at all. Based on the GFI and AGFI values reported in Table 3.5 (.933 and .906, respectively), we can once again conclude that our hypothesized model fits the sample data fairly well.

The last index of fit in this group, the parsimony goodness-of-fit index (PGFI), was introduced by James, Mulaik, and Brett (1982) to address the issue of parsimony in SEM. As the first of a series of "parsimony-based indexes of fit" (see Williams & Holahan, 1994), the PGFI takes into account the complexity (i.e., number of estimated parameters) of the hypothesized model in the assessment of overall model fit. As such, "two logically interdependent pieces of information," the goodness of fit of the model (as measured by the GFI) and the parsimony of the model, are represented by a single index (the PGFI), thereby providing a more realistic evaluation of the hypothesized model (Mulaik et al., 1989, p. 439). Typically, parsimony-based indexes have lower values than the threshold level generally perceived as "acceptable" for other normed indices of fit. Mulaik et al. suggested that nonsignificant χ^2 statistics and goodness-of-fit indexes in the .90s, accompanied by parsimonious-fit indices in the .50s, are not unexpected. Thus, our finding of a PGFI value of .672 would seem to be consistent with our previous fit statistics.

We turn now to the next set of goodness-of-fit statistics, which can be classified as incremental or comparative indexes of fit (Hu & Bentler, 1995; Marsh et al., 1988). As with the GFI and AGFI, incremental indexes of fit are based on a comparison of the hypothesized model against some standard. However, whereas this standard represents no model at all for the GFI and AGFI, for the incremental indices, it represents a baseline model (typically the independence or null model noted earlier).[5] We now review these incremental indices.

For the better part of a decade, Bentler and Bonett's (1980) normed fit index (NFI) has been the practical criterion of choice, as evidenced in large part by the current "classic" status of its original paper (see Bentler, 1992; Bentler & Bonett, 1987). However, addressing evidence that the NFI has shown a tendency to underestimate fit in small samples, Bentler (1990) revised the NFI to take sample size into account and proposed the comparative fit index (CFI; see last column). Values for both the NFI and CFI range from zero to 1.00 and are derived from the comparison of an hypothesized model with the independence model, as described earlier. As such, each provides a measure of complete covariation in the data, Although a value >.90 was originally considered representative of a well-fitting model (see Bentler, 1992), a revised cutoff value close to .95 has recently been advised (Hu & Bentler, 1999). Both indices of fit are reported in the AMOS output; however, Bentler (1990) has suggested that the CFI should be the index of choice. As shown in Table 3.5, both the NFI (.907) and CFI (.962) were consistent in suggesting that the hypothesized model represented an adequate fit to the data.

The relative fit index (RFI; Bollen, 1986) represents a derivative of the NFI; as with both the NFI and CFI, the RFI coefficient values range from zero to 1.00, with values close to .95 indicating superior fit (see Hu & Bentler, 1999). The incremental index of fit (IFI) was developed by Bollen (1989b) to address the issues of parsimony and sample size which were known to be associated with the NFI. As such, its computation is basically the same as the NFI, except that degrees of freedom are taken into account. Thus, it is not surprising that our finding of IFI = .962 is consistent with that of the CFI in reflecting a well-fitting model. Finally, the Tucker–Lewis index (TLI; Tucker & Lewis, 1973), consistent with the other indexes noted here, yields values ranging from zero to 1.00, with values close to .95 (for large samples) being indicative of good fit (see Hu & Bentler, 1999).

The next cluster of fit indexes all relate to the issue of model parsimony. The first fit index (PRATIO) relates to the initial parsimony ratio proposed by James et al. (1982). More appropriately, however, the index has subsequently been tied to other goodness-of-fit indexes (see the PGFI noted earlier). Here, it is computed relative to the NFI and CFI. In both cases, as was true for PGFI, the complexity of the model is taken into account in the assessment of model fit (see James et al., 1982;

---

[5]For alternate approaches to formulating baseline models, see Cudeck and Browne (1983) and Sobel and Bohrnstedt (1985).

Mulaik et al., 1989). Again, a PNFI of .740 and PCFI of .785 (see Table 3.5) fall in the range of expected values.[6]

The next set of fit statistics provides us with the noncentrality parameter (NCP) estimate. In our initial discussion of the χ^2 statistic, we focused on the extent to which the model was tenable and could not be rejected. Now, however, let's look a little more closely at what happens when the hypothesized model is incorrect [i.e., $\Sigma \neq \Sigma(\theta)$]. In this circumstance, the χ^2 statistic has a noncentral χ^2 distribution, with a noncentrality parameter, λ, that is estimated by the noncentrality parameter (Bollen, 1989a; Hu & Bentler, 1995; Satorra & Saris, 1985). The noncentrality parameter is a fixed parameter with associated degrees of freedom, and can be denoted as $\chi^2_{(df,\lambda)}$. Essentially, it functions as a measure of the discrepancy between Σ and $\Sigma(\theta)$ and thus can be regarded as a "population badness-of-fit" (Steiger, 1990). As such, the greater the discrepancy between Σ and $\Sigma(\theta)$, the larger is the λ value. (For a presentation of the various types of error associated with discrepancies among matrices, see Browne & Cudeck, 1993, Cudeck & Henly, 1991, and MacCallum et al., 1994.) It is now easy to see that the central χ^2 statistic is a special case of the noncentral χ^2 distribution when $\lambda = 0.0$. (For an excellent discussion and graphic portrayal of differences between the central and noncentral χ^2 statistics, see MacCallum et al., 1996.) As a means to establishing the precision of the noncentrality parameter estimate, Steiger (1990) suggested that it be framed within the bounds of confidence intervals. Turning to Table 3.5, we find that our hypothesized model yielded a noncentrality parameter of 60.511. This value represents the χ^2 value minus its degrees of freedom (158.51 − 98). The confidence interval indicates that we can be 90% confident that the population value of the noncentrality parameter (λ) lies between 29.983 and 98.953.

For those who may wish to use this information, values related to the minimum discrepancy function (FMIN) and the population discrepancy (FO) are presented next. The columns labeled LO90 and HI90 contain the lower and upper limits, respectively, of a 90% confidence interval around FO.

The next set of fit statistics focus on the root mean square error of approximation (RMSEA). Although this index, and the conceptual framework within which it is embedded, was first proposed by Steiger and Lind in 1980, it has only recently been recognized as one of the most informative criteria in covariance structure modeling. The RMSEA takes into account the error of approximation in the population and asks the question, "How well would the model, with unknown but optimally chosen parameter values, fit the population covariance matrix if it were available?" (Browne & Cudeck, 1993, pp. 137–138). This discrepancy, as measured by the RMSEA, is expressed per degree of freedom, thus making the index sensitive to the number of estimated parameters in the model (i.e., the complexity of the

---

[6]More recently, in keeping with Bentler's recommendation regarding use of the CFI over the NFI, the PCFI has been the index of choice (see Byrne, 1994a; Carlson & Mulaik, 1993; Williams & Holahan, 1994).

model); values less than .05 indicate good fit, and values as high as .08 represent reasonable errors of approximation in the population (Browne & Cudeck, 1993). MacCallum et al. (1996) recently elaborated on these cutpoints and noted that RMSEA values ranging from .08 to .10 indicate mediocre fit, and those greater than .10 indicate poor fit. Although Hu and Bentler (1999) suggested a value of .06 to be indicative of good fit between the hypothesized model and the observed data, they cautioned that when sample size is small, the RMSEA (and TLI) tend to over-reject true population models (but see Fan et al., 1999, for comparisons with other indices of fit). Although these criteria are based solely on subjective judgment, and therefore cannot be regarded as infallible or correct, Browne and Cudeck (1993) and MacCallum et al. (1996) argued that they would appear to be more realistic than a requirement of exact fit, where RMSEA = 0.0. (For a generalization of the RMSEA to multiple independent samples, see Steiger, 1998.)

Addressing Steiger's (1990) call for the use of confidence intervals to assess the precision of RMSEA estimates, AMOS reports a 90% interval around the RMSEA value. In contrast to point estimates of model fit (which do not reflect the impreci-sion of the estimate), confidence intervals can yield this information, thereby pro-viding the researcher with more assistance in the evaluation of model fit. Thus, MacCallum et al. (1996) strongly urge the use of confidence intervals in practice. Presented with a small RMSEA, but a wide confidence interval, a researcher would conclude that the estimated discrepancy value is quite imprecise thereby negating any possibility to determine accurately the degree of fit in the population. In con-trast, a very narrow confidence interval would argue for good precision of the RMSEA value in reflecting model fit in the population (MacCallum et al., 1996).

In addition to reporting a confidence interval around the RMSEA value, the AMOS program tests for the closeness of fit. That is, it tests the hypothesis that the RMSEA is "good" in the population (specifically, that it is <.05). Joreskog and Sor-bom (1996a) suggested that the p value for this test should be >.50.

Turning to Table 3.5, we see that the RMSEA value for our hypothesized model is .048, with the 90% confidence interval ranging from .034 to .062 and the p value for the test of closeness of fit equal to .562. Interpretation of the confidence inter-val indicates that we can be 90% confident that the true RMSEA value in the pop-ulation will fall within the bounds of .034 and .062, which represents a good degree of precision. Given that (a) the RMSEA point estimate is <.05 (.048), (b) the upper bound of the 90% interval is .06, which is less than the value suggested by Browne and Cudeck (1993), although equal to the cutoff value proposed by Hu and Bentler (1999), and (c) the probability value associated with this test of close fit is >.50 (p = .562), we can conclude that the initially hypothesized model fits the data well.[7]

Before leaving this discussion of the RMSEA, it is important to note that con-fidence intervals can be influenced seriously by sample size, as well as model com-

---

[7]One possible limitation of the RMSEA, as noted by Mulaik (see Byrne, 1994a), is that it ignores the complexity of the model.

plexity (MacCallum et al., 1996). For example, if sample size is small and the number of estimated parameters is large, the confidence interval will be wide. Given a complex model (i.e., a large number of estimated parameters), a very large sample size would be required in order to obtain a reasonably narrow confidence interval. On the other hand, if the number of parameters is small, then the probability of obtaining a narrow confidence interval is high, even for samples of rather moderate size (MacCallum et al., 1996).

Let's turn to the next cluster of statistics. The first of these is Akaike's (1987) information criterion (AIC), with Bozdogan's (1987) consistent version of the AIC (CAIC) shown at the end of the row. Both criteria address the issue of parsimony in the assessment of model fit; as such, statistical goodness of fit and number of estimated parameters are taken into account. Bozdogan (1987), however, noted that the AIC carried a penalty only as it related to degrees of freedom (thereby reflecting the number of estimated parameters in the model), and not to sample size. Presented with factor-analytic findings that revealed the AIC to yield asymptotically inconsistent estimates, he proposed the CAIC, which takes sample size into account (Bandalos, 1993). The AIC and CAIC are used in the comparison of two or more models, with smaller values representing a better fit of the hypothesized model (Hu & Bentler, 1995). The AIC and CAIC indices also share the same conceptual framework; as such, they reflect the extent to which parameter estimates from the original sample will cross-validate in future samples (Bandalos, 1993). The Browne-Cudeck criterion (BCC; Browne & Cudeck, 1989) and the Bayes information criterion (BIC; Raftery, 1993; Schwarz, 1978) operate in the same manner as the AIC and CAIC. The basic difference among these indexes is that both the BCC and BIC impose greater penalties than either the AIC and CAIC for model complexity. Turning to the output once again, we see that in the case of all four of these fit indices, the fit statistics for the hypothesized model are substantially smaller than they are for either the independence or the saturated models.

The expected cross-validation index (ECVI) is central to the next cluster of fit statistics. The ECVI was proposed, initially, as a means to assessing, in a single sample, the likelihood that the model cross-validates across similar-sized samples from the same population (Browne & Cudeck, 1989). Specifically, it measures the discrepancy between the fitted covariance matrix in the analyzed sample, and the expected covariance matrix that would be obtained in another sample of equivalent size. Application of the ECVI assumes a comparison of models whereby an ECVI index is computed for each model and then all ECVI values are placed in rank order; the model having the smallest ECVI value exhibits the greatest potential for replication. Because ECVI coefficients can take on any value, there is no determined appropriate range of values. In assessing our hypothesized four-factor model, we compare its ECVI value of .888 with that of both the saturated model (ECVI = 1.030) and the independence model (ECVI = 6.548). Given the lower ECVI value for the hypothesized model, compared with both the independence and saturated models, we conclude that it represents the best fit to the data. Beyond this comparison, Browne and Cudeck (1993) showed that it is now possible to take the precision of the estimated ECVI value into account through the formulation of confidence intervals. Turning to Table 3.5 again, we see that this interval ranges from .773 to 1.034. Taken together, these results suggest that the hypothesized model is well-fitting and represents a reasonable approximation to the population. The last fit statistic, the MECVI, is actually identical to the BCC, except for a scale factor (Arbuckle & Wothke, 1999).

The last goodness-of-fit statistic appearing on the AMOS output is Hoelter's (1983) critical N (CN) (labeled as Hoelter's .05 and .01 indexes). This fit statistic differs substantially from those previously discussed in that it focuses directly on the adequacy of sample size, rather than on model fit. Development of Hoelter's index arose from an attempt to find a fit index that is independent of sample size. Specifically, its purpose is to estimate a sample size that would be sufficient to yield an adequate model fit for a χ^2 test (Hu & Bentler, 1995). Hoelter (1983) proposed that a value in excess of 200 is indicative of a model that adequately represents the sample data. As shown in Table 3.5, both the .05 and .01 CN values for our hypothesized SC model were >200 (204 and 223, respectively). Interpretation of this finding leads us to conclude that the size of our sample ($N = 265$) was satisfactory according to Hoelter's benchmark that the CN should exceed 200.

Having worked your way through this smorgasbord of goodness-of-fit measures, you are no doubt feeling totally overwhelmed and wondering what you do with all this information! Although you certainly don't need to report the entire set of fit indexes, such an array can give you a good sense of how well your model fits the sample data. But how does one choose which indexes are appropriate in the assessment of model fit? Unfortunately, this choice is not a simple one, largely because particular indexes have been shown to operate somewhat differently given the sample size, estimation procedure, model complexity, and/or violation of the underlying assumptions of multivariate normality and variable independence. Thus, Hu and Bentler (1995) cautioned that in choosing which goodness-of-fit indexes to use in the assessment of model fit, careful consideration of these critical factors is essential. For further elaboration on these goodness-of-fit statistics with respect to their formulas and functions, or the extent to which they are affected by sample size, estimation procedures, misspecification, and/or violations of assumptions, readers are referred to: Arbuckle and Wothke (1999), Bandalos (1993), Bentler and Yuan (1999), Bollen (1989a), Browne and Cudeck (1993), Curran, West, and Finch (1996), Fan et al. (1999), Finch et al. (1997), Gerbing and Anderson (1993), Hu and Bentler (1995, 1998, 1999), Hu, Bentler, and Kano (1992), Joreskog and Sorbom (1993), La Du and Tanaka (1989), Marsh et al. (1988), Mulaik et al. (1989), Raykov and Widaman (1995), Sugawara and MacCallum (1993), Weng and Cheng (1997), West et al. (1995), Wheaton (1987), Williams and Holahan (1994), and for an annotated bibliography, see Austin and Calderón (1996).

In finalizing this section on model assessment, I wish to leave you with this important reminder—that global fit indexes alone cannot possibly envelop all that needs to be known about a model in order to judge the adequacy of its fit to the sample data. As Sobel and Bohrnstedt (1985, p. 158) so cogently stated well over a decade ago, "Scientific progress could be impeded if fit coefficients (even appropriate ones) are used as the primary criterion for judging the adequacy of a model." They further posited that, despite the problematic nature of the χ^2 statistic, exclusive reliance on goodness-of-fit indexes is unacceptable. Indeed, fit indexes provide no guarantee whatsoever that a model is useful. In fact, it is entirely possible for a model to fit well and yet still be incorrectly specified (Wheaton, 1987). (For an excellent review of ways by which such a seemingly dichotomous event can happen, readers are referred to Bentler & Chou, 1987.) Fit indexes yield information bearing only on the model's *lack of fit*. More importantly, they can in no way reflect the extent to which the model is plausible; *this judgment rests squarely on the shoulders of the researcher*. Thus, assessment of model adequacy must be based on multiple criteria that take into account theoretical, statistical, and practical considerations.

Model Misspecification

Although, in general, we could conclude that our hypothesized four-factor CFA model fit the data well, our next task is to identify any areas of misfit in the model (Joreskog, 1993). In this regard, AMOS yields two types of information that can be helpful in detecting model misspecification—the standardized residuals, and the modification indices. Because this information was not provided as default output in our initial test of the model, we return to AMOS Graphics and request this optional output. To obtain this information, we click on the Analysis Properties icon ▦, which triggers an output tab that offers a variety of options. Figure 3.8 shows this card with the "Output" tab in a forward position. For our purposes here, we select residuals and modification indices as our only options.

Residuals.   Recall that the essence of SEM is to determine the fit between the restricted covariance matrix $[\Sigma(\theta)]$, implied by the hypothesized model, and the sample covariance matrix (S); any discrepancy between the two is captured by the residual covariance matrix. Each element in this residual matrix, then, represents the discrepancy between the covariances in $\Sigma(\theta)$ and those in S [i.e., $\Sigma(\theta) - S$]; that is to say, there is one residual for each pair of observed variables (Joreskog, 1993). In the case of our hypothesized model, for example, the residual matrix would contain $[(16 \times 17)/2] = 136$ elements. It may be worth noting that, as in conventional regression analysis, the residuals are not independent of one another. Thus, any attempts to test them (in the strict statistical sense) would be inappropriate. In essence, only their magnitude is of interest in alerting the researcher to possible areas of model misfit.

Both the matrix of unstandardized residuals and that of standardized residuals are presented in the optional AMOS output. However, because the fitted residuals are dependent on the unit of measurement of the observed variables, they can be

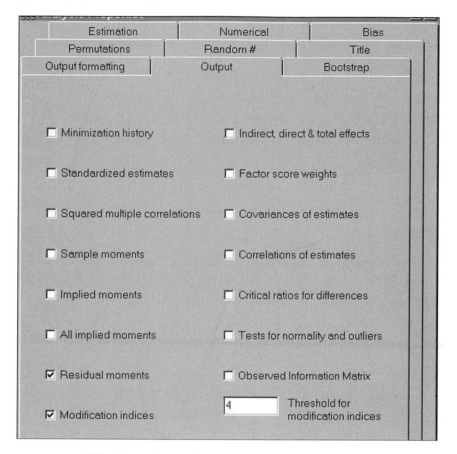

FIG. 3.8.   AMOS Graphics: the Analysis Properties dialog box.

difficult to interpret and, thus their standardized values are typically examined. As such, only the latter are presented in Table 3.6. Standardized residuals are fitted residuals divided by their asymptotically (large sample) standard errors (Joreskog & Sorbom, 1988). As such, they are analogous to Z scores and are therefore the easier of the two sets of residual values to interpret. In essence, they represent estimates of the number of standard deviations the observed residuals are from the zero residuals that would exist if model fit were perfect [i.e., $\Sigma(\theta) - S = 0.0$]. Values >2.58 are considered to be large (Joreskog & Sorbom, 1988). In examining the standardized residual values presented in Table 3.6, we observe only one that exceeds the cutpoint of 2.58. As such, the residual value of -2.942 represents the covariance between the observed variables SDQ2N07 and SDQ2N34. From this information, we can conclude that the only statistically significant discrepancy of note lies with the covariance between the two variables noted.

TABLE 3.6

AMOS Text Output for Hypothesized Four-Factor CFA Model: Standardized Residual Covariances

	SDQ2N07	SDQ2N19	SDQ2N31	SDQ2N43	SDQ2N10	SDQ2N22	SDQ2N34
SDQ2N07	0.000						
SDQ2N19	0.251	0.000					
SDQ2N31	0.189	-0.457	0.000				
SDQ2N43	-0.458	1.013	-0.071	0.000			
SDQ2N10	-0.668	0.582	0.218	0.087	-0.000		
SDQ2N22	-0.408	1.027	0.845	-0.072	-0.121	0.000	
SDQ2N34	-2.942	-1.503	-2.030	-1.446	0.501	-0.440	0.000
SDQ2N46	-0.466	-0.548	0.514	1.457	-0.209	0.267	0.543
SDQ2N04	0.057	-0.061	0.333	-0.645	1.252	-0.442	-0.544
SDQ2N16	-0.645	0.422	0.059	0.100	-0.131	0.563	-1.589
SDQ2N28	-0.711	0.959	0.579	0.250	-0.609	-0.095	-2.184
SDQ2N40	-1.301	0.729	-0.227	0.909	0.516	0.574	-0.455
SDQ2N01	-0.496	-0.270	-0.229	-1.206	-0.052	-0.549	0.873
SDQ2N13	-1.141	-0.100	-0.037	0.175	0.248	0.001	1.423
SDQ2N25	0.011	-0.827	0.505	-0.220	-0.564	-0.135	0.621
SDQ2N37	-0.099	-0.190	1.285	-0.449	-0.099	0.060	0.756

	SDQ2N46	SDQ2N04	SDQ2N16	SDQ2N28	SDQ2N40	SDQ2N01	SDQ2N13
SDQ2N46	0.000						
SDQ2N04	-0.382	0.001					
SDQ2N16	-0.276	0.272	0.000				
SDQ2N28	-0.350	-0.084	0.427	0.000			
SDQ2N40	0.983	-1.545	-0.240	0.358	0.000		
SDQ2N01	0.721	0.027	-0.620	-1.240	-0.611	-0.000	
SDQ2N13	0.443	1.777	-0.203	-0.719	-0.217	0.145	0.000
SDQ2N25	-0.818	-0.493	-0.600	-0.894	-0.112	2.132	-0.588
SDQ2N37	-0.598	0.796	0.884	0.568	1.727	-0.971	0.327

	SDQ2N25	SDQ2N37
SDQ2N25	0.000	
SDQ2N37	-0.645	0.000

Modification Indexes.   The second type of information related to misspecification reflects the extent to which the hypothesized model is appropriately described. Evidence of misfit in this regard is captured by the modification indexes (MIs), which can be conceptualized as a χ^2 statistic with one degree of freedom (Joreskog & Sorbom, 1988). Specifically, for each *fixed* parameter specified, AMOS provides an MI, the value of which represents the expected drop in overall χ^2 value if the parameter were to be freely estimated in a subsequent run; all freely estimated parameters automatically have MI values equal to zero. Although this decrease in χ^2 is expected to approximate the MI value, the actual differential can be larger. Associated with each MI is an expected parameter change (EPC) value (Saris, Satorra, & Sorbom, 1987), which is reported in the accompanying column labeled Par Change. This latter statistic represents the predicted estimated change, in either a positive or negative direction, for each fixed parameter in the model and yields important information regarding the sensitivity of the evaluation of fit to any reparameterization of the model.[8] The MIs and accompanying expected parameter change statistics related to our hypothesized model are presented in Table 3.7.

As shown in Table 3.7, the MIs and EPCs are presented first for possible covariances, followed by those for the regression weights. Recall that the only model parameters for which the MIs are applicable are those that were fixed to a value of 0.0. Thus, no values appear under the heading "Variances," as all parameters representing variances (factors and measurement errors) were freely estimated.

In reviewing the parameters in the Covariance section, the only ones that make any substantive sense are those representing error covariances. In this regard, only the parameter representing a covariance between err25 and err01 appears to be of any interest. Nonetheless, an MI value of this size (13.487), with an EPC value of .285, particularly as they relate to an error covariance, can be considered of little concern. Turning to the Regression Weights section, I consider only two to make any substantive sense; these are SDQ2N07 ← ESC, and SDQ2N34 ← MSC. Both parameters represent cross-loadings. However, again, the MIs, and their associated EPC values, are not worthy of inclusion in a subsequently specified model.

POST HOC ANALYSES

At this point, the researcher can decide whether or not to respecify and reestimate the model. If he or she elects to follow this route, it is important to realize that analyses are now framed within an *exploratory*, rather than a *confirmatory*, mode. In other words, once an hypothesized CFA model, for example, has been rejected, this spells the end of the confirmatory factor-analytic approach, in its truest sense. Although CFA procedures continue to be used in any respecification and reestimation of the model, these analyses are exploratory in the sense that they focus on the detection of misfitting parameters in the originally hypothesized model. Such post hoc analyses are conventionally termed "specification searches" (see MacCallum, 1986). (The issue of post hoc model fitting is addressed further in chap. 10 in the section dealing with cross-validation).

The ultimate decision underscoring whether or not to proceed with a specification search is twofold. First and foremost, the researcher must determine whether the estimation of the targeted parameter is substantively meaningful. If, indeed, it makes no sound substantive sense to free up the parameter exhibiting the largest MI, then one may wish to consider the parameter having the next largest MI value (Joreskog, 1993). Second, one needs to consider whether or not the respecified model would lead to an overfitted model. The issue here is tied to the

---

[8]Bentler (1995) noted, however, that because these parameter change statistics are sensitive to the way by which variables and factors are scaled or identified, their absolute value is sometimes difficult to interpret.

TABLE 3.7
AMOS Text Output for Hypothesized Four-Factor CFA Model:
Modification Indexes and Parameter Change Statistics

Covariances:			M.I.	Par Change
err31	<------->	err19	8.956	-0.167
err43	<------->	err19	7.497	0.201
err34	<--------->	GSC	8.192	0.225
err46	<------->	err43	4.827	0.159
err04	<------->	err10	5.669	0.162
err40	<------->	err43	5.688	0.155
err40	<------->	err04	8.596	-0.224
err13	<------->	err04	6.418	0.217
err25	<------->	err01	13.487	0.285
err37	<--------->	ASC	6.873	0.079
err37	<------->	err31	4.041	0.097
err37	<------->	err40	5.331	0.141

Variances:	M.I.	Par Change

Regression Weights:			M.I.	Par Change
SDQ2N07	<--------	**ESC**	7.427	-0.242
SDQ2N07	<----	SDQ2N34	4.897	-0.083
SDQ2N07	<----	SDQ2N28	5.435	-0.112
SDQ2N07	<----	SDQ2N40	6.323	-0.119
SDQ2N31	<----	SDQ2N37	5.952	0.107
SDQ2N10	<----	SDQ2N04	4.038	0.081
SDQ2N34	<--------	**MSC**	6.323	-0.173
SDQ2N34	<----	SDQ2N07	7.695	-0.157
SDQ2N34	<----	SDQ2N31	5.316	-0.148
SDQ2N34	<----	SDQ2N28	4.887	-0.167
SDQ2N04	<----	SDQ2N13	5.029	0.123
SDQ2N40	<----	SDQ2N04	5.883	-0.110
SDQ2N01	<----	SDQ2N25	8.653	0.173
SDQ2N13	<----	SDQ2N04	4.233	0.104
SDQ2N25	<----	SDQ2N01	7.926	0.140
SDQ2N37	<----	SDQ2N40	5.509	0.103

Execution time summary:	
Minimization:	0.220
Miscellaneous:	5.050
Bootstrap:	0.000
Total:	5.270

idea of knowing when to stop fitting the model, or as Wheaton (1987, p. 123) phrased the problem, "knowing . . . how much fit is enough without being too much fit." In general, overfitting a model involves the specification of additional parameters in the model after having determined a criterion that reflects a minimally adequate fit. For example, an overfitted model can result from the inclusion of additional parameters that (a) are "fragile" in the sense of representing weak effects that are not likely replicable, (b) lead to a significant inflation of standard errors, and (c) influence primary parameters in the model, although their own substantive meaningfulness is somewhat equivocal (Wheaton, 1987). Although correlated errors often fall into this latter category,[9] there are many situations, particularly with respect to social psychological research, where these parameters can make strong substantive sense and therefore should be included in the model (Joreskog & Sorbom, 1993).

Having laboriously worked our way through the process involved in evaluating the fit of an hypothesized model, what can we conclude regarding the CFA model under scrutiny in this chapter? In answering this question, we must necessarily pool all the information gleaned from our study of the AMOS text output. Taking into account (a) the feasibility and statistical significance of all parameter estimates, (b) the substantially good fit of the model, with particular reference to the CFI (.962) and RMSEA (.048) values, and (c) the lack of any substantial evidence of model misfit, I conclude that any further incorporation of parameters into the model would result in an overfitted model. Indeed, MacCallum et al. (1992, p. 501) cautioned that "when an initial model fits well, it is probably unwise to modify it to achieve even better fit because modifications may simply be fitting small idiosyncratic characteristics of the sample." Adhering to this caveat, I concluded that the four-factor model schematically portrayed in Fig. 3.1 represents an adequate description of self-concept structure for Grade 7 adolescents.

HYPOTHESIS 2: SELF-CONCEPT IS A TWO-FACTOR STRUCTURE

The model to be tested here postulates a priori that SC is a two-factor structure consisting of GSC and ASC. As such, it argues against the viability of subject-specific academic SC factors. As with the four-factor model, the four GSC measures load onto the GSC factor; in contrast, all other measures load onto the ASC factor. This hypothesized model is represented schematically in Fig. 3.9, which serves as the model specification for AMOS Graphics. The input file for AMOS Basic is shown in Table 3.8.

In reviewing these graphical and equation model specifications, two points relative to the modification of the input file are of interest. First, while the pattern of factor loadings remains the same for the GSC and ASC measures, it changes for both the ESC and MSC measures in allowing them to load onto the ASC factor. Second, because only one of these eight ASC factor loadings needs to be fixed to 1.0, the two previously constrained parameters (SDQ2N10 ← ESC; SDQ2N07 ← MSC) are now freely estimated.

---

[9]Typically, the misuse in this instance arises from the incorporation of correlated errors into the model purely on the basis of statistical fit and for the purpose of achieving a better fitting model.

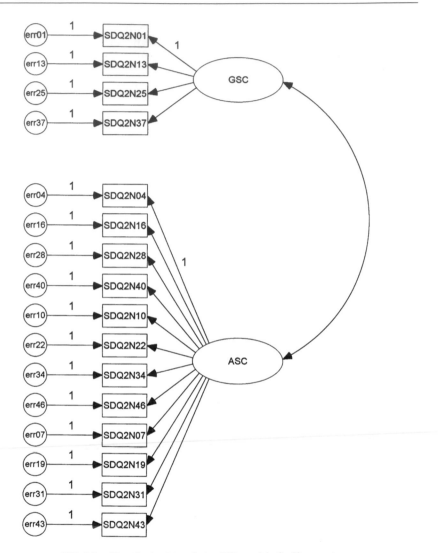

FIG. 3.9.   Hypothesized two-factor CFA model of self-concept.

AMOS Text Output: Hypothesized Two-Factor Model

Only the goodness-of-fit statistics are relevant to the present application, and a selected group of these is presented in Table 3.9.

As indicated in the output, the $\chi^2_{(103)}$ value of 455.926 represents a poor fit to the data, and a substantial decrement from the overall fit of the four-factor model ($\chi^2_{(5)}$ = 297.415). The gain of five degrees of freedom can be explained by the estima-

TABLE 3.8
AMOS BASIC Input for Hypothesized Two-Factor CFA Model

Sub Main

Dim Sem as new AmosEngine
'Testing for Multidimensionality of SC for Grade 7 Sample'
'Model 2'

SEM.TextOutput
SEM.Mods 4

SEM.BeginGroup "asc7indm.txt"

    SEM.Structure "SDQ2N01 ← GSC (1)"
    SEM.Structure "SDQ2N13 ← GSC"
    SEM.Structure "SDQ2N25 ← GSC"
    SEM.Structure "SDQ2N37 ← GSC"

    SEM.Structure "SDQ2N04 ← ASC (1)"
    SEM.Structure "SDQ2N16 ← ASC"
    SEM.Structure "SDQ2N28 ← ASC"
    SEM.Structure "SDQ2N40 ← ASC"
    SEM.Structure "SDQ2N10 ← ASC"
    SEM.Structure "SDQ2N22 ← ASC"
    SEM.Structure "SDQ2N34 ← ASC"
    SEM.Structure "SDQ2N46 ← ASC"
    SEM.Structure "SDQ2N07 ← ASC"
    SEM.Structure "SDQ2N19 ← ASC"
    SEM.Structure "SDQ2N31 ← ASC"
    SEM.Structure "SDQ2N43 ← ASC"

    SEM.Structure "SDQ2N01 ← err01 (1)"
    SEM.Structure "SDQ2N13 ← err13 (1)"
    SEM.Structure "SDQ2N25 ← err25 (1)"
    SEM.Structure "SDQ2N37 ← err37 (1)"
    SEM.Structure "SDQ2N04 ← err04 (1)"
    SEM.Structure "SDQ2N16 ← err16 (1)"
    SEM.Structure "SDQ2N28 ← err28 (1)"
    SEM.Structure "SDQ2N40 ← err40 (1)"
    SEM.Structure "SDQ2N10 ← err10 (1)"
    SEM.Structure "SDQ2N22 ← err22 (1)"
    SEM.Structure "SDQ2N34 ← err34 (1)"
    SEM.Structure "SDQ2N46 ← err46 (1)"
    SEM.Structure "SDQ2N07 ← err07 (1)"
    SEM.Structure "SDQ2N19 ← err19 (1)"
    SEM.Structure "SDQ2N31 ← err31 (1)"
    SEM.Structure "SDQ2N43 ← err43 (1)"

End Sub

TABLE 3.9
Selected AMOS Text Output for Hypothesized Two-Factor Model: Goodness-of-Fit Statistics

Summary of Models

Model	NPAR	CMIN	DF	P	CMIN/DF
Your model	33	455.926	103	0.000	4.426
Saturated model	136	0.000	0		
Independence model	16	1696.728	120	0.000	14.139

Model	RMR	GFI	AGFI	PGFI
Your model	0.182	0.754	0.675	0.571
Saturated model	0.000	1.000		
Independence model	0.628	0.379	0.296	0.334

Model	DELTA1 NFI	RHO1 RFI	DELTA2 IFI	RHO2 TLI	CFI
Your model	0.731	0.687	0.779	0.739	0.776
Saturated model	1.000		1.000		1.000
Independence model	0.000	0.000	0.000	0.000	0.000

Model	PRATIO	PNFI	PCFI
Your model	0.858	0.628	0.666
Saturated model	0.000	0.000	0.000
Independence model	1.000	0.000	0.000

Model	NCP	LO 90	HI 90
Your model	352.926	290.500	422.898
Saturated model	0.000	0.000	0.000
Independence model	1576.728	1447.292	1713.561

Model	RMSEA	LO 90	HI 90	PCLOSE
Your model	0.114	0.103	0.125	0.000
Independence model	0.223	0.214	0.233	0.000

Model	AIC	BCC	BIC	CAIC
Your model	521.926	526.469	731.553	673.057
Saturated model	272.000	290.721	1135.915	894.843
Independence model	1728.728	1730.931	1830.365	1802.004

Model	ECVI	LO 90	HI 90	MECVI
Your model	1.977	1.741	2.242	1.994
Saturated model	1.030	1.030	1.030	1.101
Independence model	6.548	6.058	7.067	6.557

tion of two fewer factor variances and five fewer factor covariances, with the estimation of two additional factor loadings (formerly SDQ2N10 ← ESC and SDQ2N07 ← MSC). As expected, all other indexes of fit reflect the fact that self-concept structure is not well represented by the hypothesized two-factor model. In particular, the CFI value of .776 and RMSEA value of .114 are strongly indicative of inferior goodness of fit between the hypothesized two-factor model and the sample data.

HYPOTHESIS 3: SELF-CONCEPT IS A ONE-FACTOR STRUCTURE

Although it now seems obvious that the structure of SC for Grade 7 adolescents is best represented by a multidimensional model, there are still researchers who contend that SC is a unidimensional construct. Thus, for purposes of completeness, and to address the issue of unidimensionality, Byrne and Worth Gavin (1996) proceeded in testing this hypothesis. However, because the one-factor model represents a restricted version of the two-factor model, and thus cannot possibly represent a better fitting model, in the interest of space, these analyses are not presented here.

In summary, it is evident from these analyses that both the two-factor and one-factor models of self-concept represent a misspecification of factorial structure for early adolescents. Based on these findings, then, Byrne and Worth Gavin (1996) concluded that SC is a multidimensional construct, which in their study comprised the four facets of general, academic, English, and mathematics self-concepts.

Application 2:
Testing for the Factorial
Validity of Scores From a
Measuring Instrument
(First-Order CFA Model)

❦

F or our second application, we once again examine a first-order confirmatory factor analysis (CFA) model. However, this time we test hypotheses bearing on a single measuring instrument, the Maslach Burnout Inventory (MBI; Maslach & Jackson, 1981, 1986), designed to measure three dimensions of burnout that the authors term emotional exhaustion (EE), depersonalization (DP), and reduced personal accomplishment (PA). The term *burnout* denotes the inability to function effectively in one's job as a consequence of prolonged and extensive job-related stress; *emotional exhaustion* represents feelings of fatigue that develop as one's energies become drained, *depersonalization* the development of negative and uncaring attitudes toward others, and *reduced personal accomplishment* a deterioration of self-confidence, and dissatisfaction in one's achievements.

The purposes of the original study from which this example is taken (Byrne, 1993) were fourfold:

1. To test for the factorial validity of the MBI separately for elementary, intermediate, and secondary teachers.
2. Given findings of inadequate fit, to propose and test an alternative factorial structure.

3. To cross-validate this structure across a second independent sample for each teacher group.
4. To test for the equivalence of item measurements and theoretical structure across the three teaching panels.

Only analyses bearing on the factorial validity of the MBI for the calibration sample of elementary teachers ($n = 580$) are of interest in the present chapter.

Confirmatory factor analysis of a measuring instrument is most appropriately applied to measures that have been fully developed and their factor structures validated. The legitimacy of CFA use, of course, is tied to its conceptual rationale as a hypothesis-testing approach to data analysis. That is to say, based on theory, empirical research, or a combination of both, the researcher postulates a model and then tests for its validity given the sample data. Thus, application of CFA procedures to assessment instruments that are still in the initial stages of development represents a serious misuse of this analytic strategy. In testing for the validity of factorial structure for an assessment measure, the researcher seeks to determine the extent to which items designed to measure a particular factor (i.e., latent construct) actually do so. In general, subscales of a measuring instrument are considered to represent the factors; all items comprising a particular subscale are therefore expected to load onto its related factor.

Given that the MBI has been commercially marketed since 1981, is the most widely used measure of occupational burnout, and has undergone substantial testing of its psychometric properties over the years (see e.g., Byrne, 1991, 1993, 1994a), it most certainly qualifies as a candidate for CFA research. Interestingly, until my 1991 study of the MBI, virtually all previous factor-analytic work had been based only on exploratory procedures. We turn now to a description of the structure of this instrument.

The Measuring Instrument Under Study.   The MBI is a 22-item instrument structured on a 7-point Likert-type scale that ranges from 0 "feeling has never been experienced" to 6 "feeling experienced daily." It is composed of three subscales, each measuring one facet of burnout; the EE subscale comprises nine items, the DP subscale five, and the PA subscale eight. The original version of the MBI (Maslach & Jackson, 1981) was constructed from data based on samples of workers from a wide range of human service organizations. Recently, however, Maslach and Jackson (1986), in collaboration with Schwab, developed the Educators' Survey (MBI Form Ed), a version of the instrument specifically designed for use with teachers. The MBI Form Ed parallels the original version of the MBI except for the modified wording of certain items to make them more appropriate to a teacher's work environment. Specifically, the generic term *recipients*, used in reference to clients, was replaced by the term *students*.

THE HYPOTHESIZED MODEL

The CFA model in the present example hypothesized a priori that: (a) responses to the MBI could be explained by three factors, (b) each item would have a nonzero loading on the burnout factor it was designed to measure, and zero loadings on all other factors, (c) the three factors would be correlated and, (d) measurement error terms would be uncorrelated. A schematic representation of this model is presented in Fig. 4.1.[1]

MODELING WITH AMOS GRAPHICS

The hypothesized three-factor model of MBI structure (see Fig. 4.1) provided the specification input for analyses using AMOS Graphics. I am a firm believer that one should always check the expected number of degrees of freedom associated with a specified model prior to testing for its validity. In chapter 2, we reviewed the process involved in computing these values and, ultimately, in determining the identification status of an hypothesized model. Although all such information (estimated/fixed parameters; degrees of freedom) is provided in the Model/Parameter Summary tables of the AMOS output, I nonetheless still encourage you to make this practice part of your routine, as I believe it forces you to think through the specification of your model.

This recommendation notwithstanding, let me now show you how AMOS Graphics has simplified this process to a mere click of a button. Using our hypothesized model in Fig. 4.1 as an example, one click on the [DF] icon on the tool palette produces the Degrees of Freedom dialog box shown in Fig. 4.2. As such, we see that the sample covariance matrix comprises a total of 253 pieces of information (i.e., number of sample moments, as derived from the observed variables in the model). Of the 72 parameters in the model, only 47 are to be freely estimated; all others (25) are fixed parameters in the model (i.e., they are constrained to equal zero or some nonzero value). As a consequence, the hypothesized model is over-identified with 206 (253 − 47) degrees of freedom.

Prior to submitting the model input to analysis, you will likely wish to review the Analysis Properties box (introduced in chapter 3) in order to tailor the type of information to be provided on the AMOS output. Recall that clicking on the Analysis Properties icon [▦] yields the dialog box shown in Fig. 4.3. For our purposes here, we request the modifications indices (MIs) and the standardized estimates (these will be in addition to the unstandardized estimates, which are default). In contrast to the MI specification in chapter 3, however, here we stipulate a threshold of 10. As such, only MI estimates equal to, or greater than 10 will be included in the output file.

---

[1] As was the case in chapter 3, the first of each congeneric set of items was constrained to a value of 1.0.

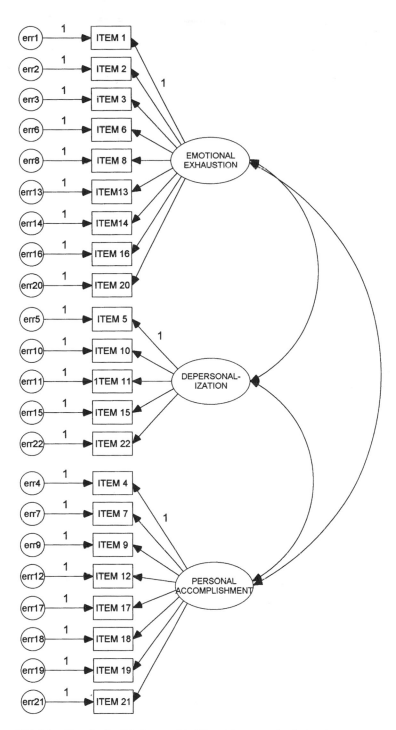

FIG. 4.1. Hypothesized 22-item model of factorial structure for the Maslach Burnout Inventory (Model 1).

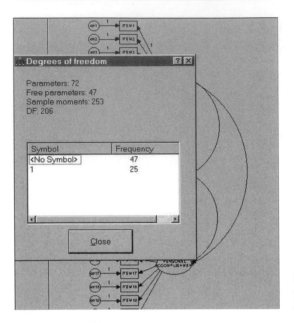

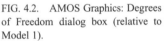

FIG. 4.2. AMOS Graphics: Degrees of Freedom dialog box (relative to Model 1).

Having specified the hypothesized three-factor CFA model of MBI structure and selected the information we wish to have included in the reporting of results, let's now review the related text output file.

AMOS Text Output File: The Hypothesized Model

In contrast to chapter 3, only selected portions of this file are reviewed and discussed. We first examine indices of fit for the model as a whole, and then review the modification indices with a view to pinpointing areas of model misspecification.

Model Assessment

Goodness-of-Fit Summary.   Because the various indices of model fit provided by the AMOS program were discussed in chapter 3, model evaluation throughout the remaining chapters is limited to those summarized in Table 4.1. These criteria were chosen on the basis of (a) their variant approaches to the assessment of model fit (see Hoyle, 1995b) and (b) their support in the literature as important indexes of fit that should be reported.[2] This selection, of course, in no way implies that the

---

[2]For example, Sugawara and MacCallum (1993) recommended that the RMSEA always be reported when maximum likelihood estimation is the only method used because it has been found to yield consistent results across estimation procedures when the model is well specified; MacCallum et al. (1996) recently extended this caveat to include confidence intervals.

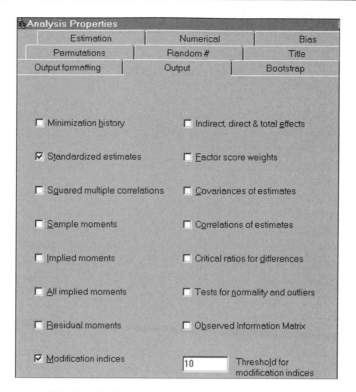

FIG. 4.3.   AMOS Graphics: Analysis Properties dialog box.

remaining criteria are unimportant. Rather, it addresses the need for users to select a subset of goodness-of-fit indexes from the generous quantity provided by the AMOS program.[3] These selected indexes of fit are presented in Table 4.1.

In reviewing these criteria in terms of their optimal values (see chap. 3), we can see that they are consistent in their reflection of an ill-fitting model. For example, values of GFI = .858 and CFI = .850 are indicative of a very poor fit of the model to the data. Thus, it is apparent that some modification in specification is needed in order to determine a model that better represents the sample data. To assist us in pinpointing possible areas of misfit, we examine the modification indexes.[4] We

---

[3]Although included here, due to the formatting of the output file, several fit indexes provide basically the same information. For example, the AIC, CAIC, and ECVI each serve the same function in addressing parsimony. With respect to the NFI, Bentler (1990) has recommended that the CFI be the index of choice.

[4]Of course, as noted in chapter 3, it is important to realize that once we have determined that the hypothesized model represents a poor fit to the data (i.e., the null hypothesis has been rejected), and subsequently embark in post hoc model fitting to identify areas of misfit in the model, we cease to operate in a confirmatory mode of analysis. All model specification and estimation henceforth represent exploratory analyses.

TABLE 4.1

Selected AMOS Text Output for Hypothesized Model: Goodness-of-Fit Statistics

```
Summary of models
- - - - - - - - - - - - - - - - -
```

Model	NPAR	CMIN	DF	P
Your model	47	1010.908	206	0.000
Saturated model	253	0.000	0	
Independence model	22	5598.461	231	0.000

Model	RMR	GFI	AGFI	PGFI
Your model	0.146	0.858	0.825	0.698
Saturated model	0.000	1.000		
Independence model	0.723	0.313	0.247	0.286

Model	DELTA1 NFI	RHO1 RFI	DELTA2 IFI	RHO2 TLI	CFI
Your model	0.819	0.798	0.851	0.832	0.850
Saturated model	1.000		1.000		1.000
Independence model	0.000	0.000	0.000	0.000	0.000

Model	PRATIO	PNFI	PCFI
Your model	0.892	0.731	0.758
Saturated model	0.000	0.000	0.000
Independence model	1.000	0.000	0.000

Model	RMSEA	LO 90	HI 90	PCLOSE
Your model	0.082	0.077	0.087	0.000
Independence model	0.200	0.196	0.205	0.000

Model	ECVI	LO 90	HI 90	MECVI
Your model	1.908	1.744	2.086	1.915
Saturated model	0.874	0.874	0.874	0.910
Independence model	9.745	9.330	10.171	9.748

turn next to these indicators of model misspecification, which are presented in Table 4.2.

Modification Indexes. Based on our CFA model, the factor loadings and error terms that were fixed to a value of 0.0 are of substantial interest; large MIs would argue for the presence of factor cross-loadings (i.e., a loading on more than one factor) and error covariances, respectively. In AMOS, however, MIs are computed for all parameters *implicitly* assumed to be zero, as well as those that are *explicitly* fixed to zero or to some nonzero value. In reviewing the list of MIs in

TABLE 4.2
Selected AMOS Text Output for Hypothesized Model: Modification Indexes

Covariances:		M.I.	Par Change
err7 <---------------------------> err4		40.818	0.175
err12 <---------> PERSONAL_ACCOMPLISHMENT		13.141	-0.065
err12 <-----------> EMOTIONAL_EXHAUSTION		73.017	-0.419
err19 <------------------------> err18		36.140	0.231
err11 <------------------------> err5		13.767	-0.207
err11 <------------------------> err10		19.088	0.194
err15 <------------------------> err5		24.104	0.255
err22 <------------------------> err5		10.468	0.247
err1 <---------> PERSONAL_ACCOMPLISHMENT		12.004	0.066
err2 <------------------------> err1		93.373	0.484
err3 <------------------------> err12		28.113	-0.287
err6 <------------------------> err5		23.690	0.337
err8 <------------------------> err12		10.025	-0.150
err13 <------------------------> err9		10.094	-0.179
err13 <------------------------> err12		12.413	0.189
err14 <---------> PERSONAL_ACCOMPLISHMENT		17.587	0.101
err14 <------------------------> err2		13.284	0.234
err14 <------------------------> err13		12.970	0.253
err16 <------------> DEPERSONAL-_IZATION		21.351	0.176
err16 <------------------------> err5		18.385	0.269
err16 <------------------------> err1		15.185	-0.216
err16 <------------------------> err2		16.800	-0.222
err16 <------------------------> err6		175.606	0.871
err20 <------------------------> err1		13.813	-0.175
err20 <------------------------> err2		16.450	-0.187
err20 < > err9		12.072	0.155
err20 <------------------------> err13		14.864	0.195

Regression Weights:		M.I.	Par Change
ITEM4 <------------------------ ITEM7		28.102	0.215
ITEM7 <------------------------ ITEM4		31.277	0.193
ITEM12 <----------- EMOTIONAL_EXHAUSTION		54.157	-0.267
ITEM12 <------------------------ ITEM1		35.411	-0.161
ITEM12 <------------------------ ITEM2		33.938	-0.166
ITEM12 <------------------------ ITEM3		74.407	-0.226
ITEM12 <------------------------ ITEM6		20.645	-0.123
ITEM12 <------------------------ ITEM8		56.289	-0.185
ITEM12 <------------------------ ITEM14		19.919	-0.110
ITEM12 <------------------------ ITEM16		28.073	-0.156
ITEM12 <------------------------ ITEM20		35.123	-0.185
ITEM18 <------------------------ ITEM19		18.867	0.160
ITEM19 <------------------------ ITEM18		19.693	0.141
ITEM19 <------------------------ ITEM8		14.603	0.081
ITEM19 <------------------------ ITEM14		10.189	0.068
ITEM5 <------------------------ ITEM15		17.029	0.193
ITEM5 <------------------------ ITEM6		19.654	0.140
ITEM5 <------------------------ ITEM16		15.759	0.137
ITEM15 <------------------------ ITEM7		10.447	-0.153
ITEM15 <------------------------ ITEM5		14.888	0.108
ITEM1 <--------- PERSONAL_ACCOMPLISHMENT		12.463	0.433
ITEM1 <------------------------ ITEM7		10.760	0.174
ITEM1 <------------------------ ITEM2		36.745	0.178
ITEM2 <--------- PERSONAL_ACCOMPLISHMENT		10.335	0.386
ITEM2 <------------------------ ITEM18		12.170	0.130
ITEM2 <------------------------ ITEM1		33.301	0.158

(Continued)

TABLE 4.2 *(Continued)*

Regression Weights:		M.I.	Par Change
ITEM3 <------------------------ ITEM12		24.266	-0.192
ITEM6 <------------------------ ITEM5		26.684	0.192
ITEM6 <------------------------ ITEM16		98.428	0.358
ITEM13 <------------------------ ITEM9		11.928	-0.129
ITEM14 <-------- PERSONAL_ACCOMPLISHMENT		16.100	0.627
ITEM14 <------------------------ ITEM18		12.674	0.173
ITEM14 <------------------------ ITEM19		13.179	0.189
ITEM16 <------------ DEPERSONAL-_IZATION		12.800	0.230
ITEM16 <------------------------ ITEM5		27.500	0.177
ITEM16 <------------------------ ITEM10		11.250	0.113
ITEM16 <------------------------ ITEM15		12.173	0.155
ITEM16 <------------------------ ITEM6		100.687	0.302

Table 4.2, for example, you see suggested covariances between error terms and factors, and suggested regression paths among the observed variables. Because the parameters associated with these additional MIs are substantively meaningless, we focus solely on those representing cross-loadings and error covariances.

Although a review of the MIs for the regression weights (i.e., factor loadings) reveals five parameters indicative of cross-loadings, I draw your attention to the one with the highest value (MI = 54.157).[5] This parameter, which represents the cross-loading of Item 12 on the EE factor, stands apart from the rest and accounts for substantial misspecification of the hypothesized factor loading. Such misspecification, for example, could mean that Item 12, in addition to measuring personal accomplishment, also measures emotional exhaustion; alternatively, it could indicate that, although Item 12 was postulated to load on the PA factor, it may load more appropriately on the EE factor.

Turning to the MIs and expected change statistics related to the covariances, we see very clear evidence of misspecification associated with the pairing of Items 1 and 2 (MI = 93.373) and items 6 and 16 (MI = 175.606). Although, admittedly, there are a few additionally quite large MI values shown, these two are substantially larger than those remaining; they represent misspecified error covariances.[6] These measurement error covariances represent systematic, rather than random, measurement error in item responses, and they may derive from characteristics specific either to the items or to the respondents (Aish & Joreskog, 1990). For example, if these parameters reflect item characteristics, they may represent a small omitted factor. If, on the other hand, they represent respondent characteristics, they may reflect bias such as yea-/nay-saying, social desirability, and the like (Aish & Joreskog, 1990). Another type of method effect that can trigger correlated errors is

---

[5]Although you will note larger MIs associated with the regression weights (e.g., 74.407; 100.687), these values pertain to the regression of Item 12 on Item 3, and Item 16 on Item 6, respectively. These MIs do *not* represent cross-loadings and are, in essence, meaningless.

[6]Although they technically represent error covariances, these parameters are typically referenced as correlated errors.

a high degree of overlap in item content. Such redundancy occurs when an item, although worded differently, essentially asks the same qestion. Indeed, based on my work with the MBI (Byrne, 1991, 1993, 1994a), I believe the latter to be true with respect to this instrument.

POST HOC ANALYSES

Provided with information related both to model fit and to possible areas of model misspecification, a researcher may wish to consider respecifying an originally hypothesized model. As emphasized in chapter 3, should this be the case, it is critically important that he or she be cognizant of both the exploratory nature of, and the dangers associated with, the process of post hoc model fitting. (For greater discussion of this topic see chap. 3; see also, e.g., Anderson & Gerbing, 1988; Cliff, 1983; Cudeck & Browne, 1983; Joreskog, 1993; MacCallum, 1986.) For didactic purposes in illustrating the various aspects of post hoc model fitting, we proceed next to respecify the initially hypothesized model of MBI structure taking into account the misspecification information given earlier.

In the original study from which this example is taken (Byrne, 1993), information derived from both exploratory and confirmatory factor analyses of the MBI led me to conclude that Item 12 and Item 16 may be inappropriate for use with teachers. As a consequence, I considered it prudent to respecify the model with these items deleted (see Anderson & Gerbing, 1988); all subsequent analyses in this chapter, then, are based on the 20-item revision, which is labeled here as Model 2.

Interestingly, although the MI value associated with the cross-loading of Item 16 on depersonalization, in the original study, was large relative to the other MIs in the same matrix, its value in the present AMOS analysis was relatively small. This discrepancy likely arose from the alternate approaches to the computation of MIs by AMOS 4.0 and LISREL 7 (Joreskog & Sorbom, 1988), the program used for the original analyses. The computation of MIs in AMOS 4.0 is based on the LISREL approach used prior to LISREL 6 (Arbuckle, personal communication, February 23, 1999). Regardless of this discrepancy, other indicators of misspecification bearing on Item 16, as well as on Item 12, were evidenced across both sets of analyses. For example, in Table 4.2, given both the number and size of MIs associated with Item 12 (9) and Item 16 (5), it is clear that these items are in some way problematic.

Let's return now to AMOS Graphics and the modification of Model 2.

AMOS Graphics: Model 2

Respecification of the hypothesized model of MBI structure from one based on 22 items to one based on 20 simply entails the deletion of the two regression paths associated with Item 12 and Item 16, along with their related observed variable rectangles and measurement error terms; these deletions are quickly imposed using AMOS Graphics. After activating the Erase icon ☒, simply position the cursor over the parameter that you wish to delete and then click. As illustrated in Fig. 4.4, the regression path arrow and the observed variable rectangle associated with Item 16 have already been deleted; the cursor is shown targeted on the related error term, which will be deleted with a single click of the mouse.

The respecified model of MBI structure, with Item 12 and Item 16 deleted, is presented in Fig. 4.5. For sake of comparison, the Degrees of Freedom dialog box is shown in Fig. 4.6. Notice that with the number of MBI items reduced from 22 to 20, the number of pieces of information with which we have to work is now 210 [20(21)/2]. Given the estimation of 43 parameters in the model, we therefore have 210 − 43 = 167 degrees of freedom.

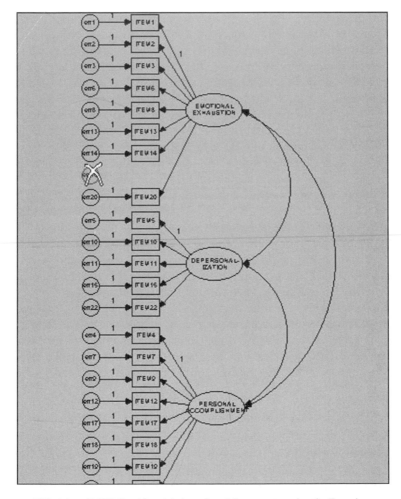

FIG. 4.4.   AMOS Graphics: deletion of model parameter using the Erase icon.

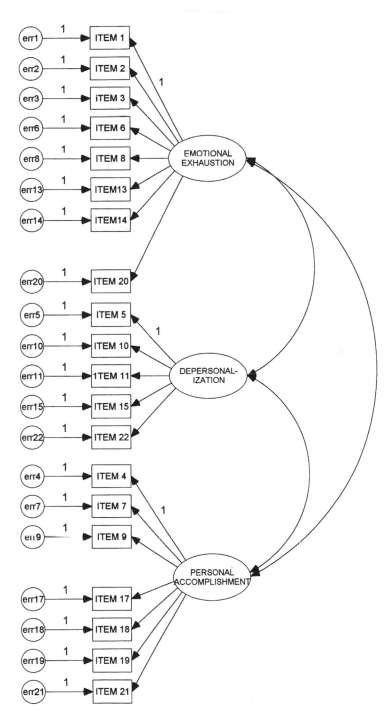

FIG. 4.5. Hypothesized 20-item model of factorial structure for the Maslach Burnout Inventory (Model 2).

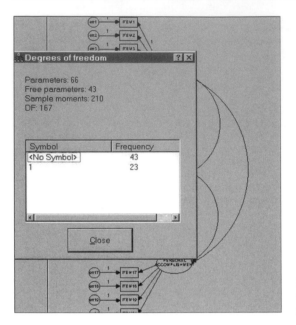

FIG. 4.6.   AMOS Graphics: Degrees of freedom dialog box (relative to model 2).

Let's turn now to Table 4.3, in which the goodness-of-fit statistics related to this respecified model (Model 2) are presented.

AMOS Text Output File: Model 2

Although a review of the various fit indexes for this model are substantially improved over those for the initial model, there is still some evidence of misfit in the model. For example, the CFI and GFI values of .901 and .899, respectively, are marginally adequate at best. To pinpoint areas of misspecification in the model, we turn now to the MIs, which are shown in Table 4.4.

As might be expected from our earlier work, the constrained parameter exhibiting the highest degree of misfit lay in the error covariance matrix and represents a correlated error between Item 1 and Item 2 (MI = 78.193). Compared with MI values for all other error covariance parameters, the one bearing on the association between Item 1 and Item 2 is exceptionally high and, thus, clearly in need of respecification.

Unquestionably, the specification of correlated error terms for purposes of achieving a better fitting model is not an acceptable practice; as with other parameters, such specification must be supported by a strong substantive and/or empirical rationale (Joreskog, 1993). It is my belief that such a case exists here. Specifically, the correlated error in the present context replicates those from my other validation work with the MBI (Byrne, 1991, 1994a), thereby arguing for the sta-

TABLE 4.3

Selected AMOS Text Output for Model 2: Goodness-of-Fit Statistics

Summary of models

Model	NPAR	CMIN	DF	P
Your model	43	618.520	167	0.000
Saturated model	210	0.000	0	
Independence model	20	4737.513	190	0.000

Model	RMR	GFI	AGFI	PGFI
Your model	0.112	0.899	0.872	0.715
Saturated model	0.000	1.000		
Independence model	0.714	0.346	0.277	0.313

Model	DELTA1 NFI	RHO1 RFI	DELTA2 IFI	RHO2 TLI	CFI
Your model	0.869	0.851	0.901	0.887	0.901
Saturated model	1.000		1.000		1.000
Independence model	0.000	0.000	0.000	0.000	0.000

Model	PRATIO	PNFI	PCFI
Your model	0.879	0.764	0.792
Saturated model	0.000	0.000	0.000
Independence model	1.000	0.000	0.000

Model	RMSEA	LO 90	HI 90	PCLOSE
Your model	0.068	0.063	0.074	0.000
Independence model	0.203	0.198	0.208	0.000

Model	ECVI	LO 90	HI 90	MECVI
Your model	1.217	1.092	1.355	1.222
Saturated model	0.725	0.725	0.725	0.753
Independence model	8.251	7.870	8.645	8.254

bility of this finding. Based on this logical and empirical rationale, the model was subsequently respecified with this parameter freely estimated.

AMOS Graphics: Model 3

The third model of MBI structure is shown in Fig. 4.7. In summary, this model was based on only 20 of the original 22 items and included a correlated error between Item 1 and Item 2. In reviewing results bearing on the analysis of this model, we turn first to Table 4.5, which summarizes the goodness-of-fit statistics.

TABLE 4.4

Selected AMOS Text Output for Model 2: Modification Indexes

Covariances:		M.I.	Par Change
err7 <-----------------------------> err4		34.212	0.158
err19 <----------------------------> err4		10.659	-0.106
err19 <--------------------------> err18		34.902	0.229
err11 <---------------------------> err5		13.137	-0.203
err11 <--------------------------> err10		18.831	0.193
err15 <---------------------------> err5		24.273	0.256
err22 <---------------------------> err5		10.471	0.248
err1 <---------> PERSONAL_ACCOMPLISHMENT		11.160	0.069
err2 <---------------------------> err1		78.193	0.426
err6 <-------------> DEPERSONAL-_IZATION		14.319	0.165
err6 <----------------------------> err5		26.153	0.366
err13 <--------------------------> err2		10.803	-0.174
err14 <--------> PERSONAL_ACCOMPLISHMENT		14.453	0.101
err14 <-------------------------> err13		11.683	0.240
err20 <--------------------------> err1		17.953	-0.197
err20 <--------------------------> err2		21.122	-0.210
err20 <--------------------------> err8		14.549	0.172
err20 <-------------------------> err13		16.651	0.209

Regression Weights:		M.I.	Par Change
ITEM4 <------------------------ ITEM7		22.550	0.191
ITEM7 <------------------------ ITEM4		25.051	0.172
ITEM18 <---------------------- ITEM19		17.648	0.156
ITEM19 <---------------------- ITEM18		18.757	0.138
ITEM5 <----------------------- ITEM15		17.144	0.194
ITEM5 <------------------------ ITEM6		20.964	0.145
ITEM15 <----------------------- ITEM7		10.165	-0.151
ITEM15 <----------------------- ITEM5		15.025	0.109
ITEM1 <--------- PERSONAL_ACCOMPLISHMENT		13.005	0.413
ITEM1 <------------------------ ITEM2		28.845	0.155
ITEM2 <--------- PERSONAL_ACCOMPLISHMENT		10.788	0.369
ITEM2 <----------------------- ITEM18		11.683	0.125
ITEM2 <------------------------ ITEM1		25.984	0.137
ITEM6 <------------ DEPERSONAL-_IZATION		11.330	0.246
ITEM6 <----------------------- ITEM19		10.194	-0.160
ITEM6 <------------------------ ITEM5		33.409	0.222
ITEM6 <----------------------- ITEM15		12.032	0.175
ITEM13 <----------------------- ITEM9		13.098	-0.135
ITEM14 <-------- PERSONAL_ACCOMPLISHMENT		14.753	0.569
ITEM14 <---------------------- ITEM18		11.597	0.165
ITEM14 <---------------------- ITEM19		11.890	0.179

AMOS Text Output File: Model 3

A review of the fit indexes presented in Table 4.5 for Model 3, and a comparison of these values with those summarized in Table 4.3 for Model 2 (the initial 20-item model of MBI structure), reveal Model 3 to be the better fitting one. In particular, note the improved CFI value of .92 (vs. .90), and the drop in RMSEA (.062 vs. .068) and ECVI (1.072 vs. 1.217) values.

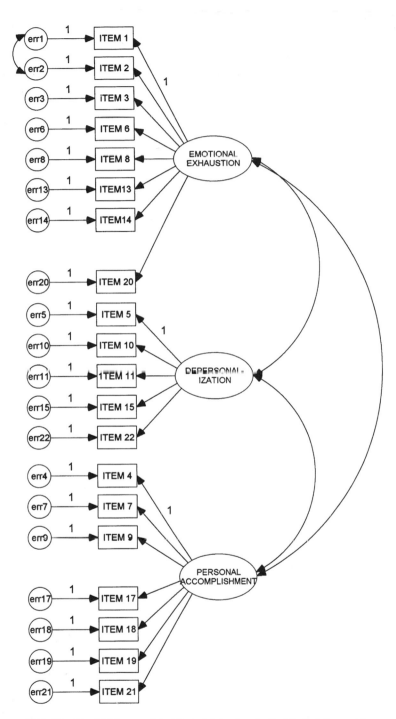

FIG. 4.7.   Final 20-item model of factorial structure for the Maslach Burnout Inventory.

TABLE 4.5

Selected AMOS Text Output for Model 3: Goodness-of-Fit Indexes

Summary of models

Model	NPAR	CMIN	DF	P
Your model	44	532.419	166	0.000
Saturated model	210	0.000	0	
Independence model	20	4737.513	190	0.000

Model	RMR	GFI	AGFI	PGFI
Your model	0.106	0.914	0.892	0.723
Saturated model	0.000	1.000		
Independence model	0.714	0.346	0.277	0.313

Model	DELTA1 NFI	RHO1 RFI	DELTA2 IFI	RHO2 TLI	CFI
Your model	0.888	0.871	0.920	0.908	0.919
Saturated model	1.000		1.000		1.000
Independence model	0.000	0.000	0.000	0.000	0.000

Model	PRATIO	PNFI	PCFI
Your model	0.874	0.775	0.803
Saturated model	0.000	0.000	0.000
Independence model	1.000	0.000	0.000

Model	RMSEA	LO 90	HI 90	PCLOSE
Your model	0.062	0.056	0.068	0.001
Independence model	0.203	0.198	0.208	0.000

Model	ECVI	LO 90	HI 90	MECVI
Your model	1.072	0.958	1.199	1.077
Saturated model	0.725	0.725	0.725	0.753
Independence model	8.251	7.870	8.645	8.254

In assessing the extent to which a respecified model exhibits improvement in fit, however, it has become customary to determine if the difference in fit between the two models is statistically significant. As such, the researcher examines the difference in χ^2 $(\Delta\chi^2)$ between the two models. Doing so, however, presumes that the two models are nested.[7] The differential between the models represents a measurement

---

[7]Nested models are hierarchically related to one another in the sense that their parameter sets are subsets of one another (i.e., particular parameters are freely estimated in one model, but fixed to zero in a second model) (Bentler & Chou, 1987; Bollen, 1989a). Thus, for example, it would be inappropriate to compare this final model with the initially hypothesized model, which was based on a 22-item MBI structure.

TABLE 4.6

Selected AMOS Text Output for Model 3: Modification Indexes

Covariances:			M.I.	Par Change
err7	<--------------------------->	err4	34.287	0.158
err19	<--------------------------->	err4	10.467	-0.105
err19	<--------------------------->	err18	35.021	0.229
err11	<--------------------------->	err5	13.571	-0.206
err11	<--------------------------->	err10	19.025	0.194
err15	<--------------------------->	err5	24.122	0.255
err22	<--------------------------->	err5	10.495	0.248
err6	<------------->	DEPERSONAL-_IZATION	12.432	0.152
err6	<--------------------------->	err5	25.427	0.359
err14	<--------->	PERSONAL_ACCOMPLISHMENT	16.881	0.110
err14	<--------------------------->	err2	14.897	0.228
err14	<--------------------------->	err13	11.139	0.233

Regression Weights:			M.I.	Par Change
ITEM4	<-------------------------	ITEM7	22.600	0.191
ITEM7	<-------------------------	ITEM4	25.128	0.172
ITEM18	<-------------------------	ITEM19	17.744	0.157
ITEM19	<-------------------------	ITEM18	18.821	0.138
ITEM5	<-------------------------	ITEM15	17.032	0.193
ITEM5	<-------------------------	ITEM6	20.513	0.143
ITEM15	<-------------------------	ITEM7	10.110	-0.150
ITEM15	<-------------------------	ITEM5	14.913	0.108
ITEM6	<-------------------------	ITEM5	30.615	0.211
ITEM6	<-------------------------	ITEM15	10.717	0.165
ITEM13	<-------------------------	ITEM9	10.424	-0.120
ITEM14	<---------	PERSONAL_ACCOMPLISHMENT	16.920	0.615
ITEM14	<-------------------------	ITEM18	13.387	0.178
ITEM14	<-------------------------	ITEM19	13.093	0.189

of the overidentifying constraints and is itself χ^2 distributed, with degrees of freedom equal to the difference in degrees of freedom (Δdf); it can thus be tested statistically, with a significant $\Delta\chi^2$ indicating substantial improvement in model fit. Comparison of Model 3 ($\chi^2_{(166)} = 532.42$) with Model 2 ($\chi^2_{(167)} = 618.52$), for example, yields a difference in χ^2 value of 86.10 ($\Delta\chi^2_{(1)} = 86.10$).[8]

The second point of interest in the output file for Model 3 relates to the MIs, which are summarized in Table 4.6. In reviewing these misspecification statistics, it is evident that the model could be further improved with the addition of possibly four more correlated errors (err7/4; err 18/19; err5/15; err5/6). However, in the interest of parsimony, together with the relative closeness of these MI values, I consider Model 3 to represent the best fitting model of MBI structure for elementary teachers.[9]

---

[8]One parameter, previously specified as fixed in the initially hypothesized model (Model 2), was specified as free in the final model, thereby using up one degree of freedom (i.e., one less degrees of freedom).

[9]In the original study, an additional correlated error between Item 10 and Item 11 was incorporated into the model on the basis of its exceptionally large MI value. (See earlier explanation regarding discrepancies in MI values as computed by the AMOS 4.0 and LISREL 7 programs.)

Having determined this final model, our interest now focuses on the parameter estimates; standardized as well as unstandardized values are presented. Turning first to the factor loading estimates in Table 4.7, we see that all are both substantively reasonable and statistically significant.

Turning next to the variance and covariance estimates shown in Table 4.8, we again can conclude that all estimates are statistically significant, as well as sub-

TABLE 4.7
Selected AMOS Text Output for Model 3: Factor Loading Parameter Estimates

Regression Weights:	Estimate	S.E.	C.R.
ITEM20 <------- EMOTIONAL_EXHAUSTION	0.861	0.048	18.103
ITEM14 <------- EMOTIONAL_EXHAUSTION	0.957	0.061	15.682
ITEM13 <------- EMOTIONAL_EXHAUSTION	1.056	0.057	18.567
ITEM8 <-------- EMOTIONAL_EXHAUSTION	1.250	0.059	21.101
ITEM6 <-------- EMOTIONAL_EXHAUSTION	0.799	0.056	14.309
ITEM3 <-------- EMOTIONAL_EXHAUSTION	1.019	0.057	18.006
ITEM2 <-------- EMOTIONAL_EXHAUSTION	0.916	0.040	23.075
ITEM1 <-------- EMOTIONAL_EXHAUSTION	1.000		
ITEM22 <-------- DEPERSONAL-_IZATION	0.637	0.088	7.215
ITEM15 <-------- DEPERSONAL-_IZATION	0.667	0.068	9.750
ITEM11 <-------- DEPERSONAL-_IZATION	1.410	0.108	13.010
ITEM10 <-------- DEPERSONAL-_IZATION	1.380	0.106	13.018
ITEM5 <--------- DEPERSONAL-_IZATION	1.000		
ITEM21 <---- PERSONAL_ACCOMPLISHMENT	1.229	0.164	7.488
ITEM19 <---- PERSONAL_ACCOMPLISHMENT	1.659	0.174	9.552
ITEM18 <---- PERSONAL_ACCOMPLISHMENT	1.726	0.183	9.421
ITEM17 <---- PERSONAL_ACCOMPLISHMENT	1.376	0.140	9.797
ITEM9 <----- PERSONAL_ACCOMPLISHMENT	1.709	0.191	8.956
ITEM7 <----- PERSONAL_ACCOMPLISHMENT	1.057	0.122	8.669
ITEM4 <----- PERSONAL_ACCOMPLISHMENT	1.000		

Standardized Regression Weights:	Estimate
ITEM20 <------- EMOTIONAL_EXHAUSTION	0.747
ITEM14 <------- EMOTIONAL_EXHAUSTION	0.655
ITEM13 <------- EMOTIONAL_EXHAUSTION	0.765
ITEM8 <-------- EMOTIONAL_EXHAUSTION	0.860
ITEM6 <-------- EMOTIONAL_EXHAUSTION	0.602
ITEM3 <-------- EMOTIONAL_EXHAUSTION	0.744
ITEM2 <-------- EMOTIONAL_EXHAUSTION	0.727
ITEM1 <-------- EMOTIONAL_EXHAUSTION	0.752
ITEM22 <-------- DEPERSONAL-_IZATION	0.351
ITEM15 <-------- DEPERSONAL-_IZATION	0.506
ITEM11 <-------- DEPERSONAL-_IZATION	0.793
ITEM10 <-------- DEPERSONAL-_IZATION	0.794
ITEM5 <--------- DEPERSONAL-_IZATION	0.575
ITEM21 <---- PERSONAL_ACCOMPLISHMENT	0.423
ITEM19 <---- PERSONAL_ACCOMPLISHMENT	0.649
ITEM18 <---- PERSONAL_ACCOMPLISHMENT	0.630
ITEM17 <---- PERSONAL_ACCOMPLISHMENT	0.690
ITEM9 <----- PERSONAL_ACCOMPLISHMENT	0.569
ITEM7 <----- PERSONAL_ACCOMPLISHMENT	0.536
ITEM4 <----- PERSONAL_ACCOMPLISHMENT	0.475

TABLE 4.8

Selected AMOS Text Output for Model 3: Variance/Covariance Parameter Estimates

Covariances:	Estimate	S.E.	C.R.
EMOTIONAL_EXHAUS <> PERSONAL_ACCOMPL	-0.226	0.035	-6.375
EMOTIONAL_EXHAUS <> DEPERSONAL-_IZAT	0.662	0.075	8.787
DEPERSONAL-_IZAT <> PERSONAL_ACCOMPL	-0.187	0.029	-6.496
err2 <----------------------> err1	0.489	0.062	7.825

Correlations:	Estimate
EMOTIONAL_EXHAUS <> PERSONAL_ACCOMPL	-0.409
EMOTIONAL_EXHAUS <> DEPERSONAL-_IZAT	0.625
DEPERSONAL-_IZAT <> PERSONAL_ACCOMPL	-0.496
err2 <----------------------> err1	0.414

Variances:	Estimate	S.E.	C.R.
EMOTIONAL_EXHAUSTION	1.557	0.151	10.294
DEPERSONAL-_IZATION	0.721	0.104	6.946
PERSONAL_ACCOMPLISHMENT	0.196	0.036	5.434
err20	0.913	0.061	14.896
err14	1.895	0.120	15.762
err13	1.233	0.084	14.652
err8	0.856	0.070	12.228
err6	1.752	0.109	16.071
err3	1.307	0.087	14.943
err2	1.165	0.078	15.019
err1	1.195	0.081	14.737
err22	2.086	0.126	16.543
err15	0.934	0.059	15.849
err11	0.849	0.077	10.964
err10	0.805	0.074	10.911
err5	1.460	0.095	15.326
err21	1.364	0.085	16.081
err19	0.742	0.054	13.849
err18	0.890	0.063	14.163
err17	0.409	0.031	13.065
err9	1.201	0.080	14.950
err7	0.546	0.036	15.280
err4	0.673	0.043	15.760

stantively reasonable. In reviewing these standardized estimates, you will want to verify that particular parameter values are consistent with the literature. For example, within the context of the present application, it is of interest to inspect correlations among the MBI factors for consistency with their previously reported values; these estimates are as expected. Of particular note is the size of the correlated error associated with Item 1 and Item 2, which can be considered substantially large within the present context ($r = .414$).

MODELING WITH AMOS BASIC

The AMOS Basic input for the final model of MBI structure, as shown in Fig. 4.7, is presented in Table 4.9. Let's briefly review the structure of this file. The three lines that follow the title request that: (a) the output be presented in text (rather than table) format, (b) the threshold level for the modification indices is set at 10, and (c) the standardized estimates are to be included in the output. The next line (SEM.BeginGroup) includes the name of the data to be used in the analysis. In this

TABLE 4.9
AMOS Basic Input File for Final Model of MBI Structure

Sub Main
Dim Sem As New AmosEngine
'Testing for Validity of the MBI for Elementary Teachers: Final Model'

SEM.TextOutput
SEM.Mods 10
SEM.Standardized

SEM.BeginGroup "cvel1.xls"

    SEM.Structure "ITEM1 ← EMOTIONAL EXHAUSTION (1)"
    SEM.Structure "ITEM2 ← EMOTIONAL EXHAUSTION"
    SEM.Structure "ITEM3 ← EMOTIONAL EXHAUSTION"
    SEM.Structure "ITEM6 ← EMOTIONAL EXHAUSTION"
    SEM.Structure "ITEM8 ← EMOTIONAL EXHAUSTION"
    SEM.Structure "ITEM13 ← EMOTIONAL EXHAUSTION"
    SEM.Structure "ITEM14 ← EMOTIONAL EXHAUSTION"
    SEM.Structure "ITEM20 ← EMOTIONAL EXHAUSTION"
    SEM.Structure "ITEM5 ← DEPERSONALIZATION (1)"
    SEM.Structure "ITEM10 ← DEPERSONALIZATION"
    SEM.Structure "ITEM11 ← DEPERSONALIZATION"
    SEM.Structure "ITEM15 ← DEPERSONALIZATION"
    SEM.Structure "ITEM22 ← DEPERSONALIZATION"
    SEM.Structure "ITEM4 ← PERSONAL ACCOMPLISHMENT (1)"
    SEM.Structure "ITEM7 ← PERSONAL ACCOMPLISHMENT"
    SEM.Structure "ITEM9 ← PERSONAL ACCOMPLISHMENT"
    SEM.Structure "ITEM17 ← PERSONAL ACCOMPLISHMENT"
    SEM.Structure "ITEM18 ← PERSONAL ACCOMPLISHMENT"
    SEM.Structure "ITEM19 ← PERSONAL ACCOMPLISHMENT"
    SEM.Structure "ITEM21 ← PERSONAL ACCOMPLISHMENT"

    SEM.Structure "ITEM1 ← err1 (1)"
    SEM.Structure "ITEM2 ← err2 (1)"
    SEM.Structure "ITEM3 ← err3 (1)"
    SEM.Structure "ITEM6 ← err6 (1)"
    SEM.Structure "ITEM8 ← err8 (1)"
    SEM.Structure "ITEM13 ← err13 (1)"

(Continued)

TABLE 4.9 *(Continued)*

SEM.Structure "ITEM14 ← err14 (1)"
SEM.Structure "ITEM20 ← err20 (1)"
SEM.Structure "ITEM5 ← err5 (1)"
SEM.Structure "ITEM10 ← err10 (1)"
SEM.Structure "ITEM11 ← err11 (1)"
SEM.Structure "ITEM15 ← err15 (1)"
SEM.Structure "ITEM22 ← err22 (1)"
SEM.Structure "ITEM4 ← err4 (1)"
SEM.Structure "ITEM7 ← err7 (1)"
SEM.Structure "ITEM9 ← err9 (1)"
SEM.Structure "ITEM17 ← err17 (1)"
SEM.Structure "ITEM18 ← err18 (1)"
SEM.Structure "ITEM19 ← err19 (1)"
SEM.Structure "ITEM21 ← err21 (1)"

SEM.Structure "err1 <> err2"

End Sub

case, the data are contained in a Microsoft Excel file (*.xls). These commands are then followed by the model specification input. As such, the first block of equations relates to the factor loadings, while the second block of equations relates to the regression weights for the measurement errors (which are fixed to 1.0 as only the error variances are of interest). Finally, the last statement specifies that the covariance between the measurement errors associated with Item 1 and Item 2 are to be computed. Consistent with the AMOS Basic input files for CFA models illustrated in chapter 3, no correlations among the factors are specified as these parameters are assumed by default. Likewise, given that AMOS Basic assumes no correlation among the error terms, it is thus necessary that we specify the error correlation related to Item 1 and Item 2.

CHAPTER 5

Application 3: Testing for the Factorial Validity of Scores From a Measuring Instrument (Second-Order CFA Model)

$\sim$

Although the two previous applications focused on CFA first-order models, the present application examines a CFA model that comprises a second-order factor. As such, we test hypotheses related to the Beck Depression Inventory (Beck, Ward, Mendelson, Mock, & Erbaugh, 1961) as it bears on the nonclinical adolescent population. The example is taken from a study by Byrne, Baron, and Campbell (1993) and represents one of a series of studies that have tested for the validity of second-order BDI factorial structure for high school adolescents in Canada (Byrne & Baron, 1993, 1994; Byrne, Baron, & Campbell, 1993, 1994), Sweden (Byrne, Baron, Larsson, & Melin, 1995, 1996), and Bulgaria (Byrne, Baron, & Balev, 1996, 1998). Although the purposes of the Byrne et al. (1993) study were to cross-validate and test for an invariant BDI structure across gender for Canadian high school students, we focus only on factorial validity as it relates to the female calibration sample. (For further details regarding the sample, analyses, and results, readers are referred to the original article.)

The Beck Depression Inventory (BDI) is a 21-item scale that measures symptoms related to cognitive, behavioral, affective, and somatic components of depression. Although originally designed for use by trained interviewers, it is now most typically used as a self-report measure. For each item, respondents are presented with four statements rated from 0 to 3 in terms of intensity and are asked to select the one that most accurately describes their own feelings; higher scores represent a more severe level of reported depression. As noted in chapter 4, the CFA of a measuring instrument is most appropriately conducted with fully developed assessment measures that have demonstrated satisfactory factorial validity. Justification for CFA procedures in the present instance is based on evidence provided by Tanaka and Huba (1984), and replicated studies by Byrne and associates (already cited), that BDI score data are most adequately represented by an hierarchical factorial structure. That is to say, the first-order factors are explained by some higher order structure which, in the case of the BDI, is a single second-order factor of general depression.

Let's turn now to a description of the BDI and its postulated structure.

THE HYPOTHESIZED MODEL

The model to be tested in the present application derives from the work of Byrne et al. (1993). As such, the CFA model hypothesized a priori that:

1. Responses to the BDI could be explained by three first-order factors (negative attitude, performance difficulty, somatic elements), and one second-order factor (general depression).
2. Each item would have a non-zero loading on the first-order factor it was designed to measure, and zero loadings on the other two first-order factors.
3. Error terms associated with each item would be uncorrelated.
4. Covariation among the three first-order factors would be explained fully by their regression on the second-order factor.

A diagrammatic representation of this model is presented in Fig. 5.1.

MODELING WITH AMOS GRAPHICS

Before examining analyses related to the input model shown in Fig. 5.1, allow me to show you another drawing feature of AMOS Graphics; this one relates to the aligning of objects in a model. In the case to be illustrated here, we focus on the vertical alignment of the first-order factors of negative attitude, performance difficulty, and somatic elements. Specifically, you will likely want to line up, vertically, the ellipses representing these three factors before you add the higher order factor of depression to the model. The approach that I illustrate here follows from the Help drop-down menu.

Once you pull down the Help menu, you will see that the first option is labeled as "Contents." Clicking on this option yields the list of available topics. Scrolling down the list, I selected "Align objects vertically," which is shown highlighted in

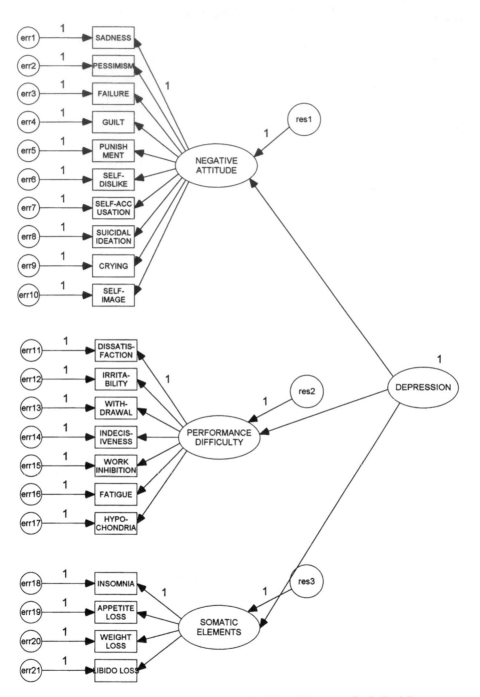

FIG. 5.1.   Hypothesized second-order model of factorial structure for the Beck Depression Inventory.

Fig. 5.2. Accompanying this selection, you will also see the parenthesized notation *obsolete*, which indicates that the method used in earlier versions of AMOS is no longer available. Clicking on the Display button immediately triggers the message shown in Fig. 5.3. Finally, clicking on the underlined topic presents a detailed list of instructions that involve use of the Drag Properties ▓ icon in the tool palette; the list of required steps is shown in Fig. 5.4. As illustrated, the menu also includes a tip with respect to the simultaneous alignment of several objects.

As suggested in previous chapters, as an initial check of the hypothesized model, we need to determine the degrees of freedom associated with this model in order to ascertain its status with respect to model identification. A simple click of the Degrees of Freedom ▓ icon yielded the summary presented in Fig. 5.5. As indicated, we have 231 sample moments and 45 freely estimated parameters, leaving us with 186 degrees of freedom. At first blush, one might feel confident that the specified model was overidentified and thus all should go well. However, as I noted in chapter 2, with hierarchical models, it is critical that one also check the identification status of the higher order portion of the model. In the present case,

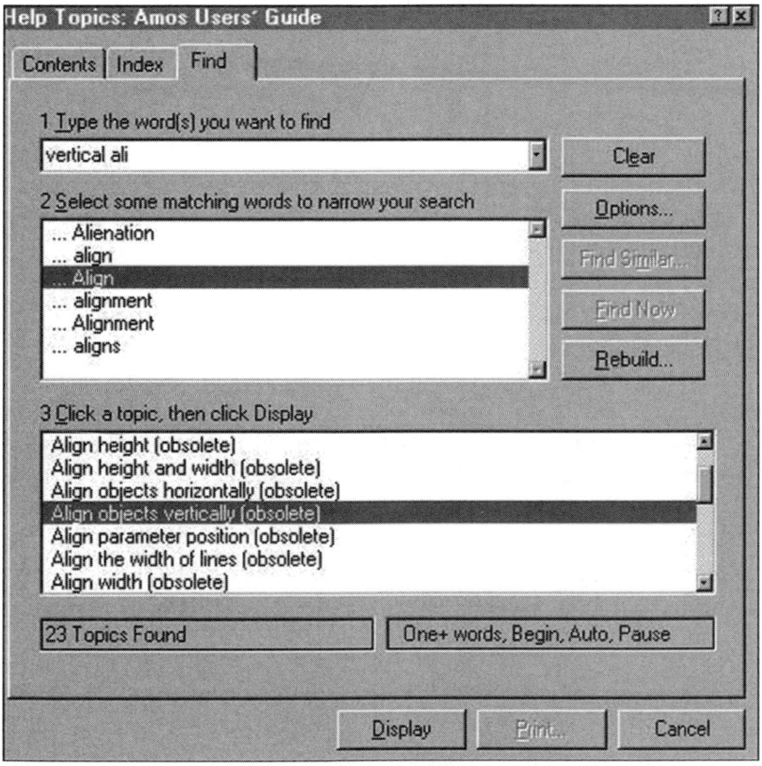

FIG. 5.2.   AMOS Graphics: Align pull-down menu.

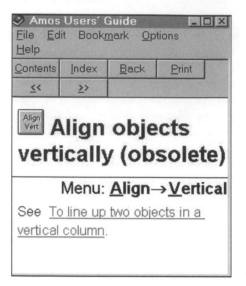

FIG. 5.3.   AMOS Graphics: Users'
Guide to the vertical alignment of
objects.

given the specification of only three first-order factors, the higher order structure
will be just-identified unless a constraint is placed on at least one parameter in this
upper level of the model (see Bentler, 1995; Rindskopf & Rose, 1988). More
specifically, with three first-order factors, we have six $[(4 \times 3)/2]$ pieces of information; the number of estimable parameters is also six (three factor loadings; three
residuals), thereby resulting in a just-identified model. Thus, prior to testing for the
validity of the hypothesized structure shown in Fig. 5.1, we need first to address
this identification issue at the upper level of the model.

One approach to resolving the issue of just-identification in the hypothesized
model is to place equality constraints on particular parameters known to yield estimates that are approximately equal. The AMOS program provides a powerful and
quite unique exploratory mechanism for separating promising from unlikely
parameter candidates for the imposition of equality constraints. This strategy,
termed the critical ratio difference (CRDIFF) method, produces a listing of critical
ratios for the pairwise differences among all parameter estimates. To determine
these values, we need first to request that critical ratios for differences among
parameters be included in the AMOS output file, and second, to calculate the
model estimates. (Because illustration related to both procedures has been demonstrated earlier, diagrams related to each are not presented here.)

AMOS Text Output File

In the initial output file, only the summary data and critical ratios of differences are
of interest. We turn first to the summary information, presented in Table 5.1, where
several points are worthy of review. First, consistent with Figure 5.1, there are three

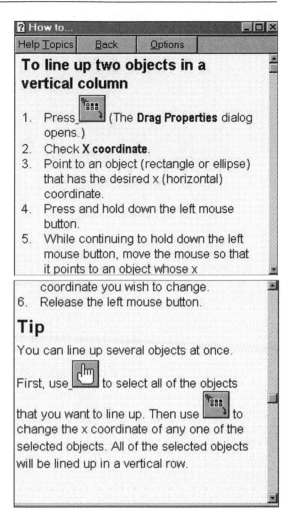

FIG. 5.4. AMOS Graphics: instructions for conducting a vertical alignment of objects.

dependent first-order factors (negative attitude, performance difficulty, somatic elements) and one independent second-order factor (depression); as shown in Table 5.1, these are labeled as unobserved endogenous and unobserved exogenous variables, respectively. Second, we see that the sample size is 321. Finally, summary information related to the computation of the degrees of freedom is presented.

Let's turn now to our second interest in the output file, the critical ratios of differences among parameters; two pieces of information are relevant. First, to assist in the identification of all such values, AMOS assigns unique labels to the model parameters; these labels are shown in Table 5.2, along with the maximum likelihood estimates, standard errors and critical ratios. Two prime candidates for the imposition of equality constraints are the higher order residuals related to the neg-

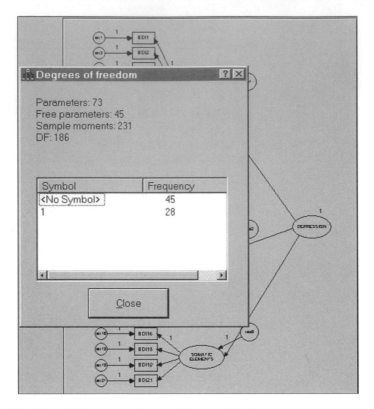

FIG. 5.5.   AMOS Graphics: Degrees of Freedom dialog box (relative to the hypothesized model).

ative attitudes and performance difficulty factors, as their estimated values are
almost identical; these values are shown under the "Variances" heading. Indeed,
these two parameters were constrained to be equal in the original study (Byrne et
al., 1993). However, we see that the estimated value of the third residual, related to
the somatic elements factor, is really not that different from the other two. A final
decision on which parameters to constrain as equal must be determined from the
actual critical ratios of difference values, which are extrapolated from the output
file and shown in Table 5.3.

The second set of information needed, then, relates to the actual computed difference values. Turning to Table 5.3, you will see only a portion of the critical ratios
of differences for the residual/measurement error parameters. For our purposes
here, we focus only on the residuals which, as indicated in Table 5.2, are labeled as
par-22, par-23, and par-24. Let's examine the first off-diagonal entry of 0.051 in
the upper left of the table. This critical ratio represents the difference between par-
22 (residual 1) and par-23 (residual 2), divided by the estimated standard error of
this difference (Arbuckle & Wothke, 1999). The critical ratio can be compared to a

```
Your model contains the following variables

                BDI14                          observed    endogenous
                BDI10                          observed    endogenous
                BDI9                           observed    endogenous
                BDI8                           observed    endogenous
                BDI7                           observed    endogenous
                BDI6                           observed    endogenous
                BDI5                           observed    endogenous
                BDI3                           observed    endogenous
                BDI2                           observed    endogenous
                BDI1                           observed    endogenous
                BDI20                          observed    endogenous
                BDI17                          observed    endogenous
                BDI15                          observed    endogenous
                BDI13                          observed    endogenous
                BDI12                          observed    endogenous
                BDI11                          observed    endogenous
                BDI4                           observed    endogenous
                BDI21                          observed    endogenous
                BDI19                          observed    endogenous
                BDI18                          observed    endogenous
                BDI16                          observed    endogenous

                NEGATIVE_ATTITUDE              unobserved  endogenous
                PERFORMANCE_DIFFICULTY         unobserved  endogenous
                SOMATIC_ELEMENTS              unobserved  endogenous

                err14                          unobserved  exogenous
                err10                          unobserved  exogenous
                err9                           unobserved  exogenous
                err8                           unobserved  exogenous
                err7                           unobserved  exogenous
                err6                           unobserved  exogenous
                err5                           unobserved  exogenous
                err3                           unobserved  exogenous
                err2                           unobserved  exogenous
                err1                           unobserved  exogenous
                err20                          unobserved  exogenous
                err17                          unobserved  exogenous
                err15                          unobserved  exogenous
                err13                          unobserved  exogenous
                err12                          unobserved  exogenous
                err11                          unobserved  exogenous
                err4                           unobserved  exogenous
                err21                          unobserved  exogenous
                err19                          unobserved  exogenous
                err18                          unobserved  exogenous
                err16                          unobserved  exogenous
                DEPRESSION                     unobserved  exogenous
                res1                           unobserved  exogenous
                res2                           unobserved  exogenous
                res3                           unobserved  exogenous

                Number of variables in your model:   49
                Number of observed variables:        21
                Number of unobserved variables:      28
                Number of exogenous variables:       25
                Number of endogenous variables:      24

The model is recursive.

Sample size:   321
```

(Continued)

TABLE 5.1 *(Continued)*

Model: Your model

Computation of Degrees of Freedom

Number of distinct sample moments: 231
Number of distinct parameters to be estimated: 45

Degrees of freedom: 186

Minimum was achieved

Chi-square =   340.078
Degrees of freedom =   186
Probability level =   0.000

table of the standard normal distribution to test whether the two parameters are equal in the population. Given that the value of 0.051 is less than 1.96, the hypothesis that the two residual variances are equal in the population could not be rejected. Likewise, the critical ratios of differences related to the remaining pairs of residuals are statistically nonsignificant. Given these findings, it seems reasonable to constrain variances related to the three residuals to be equal. As such, the higher order level of the model will be overidentified with two degrees of freedom. That is to say, the variance will be estimated for one residual, and then the same value will be held constant across the other two residual variances. The degrees of freedom for the model, as a whole, then should increase from 186 to 188.

Having determined which parameters in the upper level of the model that we wish to constrain, we now need to include this information in the model to be tested. The specification of equality constraints is accomplished, in AMOS Graphics, by assigning the same label to all parameters to be constrained equal. Let's return to our hypothesized model and assign these equality constraints to the three factor residuals associated with the first-order factors. Turning to the first residual, a right-click on the mouse will produce the dialog box shown in Fig. 5.6. We then click on the Object Properties option which, in turn, yields the dialog box shown in Fig. 5.7. Clicking on the Parameters tab will then produce a blank space under Variance, where you can enter any arbitrary label (although typically, in AMOS, these include an underscore). In the present case, we'll use the label "var_a." This same label is subsequently assigned to the remaining residuals and indicates to the AMOS 4.0 program that the variances of the three residual parameters are to be constrained equal.

The hypothesized model, with these equality constraints specified, is presented in Fig. 5.8. Analyses are now based on this respecified model. (Note that the actual item numbers have replaced their related content as labels for the observed variables.)

TABLE 5.2
Selected AMOS Text Output for Hypothesized Model: Labels for Critical Ratios of Differences

Regression Weights:	Estimate	S.E.	C.R.	Label
PERFORMANCE_DIFFICULTY <- DEPRESSION	0.477	0.052	9.089	par-19
NEGATIVE_ATTITUDE <------ DEPRESSION	0.419	0.044	9.625	par-20
SOMATIC_ELEMENTS <------- DEPRESSION	0.349	0.049	7.106	par-21
BDI14 <----------- NEGATIVE_ATTITUDE	1.037	0.153	6.766	par-1
BDI10 <----------- NEGATIVE_ATTITUDE	1.177	0.158	7.454	par-2
BDI9 <----------- NEGATIVE_ATTITUDE	0.765	0.092	8.298	par-3
BDI8 <----------- NEGATIVE_ATTITUDE	0.856	0.118	7.252	par-4
BDI7 <----------- NEGATIVE_ATTITUDE	1.127	0.117	9.610	par-5
BDI6 <----------- NEGATIVE_ATTITUDE	1.194	0.151	7.919	par-6
BDI5 <----------- NEGATIVE_ATTITUDE	0.633	0.089	7.117	par-7
BDI3 <----------- NEGATIVE_ATTITUDE	1.004	0.112	9.000	par-8
BDI2 <----------- NEGATIVE_ATTITUDE	0.886	0.112	7.893	par-9
BDI1 <----------- NEGATIVE_ATTITUDE	1.000			
BDI20 <------ PERFORMANCE_DIFFICULTY	0.622	0.099	6.262	par-10
BDI17 <------ PERFORMANCE_DIFFICULTY	0.764	0.103	7.432	par-11
BDI15 <------ PERFORMANCE_DIFFICULTY	0.710	0.103	6.901	par-12
BDI13 <------ PERFORMANCE_DIFFICULTY	1.106	0.136	8.117	par-13
BDI12 <------ PERFORMANCE_DIFFICULTY	0.444	0.070	6.361	par-14
BDI11 <------ PERFORMANCE_DIFFICULTY	0.535	0.119	4.474	par-15
BDI4 <------- PERFORMANCE_DIFFICULTY	1.000			
BDI21 <----------- SOMATIC_ELEMENTS	0.380	0.105	3.608	par-16
BDI19 <----------- SOMATIC_ELEMENTS	-0.065	0.099	-0.651	par-17
BDI18 <----------- SOMATIC_ELEMENTS	1.200	0.204	5.876	par-18
BDI16 <----------- SOMATIC_ELEMENTS	1.000			

Variances:	Estimate	S.E.	C.R.	Label
DEPRESSION	1.000			
res1	0.034	0.018	1.928	par-22
res2	0.036	0.024	1.483	par-23
res3	0.047	0.028	1.686	par-24
err14	0.927	0.076	12.124	par-25
err10	0.887	0.074	11.942	par-26
err9	0.258	0.022	11.618	par-27
err8	0.512	0.043	12.001	par-28
err7	0.286	0.027	10.621	par-29
err6	0.744	0.063	11.781	par-30
err5	0.297	0.025	11.030	par-31
err3	0.316	0.028	11.199	par-32
err2	0.415	0.035	11.791	par-33
err1	0.369	0.032	11.418	par-34
err20	0.440	0.037	11.925	par-35
err17	0.370	0.033	11.332	par-36
err15	0.419	0.036	11.652	par-37
err13	0.528	0.049	10.683	par-38
err12	0.214	0.018	11.889	par-39
err11	0.799	0.065	12.357	par-40
err4	0.528	0.048	11.058	par-41
err21	0.318	0.026	12.172	par-42
err19	0.361	0.029	12.638	par-43
err18	0.573	0.062	9.308	par-44
err16	0.518	0.051	10.255	par-45

TABLE 5.3
Selected AMOS Text Output for Hypothesized Model:
Critical Ratios of Differences Among Residual Variances

	par-22	par-23	par-24	par-25	par-26	par-27	par-28	
par-22	0.000							
par-23	0.051	0.000						
par-24	0.381	0.304	0.000					
par-25	11.356	11.102	10.799	0.000				
par-26	11.142	10.885	10.573	-0.377	0.000			
par-27	7.810	6.724	5.876	-8.401	-8.108	0.000		
par-28	10.308	9.687	9.097	-4.735	-4.371	5.282	0.000	
par-29	7.691	6.881	6.133	-7.890	-7.583	0.807	-4.463	
par-30	10.785	10.458	10.079	-1.843	-1.463	7.254	3.038	
par-31	8.612	7.522	6.676	-7.839	-7.534	1.181	-4.362	
par-32	8.374	7.512	6.752	-7.481	-7.165	1.626	-3.815	
par-33	9.612	8.850	8.163	-6.079	-5.736	3.770	-1.755	
par-34	8.803	8.226	7.514	-6.711	-6.379	2.833	-2.664	
par-35	9.912	9.014	8.466	-5.739	-5.391	4.233	-1.281	
par-36	9.037	7.988	7.491	-6.700	-6.371	2.846	-2.645	
par-37	9.599	8.655	8.147	-6.010	-5.667	3.822	-1.664	
par-38	9.403	8.634	8.453	-4.388	-4.028	4.987	0.238	
par-39	7.116	5.790	4.996	-9.077	-8.805	-1.526	-6.435	
par-40	11.407	11.000	10.663	-1.278	-0.891	7.920	3.705	
par-41	9.695	8.717	8.676	-4.427	-4.065	5.135	0.248	
par-42	8.982	7.884	6.871	-7.544	-7.232	1.750	-3.889	
par-43	9.720	8.654	7.825	-6.934	-6.608	2.860	-2.941	
par-44	8.410	8.108	6.925	-3.613	-3.260	4.816	0.807	
par-45	9.036	8.592	7.046	-4.466	-4.109	4.718	0.087	

Let's turn to goodness-of fit statistics and modification indexes (MIs) related to the hypothesized model as shown in Fig. 5.8. These values are presented in Tables 5.4 and 5.5, respectively.

Model Assessment

Goodness-of-Fit Summary. In reviewing the goodness-of-fit statistics in Table 5.4, we can see that the imposition of equality constraints across the three residual variances resulted in only a trivial degradation of fit ($\chi^2_{(186)}$ = 340.211 versus $\chi^2_{(188)}$ = 340.078; see Table 5.1). Based on the GFI and CFI values of .908 and .885, respectively, however, we can determine that there is some degree of misfit in the hypothesized second-order model structure. To locate the source of this misfit, we turn now to the relevant MIs shown in Table 5.5.

Modification Indexes. In reviewing this table, it is evident that the only modification indexes (MIs) of any substantial note appear in the covariances portion of the output. Interestingly, there are no significant MIs suggested for the factor loadings; those specified (under the heading of Regression Weights) cannot be consid-

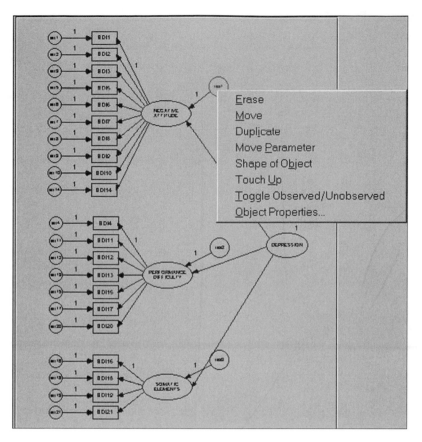

FIG. 5.6.   AMOS Graphics: menu provided by a right-click of the mouse.

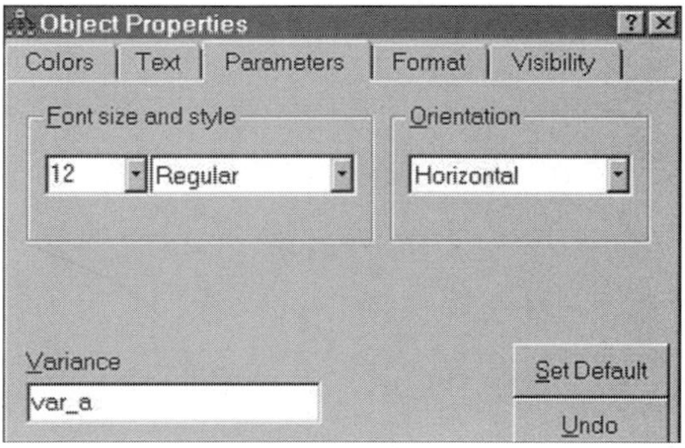

FIG. 5.7.   AMOS Graphics: Object Properties dialog box with parameters tab selected.

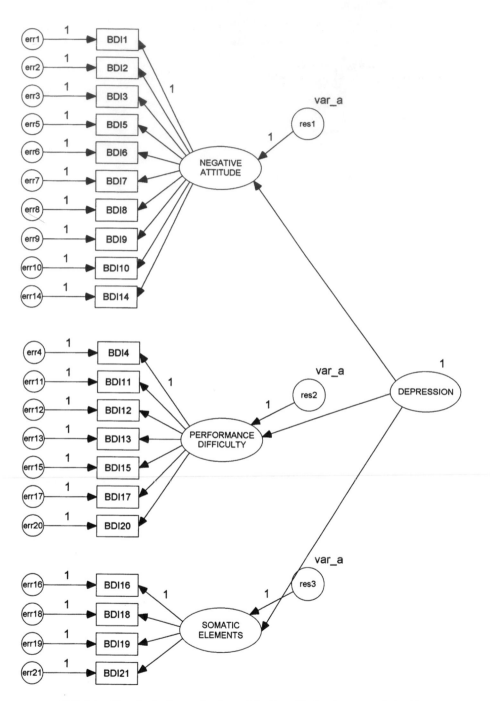

FIG. 5.8. Hypothesized second-order model with residual variances constrained to be equal.

TABLE 5.4
Selected AMOS Text Output for Hypothesized Model: Goodness-of-Fit Statistics

Summary of models

Model	NPAR	CMIN	DF	P
Your model	43	340.211	188	0.000
Saturated model	231	0.000	0	
Independence model	21	1530.116	210	0.000

Model	RMR	GFI	AGFI	PGFI
Your model	0.036	0.908	0.886	0.739
Saturated model	0.000	1.000		
Independence model	0.149	0.472	0.419	0.429

Model	DELTA1 NFI	RHO1 RFI	DELTA2 IFI	RHO2 TLI	CFI
Your model	0.778	0.752	0.887	0.871	0.885
Saturated model	1.000		1.000		1.000
Independence model	0.000	0.000	0.000	0.000	0.000

Model	PRATIO	PNFI	PCFI
Your model	0.895	0.696	0.792
Saturated model	0.000	0.000	0.000
Independence model	1.000	0.000	0.000

Model	RMSEA	LO 90	HI 90	PCLOSE
Your model	0.050	0.042	0.059	0.466
Independence model	0.140	0.134	0.147	0.000

Model	ECVI	LO 90	HI 90	MECVI
Your model	1.332	1.183	1.506	1.352
Saturated model	1.444	1.444	1.444	1.550
Independence model	4.913	4.536	5.313	4.923

ered as they are substantively meaningless. Likewise, the MIs related to the residuals (in the covariance matrix) are uninterpretable. In the covariance portion of the output file, then, we find the largest MI to be 22.347, which relates to an error covariance between Item 20 (hypochondria) and Item 21 (libido loss); the corresponding EPC statistic is 0.102. From this information, we can anticipate that if the model were to be reestimated with this parameter specified as free, we could expect

TABLE 5.5

Selected AMOS Text Output for Hypothesized Model: Modification Indexes

Covariances:			M.I.	Par Change
err19	<--------------------------->	res3	8.306	0.050
err20	<--------------------------->	res2	12.072	-0.059
err20	<--------------------------->	res1	10.501	0.046
err20	<--------------------------->	err21	22.347	0.102
err20	<--------------------------->	err4	10.619	-0.094
err1	<--------------------------->	err17	10.200	0.072
err2	<--------------------------->	err11	9.574	-0.104
err6	<--------------------------->	err20	9.314	0.103
err7	<--------------------------->	err11	6.047	-0.071
err8	<--------------------------->	res2	6.570	0.048
err8	<--------------------------->	err13	11.861	0.109
err9	<--------------------------->	err18	9.130	0.072
err9	<--------------------------->	err3	7.511	-0.048
err10	<--------------------------->	err11	11.060	0.162

Regression Weights:			M.I.	Par Change
BDI18	<---------------------------	BDI9	6.326	0.186
BDI21	<---------------------------	BDI20	19.247	0.190
BDI4	<---------------------------	BDI20	8.334	-0.168
BDI11	<---------------------------	BDI10	8.464	0.135
BDI13	<---------------------------	BDI8	9.312	0.162
BDI20	<---------------------------	BDI21	21.966	0.304
BDI20	<---------------------------	BDI4	6.405	-0.108
BDI20	<---------------------------	BDI6	9.989	0.117
BDI1	<---------------------------	BDI17	7.645	0.136
BDI2	<---------------------------	BDI11	9.392	-0.122
BDI6	<---------------------------	BDI20	6.560	0.173
BDI7	<---------------------------	BDI11	6.190	-0.086
BDI8	<---------------------------	BDI13	9.574	0.137
BDI9	<---------------------------	BDI18	6.069	0.080
BDI10	<---------------------------	BDI11	11.165	0.193

the overall χ^2 value to drop by at least 22.35, and the value of the estimate itself to be approximately 0.10.

As I emphasize throughout this book, the decision to reparameterize a model on the basis of MI information must make sound substantive sense; error covariances are no exception to this edict. Indeed, Joreskog (1993, p. 297) admonished that "Every correlation between error terms must be justified and interpreted substantively." Given that the sample under study is composed of adolescent girls only, and within the framework of the depression literature bearing on this population, I believe that the specification of an error correlation between Item 20 and Item 21 can be substantiated. Error correlations between item pairs are often an indication of perceived redundancy in item content. As such, in the original article (Byrne et al., 1993), we argued that, for adolescent females, the BDI Item 20 and Item 21 appear to elicit responses reflective of the same mental set. Considering the degree of social attention accorded sexually transmitted diseases in general, and AIDS in particular in recent years, it is not surprising that young people develop health concerns relative to sexual activity. Of particular relevance is the fact that caveats conveyed by various media have focused more on young females than on young males. On the basis of this substantiated rationale, then, I consider it appropriate to reestimate the model with the error covariance between Item 20 and Item 21 specified as a free parameter; the respecified model is labeled as Model 2. Results from this analysis are discussed in the next section.

POST HOC ANALYSES

AMOS Graphics: Model 2

With one exception, Model 2 replicates the hypothesized model portrayed in Fig. 5.8; the exception involves the specification of an error covariance between items 20 and 21. This respecified model is schematically presented in Fig. 5.9.

Model Assessment

Goodness-of-Fit Summary.   In reviewing the goodness-of-fit statistics presented in Table 5.6, you will observe that the estimation of Model 2 resulted in an overall fit of $\chi^2_{(187)} = 316.938$, with the GFI increasing slightly to .913 and the CFI to .902. Thus, the expected drop in the $\chi^2_{(1)}$ value (EPC = 22.35) slightly underestimated the actual value ($\chi^2_{(1)} = 23.28$). On the other hand, the value of the parameter estimate for the error covariance between Item 20 and Item 21 was basically as predicted (.104 vs. .102) (see Table 5.9).

Modification Indexes.   Let's turn now to Table 5.7, where the MIs associated with Model 2 are summarized. A perusal of these values shows none of the factor loadings to be substantively meaningful. Likewise, the MIs associated with covariances among the residual parameters make little sense; those associated with error covariances are of relatively modest value, and arguments in support of their implementation are weak. On the basis of these findings, I see no rationale for further respecification of Model 2.

Although, admittedly, the fit of this model can be considered to be only marginally good, Model 2 nevertheless reflects a reasonable fit to the data, as judged by the CFI and the other fit indexes. More specifically, in comparison with the hypothesized model in which no error covariance was specified, the RMSEA has dropped to .047 (from .050), the ECVI has dropped to 1.26 (from 1.33), the GFI has increased to .913 (from .908), and the CFI has increased to .902 (from .885). Indeed, on the basis of the AMOS MIs, there is really no justification for any further model fitting.

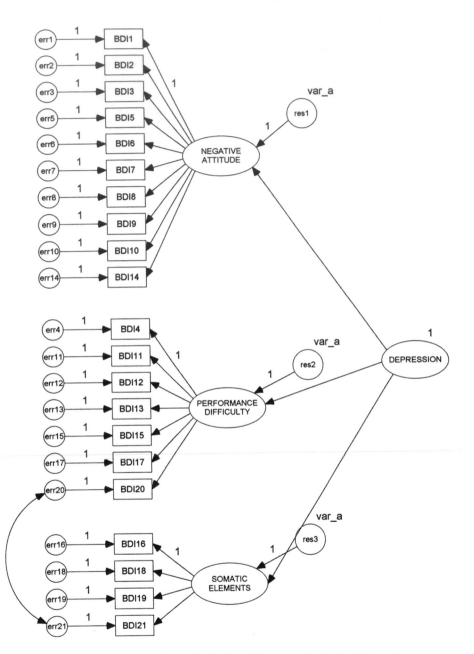

FIG. 5.9. Final model of second-order factorial structure for the Beck Depression Inventory.

TABLE 5.6
Selected AMOS Text Output for Model 2: Goodness-of-Fit Statistics

Summary of models

Model	NPAR	CMIN	DF	P
Your model	44	316.938	187	0.000
Saturated model	231	0.000	0	
Independence model	21	1530.116	210	0.000

Model	RMR	GFI	AGFI	PGFI
Your model	0.036	0.913	0.893	0.739
Saturated model	0.000	1.000		
Independence model	0.149	0.472	0.419	0.429

Model	DELTA1 NFI	RHO1 RFI	DELTA2 IFI	RHO2 TLI	CFI
Your model	0.793	0.767	0.903	0.889	0.902
Saturated model	1.000		1.000		1.000
Independence model	0.000	0.000	0.000	0.000	0.000

Model	PRATIO	PNFI	PCFI
Your model	0.890	0.706	0.803
Saturated model	0.000	0.000	0.000
Independence model	1.000	0.000	0.000

Model	RMSEA	LO 90	HI 90	PCLOSE
Your model	0.047	0.038	0.055	0.730
Independence model	0.140	0.134	0.147	0.000

Model	ECVI	LO 90	HI 90	MECVI
Your model	1.265	1.124	1.432	1.286
Saturated model	1.444	1.444	1.444	1.550
Independence model	4.913	4.536	5.313	4.923

TABLE 5.7

Selected AMOS Text Output for Model 2: Modification Indexes

Covariances:			M.I.	Par Change
err19 <--------------------------->	res3		8.636	0.051
err20 <--------------------------->	res2		12.048	-0.057
err20 <--------------------------->	res1		15.598	0.054
err20 <--------------------------->	err4		9.589	-0.086
err1 <--------------------------->	err17		10.243	0.072
err2 <--------------------------->	err11		9.648	-0.104
err6 <--------------------------->	err20		10.869	0.107
err7 <--------------------------->	err11		6.055	-0.071
err8 <--------------------------->	res2		6.707	0.048
err8 <--------------------------->	err13		11.650	0.108
err9 <--------------------------->	err18		8.828	0.071
err9 <--------------------------->	err3		7.631	-0.048
err10 <--------------------------->	err11		11.150	0.163

(Continued)

TABLE 5.7 *(Continued)*

Regression Weights:		M.I.	Par Change
BDI18 <------------------------- BDI9		6.098	0.182
BDI4 <------------------------- BDI20		7.836	-0.163
BDI11 <------------------------- BDI10		8.555	0.136
BDI13 <------------------------- BDI8		9.112	0.160
BDI20 <------------------------- BDI6		11.869	0.123
BDI1 <------------------------- BDI17		7.653	0.136
BDI2 <------------------------- BDI11		9.414	-0.122
BDI6 <------------------------- BDI20		7.026	0.179
BDI7 <------------------------- BDI11		6.181	-0.085
BDI8 <------------------------- BDI13		9.508	0.137
BDI10 <------------------------- BDI11		11.212	0.193

In reviewing these estimates in Table 5.8 (factor loadings) and Table 5.9 (variances/covariances), we see that, with one exception, all are both reasonable and statistically significant (including the one error covariance between Item 20 and Item 21), and all standard errors are acceptable. The one exception relates to the loading of Item 19 (weight loss) on the somatic elements factor, which is not statistically significant (−0.08; C.R. = −0.784). Overall, however, on the basis of (a) the adequacy of the fit statistics and unstandardized/standardized solutions, (b) the fact that the model represents a substantively reasonable fit to the data, and (c) little to no justification for freeing up parameters on the basis of the MIs, Model 2 can be considered to best represent the structure of BDI item scores for adolescent females.

In concluding this chapter, I wish to note that, given the same number of estimable parameters, fit statistics related to a model parameterized either as a first-order structure or as a second-order structure will be equivalent. The difference between the two specifications is that the second-order model is a special case of the first-order model, with the added restriction that structure be imposed on the correlational pattern among the first-order factors (Rindskopf & Rose, 1988). However, judgment as to whether or not a measuring instrument should be modeled as a first-order or as a second-order structure ultimately rests on substantive meaningfulness as dictated by the underlying theory.

MODELING WITH AMOS BASIC

Taking the final model of BDI structure for adolescent girls as our example here, let's now examine the related AMOS Basic input file, which is shown in Table 5.10.

Several aspects of this file are noteworthy. First, for the sake of variety, the input file has been structured in an alternate format. Although there are no arrows, the information conveyed via the equation statements remains the same. For example,

TABLE 5.8

Selected AMOS Text Output for Model 2: Factor Loading Parameter Estimates

Regression Weights:	Estimate	S.E.	C.R.
PERFORMANCE_DIFFICULTY <- DEPRESSION	0.482	0.051	9.446
NEGATIVE_ATTITUDE <------ DEPRESSION	0.419	0.042	9.941
SOMATIC_ELEMENTS <------- DEPRESSION	0.349	0.049	7.106
BDI14 <----------- NEGATIVE_ATTITUDE	1.031	0.151	6.818
BDI10 <----------- NEGATIVE_ATTITUDE	1.167	0.155	7.506
BDI9 <------------ NEGATIVE_ATTITUDE	0.764	0.091	8.419
BDI8 <------------ NEGATIVE_ATTITUDE	0.852	0.116	7.322
BDI7 <------------ NEGATIVE_ATTITUDE	1.122	0.115	9.764
BDI6 <------------ NEGATIVE_ATTITUDE	1.186	0.148	7.998
BDI5 <------------ NEGATIVE_ATTITUDE	0.628	0.088	7.168
BDI3 <------------ NEGATIVE_ATTITUDE	0.997	0.109	9.115
BDI2 <------------ NEGATIVE_ATTITUDE	0.883	0.111	7.988
BDI1 <------------ NEGATIVE_ATTITUDE	1.000		
BDI20 <------ PERFORMANCE_DIFFICULTY	0.590	0.096	6.133
BDI17 <------ PERFORMANCE_DIFFICULTY	0.754	0.100	7.521
BDI15 <------ PERFORMANCE_DIFFICULTY	0.705	0.101	7.008
BDI13 <------ PERFORMANCE_DIFFICULTY	1.096	0.133	8.257
BDI12 <------ PERFORMANCE_DIFFICULTY	0.440	0.068	6.436
BDI11 <------ PERFORMANCE_DIFFICULTY	0.528	0.118	4.492
BDI4 <------- PERFORMANCE_DIFFICULTY	1.000		
BDI21 <------------ SOMATIC_ELEMENTS	0.350	0.104	3.347
BDI19 <------------ SOMATIC_ELEMENTS	-0.080	0.102	-0.784
BDI18 <------------ SOMATIC_ELEMENTS	1.212	0.204	5.935
BDI16 <------------ SOMATIC_ELEMENTS	1.000		

Standardized Regression Weights:	Estimate
PERFORMANCE_DIFFICULTY <- DEPRESSION	0.929
NEGATIVE_ATTITUDE <------ DEPRESSION	0.909
SOMATIC_ELEMENTS <------- DEPRESSION	0.876
BDI14 <----------- NEGATIVE_ATTITUDE	0.443
BDI10 <----------- NEGATIVE_ATTITUDE	0.496
BDI9 <------------ NEGATIVE_ATTITUDE	0.571
BDI8 <------------ NEGATIVE_ATTITUDE	0.481
BDI7 <------------ NEGATIVE_ATTITUDE	0.696
BDI6 <------------ NEGATIVE_ATTITUDE	0.535
BDI5 <------------ NEGATIVE_ATTITUDE	0.469
BDI3 <------------ NEGATIVE_ATTITUDE	0.633
BDI2 <------------ NEGATIVE_ATTITUDE	0.534
BDI1 <------------ NEGATIVE_ATTITUDE	0.605
BDI20 <------ PERFORMANCE_DIFFICULTY	0.417
BDI17 <------ PERFORMANCE_DIFFICULTY	0.540
BDI15 <------ PERFORMANCE_DIFFICULTY	0.493
BDI13 <------ PERFORMANCE_DIFFICULTY	0.617
BDI12 <------ PERFORMANCE_DIFFICULTY	0.443
BDI11 <------ PERFORMANCE_DIFFICULTY	0.293
BDI4 <------- PERFORMANCE_DIFFICULTY	0.582
BDI21 <------------ SOMATIC_ELEMENTS	0.239
BDI19 <------------ SOMATIC_ELEMENTS	-0.053
BDI18 <------------ SOMATIC_ELEMENTS	0.534
BDI16 <------------ SOMATIC_ELEMENTS	0.482

TABLE 5.9
Selected AMOS Text Output for Model 2: Variance/Covariance Parameter Estimates

Covariances:	Estimate	S.E.	C.R.
err20 <---------------------> err21	0.104	0.023	4.569

Correlations:	Estimate		
err20 <---------------------> err21	0.274		

Variances:		Estimate	S.E.	C.R.	Label
	DEPRESSION	1.000			
	res1	0.037	0.009	4.129	var_a
	res2	0.037	0.009	4.129	var_a
	res3	0.037	0.009	4.129	var_a
	err14	0.927	0.077	12.122	
	err10	0.889	0.074	11.944	
	err9	0.257	0.022	11.601	
	err8	0.512	0.043	11.996	
	err7	0.286	0.027	10.606	
	err6	0.745	0.063	11.778	
	err5	0.297	0.025	12.038	
	err3	0.317	0.028	11.199	
	err2	0.414	0.035	11.782	
	err1	0.369	0.032	11.409	
	err20	0.445	0.037	11.989	
	err17	0.371	0.033	11.336	
	err15	0.418	0.036	11.634	
	err13	0.527	0.049	10.674	
	err12	0.214	0.018	11.880	
	err11	0.799	0.065	12.355	
	err4	0.524	0.047	11.048	
	err21	0.322	0.026	12.307	
	err19	0.361	0.029	12.634	
	err18	0.583	0.058	10.079	
	err16	0.524	0.047	11.143	

the first line of the model specification states that (the observed variable) BDI is equal to (the factor) negative attitude plus the error term err1; the (1) preceding "Negative Attitude" indicates that this regression path is to be fixed to a value of 1.0. Second, following the 21 regression equations, the three statements that follow state that regression paths associated with the residuals are to be fixed to a value of 1.0. Third, as indicated by the next statement, the variance of the higher order factor of depression is to be fixed to 1.0. Fourth, the next three statements relate to the equality constraint placed on the residuals. This equality is indicated by attaching the same label to each residual. Finally, the last statement specifies that the error terms associated with Item 20 and Item 21 are to be correlated.

TABLE 5.10
AMOS Basic Input File for Final Model of BDI Structure

Sub Main
Dim sem As New AmosEngine

SEM.TextOutput
SEM.Mods 6
SEM.Standardized

SEM.BeginGroup "bdigirl.txt"

SEM.Structure "BDI1 = (1)   NEGATIVE_ATTITUDE + (1) err1"
SEM.Structure "BDI2 =   NEGATIVE_ATTITUDE + (1) err2"
SEM.Structure "BDI3 =   NEGATIVE_ATTITUDE + (1) err3"
SEM.Structure "BDI5 =   NEGATIVE_ATTITUDE + (1) err5"
SEM.Structure "BDI6 =   NEGATIVE_ATTITUDE + (1) err6"
SEM.Structure "BDI7 =   NEGATIVE_ATTITUDE + (1) err7"
SEM.Structure "BDI8 =   NEGATIVE_ATTITUDE + (1) err8"
SEM.Structure "BDI9 =   NEGATIVE_ATTITUDE + (1) err9"
SEM.Structure "BDI10 =   NEGATIVE_ATTITUDE + (1) err10"
SEM.Structure "BDI14 =   NEGATIVE_ATTITUDE + (1) err14"

SEM.Structure "BDI4 = (1) PERFORMANCE_DIFFICULTY + (1) err4"
SEM.Structure "BDI11 =   PERFORMANCE_DIFFICULTY + (1) err11"
SEM.Structure "BDI12 =   PERFORMANCE_DIFFICULTY + (1) err12"
SEM.Structure "BDI13 =   PERFORMANCE_DIFFICULTY + (1) err13"
SEM.Structure "BDI15 =   PERFORMANCE_DIFFICULTY + (1) err15"
SEM.Structure "BDI17 =   PERFORMANCE_DIFFICULTY + (1) err17"
SEM.Structure "BDI20 =   PERFORMANCE_DIFFICULTY + (1) err20"

SEM.Structure "BDI16 = (1) SOMATIC_ELEMENTS + (1) err16"
SEM.Structure "BDI18 =   SOMATIC_ELEMENTS + (1) err18"
SEM.Structure "BDI19 =   SOMATIC_ELEMENTS + (1) err19"
SEM.Structure "BDI21 =   SOMATIC_ELEMENTS + (1) err21"

SEM.Structure "NEGATIVE_ATTITUDE = DEPRESSION + (1) res1"
SEM.Structure "PERFORMANCE_DIFFICULTY = DEPRESSION + (1) res2"
SEM.Structure "SOMATIC_ELEMENTS = DEPRESSION + (1) res3"

SEM.Structure "DEPRESSION (1)"

SEM.Structure "res1 (var_a)"
SEM.Structure "res2 (var_a)"
SEM.Structure "res3 (var_a)"

SEM.Structure "err20 ↔ err21"

End Sub

CHAPTER 6

Application 4:
Testing for the Validity
of a Causal Structure

$\mathbf{I}$n this chapter, we take our first look at a full structural equation model (SEM). The hypothesis to be tested relates to the pattern of causal structure linking several stressor variables that bear on the construct of burnout. The original study from which this application is taken (Byrne, 1994b) tested and cross-validated the impact of organizational and personality variables on three dimensions of burnout for elementary, intermediate, and secondary teachers. For purposes of illustration here, however, the application is limited to the calibration sample of elementary teachers only.

As was the case with the factor analytic applications illustrated in chapters 3 through 5, those structured as full SEMs are presumed to be of a confirmatory nature. That is to say, postulated causal relations among all variables in the hypothesized model must be grounded in theory and/or empirical research. Typically, the hypothesis to be tested argues for the validity of specified causal linkages among the variables of interest. Let's turn now to an in-depth examination of the hypothesized model under study in the current chapter.

THE HYPOTHESIZED MODEL

Formulation of the hypothesized model shown in Fig. 6.1 derived from the consensus of findings from a review of the burnout literature, as it bears on the teaching profession. [Readers wishing a more detailed summary of this research are referred to Byrne (1994b, 1999).] In reviewing this model, you will note that burnout is represented as a multidimensional construct with emotional exhaustion

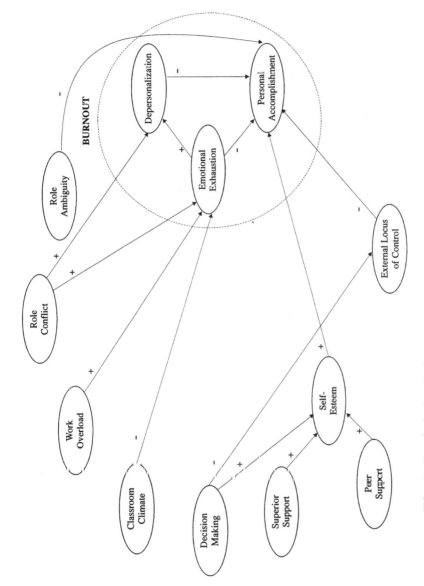

FIG. 6.1. Hypothesized model of causal structure related to teacher burnout. Reprinted from Byrne, B. M. (1994). Burnout: Testing for the validity, replication, and invariance of causal structure across elementary, intermediate, and secondary teachers. *American Educational Research Journal, 31*, pp. 645–673 (Figure 1, p. 656). Copyright (1994) by the American Educational Research Association. Reprinted by permission of the publisher.

(EE), depersonalization (DP), and personal accomplishment (PA) operating as conceptually distinct factors. This part of the model is based on the work of Leiter (1991) in conceptualizing burnout as a cognitive-emotional reaction to chronic stress. The paradigm argues that EE holds the central position because it is considered to be the most responsive of the three facets to various stressors in the teacher's work environment. Depersonalization and reduced PA, on the other hand, represent the cognitive aspects of burnout in that they are indicative of the extent to which teachers' perceptions of their students, their colleagues, and themselves become diminished. As indicated by the signs associated with each path in the model, EE is hypothesized to impact positively on DP, but negatively on PA; DP is hypothesized to impact negatively on PA.

The paths (and their associated signs) leading from the organizational (role ambiguity, role conflict, work overload, classroom climate, decisionmaking, superior support, peer support) and personality (self-esteem, external locus of control) variables to the three dimensions of burnout reflect findings in the literature.[1] For example, high levels of role conflict are expected to cause high levels of emotional exhaustion; in contrast, high (i.e., good) levels of classroom climate are expected to generate low levels of emotional exhaustion.

MODELING WITH AMOS GRAPHICS

In viewing the model shown in Fig. 6.1 we can see that it represents only the structural portion of the full structural equation model. Thus, before being able to test this model, we need to know the manner by which each of the constructs in this model is to be measured. In other words, we have to establish the measurement portion of the structural equation model (see chap. 1). In contrast to the CFA models studied previously, the task involved in developing the measurement model of a full SEM is twofold: (a) to determine the number of indicators to use in measuring each construct, and (b) to identify which items to use in formulating each indicator.

Formulation of Indicator Variables

In t! applications examined in chapters 3 through 5, the formulation of measurement indicators has been relatively straightforward; all examples have involved CFA models and, as such, comprised only measurement models. In the measurement of multidimensional facets of self-concept (chap. 3), each indicator represented a paired item score (i.e., all paired items designed to measure a particular self-concept facet). In chapters 4 and 5, our interest focused on the factorial valid-

---

[1]To facilitate interpretation, particular items were reflected such that high scores on role ambiguity, role conflict, work overload, EE, DP, and external locus of control represented negative perceptions, and high scores on the remaining constructs represented positive perceptions.

ity of a measuring instrument. As such, we were concerned with the extent to which items loaded onto their targeted factor. Adequate assessment of this phenomenon demanded that each item be included in the model. Thus, the indicator variables in these cases each represented one item in the measuring instrument under study.

In contrast to these previous examples, formulation of the indicator variables in the present application was slightly more complex. Specifically, multiple indicators of each construct were formulated through the judicious combination of particular items. As such, items were carefully grouped according to content in order to equalize the measurement weighting across indicators. For example, the Classroom Environment Scale (Bacharach, Bauer, & Conley, 1986), used to measure classroom climate, is comprised of items that tap classroom size, ability/interest of students, and various types of abuse by students. Indicators of this construct were formed such that each item in the composite of items measured a different aspect of classroom climate. In the measurement of classroom climate, self-esteem, and external locus of control, indicator variables comprised items from a single unidimensional scale; all other indicators comprised items from subscales of multidimensional scales. (For an extensive description of the measuring instruments, see Byrne, 1994b.) In total, 32 indicators were used to measure the hypothesized structural model. A schematic presentation of the full structural equation model is presented in Fig. 6.2. It is important to note that, in the interest of clarity, all double-headed arrows representing correlations among the independent (i.e., exogenous) factors, as well as error terms associated with the observed (i.e., indicator) variables have been excluded from the figure.[2] (For detailed discussions regarding both the number and composition of indicator variables in SEM, see Little, Lindenberger, & Nesselroade, 1999, and Marsh, Hau, Balla, & Grayson, 1998.)

The hypothesized model in Fig. 6.2 is most appropriately presented within the framework of the landscape layout. In AMOS Graphics, this is accomplished by either clicking on the Interface Properties icon , or by making this selection from the View/Set drop-down menu. Once selected, the Interface Properties dialog box, as shown in Fig. 6.3, provides you with a number of options. Note that the landscape orientation has been selected; portrait orientation is the default selection.

Confirmatory Factor Analyses

Because (a) the structural portion of a full structural equation model involves relations among only latent variables, and (b) the primary concern in working with a full model is to assess the extent to which these relations are valid, it is critical that the measurement of each latent variable is psychometrically sound. Thus, an impor-

---

[2]Of course, given that AMOS Graphics operates on the WYSIWYG principle, these parameters must be included in the model to be submitted for analysis.

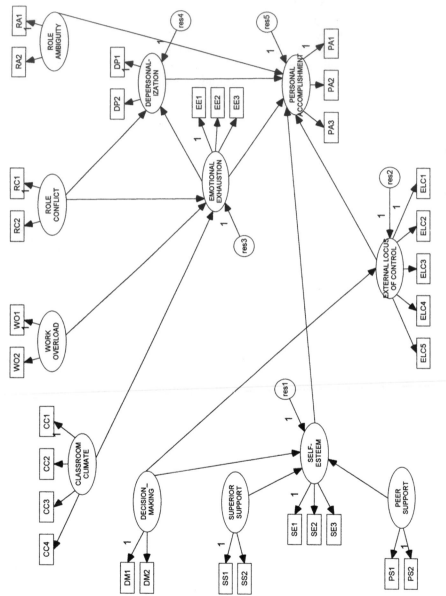

FIG. 6.2.   Hypothesized model of teacher burnout: Measurement and structural components.

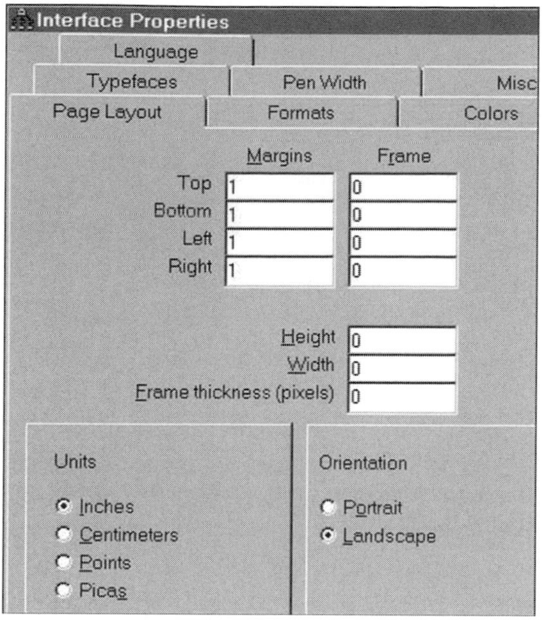

FIG. 6.3. AMOS Graphics: Interface Properties dialog box.

tant preliminary step in the analysis of full latent variable models is to test first for the validity of the measurement model before making any attempt to evaluate the structural model. Accordingly, CFA procedures are used in testing the validity of the indicator variables. Once it is known that the measurement model is operating adequately,[3] one can then have more confidence in findings related to the assessment of the hypothesized structural model.

In the present case, CFAs were conducted for indicator variables derived from each of the two multidimensional scales; these were the Teacher Stress Scale (TSS; Pettegrew & Wolf, 1982), which included all organizational indicator variables except classroom climate, and the Maslach Burnout Inventory (MBI; Maslach & Jackson, 1986), measuring the three facets of burnout. The hypothesized CFA model of the TSS is portrayed in Fig. 6.4.

Of particular note here is the presence of double-headed arrows among all six factors. Recall from chapter 2 that, in contrast to AMOS Basic, AMOS Graphics assumes no correlations among the factors. Thus, should you wish to estimate these values in accordance with the related theory, they must be present in the model. Nonetheless, despite this requirement, AMOS Graphics will prompt you should you neglect to include one or more factor correlations in the model. For example,

---

[3]For example, it may be that to attain a better fitting CFA model, the specification of a cross-loading is needed.

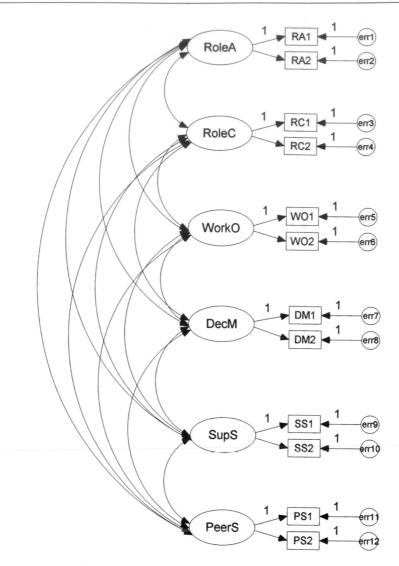

FIG. 6.4.   Hypothesized CFA model of the teacher stress scale.

Fig. 6.5 presents the error message triggered by my failure to include a correlation between Role Conflict (RoleC) and Decisionmaking (DecM).

Although goodness of fit for both the MBI (CFI = .98) and TSS (CFI = .97) was found to be exceptionally good, the solution for the TSS was somewhat problematic. More specifically, an error message in the output warned that the covariance matrix among the factors was not positive definite; as a consequence, the solution was considered to be inadmissible. This message is shown in Table 6.1.

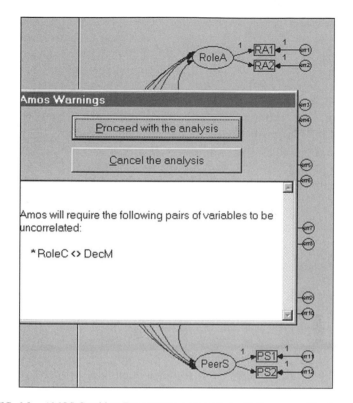

FIG. 6.5.   AMOS Graphics: Error message associated with the nonspecification of correlations among exogenous factors.

TABLE 6.1
Selected AMOS Text Output for CFA Model
of the Teacher Stress Scale: Nonpositive Definite Matrix

The following covariance matrix is not positive definite

	PeerS	SupS	DecM	WorkO	RoleC	RoleA
PeerS	0.626					
SupS	0.436	1.204				
DecM	0.393	0.799	0.622			
WorkO	-0.281	-0.522	-0.407	0.712		
RoleC	-0.255	-0.499	-0.377	0.675	0.590	
RoleA	-0.281	-0.500	-0.406	0.446	0.444	0.471

This solution is not admissible.

Multicollinearity is often the major contributing factor to the formulation of a nonpositive definite matrix. This condition arises from the situation where two or more variables are so highly correlated that they both, essentially, represent the same underlying construct. Indeed, in checking out this possibility, I found the correlation between role conflict (RoleC) and work overload (WorkO) to be 1.041, which definitely signals a problem of multicollinearity. Substantively, this finding is not surprising as there appears to be substantial content overlap among TSS items measuring role conflict and work overload. Of course, the very presence of a correlation >1.00 is indicative of a solution that is clearly inadmissible. However, the flip side of the coin regarding inadmissible solutions is that they alert the researcher to serious model misspecifications.

In an effort to address this problem of multicollinearity, a second CFA model of the TSS was specified in which the factor of work overload was deleted, but its two observed indicator variables were loaded onto the role conflict factor. Goodness of fit related to this five-factor model of the TSS ($\chi^2_{(44)}$ = 152.37; CFI = .973; RMSEA = .064) was almost identical to the six-factor hypothesized model ($\chi^2_{(39)}$ = 145.95; CFI = .973; RMSEA = .068). Furthermore, the factor covariance matrix was no longer nonpositive definite. Thus, this five-factor structure served as the measurement model for the TSS throughout analyses related to the full causal model. However, as a consequence of this measurement restructuring, the revised model of burnout shown in Fig. 6.6 replaced the originally hypothesized model (see Fig. 6.2) in serving as the hypothesized model to be tested. Once again, in the interest of clarity, the factor correlations and errors of measurement are not included.

AMOS Text Output: Hypothesized Model

Before examining the results of our testing of the hypothesized model, I consider it important to review, first, the status of all factors comprising this model. Turning to Table 6.2 we can see that there are five dependent factors in the model (depersonalization [DP], external locus of control [ELC], emotional exhaustion [EE], personal accomplishment [PA], self-esteem [SE]); each of these factors has single-headed arrows pointing at it, thereby easily identifying it as a dependent factor in the model. The independent factors are those hypothesized as exerting an influence on the dependent factors; these are role ambiguity (RA), role conflict (RC), decision making (DM), superior support (SS), peer support (PS), and classroom climate (CC). Additional information from this table informs us there are 599 cases, that the correct number of degrees of freedom is 436, and that the minimum was achieved in reaching a convergent solution.

Model Assessment

Goodness-of-Fit Summary.   Selected goodness-of-fit statistics related to the hypothesized model are presented in Table 6.3. Here, we see that the overall χ^2 value, with 436 degrees of freedom, is 1030.892. Given the known sensitivity of

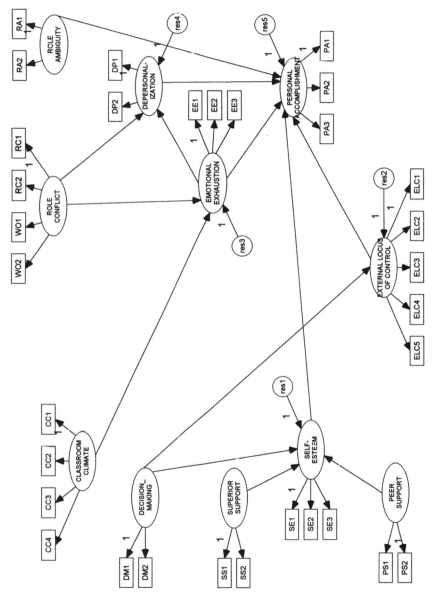

FIG. 6.6.   Revised hypothesized model of teacher burnout: Measurement and structural components.

TABLE 6.2
Selected AMOS Text Output for Hypothesized Model: Model Summary

Dependent Factors

DP	unobserved endogenous
ELC	unobserved endogenous
EE	unobserved endogenous
PA	unobserved endogenous
SE	unobserved endogenous

Independent Factors

RA	unobserved exogenous
RC	unobserved exogenous
DM	unobserved exogenous
SS	unobserved exogenous
PS	unobserved exogenous
CC	unobserved exogenous

Number of variables in your model:	80
Number of observed variables:	32
Number of unobserved variables:	48
Number of exogenous variables:	43
Number of endogenous variables:	37

Sample size: 599

Computation of Degrees of Freedom

Number of distinct sample moments:	528
Number of distinct parameters to be estimated:	92

Degrees of freedom:	436

Minimum was achieved

this statistic to sample size, however, use of the χ^2 index provides little guidance in determining the extent to which the model does not fit. Thus, it is more beneficial to rely on other indexes of fit. Primary among these are the GFI, CFI, and RMSEA. Furthermore, given that we shall be comparing a series of models in our quest to obtain a final well-fitting model, the ECVI is also of interest.

Interestingly, although the GFI (.903) suggests that model fit was only marginally adequate, the CFI (.941) suggests that it is relatively well-fitting. In addition, the RMSEA value of .048 is well within the recommended range of acceptability (<.05 to .08). Finally, the ECVI value for this initially hypothesized model is 2.032. This value, as noted earlier in the book, has no substantive meaning; rather, it is

TABLE 6.3

Selected AMOS Output Text for Hypothesized Model: Goodness-of-Fit Statistics

Summary of models

Model	NPAR	CMIN	DF	P
Default model	92	1030.892	436	0.000
Saturated model	528	0.000	0	
Independence model	32	10590.438	496	0.000

Model	RMR	GFI	AGFI	PGFI
Default model	0.050	0.903	0.883	0.746
Saturated model	0.000	1.000		
Independence model	0.324	0.256	0.208	0.240

Model	DELTA1 NFI	RHO1 RFI	DELTA2 IFI	RHO2 TLI	CFI
Default model	0.903	0.889	0.941	0.933	0.941
Saturated model	1.000		1.000		1.000
Independence model	0.000	0.000	0.000	0.000	0.000

Model	PRATIO	PNFI	PCFI
Default model	0.879	0.793	0.827
Saturated model	0.000	0.000	0.000
Independence model	1.000	0.000	0.000

Model	RMSEA	LO 90	HI 90	PCLOSE
Default model	0.048	0.044	0.052	0.833
Independence model	0.184	0.181	0.188	0.000

Model	ECVI	LO 90	HI 90	MECVI
Default model	2.032	1.881	2.195	2.050
Saturated model	1.766	1.766	1.766	1.869
Independence model	17.817	17.263	18.382	17.823

used within a relative framework. (For a review of these rule-of-thumb guidelines, you may wish to consult chap. 3, where goodness-of-fit indexes are described in more detail.)

Modification Indexes.   Over and above the fit of the model as a whole, however, a review of the modification indices reveals some evidence of misfit in the model. Because we are interested solely in the causal paths of the model at this point, only a subset of indexes related to the regression weights is included in Table

6.4. Turning to this table, you will note that the first 10 modification indexes (MIs) are enclosed in a rectangle. These parameters represent the structural (i.e., causal) paths in the model and are the only MIs of interest. Some of the remaining MIs in Table 6.4 represent the cross-loading of an indicator variable onto a factor other than the one it was designed to measure (EE3 ← CC). Others represent the regression of one indicator variable on another; these MIs are substantively meaningless.[4]

In reviewing the information provided in the rectangle, note that the maximum MI is associated with the regression path flowing from classroom climate to depersonalization (DP ← CC). The value of 24.776 indicates that, if this parameter were to be freely estimated in a subsequent model, the overall χ^2 value would drop by at least this amount. If you turn now to the expected parameter change statistic related to this parameter, you will find a value of −0.351; this value represents the approximate value that the newly estimated parameter would assume.

In data preparation, the TSS items measuring classroom climate were reflected such that low scores were indicative of a poor classroom milieu, and high scores, of a good classroom milieu. From a substantive perspective, it would seem perfectly reasonable that elementary school teachers whose responses yielded low scores for classroom climate should concomitantly display high levels of depersonalization. Given the meaningfulness of this influential flow, the model was reestimated with the path from classroom climate to depersonalization specified as a free parameter; this model is subsequently labeled as Model 2. Results related to this respecified model are discussed within the framework of post hoc analyses in the next section.

POST HOC ANALYSES

AMOS Text Output: Model 2

In the interest of space, only the final model of burnout, as determined from the following post hoc model-fitting procedures, is displayed. However, relevant portions of the AMOS output, pertinent to each respecified model, are presented and discussed.

Model Assessment

Goodness-of-Fit Summary.   The estimation of Model 2 yielded an overall $\chi^2_{(435)}$ value of 995.019, a GFI of .906, a CFI of .945, and an RMSEA of .046; the ECVI value was 1.975. Although the improvement in model fit for Model 2, compared with the originally hypothesized model, would appear to be trivial on the basis of the GFI, CFI, and RMSEA values, the model difference nonetheless was statistically significant ($\Delta\chi^2_{(1)}$ = 35.873). Moreover, the parameter estimate for the

---

[4]As previously noted, the present version of AMOS provides no mechanism for excluding MIs such as these.

Regression Weights:

	M.I.	Par Change
	-----	-----------
SE <-------- EE	10.039	-0.047
SE <------- ELC	9.253	-0.138
SE <-------- DP	17.320	-0.099
ELC <------- RC	19.554	0.108
ELC <------- RA	6.905	0.060
ELC <------- EE	10.246	0.047
ELC <------- SE	20.273	-0.184
ELC <------- DP	8.513	0.068
DP <-------- CC	24.776	-0.351
DP <-------- SE	12.249	-0.260
EE3 <------- CC	9.711	-0.220
EE3 <------- DM	6.915	-0.085
EE3 <------- RA	10.453	0.135
EE3 <------- SE	16.223	-0.299
EE3 <------ ELC	10.072	0.257
EE3 <------- PA	22.665	-0.270
EE3 <------ PA1	19.682	-0.172
EE3 <----- ELC5	7.369	0.123
EE3 <----- ELC3	6.417	0.133
EE3 <------ CC1	6.553	-0.143
EE3 <------ CC2	8.719	-0.153
EE3 <------ CC4	9.198	-0.134
EE3 <------ SE3	13.770	-0.205
EE3 <------ SE1	13.822	-0.247
EE3 <------ SE2	8.392	-0.166
EE3 <------ PA3	14.263	-0.136
EE3 <------ PA2	12.137	-0.127
EE3 <----- ELC2	9.445	0.157
EE3 <------ SS1	6.351	-0.064
EE3 <------ RA2	12.153	0.110
ELC5 <------ SE	13.007	-0.173
ELC5 <----- SE3	9.986	0.113
ELC5 <----- SE1	9.341	-0.131
ELC5 <----- SE2	14.237	-0.140
ELC5 <----- EE2	6.772	0.038
ELC4 <------ CC	9.809	-0.152
ELC4 <----- CC3	8.790	-0.120
ELC4 <----- CC4	10.076	-0.096
ELC4 <----- PS1	6.086	-0.054
CC1 <------- RC	7.601	-0.075
CC1 <------- EE	8.622	-0.048
CC1 <------- DP	8.350	-0.075

.
.
.

path from classroom climate to depersonalization was slightly higher than the one predicted by the expected parameter change statistic (-0.479 vs. -0.351) and it was statistically significant (C.R. $= -5.712$). Modification indexes related to the structural parameters for Model 2 are shown in Table 6.5.

TABLE 6.5
Selected AMOS Text Output for Model 2: Modification Indexes

Regression Weights:		M.I.	Par Change
		-----	----------
SE	<-------- EE	9.898	-0.047
SE	<------- ELC	9.156	-0.138
SE	<-------- DP	14.692	-0.092
ELC	<------- RC	19.604	0.108
ELC	<------- RA	6.906	0.060
ELC	<------- EE	10.291	0.047
ELC	<------- SE	20.311	-0.184
ELC	<------- DP	7.774	0.066
DP	<-------- SE	11.422	-0.236
EE3	<------- CC	14.843	-0.274
EE3	<------- DM	7.568	-0.089
EE3	<------- RA	11.108	0.140
EE3	<------- SE	16.844	-0.306
EE3	<------ ELC	10.405	0.263
EE3	<------- PA	24.665	-0.282
EE3	<------- PA1	21.194	-0.180
EE3	<----- ELC5	7.325	0.124
EE3	<----- ELC3	6.607	0.136
EE3	<------ CC1	8.759	-0.166
EE3	<------ CC2	12.172	-0.181
EE3	<------ CC4	12.360	-0.156
EE3	<------ SE3	14.203	-0.209
EE3	<------ SE1	14.339	-0.252
EE3	<------ SE2	8.655	-0.170
EE3	<------ PA3	15.286	-0.142
EE3	<------ PA2	13.297	-0.134
EE3	<----- ELC2	9.637	0.159
EE3	<------ SS1	6.630	-0.065
EE3	<------ RA2	12.612	0.112
ELC5	<------ SE	13.021	-0.173
ELC5	<----- SE3	9.983	-0.113
ELC5	<----- SE1	9.343	-0.131
ELC5	<----- SE2	14.239	-0.140
ELC5	<----- EE2	6.773	0.038
ELC4	<------ CC	10.922	-0.160
ELC4	<----- CC3	8.821	-0.120
ELC4	<----- CC4	10.112	-0.096
ELC4	<----- PS1	6.087	-0.054
CC1	<------- RC	7.554	-0.075
CC1	<------- EE	8.664	-0.048
CC1	<------ EE3	8.713	-0.041

Modification Indexes.   In reviewing the boxed statistics presented in Table 6.5, we see that there are still nine MIs that can be taken into account in the determination of a well-fitting model of burnout. The largest of these (MI = 20.311) is associated with a path flowing from self-esteem to external locus of control (ELC ← SE), and the expected value is estimated to be −0.184. Substantively, this path again makes good sense. Indeed, it seems likely that teachers who exhibit high levels of self-esteem also exhibit low levels of external locus of control. On the basis of this rationale, and despite the fact that the Expected Parameter Change statistic is larger for the DP ← SE path, we remain consistent in focusing on the path associated with the largest MI. (Recall Bentler's 1995 caveat, noted in chap. 3, that these values can be affected by both the scaling and identification of factors and variables.) Thus, the causal structure was again respecified—this time, with the path from self-esteem to external locus of control freely estimated (Model 3).

AMOS Text Output: Model 3

Goodness-of-Fit Summary.   Model 3 yielded an overall $\chi^2_{(434)}$ value of 967.244, with GFI = .909, CFI = .947, and RMSEA = .045; the ECVI was 1.932. Again, the χ^2 difference between Model 2 and Model 3 was statistically significant ($\Delta\chi^2_{(1)}$ = 27.775). Modification indexes related to Model 3 are shown in Table 6.6. Of initial import here is the fact that the number of MIs has now dropped from nine to only four. This discrepancy in the number of MI values between Model 2 and Model 3 serves as a perfect example of why the incorporation of additional parameters into the model must be done one at a time.

Modification Indexes.   Reviewing the boxed statistics here, we see that the largest MI (17.074) is associated with a path from self-esteem to emotional exhaustion (EE ← SE). However, it is important that you note that an MI (9.642) related to the reverse path involving these factors (SE ← EE) is also included as an MI. As emphasized in chapter 3, parameters identified by AMOS as belonging in a model are based on statistical criteria only; of more import is that their inclusion be substantively meaningful. Within the context of the original study, the incorporation of this latter path (SE ← EE) into the model would make no sense whatsoever because its primary purpose was to validate the impact of organizational and personality variables on burnout, and not the reverse. Thus, we ignore this suggested model modification.[5] Because it seems reasonable that teachers who exhibit high levels of self-esteem may, concomitantly, exhibit low levels of emotional exhaustion, the model was reestimated once again, with this path freely estimated (Model 4).

---

[5]Of course, had a nonrecursive model represented the hypothesized model, such feedback paths would be of interest.

TABLE 6.6
Selected AMOS Text Output for Model 3: Modification Indexes

Regression Weights:			M.I.	Par Change
SE	<-------	EE	9.642	-0.046
EE	<-------	SE	17.074	-0.408
ELC	<-------	RC	14.322	0.090
DP	<--------	SE	11.467	-0.236
EE3	<-------	CC	14.858	-0.274
EE3	<-------	DM	6.916	-0.085
EE3	<-------	RA	11.117	0.140
EE3	<-------	SE	17.121	-0.308
EE3	<------	ELC	11.174	0.273
EE3	<-------	PA	24.481	-0.280
EE3	<------	PA1	21.090	-0.179
EE3	<-----	ELC5	7.323	0.124
EE3	<-----	ELC3	6.611	0.136
EE3	<------	CC1	8.764	-0.166
EE3	<------	CC2	12.175	-0.181
EE3	<------	CC4	12.366	-0.156
EE3	<------	SE3	14.137	-0.209
EE3	<------	SE1	14.283	-0.252
EE3	<------	SE2	8.608	-0.169
EE3	<------	PA3	15.230	-0.141
EE3	<------	PA2	13.251	-0.133
EE3	<-----	ELC2	9.645	0.159
EE3	<------	SS1	6.625	-0.065
EE3	<------	RA2	12.608	0.112
ELC5	<-----	CC2	6.493	0.084
ELC5	<-----	SE2	6.226	-0.092
ELC4	<------	CC	10.455	-0.156
ELC4	<-----	CC3	8.793	-0.119
ELC4	<-----	CC4	10.088	-0.096
CC1	<-------	RC	7.553	-0.075
CC1	<-------	EE	8.685	-0.048
CC1	<------	EE3	8.731	-0.041

.
.
.

AMOS Text Output: Model 4

Goodness-of-Fit Summary.   The estimation of Model 4 yielded a χ^2 value of 943.243, with 433 degrees of freedom. Values related to the GFI, CFI, and RMSEA were .911, .949, and .044, respectively; the ECVI value was 1.895. Again, the difference in fit between this model (Model 4) and its predecessor (Model 3) was statistically significant ($\Delta\chi^2_{(1)} = 24.001$). Modification indexes related to the estimation of Model 4 are presented in Table 6.7.

Modification Indexes.   In reviewing these boxed statistics, note that the MI associated with the regression path flowing from emotional exhaustion to self-esteem (SE ← EE) is no longer present. We are left only with the paths leading from role conflict to external locus of control (ELC ← RC), and from self-esteem to depersonalization (DP ← SE), with the former being the larger of the two (MI = 15.170). Because the estimation of this parameter is substantively meaningful, and the sign of the expected change statistic (0.093) is perfectly reasonable, Model 4 was respecified to include the estimation of a regression path leading from role conflict to external locus of control (ELC ← RC) (Model 5).

TABLE 6.7
Selected AMOS Text Output for Model 4: Modification Indexes

Regression Weights:	M.I.	Par Change
	---------	----------
ELC <------- RC	15.170	0.093
DP <-------- SE	10.277	-0.225
EE3 <------- CC	14.213	-0.266
EE3 <------- DM	6.419	-0.081
EE3 <------- RA	10.156	0.133
EE3 <------- SE	9.979	-0.235
EE3 <------ ELC	9.428	0.249
EE3 <------- PA	21.448	-0.259
EE3 <------ PA1	18.912	-0.168
EE3 <----- ELC5	6.092	0.112
EE3 <------ CC1	8.814	-0.166
EE3 <------ CC2	12.026	-0.179
EE3 <------ CC4	12.422	-0.155
EE3 <------ SE3	8.433	-0.160
EE3 <------ SE1	9.199	-0.201
EE3 <------ PA3	13.426	-0.131
EE3 <------ PA2	12.100	-0.126
EE3 <----- ELC2	9.274	0.155
EE3 <------ SS1	6.415	-0.064
EE3 <------ RA2	12.044	0.109
ELC5 <----- CC2	6.516	0.084
ELC5 <----- SE2	6.322	-0.092
ELC4 <------- CC	10.390	-0.156
ELC4 <----- CC3	8.788	-0.119
ELC4 <----- CC4	10.081	-0.096
CC1 <------- RC	7.423	-0.074
CC1 <------- EE	8.896	-0.049
·		
·		
·		

AMOS Text Output: Model 5

Goodness-of-Fit Summary.   Results from the estimation of Model 5 yielded a $\chi^2_{(432)}$ value of 904.724, a GFI of .913, a CFI of .953, and an RMSEA of .043; the ECVI value was 1.834. Again, the improvement in model fit was found to be statistically significant ($\Delta\chi^2_{(1)} = 38.519$. Finally, the estimated parameter value (0.220) was also statistically significant (C.R. = 5.957). Modification indexes related to this model are presented in Table 6.8.

Modification Indexes.   Not unexpectedly, a review of the output related to Model 5 reveals an MI associated with the path from self-esteem to depersonalization (DP ← SE); note that the expected parameter change statistic has remained minimally unchanged (−0.225 vs. −0.223). Once again, from a substantively meaningful perspective, we could expect that high levels of self-esteem would generate

TABLE 6.8
Selected AMOS Text Output for Model 5: Modification Indexes

Regression Weights:		M.I.	Par Change
DP <-------- SE		10.147	-0.223
EE3 <------- CC		14.216	-0.266
EE3 <------- DM		6.282	-0.080
EE3 <------- RA		10.328	0.134
EE3 <------- SE		9.920	-0.234
EE3 <------ ELC		8.577	0.238
EE3 <------ PA		21.217	-0.257
EE3 <------ PA1		18.806	-0.167
EE3 <------ CC1		8.867	-0.166
EE3 <------ CC2		12.039	-0.179
EE3 <------ CC4		12.437	-0.155
EE3 <------ SE3		8.441	-0.161
EE3 <------ SE1		9.246	-0.201
EE3 <------ PA3		13.213	-0.130
EE3 <------ PA2		11.998	-0.126
EE3 <----- ELC2		8.752	0.151
EE3 <------ SS1		6.493	-0.064
EE3 <------ RA2		12.122	0.110
ELC5 <----- CC2		8.462	0.096
ELC5 <----- SE2		6.287	-0.091
ELC4 <------ CC		8.891	-0.144
ELC4 <----- CC3		8.303	-0.116
ELC4 <----- CC4		9.222	-0.092
CC1 <------- RC		7.029	-0.071
CC1 <------- EE		8.870	-0.049
CC1 <------ EE3		9.118	-0.042
.			
.			
.			

low levels of depersonalization thereby yielding a negative expected parameter change statistic value. Thus, Model 5 was respecified with the path (DP ← SE) freely estimated, and was labeled as Model 6.

AMOS Text Output: Model 6

Goodness-of-Fit Summary.   Estimation of Model 6 yielded an overall $\chi^2_{(431)}$ value of 890.619; again, the χ^2 difference between Models 3 and 4 was statistically significant ($\Delta\chi^2_{(1)}$ = 14.105), as was the estimated parameter (−0.310, C.R. = −3.766). Furthermore, there was virtually no change in the GFI (.913), CFI (.953), and RMSEA (.043) values; the ECVI dropped a little further to 1.814, thereby indicating that Model 6 represented the best fit to the data thus far in the analyses. As expected, and as can be seen in Table 6.9, no MIs associated with structural paths were present in the output; only MIs related to the regression weights of factor loadings were presented. As you will note, there are no outstanding values suggestive of model misfit. Taking each of these factors into account, no further consideration was given to the inclusion of additional parameters.

Model Parsimony.   Thus far, discussion related to model fit has considered only the addition of parameters to the model. However, another side to the question of fit, particularly as it pertains to a full model, is the extent to which certain initially hypothesized paths may be irrelevant to the model. One way of determining such irrelevancy is to examine the statistical significance of all structural parameter estimates. This information, as derived from the estimation of Model 6, is presented in Table 6.10.

In reviewing the structural parameter estimates for Model 6, we can see five parameters that are nonsignificant; these parameters represent the paths from peer support to self-esteem (SE ← PS; C.R. = −0.595); role conflict to depersonalization (DP ← RC; C.R. = −0.839); decision making to external locus of control (ELC ← DM; −1.400); emotional exhaustion to personal accomplishment (PA ← EE;

TABLE 6.9
Selected AMOS Text Output for Model 6: Modification Indexes

Regression Weights:		M.I.	Par Change
EE3 <------- CC		14.167	-0.266
EE3 <------- DM		6.611	-0.083
EE3 <------- RA		10.825	0.138
EE3 <------- SE		12.454	-0.264
EE3 <------ ELC		9.215	0.247
EE3 <------- DP		6.368	0.108
.			
.			
.			

TABLE 6.10

Selected AMOS Text Output for Model 6: Maximum Likelihood Estimates for Structural Paths

Regression Weights:			Estimate	S.E.	C.R.
SE	<--------	DM	0.734	0.204	3.592
SE	<--------	SS	-0.475	0.151	-3.147
✓SE	<--------	PS	-0.042	0.071	-0.595
EE	<--------	RC	0.782	0.081	9.694
EE	<--------	CC	-0.361	0.109	-3.309
EE	<--------	SE	-0.544	0.111	-4.889
DP	<--------	EE	0.326	0.040	8.217
✓DP	<--------	RC	-0.051	0.061	-0.839
✓ELC	<-------	DM	-0.035	0.025	-1.400
DP	<--------	CC	-0.469	0.083	-5.636
ELC	<-------	SE	-0.182	0.045	-4.056
ELC	<-------	RC	0.220	0.037	5.938
DP	<--------	SE	-0.310	0.082	-3.766
PA	<--------	DP	-0.229	0.051	-4.476
✓PA	<--------	EE	-0.058	0.033	-1.773
PA	<--------	RA	-0.096	0.045	-2.145
PA	<--------	SE	0.217	0.071	3.042
✓PA	<-------	ELC	-0.068	0.076	-0.895

−1.773); external locus of control to personal accomplishment (PA ← ELC; −0.895). In the interest of parsimony, a final model of burnout was estimated with these five structural paths deleted from the model.

Because standardized estimates are typically of interest in presenting results from structural equation models, it is usually of interest to request these statistics when you have determined your final model. Given that Model 7 will serve as our final model of teacher burnout, this request was made by clicking on the Analysis Properties ▦ icon, which, in turn, yielded the dialog box shown in Fig. 6.7; you observe that I also requested the squared multiple correlations.

AMOS Text Output: Model 7

Goodness-of-Fit Summary.   Estimation of this final model (Model 7) resulted in an overall $\chi^2_{(436)}$ value of 897.581. At this point, you may have some concern over the slight erosion in model fit from $\chi^2_{(431)} = 890.619$ for Model 4, to $\chi^2_{(436)} = 897.581$ for Model 7, the final model. However, with deletion of any parameters from a model, such a change is to be expected. The important aspect of this change in model fit is that the χ^2 difference between the two models is not significant $(\Delta\chi^2_{(5)} = 6.962)$. Furthermore, from a review of the goodness-of-fit statistics in Table 6.11, you will note that values for the other fit indexes of interest remained virtually unchanged from those related to Model 6 (GFI = .914; CFI = .954; RMSEA = .042); the slight drop in the ECVI value signals that this final and most parsimonious model represents the best fit to the data overall.

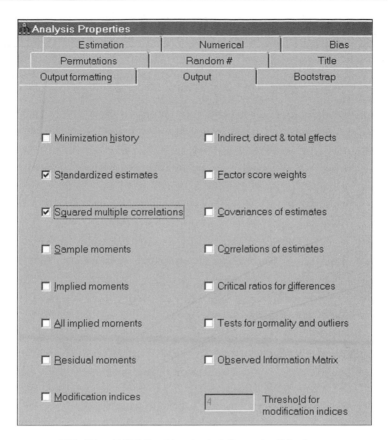

FIG. 6.7.   AMOS Graphics: Analysis Properties dialog box.

A schematic representation of this final model of burnout for elementary teachers is displayed in Fig. 6.8, and the unstandardized, as well as standardized, maximum likelihood parameter estimates are presented in Table 6.12. It is important to draw your attention to the fact that all parameter estimates are statistically significant and substantively meaningful.

Taking one last look at this final model of burnout, let's review the squared multiple correlations (SMCs) shown in Table 6.13. The SMC is a useful statistic that is independent of all units of measurement. Once it is requested, AMOS 4.0 will provide a SMC for each endogenous variable in the model. Thus, in Table 6.13, you see SMCs for the dependent factors in the model (SE, EE, DP, PA, ELC) and for each of the factor loading regression paths (CC1–SS2). The SMC value represents the proportion of variance that is explained by the predictors of the variable in question. For example, in order to interpret the SMC associated with self-esteem (SE), we need first to review Fig. 6.8 to ascertain which factors in the model serve

TABLE 6.11

Selected AMOS Text Output for Model 7: Goodness-of-Fit Statistics

Summary of models

Model	NPAR	CMIN	DF	P
Default model	92	897.581	436	0.000
Saturated model	528	0.000	0	
Independence model	32	10590.438	496	0.000

Model	RMR	GFI	AGFI	PGFI
Default model	0.040	0.914	0.896	0.755
Saturated model	0.000	1.000		
Independence model	0.324	0.256	0.208	0.240

Model	DELTA1 NFI	RHO1 RFI	DELTA2 IFI	RHO2 TLI	CFI
Default model	0.915	0.904	0.955	0.948	0.954
Saturated model	1.000		1.000		1.000
Independence model	0.000	0.000	0.000	0.000	0.000

Model	PRATIO	PNFI	PCFI
Default model	0.879	0.805	0.839
Saturated model	0.000	0.000	0.000
Independence model	1.000	0.000	0.000

Model	RMSEA	LO 90	HI 90	PCLOSE
Default model	0.042	0.038	0.046	1.000
Independence model	0.184	0.181	0.188	0.000

Model	ECVI	LO 90	HI 90	MECVI
Default model	1.809	1.672	1.959	1.827
Saturated model	1.766	1.766	1.766	1.869
Independence model	17.817	17.263	18.382	17.823

as its predictors. Accordingly, we determine that 24.6% of the variance associated with self-esteem is accounted for by its two predictors: decision making and superior support. Likewise, we can determine that the factor of superior support explains 90.2% of the variance associated with its second indicator variable, SS2.

In working with structural equation models, it is very important to know when to stop fitting a model. Although there are no firm rules or regulations to guide this decision, the researcher's best yardsticks include (a) a thorough knowledge of the sub-

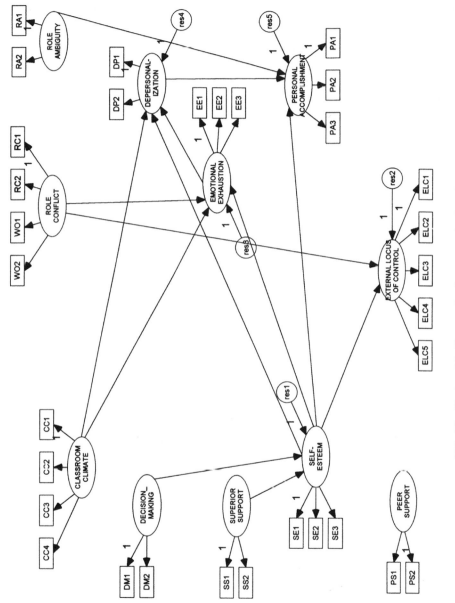

FIG. 6.8.   Final model of burnout for elementary school teachers.

Regression Weights:

		Unstandardized Estimate	S.E.	C.R.	Standardized Estimate
SE <--------	DM	0.628	0.108	5.825	1.418
SE <--------	SS	-0.402	0.092	-4.377	-1.063
EE <--------	RC	0.777	0.080	9.730	0.490
EE <--------	CC	-0.363	0.109	-3.334	-0.147
EE <--------	SE	-0.555	0.111	-5.021	-0.203
DP <--------	EE	0.316	0.034	9.390	0.475
DP <--------	CC	-0.451	0.080	-5.632	-0.276
DP <--------	SE	-0.293	0.081	-3.619	-0.161
PA <--------	DP	-0.285	0.044	-6.480	-0.374
PA <--------	RA	-0.134	0.040	-3.376	-0.177
ELC <-------	SE	-0.194	0.044	-4.405	-0.207
PA <-------	SE	0.242	0.070	3.440	0.174
ELC <-------	RC	0.252	0.030	8.466	0.463
DP2 <-------	DP	1.000			0.749
DP1 <-------	DP	1.156	0.072	16.026	0.833
RA2 <-------	RA	1.000			0.819
RA1 <-------	RA	0.853	0.050	16.976	0.721
RC2 <-------	RC	1.341	0.081	16.523	0.789
RC1 <-------	RC	1.000			0.682
DM2 <-------	DM	1.000			0.801
DM1 <-------	DM	0.773	0.040	19.228	0.714
SS2 <-------	SS	1.000			0.950
SS1 <-------	SS	0.941	0.028	33.710	0.891
PS2 <-------	PS	1.000			0.889
PS1 <-------	PS	0.976	0.057	17.252	0.822
ELC1 <-----	ELC	1.000			0.693
ELC2 <-----	ELC	0.845	0.068	12.500	0.577
EE1 <-------	EE	1.000			0.890
EE2 <-------	EE	1.027	0.032	32.590	0.917
PA2 <-------	PA	1.000			0.713
PA3 <-------	PA	1.019	0.066	15.443	0.718
SE2 <-------	SE	1.000			0.816
SE1 <-------	SE	0.821	0.040	20.429	0.774
SE3 <-------	SE	1.137	0.049	23.009	0.894
CC4 <-------	CC	1.000			0.697
CC3 <-------	CC	0.711	0.053	13.445	0.662
CC2 <-------	CC	0.939	0.064	14.776	0.767
CC1 <-------	CC	0.702	0.055	12.735	0.619
ELC3 <-----	ELC	1.046	0.068	15.486	0.735
ELC4 <-----	ELC	1.048	0.074	14.219	0.665
ELC5 <-----	ELC	1.309	0.080	16.409	0.795
EE3 <-------	EE	0.975	0.033	29.521	0.867
PA1 <-------	PA	1.131	0.068	16.579	0.856
WO1 <-------	RC	1.138	0.071	16.006	0.757
WO2 <-------	RC	1.019	0.074	13.825	0.639

Covariances:

		Unstandardized Estimate	S.E.	C.R.	Standardized Estimate
RA <------->	RC	0.490	0.044	11.056	0.798
DM <------->	CC	0.186	0.028	6.744	0.381
DM <------->	SS	1.115	0.077	14.503	0.960
SS <------->	PS	0.478	0.049	9.761	0.503
DM <------->	PS	0.530	0.049	10.874	0.653
PS <------->	CC	0.101	0.021	4.825	0.252
RA <------->	DM	-0.631	0.053	-11.866	-0.785
RA <------->	SS	-0.629	0.054	-11.562	-0.668
RA <------->	PS	-0.346	0.038	-9.175	-0.525
RA <------->	CC	-0.149	0.023	-6.526	-0.378
RC <------->	DM	-0.515	0.050	-10.229	-0.680
RC <------->	SS	-0.504	0.051	-9.829	-0.568
RC <------->	PS	-0.266	0.034	-7.721	-0.429
RC <------->	CC	-0.152	0.022	-6.914	-0.407
SS <------->	CC	0.161	0.029	5.582	0.282

(Continued)

TABLE 6.12 *(Continued)*

Variances:

	Unstandardized Estimate	S.E.	C.R.

Exogenous Factors

	Unstandardized Estimate	S.E.	C.R.
RA	0.652	0.060	10.873
RC	0.578	0.065	8.924
DM	0.991	0.086	11.558
SS	1.361	0.090	15.107
PS	0.665	0.057	11.589
CC	0.240	0.028	8.716

Endogenous Factor Residuals

rse	0.147	0.015	9.995
ree	0.802	0.065	12.295
rdp	0.311	0.038	8.252
rel	0.116	0.014	8.545
rpa	0.247	0.028	8.701

Errors of Measurement

edp2	0.504	0.043	11.685
edp1	0.375	0.047	7.930
era2	0.319	0.033	9.539
era1	0.439	0.033	13.466
erc2	0.632	0.050	12.751
erc1	0.665	0.045	14.916
ewo2	0.870	0.056	15.413
ewo1	0.556	0.041	13.585
edm2	0.552	0.038	14.614
edm1	0.568	0.036	15.960
ess2	0.148	0.025	5.845
ess1	0.313	0.028	11.198
eps2	0.176	0.034	5.247
eps1	0.305	0.035	8.643
eel1	0.186	0.013	14.317
eel2	0.246	0.016	15.710
eee1	0.381	0.032	11.750
eee2	0.291	0.030	9.779
epa2	0.361	0.027	13.402
epa3	0.364	0.027	13.274
ese2	0.098	0.008	12.175
ese1	0.088	0.006	13.645
ese3	0.063	0.008	7.857
ecc4	0.255	0.019	13.160
ecc3	0.156	0.011	13.905
ecc2	0.148	0.013	11.052
ecc1	0.190	0.013	14.609
eel3	0.159	0.012	13.480
eel4	0.237	0.016	14.751
eel5	0.171	0.015	11.727
eee3	0.456	0.035	12.992
epa1	0.175	0.023	7.693

stantive theory, (b) an adequate assessment of statistical criteria based on information pooled from various indexes of fit, and (c) a watchful eye on parsimony. In this regard, the SEM researcher must walk a fine line between incorporating a sufficient number of parameters to yield a model that adequately represents the data, and falling prey to the temptation of incorporating too many parameters in a zealous attempt to attain the best fitting model, statistically. Two major problems with the latter tack are that (a) the

TABLE 6.13
Selected AMOS Text Output for Model 7: Squared Multiple Correlations

	Estimate
SE	0.246
EE	0.448
DP	0.517
PA	0.338
ELC	0.325
PA1	0.732
EE3	0.752
ELC5	0.633
ELC4	0.442
ELC3	0.541
CC1	0.384
CC2	0.589
CC3	0.438
CC4	0.485
SE3	0.800
SE1	0.599
SE2	0.666
PA3	0.515
PA2	0.509
EE2	0.841
EE1	0.792
ELC2	0.332
ELC1	0.480
PS1	0.675
PS2	0.790
SS1	0.794
SS2	0.902
DM1	0.510
DM2	0.642
WO1	0.574
WO2	0.408
RC1	0.465
RC2	0.622
RA1	0.519
RA2	0.671
DP1	0.696
DP2	0.561

model can comprise parameters that actually contribute only trivially to its structure, and (b) the more parameters there are in a model, the more difficult it is to replicate its structure should future validation research be conducted.

In the case of the model tested in this chapter, I considered the addition of five structural paths to be justified both substantively and statistically. From the statistical perspective, it was noted that the addition of each new parameter resulted in a statistically significant difference in fit from the previously specified model. The inclusion of these five additional paths, and the deletion of five originally specified paths, resulted in a final model that fitted the data well (GFI = .914; CFI = .954; RMSEA = .042). Furthermore, based on the ECVI index, it appears that the final model (Model 7) has the greatest potential for replication in other samples of elementary teachers, compared with Models 1 through 6.

In concluding this chapter, let's now summarize and review findings from the various models tested. First, of 13 causal paths specified in the revised hypothesized model (see Fig. 6.6), 8 were found to be statistically significant for elementary teachers. These paths reflected the impact of (a) classroom climate and role conflict on emotional exhaustion, (b) decision making and superior support on self-esteem, (c) self-esteem, role ambiguity, and depersonalization on perceived personal accomplishment, and (d) emotional exhaustion on depersonalization. Second, five paths, not specified a priori (classroom climate → depersonalization; self-esteem → external locus of control; self-esteem → emotional exhaustion; role conflict → external locus of control; self-esteem → depersonalization), proved to be essential components of the causal structure; they were therefore added to the model. Finally, five hypothesized paths (peer support → self-esteem; role conflict → depersonalization; decision making → external locus of control; emotional exhaustion → personal accomplishment; external locus of control → personal accomplishment) were not significant and were subsequently deleted from the model.

In general, we can conclude from this application that role ambiguity, role conflict, classroom climate, participation in the decision-making process, and the support of one's superiors are potent organizational determinants of burnout for elementary school teachers. The process, however, appears to be strongly tempered by ones sense of self-worth.

MODELING WITH AMOS BASIC

For an example of an AMOS Basic file in this chapter, let's examine one related to the final model of burnout schematically displayed in Fig. 6.8. This input file is presented in Table 6.14.

Although most of the setup here will be familiar to you at this point, a couple of points are perhaps worthy of comment. First, note that the first three SEM lines request that the output be in text format, and that both the squared multiple correlations and the standardized estimates be included. The fourth SEM line identifies the file "elind11.txt" as the data source. Second, for purposes of clarity, I have separated equations related to the measurement model (RA1–PA3) from those representing the structural model. Finally, I wish to point out that, although I have located the parenthesized values of 1, representing constrained parameters to precede the parameter in question, these values can also follow the related parameter; preference related to this specification in the structuring of an AMOS Basic input file is purely arbitrary.

TABLE 6.14
AMOS Basic Input File for Final Model of Burnout for Elementary Teachers

---

Sub Main
Dim Sem As New AmosEngine

SEM.TextOutput
SEM.Smc
SEM.Standardized
SEM.BeginGroup "elind1l.txt"

```
    SEM.Structure "RA1 = (1)  ROLE AMBIGUITY + (1) era1"
    SEM.Structure "RA2 =      ROLE AMBIGUITY + (1) era2"
    SEM.Structure "RC1 = (1)  ROLE CONFLICT + (1) erc1"
    SEM.Structure "RC2 =      ROLE CONFLICT + (1) erc2"
    SEM.Structure "WO1 =      ROLE CONFLICT + (1) erc3"
    SEM.Structure "WO2 =      ROLE CONFLICT + (1) erc4"
    SEM.Structure "CC1 = (1)  CLASSROOM CLIMATE + (1) ecc1"
    SEM.Structure "CC2 =      CLASSROOM CLIMATE + (1) ecc2"
    SEM.Structure "CC3 =      CLASSROOM CLIMATE + (1) ecc3"
    SEM.Structure "CC4 =      CLASSROOM CLIMATE + (1) ecc4"
    SEM.Structure "DM1 = (1)  DECISIONMAKING + (1) edm1"
    SEM.Structure "DM2 =      DECISIONMAKING + (1) edm2"
    SEM.Structure "SS1 = (1)  SUPERIOR SUPPORT + (1) ess1"
    SEM.Structure "SS2 =      SUPERIOR SUPPORT + (1) ess2"
    SEM.Structure "SE1 = (1)  SELF-ESTEEM + (1) ese1"
    SEM.Structure "SE2 =      SELF-ESTEEM + (1) ese2"
    SEM.Structure "SE3 =      SELF-ESTEEM + (1) ese3"
    SEM.Structure "PS1 =      PEER SUPPORT + (1) eps1"
    SEM.Structure "PS2 = (1)  PEER SUPPORT + (1) eps2"
    SEM.Structure "ELC1 = (1) EXTERNAL LOCUS OF CONTROL + (1) eel1"
    SEM.Structure "ELC2 =     EXTERNAL LOCUS OF CONTROL + (1) eel2"
    SEM.Structure "ELC3 =     EXTERNAL LOCUS OF CONTROL + (1) eel3"
    SEM.Structure "ELC4 =     EXTERNAL LOCUS OF CONTROL + (1) eel4"
    SEM.Structure "ELC5 =     EXTERNAL LOCUS OF CONTROL + (1) eel5"
    SEM.Structure "EE1 = (1)  EMOTIONAL EXHAUSTION + (1) eee1"
    SEM.Structure "EE2 =      EMOTIONAL EXHAUSTION + (1) eee2"
    SEM.Structure "EE3 =      EMOTIONAL EXHAUSTION + (1) eee3"
    SEM.Structure "DP1 = (1)  DEPERSONALIZATION + (1) edp1"
    SEM.Structure "DP2 =      DEPERSONALIZATION + (1) edp2"
    SEM.Structure "PA1 = (1)  PERSONAL ACCOMPLISHMENT + (1) epa1"
    SEM.Structure "PA2 =      PERSONAL ACCOMPLISHMENT + (1) epa2"
    SEM.Structure "PA3 =      PERSONAL ACCOMPLISHMENT + (1) epa3"

    SEM.Structure "SELF-ESTEEM = DECISIONMAKING + SUPERIOR SUPPORT + (1) res1"
    SEM.Structure "EXTERNAL LOCUS OF CONTROL = ROLE CONFLICT + SELF-ESTEEM + (1)
              res2"
    SEM.Structure "EMOTIONAL EXHAUSTION = ROLE CONFLICT + CLASSROOM CLIMATE
              + SELF-ESTEEM + (1) res3"
    SEM.Structure "DEPERSONALIZATION = EMOTIONAL EXHAUSTION + CLASSROOM CLI-
              MATE + SELF-ESTEEM + (1) res4"
    SEM.Structure "PERSONAL ACCOMPLISHMENT = SELF-ESTEEM + DEPERSONALIZA-
              TION + ROLE AMBIGUITY + (1) res5"
```

End Sub

III

MULTIPLE-GROUP
ANALYSES

❧

Application 5: Testing for Invariant Factorial Structure of a Measuring Instrument (First-Order CFA Model)

U p to this point, all applications have illustrated analyses based on single samples. In this section, however, we focus on applications involving more than one sample where the central concern is whether or not components of the measurement model and/or the structural model are invariant (i.e., equivalent) across particular groups.

In seeking evidence of multigroup invariance, researchers are typically interested in finding the answer to one of five questions. First, do the items comprising a particular measuring instrument operate equivalently across different populations (e.g., gender, age, ability)? In other words, is the measurement model group-invariant? Second, is the factorial structure of a single instrument, or of a theoretical construct measured by multiple instruments, equivalent across populations? Here, invariance of the structural model is of primary interest and, in particular, the equivalency of relations among the theoretical constructs. Third, are certain paths in a specified causal structure invariant across populations? Fourth, are the latent means of particular constructs in a model different across populations? Finally, does the factorial structure of a measuring instrument replicate across independent samples of the same population? This latter question, of course, addresses the issue of cross-validation. Applications presented in the next four chapters provide specific examples of how each of these questions can be answered using structural equation modeling based on AMOS 4.0.

In our first multigroup application, we test hypotheses related to the invariance of a single measuring instrument across three groups of teachers. Specifically, we test for equivalency of the factorial measurement (i.e., scale items) of the Maslach Burnout Inventory (MBI; Maslach & Jackson, 1986) and its underlying latent structure (i.e., relations among dimensions of burnout) across elementary, inter- mediate, and secondary teachers. Purposes of the original study, from which this example is taken (Byrne, 1993), were (a) to test for the factorial validity of the MBI separately for each of these teacher groups, (b) given findings of inadequate fit, to propose and test an alternative factorial structure, (c) to cross-validate this struc- ture over independent samples within each teacher group, and (d) to test for the equivalence of item measurements and theoretical structure across the three teach- ing panels.[1] Only analyses related to the last are central to the present chapter. Before reviewing the model under scrutiny in this chapter, let's turn first to a review of the general procedure involved in tests for invariance (or equivalence) across groups.

TESTING FOR MULTIGROUP INVARIANCE

Development of a procedure capable of testing for invariance simultaneously across groups derives from the seminal work of Joreskog (1971b). Accordingly, Joreskog recommended that all tests of invariance begin with a global test of the equality of covariance structures across groups. In other words, one tests the null hypothesis (H_0) that $\Sigma_1 = \Sigma_2 = \cdots = \Sigma_G$, where Σ is the population variance–covari- ance matrix, and G is the number of groups. Rejection of the null hypothesis then argues for the nonequivalence of the groups and, thus, for the subsequent testing of increasingly restrictive hypotheses in order to identify the source of noninvariance. On the other hand, if H_0 cannot be rejected, the groups are considered to be equiv- alent and thus tests for invariance are unjustified; group data should be pooled and all subsequent investigative work should be based on single-group analyses.

Although this omnibus test appears to be reasonable and is fairly straightfor- ward, it often leads to contradictory findings with respect to equivalencies across groups. For example, sometimes the null hypothesis is found tenable, yet subse- quent tests of hypotheses related to the invariance of particular measurement or structural parameters must be rejected (see Joreskog, 1971b). Alternatively, the global null hypothesis may be rejected, yet tests for the invariance of measurement and structural invariance hold (see Byrne, 1988a). Such inconsistencies in the glob- al test for invariance stem from the fact that there is no baseline model for the test of invariant variance–covariance matrices, thereby making it substantially more

---

[1]For a detailed description of the MBI, readers are referred to chapter 4 of this volume.

stringent than is the case for tests of invariance related to sets of parameters in the model (Muthén, personal communication, October 1988). Indeed, Muthén contended that the omnibus test provides little guidance in testing for equality across groups and thus should not be regarded as a necessary prerequisite to the testing of more specific hypotheses related to group invariance.

In testing for equivalencies across groups, sets of parameters are put to the test in a logically ordered and increasingly restrictive fashion. Depending on the model and hypotheses to be tested, the following sets of parameters are most commonly of interest in answering questions related to group invariance: (a) factor loading paths, (b) factor variances/covariances, and (c) structural regression paths; of less interest are tests for the invariance of error variances/covariances and residual (i.e., disturbance) terms. In general, except in particular instances when, for example, it might be of interest to test for the invariant reliability of an assessment measure across groups (see Byrne, 1988a), the equality of error variances and covariances is probably the least important hypothesis to test (Bentler, 1995). Although the Joreskog tradition of invariance testing holds that the equality of these parameters should be tested, it is now widely accepted that to do so represents an overly restrictive test of the data.

The General Procedure

In the Joreskog tradition, tests of hypotheses related to group invariance typically begin with scrutiny of the measurement model. In particular, the pattern of factor loadings for each observed measure is tested for its equivalence across the groups. Once it is known which measures are group-invariant, these parameters are constrained equal while subsequent tests of the structural parameters are conducted. As each new set of parameters is tested, those known to be group-invariant are constrained equal. Thus, the process of determining nonequivalence of measurement and structural parameters across groups involves the testing of a series of increasingly restrictive hypotheses. Given the univariate approach to the testing of these hypotheses, as implemented in the AMOS program, the orderly sequence of analytic steps is both necessary and strongly recommended.

Preliminary Single-Group Analyses

As a prerequisite to testing for factorial invariance, it is customary to consider a baseline model that is estimated for each group separately. This model represents the one that best fits the data from the perspectives of both parsimony and substantive meaningfulness. Given that the χ^2 statistic and its degrees of freedom are additive, the sum of the χ^2 values derived from the model-fitting process for each group separately reflects the extent to which the underlying structure fits the data across groups when no cross-group constraints are imposed. Nonetheless, because measuring instruments are often group specific in the way they operate, baseline models are not expected to be completely identical across groups. For example, whereas the baseline model for one group might include cross-loadings[2] and/or error covariances, this may not be so for other groups under study. A priori knowledge of such group differences, as illustrated in chapter 8, is critical to the application of invariance-testing procedures. Although the bulk of the literature suggests that the number of factors must be equivalent across groups before further tests of invariance can be conducted, this strategy represents a logical starting point only, and is *not* a necessary condition; indeed, only the similarly specified parameters within the same factor need be equated (Werts, Rock, Linn, & Joreskog, 1976).

Because the estimation of baseline models involves no between-group constraints, the data can be analyzed separately for each group. However, in testing for invariance, equality constraints are imposed on particular parameters, and thus the data for all groups must be analyzed simultaneously to obtain efficient estimates (Bentler, 1995; Joreskog & Sorbom, 1996b); the pattern of fixed and free parameters nonetheless remains consistent with the baseline model specification for each group.

In summary, tests for invariance can involve both measurement and structural components of a model, with the particular combination varying in accordance with the model under study. For example, in the case of first-order CFA models, the pattern of factor loadings and structural relations among the factors are typically of most interest; with second-order models, the focus is on both the lower and higher order factor loadings; and with full SEM models, the structural paths among the factors are of primary concern.

TESTING FOR INVARIANCE
ACROSS TEACHING PANELS

The Hypothesized Model

In my preliminary single-group analyses reported in Byrne (1993), I found that, for each teacher group, MBI Item 12 and Item 16 were problematic; these items were subsequently deleted and a model was proposed in which only the remaining 20 items were used to measure the underlying construct of burnout.[3] As noted earlier, however, prior to testing for invariance across multigroup samples, it is customary to first establish baseline models separately, for each group under study. Thus, the 20-item MBI model described here was tested separately for each teacher group. We turn now to the results of these analyses.

---

[2]A variable's measurement loading on more than one factor.

[3]For a more detailed account of analyses leading up to the 20-item model, readers are referred to chapter 4 (this volume) and to the original article (Byrne, 1993).

The Baseline Models

In testing for the validity of the revised 20-item MBI model for each teacher group, findings were consistent across panels in revealing exceptionally large correlated errors between Items 1 and 2, and between items 10 and 11. Scrutiny of the content for each of these items revealed evidence of substantial overlap between the targeted pairs. Given that these error terms could be substantively justified, they were subsequently specified as free parameters in the model for each teacher group. A final model that reflected these modifications was fully cross-validated for independent samples of elementary, intermediate, and secondary teachers.

Findings from this testing for a baseline model yielded one that was identically specified for each of the three teaching panels. However, it is important to point out that just because the revised model was similarly specified for elementary, intermediate, and secondary teachers, this in no way guarantees the equivalence of item measurements and underlying theoretical structure across teacher groups; these hypotheses must be tested statistically. For example, despite an identically specified factor loading, it is possible that, with the imposition of equality constraints across groups, the tenability of invariance does not hold; that is, the link between the item and its target factor differs across the groups. Such postulated equivalencies must be tested statistically.

The hypothesized model under test in the present example is the revised 20-item MBI structure as schematically depicted in Fig. 7.1. At issue, is the extent to which this revised structure of burnout, as measured by the modified 20-item MBI, is equivalent across elementary ($n = 1,159$), intermediate ($n = 388$), and secondary ($n = 1,384$) school teachers. In other words, the invariance of both the measurement and structural models related to the revised MBI is of primary interest.

MODELING WITH AMOS GRAPHICS

When working with analysis of covariance structures that involve multiple groups, the data related to each must, of course, be made known to the program. Typically, for most SEM programs, the data reside in some external file, the location of which is specified in an input file; indeed, such is the case for AMOS Basic. In contrast, however, given that no input file is used with AMOS Graphics, both the name of each group and the location of its data file, must be communicated to the program prior to any analyses involving multiple groups. This procedure is easily accomplished in AMOS Graphics via the Manage Groups dialog box, which, in turn, is made available either by pulling down the Model-Fit menu and selecting the "Manage Groups" option, or by using the Manage Groups icon ▦. To begin, click on "New" in the Manage Groups dialog box, which is shown in Fig. 7.2. Each click will yield the name "Group," along with an assigned number. In the case of Fig. 7.2, the group number (3) pertains to secondary teachers; this name change is invoked simply by typing over the former name (see Fig. 7.3).

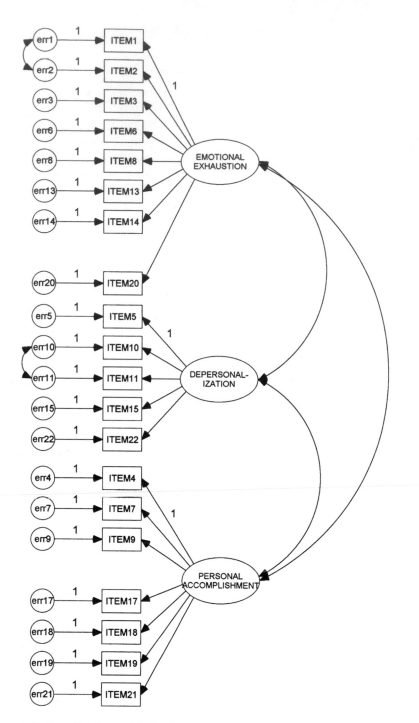

FIG. 7.1. Baseline model of revised 20-item MBI structure for elementary, inter-mediate, and secondary teachers.

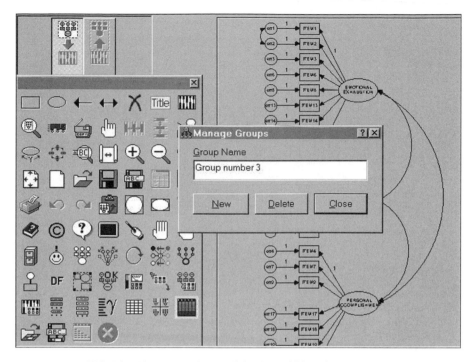

FIG. 7.2.   The Manage Groups dialog box: addition of a new group.

FIG. 7.3.   The Manage Groups dialog box: labeling of a new group.

Once the group names have been established, the next task is to identify a data file for each. This procedure is the same as the one demonstrated earlier in the book for single groups; the only difference is that a file name for each group to be included in the analysis must be selected. The Data File dialog box for this application is shown in Fig. 7.4.

Finally, specification of multigroup models is guided by several basic default rules. One such default is that all groups in the analysis will have the identical path diagram structure, unless explicitly declared otherwise. As a consequence, a model structure needs only to be drawn for the first group. All other groups will have the same structure by default.

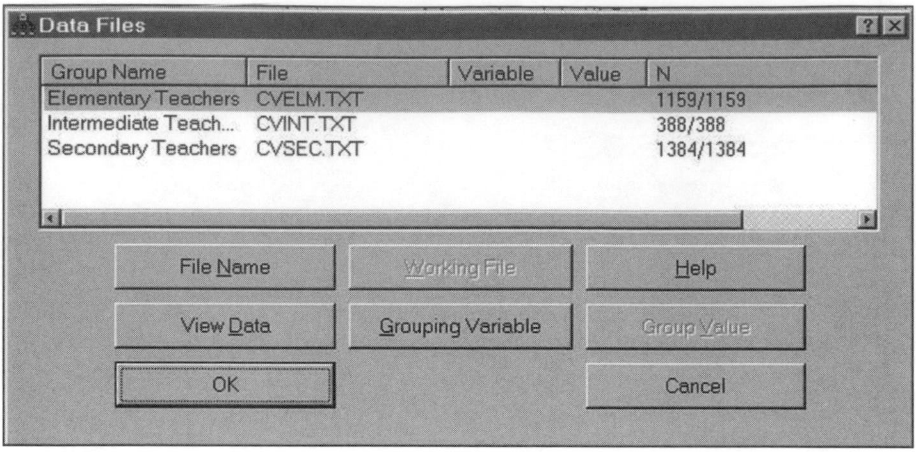

FIG. 7.4.   The Data Files dialog box: identification of data files.

Testing for the Validity of a Three-Factor Structure

Having keyed in the name associated with each group, together with the related data files, we are now ready to proceed with the analyses. As a preliminary step in testing for invariance across groups, we test for the validity of MBI structure as best represented by three factors. Given that we have already conducted this test in the establishment of baseline models, you will no doubt wonder why it is necessary to repeat the process. There are two important reasons for doing so. First, although the former tests were conducted for each group separately, tests for the validity of factorial structure in this instance are conducted across the three groups simultaneously. In other words, parameters will be estimated for all three groups at the same time. Second, in testing for invariance using the AMOS program, as with the LISREL program, the fit of this simultaneously estimated model provides the baseline value against which all subsequently specified models are compared. In contrast to single-group analyses, however, this multigroup analysis yields only one set of fit statistics for overall model fit. Given that χ^2 statistics are summative, the overall χ^2 value for the multigroup model should equal the sum of the χ^2 values obtained when the baseline model is tested separately for each group of teachers (with no cross-group constraints imposed).[4] We turn now to Table 7.1, where there are selected portions of the AMOS output file related to this simultaneous test of the hypothesized model in Fig. 7.1.

---

[4]Although this fact is always exactly true in LISREL and EQS (at least), it is exactly true in AMOS if, and only if, a checkmark is placed next to Emulisrel6 on the Estimations tab of View/Set → Analysis Properties; otherwise, it is almost, but not quite exactly, true.

TABLE 7.1
Selected AMOS Text Output for Simultaneous
Test of Hypothesized Model: Model and Sample Summary

```
Number of variables in model:    43

          Number of observed variables:      20
          Number of unobserved variables:    23
          Number of exogenous variables:     23
          Number of endogenous variables:    20
```

Summary of Parameters

	Weights	Covariances	Variances	Means	Intercepts	Total
Fixed:	23	0	0	0	0	23
Labeled:	0	0	0	0	0	0
Unlabeled:	17	5	23	0	0	45
Total:	40	5	23	0	0	68

Elementary Teachers

```
Sample size:  1159
```

Intermediate Teachers

```
Sample size:   388
```

Secondary Teachers

```
Sample size:  1384
```

Computation of Degrees of Freedom

```
              Number of distinct sample moments:   630
    Number of distinct parameters to be estimated:  135
              ----------------------------------
                         Degrees of freedom:   495
```

```
Minimum was achieved
```

AMOS Text Output: Three-Group Model
With No Equality Constraints Imposed

In reviewing the text presented in Table 7.1, the AMOS output first summarizes the number of variables in the model and then summarizes the number of parameters in the model. Under the heading "Number of Variables in the Model," we see that there are 43 variables in the model. Twenty of these variables are observed (and endogenous) and represent the MBI items; 23 are unobserved (and exogenous) and represent the 20 error variances and 3 factor variances. Under the rubric "Summary of Parameters," AMOS focuses on those that are fixed and those that are freely estimated (termed in the output as *unlabeled*). Turning to the regression paths, or *weights*, as they are termed in the output, we note that 23 are fixed, and 17 are freely estimated. The fixed parameters represent the 20 error terms, in addition to the three-factor regression paths fixed to 1.00 for purposes of model identification; the 17 unlabeled parameters represent the estimated factor loadings. Continuing through the remainder of the table, the 5 covariances refer to those associated with the factors (3), and those associated with the two error covariances (2); the 23 variances refer to both the error (20) and the factor (3) variances. In summarizing the number of parameters associated with the hypothesized model of MBI structure shown in Fig. 7.1, we see that, in total, there are 68: 23 of which are fixed, and 45 of which are freely estimated.

The next portion of the output summarizes the sample sizes related to each group under study. As you can readily see, there are 1,159, 388, and 1,384 elementary, intermediate, and secondary teachers, respectively.

The final piece of information provided in this summary table relates to the number of degrees of freedom. Although at this point in the book you will be familiar with the manner by which this number is derived, it may be helpful to review the computation relative to a multigroup application. Given that there are 20 observed variables in the hypothesized model (i.e., 20 items), we know that, for one group, this would yield 210 ($20 \times 21/2$) pieces of information (or, in other words, sample moments). Thus, for three groups, this number would be 630. Likewise, we know that there are 45 parameters to be estimated; given three groups, this number would be 135. Overall, then, a simultaneous estimation of this model for three teacher groups should yield a χ^2 value with associated 495 degrees of freedom.

Model Assessment

Goodness-of-Fit Statistics.   Let's turn now to Table 7.2 in which the goodness-of-fit indexes bearing on this multigroup model are reported. The key indexes here are the χ^2 statistic and the CFI and RMSEA values. As noted earlier, the χ^2 value of 2243.206, with 495 degrees of freedom, provides the baseline value against which all subsequent tests for invariance will be compared. The CFA and RMSEA values of .925 and .035, respectively, are indicative that the hypothesized three-factor model of MBI structure is well-fitting across the three panels of teachers. Having established the good fit of this model, we can now proceed in testing for the invariance of factorial measurement and structure across groups. However, first, we need to review the manner by which tests for invariance are conducted using AMOS Graphics.

TABLE 7.2
Selected AMOS Text Output for Simultaneous Test
of Hypothesized Model: Goodness-of-Fit Statistics

Summary of models

Model	NPAR	CMIN	DF	P
Your model	135	2243.206	495	0.000
Saturated model	630	0.000	0	
Independence model	60	23811.283	570	0.000

Model	RMR	GFI	AGFI	PGFI
Your model	0.117	0.926	0.906	0.728
Saturated model	0.000	1.000		
Independence model	0.706	0.354	0.286	0.320

Model	DELTA1 NFI	RHO1 RFI	DELTA2 IFI	RHO2 TLI	CFI
Your model	0.906	0.892	0.925	0.913	0.925
Saturated model	1.000		1.000		1.000
Independence model	0.000	0.000	0.000	0.000	0.000

Model	PRATIO	PNFI	PCFI
Your model	0.868	0.787	0.803
Saturated model	0.000	0.000	0.000
Independence model	1.000	0.000	0.000

Model	RMSEA	LO 90	HI 90	PCLOSE
Your model	0.035	0.033	0.036	1.000
Independence model	0.118	0.117	0.119	0.000

Model	ECVI	LO 90	HI 90	MECVI
Your model	0.858	0.809	0.910	0.861
Saturated model	0.430	0.430	0.430	0.444
Independence model	8.173	8.002	8.347	8.175

Testing for Invariance: The Specification of Equality Constraints

In structural equation modeling, testing for the invariance of parameters across groups is accomplished by placing constraints on particular parameters. That is to say, the parameters are specified as being invariant (i.e., equivalent) across groups. In AMOS Graphics, constraints are specified through a labeling mechanism whereby each parameter to be held equal across groups is given a label. Thus, in analyzing multigroup models, any parameters that are unlabeled will be freely estimated thereby taking on different values across groups. To initiate this labeling process, we first select the hypothesized model shown in Fig. 7.1 and then, using the Object Properties dialog box, begin the task of labeling the parameters of interest. Shown in Fig. 7.5 is the menu yielded through a right-click of the mouse, from which Object Properties is selected. More specifically, the Object Properties dialog box was triggered by first clicking on the second factor loading path (which then becomes highlighted in red), and then clicking on the right mouse button. Figure 7.6 illustrates the labeling of the first estimated parameter (p2), which represents the factor loading of MBI Item 2 on the factor of emotional exhaustion (EE).

Turning to Fig. 7.7, you see the hypothesized model of MBI structure, completely labeled, and ready for a statistical testing of the invariance of its factorial

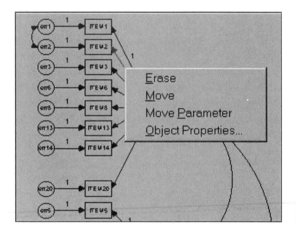

FIG. 7.5.   Selection of Object Properties via the mouse right-click.

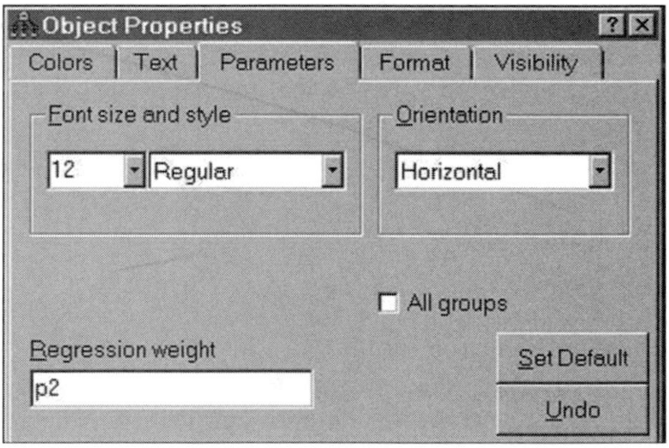

FIG. 7.6.   The Object Properties dialog box: labeling the parameters.

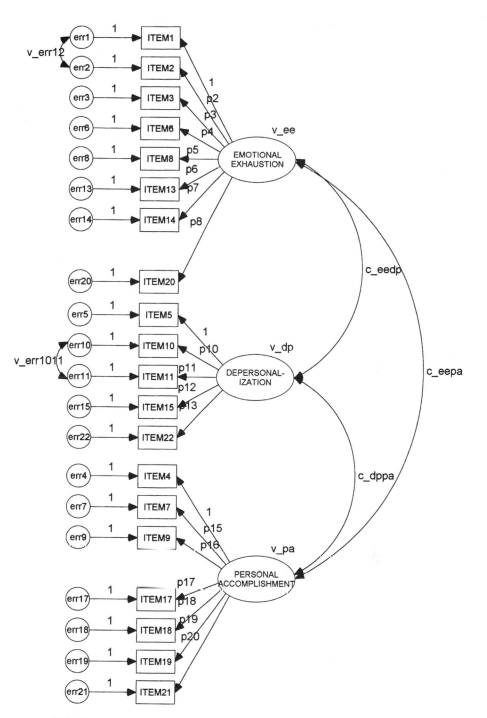

FIG. 7.7. Baseline model with equality constraints specified for factor loadings, variances and covariances, and in addition, two error covariances.

structure across the three panels of teachers. As labeled, this model specifies that (a) all factor loadings, (b) all factor variances, (c) all factor covariances, and (d) the two error covariances be constrained equal across elementary, intermediate, and secondary teachers. Although, in general, testing for the equality of error variances across groups is considered to be excessively stringent, I believe that testing related to the error covariances specified in the present context is well justified both statistically and substantively. I base this decision on the fact that, for each teacher group, the two error covariances were found to be excessively large. Scrutiny of the items associated with these error terms revealed highly overlapping content across each aberrant pair of items. Such redundancy can reflect itself in the form of error covariation, thereby offering support for the substantive rationale. Taking these two perspectives into account, it seems prudent to ascertain whether the two error covariance parameters hold across teaching panels.

Three aspects of Fig. 7.7 are worthy of particular note. First, selected labeling of parameters is purely arbitrary. In the present case, I chose to label the factor loading regression paths as p, the factor variances as v_, the factor covariances as c_, and the error covariances as v_err. Thus, for example, v_ee represents the variance of the Emotional Exhaustion factor, c_eepa represents the covariance between the factors of Emotional Exhaustion and Personal Accomplishment, v_err1011 represents the covariance between the error terms associated with items 10 and 11, and so on. Second, note that the value of 1.00, assigned to the first of each congeneric set of indicator variables (for purposes of identification), remains as such and has not been relabeled with a "p"; given that this parameter is already constrained to equal 1.00, its value will be constant across the three groups. Finally, the somewhat erratic labeling of the factor loading paths is a function of the automated labeling process provided by the program. Although, technically, it should be possible to shift these labels to a more appropriate location using the Move Parameters tool 🔍 (to be demonstrated in chap. 8), this transition does not seem to work well when there are several labeled parameters located in close proximity to one another, as is the case here. This malfunction would appear to be related to the restricted space allotment assigned to each parameter.

AMOS Text Output: Three-Group Model With Equality Constraints Imposed

Model Assessment

Goodness-of-Fit Statistics.   Goodness-of fit statistics related to this constrained three-group model are presented in Table 7.3. Of primary importance, however, is the χ^2 value, as it provides the basis of comparison with previously fitted models. In testing for the invariance of this constrained model, we compare its χ^2 value of 2344.752 (545 df) with that for the initial model in which no equality constraints were imposed ($\chi^2_{(495)} = 2243.21$). As noted earlier with single-group applications, when models are nested, this difference in χ^2 values (in large samples) is

TABLE 7.3

Selected AMOS Text Output for Test of Invariant Factor Loadings,
Variances, and Covariances: Goodness-of-Fit Statistics

Summary of models

Model	NPAR	CMIN	DF	P
Your model	85	2344.752	545	0.000
Saturated model	630	0.000	0	
Independence model	60	23811.283	570	0.000

Model	RMR	GFI	AGFI	PGFI
Your model	0.136	0.923	0.911	0.799
Saturated model	0.000	1.000		
Independence model	0.706	0.354	0.286	0.320

Model	DELTA1 NFI	RHO1 RFI	DELTA2 IFI	RHO2 TLI	CFI
Your model	0.902	0.897	0.923	0.919	0.923
Saturated model	1.000		1.000		1.000
Independence model	0.000	0.000	0.000	0.000	0.000

Model	PRATIO	PNFI	PCFI
Your model	0.956	0.862	0.882
Saturated model	0.000	0.000	0.000
Independence model	1.000	0.000	0.000

Model	RMSEA	LO 90	HI 90	PCLOSE
Your model	0.034	0.032	0.035	1.000
Independence model	0.118	0.117	0.119	0.000

Model	ECVI	LO 90	HI 90	MECVI
Your model	0.859	0.809	0.911	0.861
Saturated model	0.430	0.430	0.430	0.444
Independence model	8.173	8.002	8.347	0.175

distributed as χ^2, with degrees of freedom equal to the difference in degrees of free-dom. Given that the constrained model is nested within the initial model, we use this comparative procedure here. This comparison yields a χ^2 difference value of 101.54 with 50 degrees of freedom, which is statistically significant at the .05 probability level. Provided with this information, we now know that some equality constraints do not hold across the three teacher groups. From here on, all subsequent tests for invariance are designed to pinpoint the location of this noninvariance.

Two-Group Model With Equality Constraints Imposed:
Elementary Versus Intermediate Teachers

Given that we are working with three groups in the present application, one approach to this series of analyses is to determine, first, if the constrained model is possibly invariant across two of the three groups. To this end, the hypothesized model (with no equality constraints; Model 7.1) is once again estimated in order to establish a comparative base. However, in contrast to the previously estimated model, specification relates only to elementary and intermediate teachers.

In AMOS Graphics, any change in the number of groups to be included in an analysis is accomplished via the Manage Groups dialog box. Figures 7.8 through 7.10 illustrate this simple process when the drop-down menu is used. In the event that you have the tool palette exposed to the left of your screen as shown in Fig. 7.2, you need either to remove or to relocate this palette in order to see your list of groups. As illustrated in Fig. 7.8, removal of the palette is accomplished by simply clicking on the "Show Tools" option on the Tools drop-down menu. Figure 7.9 exhibits the "Manage Groups" option on the Model-fit drop-down menu, and Fig. 7.10 shows the list of groups. Secondary school teachers are deleted from the list by a simple highlighting and deletion process.

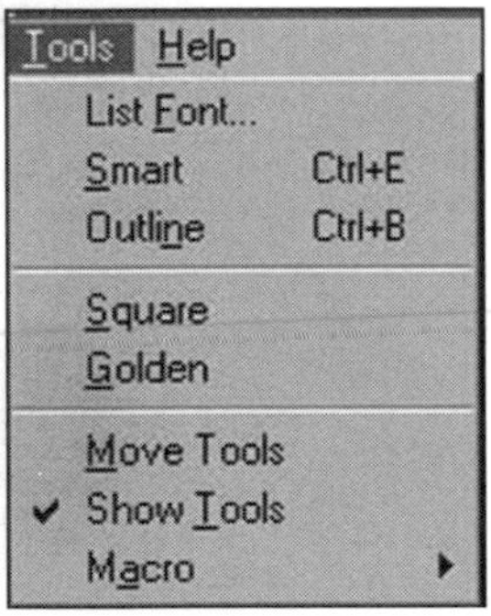

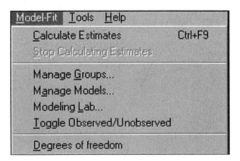

FIG. 7.8.   The Tools drop-down menu: removal of tool palette.

FIG. 7.9.   The Model-Fit drop-down menu: the Manage Groups option.

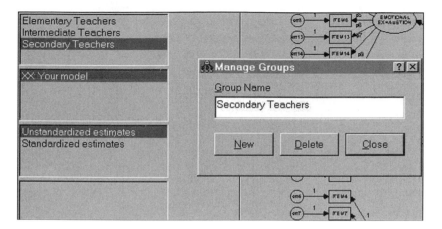

FIG. 7.10.   The Manage Groups dialog box: deletion of the secondary teacher group.

Model Assessment

Goodness-of-Fit Statistics.   Table 7.4 provides a summary of χ^2 values, and χ^2 difference values related to the series of analyses involved in testing for invariance. As such, the first entry shows the fit of the initially hypothesized model of MBI structure (Model 1) when tested simultaneously, although with no imposed equality constraints, across elementary, intermediate, and secondary teachers. Reported in the second entry, then, is the fit of Model 1 when equality constraints were specified; also reported is the difference in χ^2 value ($\Delta\chi^2$) related to its comparison with the unconstrained model. The next two entries bear on the testing of Model 1a (with no equality constraints imposed) for elementary and intermediate teachers and on its comparison with the related constrained model.[5] As you can readily observe, this comparison of models was not statistically significant. Given this finding, we conclude that all factor loadings, variances, and covariances, in addition to the two error covariances, are invariant across elementary and intermediate teachers. As a consequence, any inequality of parameters across the three groups of teachers, as determined in our first two tests for invariance, and to be determined in subsequent tests for invariance, must logically lie between secondary teachers and their elementary/intermediate school counterparts.

Two-Group Model With Equality Constraints Imposed: Elementary/Intermediate Versus Secondary Teachers

Having established the equality of measurement and structure between elementary and intermediate teachers, the next step in the process involves testing for the equivalence of factor loadings across the three panels of teachers. In using AMOS

---

[5]This multigroup model has been labeled Model 1a to distinguish it from the original multigroup model that included the three teacher groups.

TABLE 7.4
Goodness-of-Fit Statistics for Tests of Invariance: A Summary

Model Description	Groups	Comparative Model	χ^2	df	$\Delta\chi^2$	Δdf	Statistical Significance
1. Hypothesized model (Model 1)	Elementary/intermediate, secondary	—	2243.21	495	—	—	—
2. Factor loadings, variances, and covariances constrained equal	Elementary/intermediate, secondary	Model 1	2344.75	545	101.54	50	$p < .05$
3. Model 1(a)	Elementary/intermediate	—	1246.24	330	—	—	—
4. Factor loadings, variances, and covariances constrained equal	Elementary/intermediate	Model 1 (a)	1282.18	355	35.94	25	NS
5. Factor loadings constrained equal	Elementary/intermediate, secondary	Model 1	2302.26	529	59.05	34	$p < .05$
6. Factor loadings on EE constrained equal (Model 2)	Elementary/intermediate, secondary	Model 1	2248.46	509	31.55	14	NS
7. Model 2 with factor loadings on DP constrained equal	Elementary/intermediate, secondary	Model 2	2276.27	517	27.81	8	$p < .01$

Model	Group	Comparison model	χ^2	df	$\Delta\chi^2$	Δdf	p
8. Model 2 with factor loading of Item 10 on DP constrained equal	Elementary/intermediate, secondary	Model 2	2248.93	511	0.47	2	NS
9. Model 2 with factor loadings of items 10 and 11 on DP constrained equal	Elementary/intermediate, secondary	Model 2	2260.66	513	12.20	4	$p < .05$
10. Model 2 with factor loadings of items 10, 11, and 15 on DP constrained equal	Elementary/intermediate, secondary	Model 2	2262.39	513	13.93	4	$p < .01$
11. Model 2 with factor loadings of items 10, 11, and 22 on DP constrained equal	Elementary/intermediate, secondary	Model 2	2251.08	513	2.62	4	NS
12. Model 3 with factor loadings on PA constrained equal	Elementary/intermediate, secondary	Model 3	2277.08	525	26.00	12	$p < .05$

Note. $\Delta\chi^2$, Difference in χ^2 values between models; Δdf, difference in number of degrees of freedom between models; EE, Emotional Exhaustion: DP, Depersonalization; PA, Personal Accomplishment.

Graphics, this necessarily means that a modification of the fully constrained model shown in Fig. 7.7 must be made in order to initiate this change in specification. Specifically, we need to erase all labels, except those representing equality-constrained parameters to be included in any particular analysis.

In testing for multigroup invariance, it is best to establish a logically organized strategy. The general scheme to be followed here is that we test first for the invariance of all factor loadings (i.e., all elements of the factor loading matrix). Given findings of noninvariance at this level, we then proceed to test for the invariance of all factor loadings comprising each subscale (i.e., all loadings related to the one particular factor), separately. Given evidence of noninvariance at the subscale level, we then test for the invariance of each factor loading (related to the factor in question), separately. Of import in this process is that, as factor loading parameters are found to be invariant across groups, their specified equality constraints are retained, cumulatively, throughout the remainder of the invariance-testing process.

Turning to our task of testing for the invariance of the MBI across three panels of teachers, we begin first by testing for the invariance of factor loadings related to all three factors: emotional exhaustion, depersonalization, and personal accomplishment. One approach to the specification of this model, in AMOS Graphics, is to simply modify the initial invariance model in which all factor loadings, variances, and covariances were constrained equal across groups (see Fig. 7.7). As such, we remove all parameter labels, except those associated with factor loadings. This task is easily accomplished by clicking on each label (to be deleted), right-clicking in order to trigger the Object Properties dialog box, and then deleting the label listed in the parameter rectangle (of the dialog box). Proceeding in this manner will result in the labeled model displayed in Fig. 7.11; all unlabeled parameters will be freely estimated for each of the three groups.

Turning to Table 7.4, we see that testing of the model displayed in Fig. 7.11 yielded a χ^2 value of 2302.26 with 529 degrees of freedom; comparison with Model 1 yielded a $\Delta\chi^2$ value of 59.05 with 34 degrees of freedom, which was statistically significant at the .05 probability level. In order to pinpoint the nonequivalent factor loadings, the next step is to test for invariance relative to each factor separately. Accordingly, the labels for Factor 2 (depersonalization) and Factor 3 (personal accomplishment) were erased, leaving only those associated with Factor 1 (emotional exhaustion). Results related to this test of invariance, as indicated in Table 7.4, revealed all factor loadings to be equivalent across elementary/intermediate and secondary teachers.[6]

Having established the equivalence of factor loadings related to emotional exhaustion, these constraints are held in place while proceeding next to test for the invariance of the factor loadings on the Depersonalization factor. As such, model

---

[6]For purposes of simplicity in describing subsequent invariance models to be tested, I label this model as Model 2. As such, it eliminates the need to specify these constraints repeatedly for each of the models that follow.

specification in the next round of analyses, using AMOS Graphics, would have all factor loadings labeled for both Factor 1 and Factor 2. Turning once again to Table 7.4, we see that this test of invariance was statistically significant ($p < .01$), thereby signaling some discrepancy in the measurement of depersonalization between elementary/intermediate teachers and their secondary school peers. In other words, one or more items in this subscale is noninvariant across the groups; the task now is to pinpoint these noninvariant items.

We begin this search by first removing all labels associated with Factor 2, except the one associated with the first estimated parameter (Item 10; p10). It is perhaps important to reconfirm that, given the invariance of all items in the emotional exhaustion factor subscale, the labeling of all factor loadings linked to Factor 1 remain intact (hence the description as Model 2, with the factor loading of Item 10 on depersonalization constrained equal). The specification of this revised model is displayed graphically in Fig. 7.12.

As reported in Table 7.4, the test for invariance related to this first factor loading parameter (Item 10) was nonsignificant, thereby indicating its equality across groups. This orderly process of testing for the invariance of parameters is continued until all targeted parameters have been tested. It is important to remember that as parameters are found to be invariant, equality constraints related to these parameters are cumulatively held in place thereby providing a very rigorous test of equality across groups. As you can readily note in Table 7.4, the results from this series of tests bearing on Factor 2 revealed only the factor loadings associated with Item 10 (p10) and Item 22 (p13) to be group-invariant. For purposes of further comparisons involving the personal accomplishment factor (as explicated earlier for comparisons related to the depersonalization factor), I choose to label this model as Model 3.

Having now established invariance related to the factor loadings for Factors 1 and 2, the next logical step would be to test for the invariance of all factor loadings related to personal accomplishment. Specification of this model is graphically displayed in Fig. 7.13. In reviewing this model, note labels associated with (a) all factor loadings associated with emotional exhaustion, (b) only those associated with Items 10 (p10) and 22 (p13) for depersonalization,[7] and (c) all factor loadings associated with personal accomplishment. As indicated by their explicit labeling, factor loadings associated with emotional exhaustion and depersonalization have been found to be group-invariant; those associated with personal accomplishment are yet to be tested.

Results related to testing for the invariance of factor loadings related to Personal Accomplishment, as can be seen in Table 7.4, indicate that certain items in this scale are not invariant across elementary/intermediate and secondary teachers. The course of action to be followed is to pinpoint these noninvariant items, as has been

---

[7]Here again, the label associated with the loading of Item 22 (p13) on Depersonalization is misplaced; it could not be moved using the Move Parameter tool.

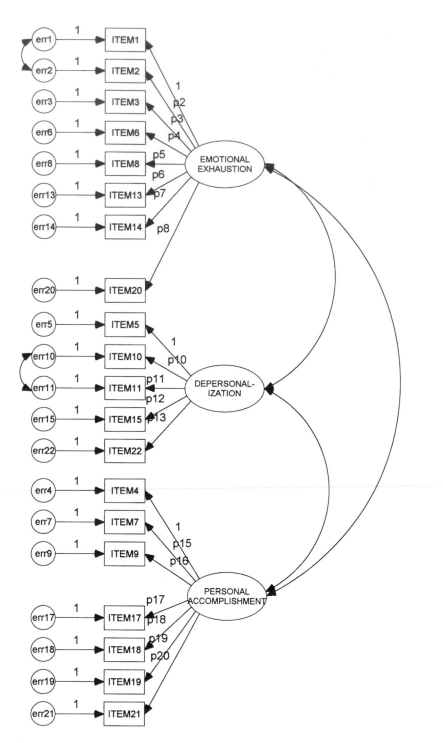

FIG. 7.11. Baseline model with equality constraints specified for all factor loadings.

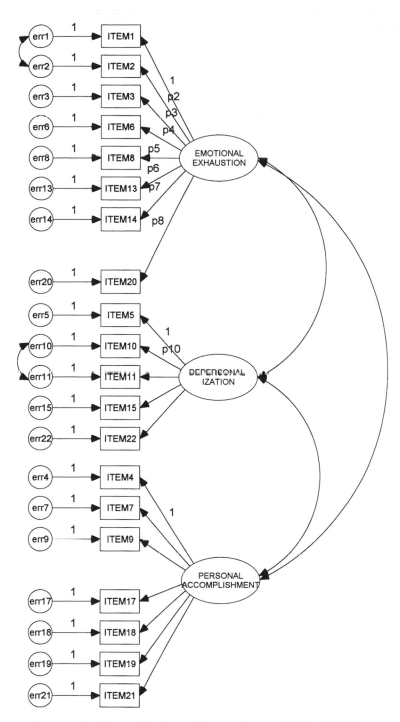

FIG. 7.12.   Baseline model with equality constraints specified for all loadings on Factor 1 and one loading for Factor 2.

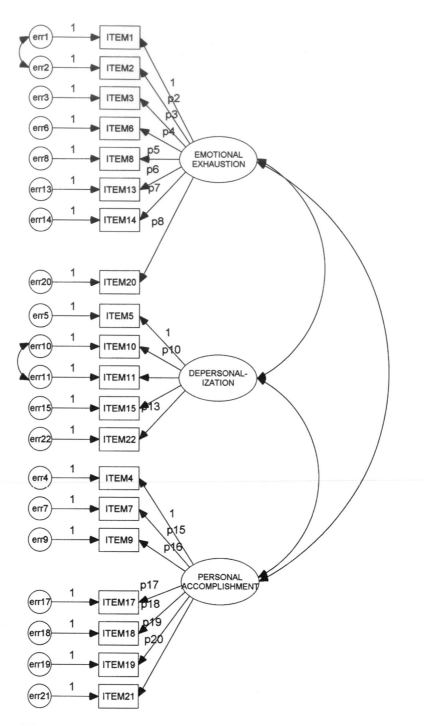

FIG. 7.13. Baseline model with equality constraints specified for all loadings on Factor 1, two of five loadings for Factor 2, and all loadings on Factor 3.

previously demonstrated. This process would be continued until all targeted parameters of interest have been tested. Once all tests for invariance related to the measurement model have been completed, one would next focus on the structural model. That is to say, one would test first for the equivalence of the two error covariances, and then for the equivalence of the three factor covariances. Due to the necessary limitation of space in describing these procedures, the latter tests of invariance are not detailed here. However, hopefully, sufficient material has been presented in this application to give you an adequate understanding of the ordered process involved.

MODELING WITH AMOS BASIC

The example AMOS Basic file to be presented in this chapter is the input file counterpart to the fully labeled baseline model displayed in Fig. 7.7; this input file is shown in Table 7.5.

TABLE 7.5

AMOS Basic Input File for Test of MBI Invariance Across
Elementary, Intermediate, and Secondary Teachers

Sub Main
Dim Sem As New AmosEngine
'Testing for Invariance of MBI Structure Across Elementary, Intermediate, and Secondary Teachers'

SEM.TextOutput

SEM.BeginGroup "cvelm.txt"
  SEM.GroupName "Elementary Teachers"

  SEM.Structure "ITEM1 ←EMOTIONAL EXHAUSTION (1)"
  SEM.Structure " ITEM2 ←EMOTIONAL EXHAUSTION (p2)"
  SEM.Structure " ITEM3 ←EMOTIONAL EXHAUSTION (p3)"
  SEM.Structure " ITEM6 ←EMOTIONAL EXHAUSTION (p4)"
  SEM.Structure " ITEM8 ←EMOTIONAL EXHAUSTION (p5)"
  SEM.Structure " ITEM13 ←EMOTIONAL EXHAUSTION (p6)"
  SEM.Structure " ITEM14 ←EMOTIONAL EXHAUSTION (p7)"
  SEM.Structure " ITEM20 ←EMOTIONAL EXHAUSTION (p8)"
  SEM.Structure "ITEM5 ←DEPERSONALIZATION (1)"
  SEM.Structure " ITEM10 ←DEPERSONALIZATION (p10)"
  SEM.Structure " ITEM11 ←DEPERSONALIZATION (p11)"
  SEM.Structure " ITEM15 ←DEPERSONALIZATION (p12)"
  SEM.Structure " ITEM22 ←DEPERSONALIZATION (p13)"
  SEM.Structure "ITEM4 ←PERSONAL ACCOMPLISHMENT (1)"
  SEM.Structure " ITEM7 ←PERSONAL ACCOMPLISHMENT (p15)"
  SEM.Structure " ITEM9 ←PERSONAL ACCOMPLISHMENT (p16)"
  SEM.Structure " ITEM17 ←PERSONAL ACCOMPLISHMENT (p17)"
  SEM.Structure " ITEM18 ←PERSONAL ACCOMPLISHMENT (p18)"
  SEM.Structure " ITEM19 ←PERSONAL ACCOMPLISHMENT (p19)"
  SEM.Structure " ITEM21 ←PERSONAL ACCOMPLISHMENT (p20)"

(Continued)

TABLE 7.5 *(Continued)*

SEM.Structure "ITEM1 ←err1 (1)"
SEM.Structure "ITEM2 ←err2 (1)"
SEM.Structure "ITEM3 ←err3 (1)"
SEM.Structure "ITEM6 ←err6 (1)"
SEM.Structure "ITEM8 ←err8 (1)"
SEM.Structure "ITEM13 ←err13 (1)"
SEM.Structure "ITEM14 ←err14 (1)"
SEM.Structure "ITEM20 ←err20 (1)"
SEM.Structure "ITEM5 ←err5 (1)"
SEM.Structure "ITEM10 ←err10 (1)"
SEM.Structure "ITEM11 ←err11 (1)"
SEM.Structure "ITEM15 ←err15 (1)"
SEM.Structure "ITEM22 ←err22 (1)"
SEM.Structure "ITEM4 ←err4 (1)"
SEM.Structure "ITEM7 ←err7 (1)"
SEM.Structure "ITEM9 ←err9 (1)"
SEM.Structure "ITEM17 ←err17 (1)"
SEM.Structure "ITEM18 ←err18 (1)"
SEM.Structure "ITEM19 ←err19 (1)"
SEM.Structure "ITEM21 ←err21 (1)"

SEM.Structure " Emotional Exhaustion (v_ee)"
SEM.Structure " Depersonalization (v_dp"
SEM.Structure " Personal Accomplishment (v_pa)"

SEM.Structure " Emotional Exhaustion ↔ Depersonalization (v_eedp)"
SEM.Structure " Emotional Exhaustion ↔ Personal Accomplishment (v_eepa)"
SEM.Structure " Depersonalization ↔ Personal Accomplishment (v_dppa)"
SEM.Structure " err1 ↔ err2 (v_e12)"
SEM.Structure " err5 ↔ err15 (v_e515)"

SEM.BeginGroup "cvint.txt"
  SEM.GroupName "Intermediate Teachers"

File Input repeated as above

SEM.BeginGroup "cvsec.txt"
  SEM.GroupName "Secondary Teachers"

File Input repeated as above

End Sub

Given that you are now familiar with the general format of the AMOS Basic input file, we focus our attention on aspects of its structure relevant to a multigroup application. In this regard, I wish to highlight three features of the file. First, note that there are three distinct sections to the file, each pertinent to one group of teachers. As such, each section identifies the data file to be used and the name of the related group. Second, note that, despite the same model specification across

groups (as is the case here), the input file must include a replication of this specification for each group separately.[8] This aspect of the AMOS Basic input file is in
direct contrast to AMOS Graphics whereby the model is graphically specified for
the first group and, by default, remains identically specified for all additional
groups in the analysis. Finally, you will quickly note that the parenthesized charac-
ter labels are consistent with those shown in Fig. 7.7 and represent parameters to
be constrained in some manner or another. The 1's represent parameters fixed to a
value of 1.00; the others represent parameters to be constrained equal across
groups. The value assigned to the latter is the parameter estimate obtained for the
first group (elementary teachers).

---

[8]Due to limitations of space, these replicated specifications are not included here.

CHAPTER 8

Application 6:
Testing for Invariant
Factorial Structure
of a Theoretical Construct
(First-Order CFA Model)

❧

$\mathbf{I}$n our second multigroup application, we test hypotheses related to the equivalencies of self-concept measurement and structure across male and female high school adolescents. In particular, we wish to determine if multidimensional facets of self-concept (general, academic, English, mathematics), and the subscale scores from multiple assessment instruments used to measure these constructs, are equivalent across gender for this population. This application is taken from a study by Byrne and Shavelson (1987) as a follow-up to their earlier work that validated the structure of self-concept for high school adolescents in general (Byrne & Shavelson, 1986).

TESTING FOR INVARIANCE ACROSS GENDER

The Hypothesized Model

The model upon which the application illustrated in the present chapter was originally based (Byrne & Shavelson, 1987) derived from an earlier construct validity study of adolescent self-concept structure (Byrne & Shavelson, 1986). In particular, the model argued for a four-factor structure comprising general self-concept, academic self-concept, English self-concept, and mathematics self-concept, with the four constructs assumed to be intercorrelated. A schematic representation of this model is shown in Fig. 8.1.

Except for academic self-concept, each of the other dimensions is measured by three independent measures. In the case of academic self-concept, findings from a preliminary factor analysis of the Affective Perception Inventory (Soares & Soares, 1979) revealed several inadequacies in its measurement of the construct, and thus it was deleted from all subsequent analyses. It was originally hypothesized that each subscale measure would have a nonzero loading on the self-concept factor it

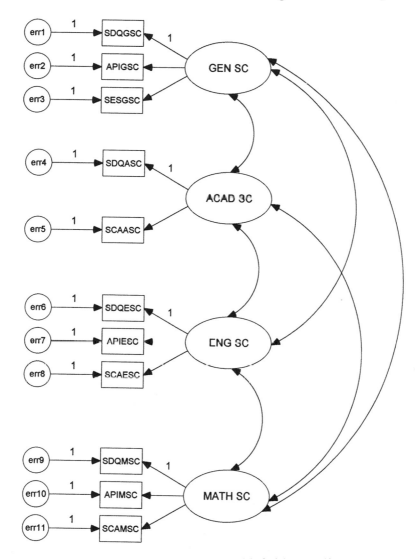

FIG. 8.1.   Hypothesized four-factor model of adolescent self-concept.

was designed to measure, and a zero loading on all other factors; error/unique-nesses associated with each of the measures were assumed to be uncorrelated. Relations among the four self-concept facets represent the structural model to be tested for its equivalency across groups.

At issue in the Byrne and Shavelson (1987) study was whether the structure of self-concept, and the instruments used in measuring components of this structure, as depicted in Fig. 8.1, were equivalent across adolescent males and females. Of primary import, then, was the invariance of both the measurement and structural models.

The Baseline Models

As noted in chapter 7, prior to testing for invariance across multigroup samples, it is customary to first establish baseline models separately, for each group under study. The baseline self-concept models for adolescent males and females, as reported by Byrne and Shavelson (1987), are shown in Fig. 8.2; these models provide the central focus of the present chapter.

In fitting the baseline model for each gender, Byrne and Shavelson (1987) reported a substantial drop in χ^2 when the English self-concept subscale (SDQESC) of the Self Description Questionnaire III (SDQIII; Marsh, 1992b) was free to cross-load onto the general SC factor. Moreover, for males only, the mathematics SC subscale of the SDQ III (SDQMSC) was allowed to cross-load onto the English SC factor. Finally, based on their substantial size and substantive reasonableness, five error covariances were included in the baseline model for males, and three in the baseline model for females. (In the interest of clarity, the two additional error covariances, for males, are not included here.) With these specifications in place, these models were considered optimal in representing the data for adolescent males and females. Overall fit of the male model was $\chi^2_{(33)} = 86.07$, with a GFI of .97 and CFI of .98; for the female model, it was $\chi^2_{(34)} = 77.30$, with a GFI of .97 and a CFI of .99.

In testing for the invariance of self-concept across gender, we consider the equivalence of its structure with respect to three issues: (a) that the number of underlying factors is equivalent, (b) that the pattern of factor loadings, including the common cross-loading, is equivalent, and (c) that structural relations among the four facets of self-concept are equivalent.[1]

MODELING WITH AMOS GRAPHICS

Testing for the Validity of a Four-Factor Structure

As I noted in the previous chapter with respect to the structure of burnout, testing that self-concept structure is best described by a four-factor structure for both adolescent girls and boys is a logical starting point in tests for invariance when using

---

[1]Given that the testing of equality constraints bearing on error variances and covariances is now considered to be excessively stringent, these analyses were not conducted.

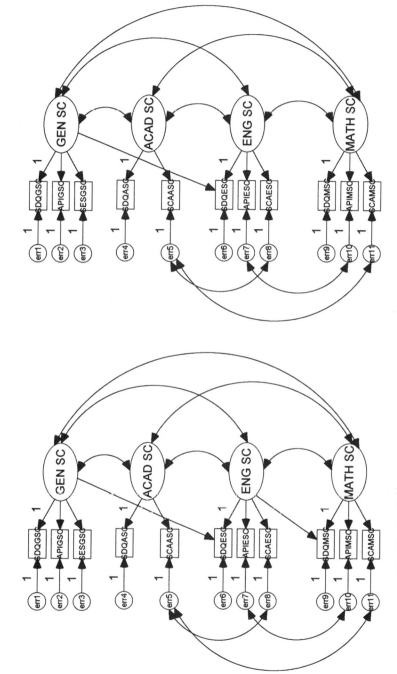

FIG. 8.2. Baseline models of self-concept for adolescent males and females. Adapted from Byrne, B. M., and Shavelson, R. J. (1987). Adolescent self-concept: Testing the assumption of equivalent structure across gender. *American Educational Research Journal, 24*, pp. 365–385 (Figure 1, p. 374), Copyright (1987) by the American Educational Research Association. Adapted by permission of the publisher.

the univariate approach employed in the AMOS (and LISREL) program. This initial test differs from the rest in that no equality constraints are specified across groups. Rather, the tenability of the hypothesized structure rests on the overall goodness of fit of the models displayed in Fig. 8.2, with a satisfactory fit arguing for an equivalent number of factors to best represent the data across groups. Because χ^2 statistics are summative when no equality constraints are imposed, the overall value for the multigroup model will equal the sum of this statistic for each group; accordingly, the χ^2 value for adolescent males and females was 163.362 with 67 degrees of freedom.[2] This χ^2 value provides the cutpoint against which all subsequent models will be compared in the series of tests to determine evidence of group invariance.

Before moving on to these subsequent tests for invariance, however, let's go back and review again the baseline models under study (Fig. 8.2). Turning first to specifications for adolescent males, we see that, over and above the initially hypothesized model, there are two cross-loadings, in addition to three error covariances.[3] By way of contrast, specifications for adolescent females include only one cross-loading, although with the same three error covariances. Thus, prior to testing for invariance, we already know that one parameter is different across the two groups. As such, this parameter is estimated freely for males, and is not constrained equal across males and females. With the exception of this parameter, then, all remaining estimated parameters can be tested for their invariance across groups. This situation serves as an excellent example of what is termed *partial measurement invariance* (see Byrne, Shavelson, & Muthén, 1989).

The models submitted for analysis are the baseline models for adolescent males and females shown in Fig. 8.2. As demonstrated in chapter 7, before conducting the simultaneous estimation of baseline models using AMOS Graphics, you need first to identify for the program the name of each group, together with its related data file; this procedure is not included again here. However, the fact that there are differential numbers of estimated parameters for males and females in the present application makes the testing for invariance less straightforward than was illustrated in chapter 7 where the baseline model was identical across groups. Because only one model can be submitted for analysis at any one time, we must determine which baseline model (male or female) will be specified. Given that the baseline model for males contains the additional parameter, this is the model of choice for reasons that become evident as we walk through the process. Accordingly, the fully constrained (i.e., labeled) model to be tested for invariance is displayed in Fig. 8.3.

Within the AMOS Graphics framework, two possible strategies may be used in specifying a constrained multigroup model in which the baseline model differs

---

[2]Recall, however, that this sum will be exact in AMOS analyses, if and only if the option 'Emulisrel6' has been selected on the Estimation tab of View/Set → Analysis Properties.

[3]Provided with evidence of excellent fit related to a model, for males, that included only the three error covariances common to both groups (see Table 8.5), the two additional error covariances specified in the original Byrne and Shavelson (1987) study were ignored.

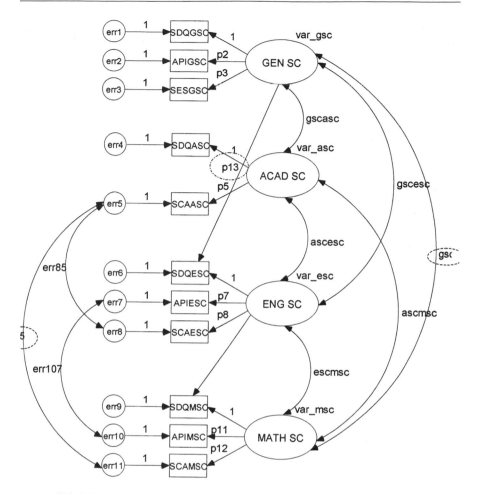

FIG. 8.3.   Model to be tested for invariance across gender with program-automated labeling.

across groups; these model-testing approaches are of central interest in this chapter. However, before turning to this topic, I wish first to demonstrate a few features of the AMOS Graphics interface that can be helpful in the drawing and labeling of models. For demonstration purposes, let's review Fig. 8.3 where we can see that (a) the label associated with the cross-loading of SDQESC on the GEN SC factor (p13) is misplaced (shown within a broken-line oval), and (b) some of the labels associated with the error covariances extend beyond the perimeter of the diagram. As an initial step in rectifying this problem, we request that the figure be displayed such that it fits the page; this modification is accomplished simply by pulling down the Edit Menu, as shown in Fig. 8.4, and selecting the Fit-to-Page option, or by

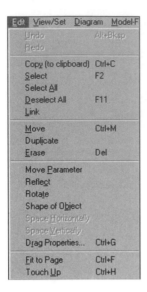

FIG. 8.4.   The AMOS Graphics Edit menu.

clicking on the Fit-to Page icon ⊡. Either action reduces the size of the figure to the one shown in Fig. 8.5.

Although the reduced version of Fig. 8.3 results in further distortion of labels, this is of no consequence as the figure will be returned to its original size, once the labels of interest have been realigned. Shown in Fig. 8.6 is the process involved in the correction of the p13 label. To move this label to a more appropriate position, we can either highlight the Move Parameter icon ⬙, or alternatively pull down the Edit Menu and make the same selection. Once you have either highlighted the icon or selected the Move Parameter option, you then need to select the parameter of interest, which in this case is the cross-loading labeled p13; as the mouse passes over parameter p13, both the label and parameter will be highlighted in red (indicating their selection). To move the parameter, simply drag the label to its new location as shown in Fig. 8.7. Similarly, we can move the two error covariances such that their labels are now within the curvature of the double-headed arrow. The final version of the hypothesized multigroup model (see Fig. 8.3) is presented in Fig. 8.8.

Having fine-tuned the labeling of the model to be tested, we turn to the issue of tailoring this model to both the male and female adolescent groups. As noted earlier, there are two approaches that can be used with AMOS Graphics. One strategy works from a *specification perspective* and calls for the additional cross-loading to be constrained to 0.00 for females, but freely estimated for males. The alternative strategy works from a *macro level* and requests the program to allow a different path diagram for each group. We turn, first, to the specification approach.

To modify the specification of a model in a multigroup analysis such that a parameter is constrained in some way for only one of the groups, we need to iden-

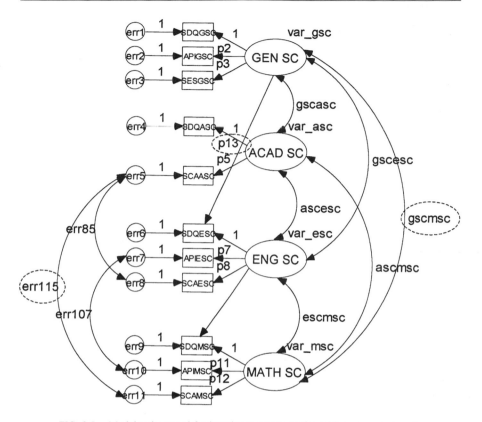

FIG. 8.5.   Model to be tested for invariance across gender, with program-automated labeling, reduced in size to fit the page.

tify two pieces of information for the program: (a) the value to which we wish to constrain the parameter, and (b) the group for which the parameter is to be constrained. This information is easily transmitted via the Object Properties and the Manage Groups dialog boxes. In essence, however, one need not even bother with the latter as the group names are automatically listed by the program in multigroup analyses; these appear to the left of the screen. Figure 8.9 shows the Object Properties dialog box that would appear after having right-clicked with the mouse on the cross-loading in question; the regression weight value has been set at 0.0. Observe, also, that the All Groups box has not been selected. Relatedly, note that, in Fig. 8.10, (a) a value of zero has been assigned to the cross-loading parameter, and (b) in the list of groups to the left of the screen, Females has been highlighted. For clarification, it is important to point out that, in order for the zero value to be assigned to the parameter only for females, this group must be highlighted prior to fixing the value. Thus, if we were to highlight "Males," we would see the same model, but with no zero value associated with the cross-loading parameter.

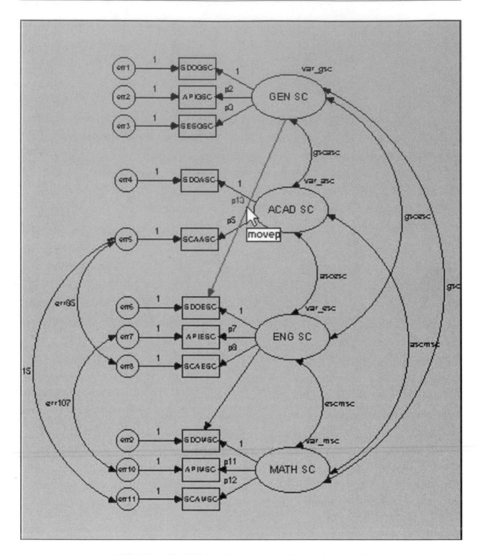

FIG. 8.6.   Highlighting the parameter value to be moved.

We turn now to the second approach to model modification, whereby the program allows the groups to have different path diagrams. To initiate this strategy, we make use of the Interface Properties dialog box, which is accessed either by clicking on its icon ▦ , or by pulling down the View/Set menu as shown in Fig. 8.11. Several choices are available within the Interface Properties dialog box, as you can readily observe in Fig. 8.12. The one of interest to us now is the Miscellaneous option. In particular, our interest is in selecting the boxed option listed at the bottom whereby different path diagrams are allowed for different groups.

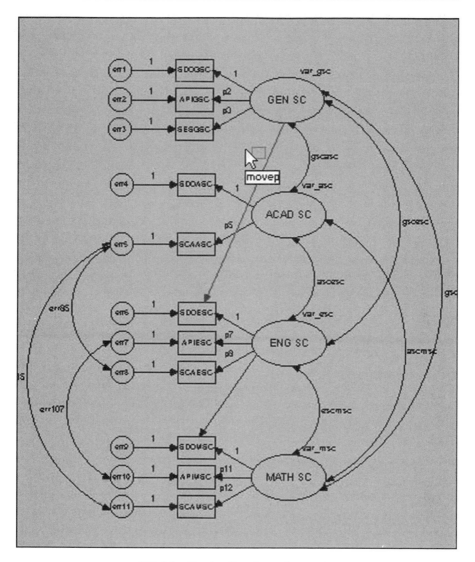

FIG. 8.7.   New location of moved parameter.

One peculiarity associated with the selection of this differential path diagram option is that it automatically triggers the warning message displayed in Fig. 8.13. Although you may feel a pang of anxiety about continuing on after having been confronted with this caveat, you must answer "yes" if you wish to use this option. Having responded in the affirmative, the model displayed, at any point in the analysis, will be consistent with the group highlighted to its left. For example, in Fig. 8.14, the model displayed relates to the female group; note the omission of a path leading from

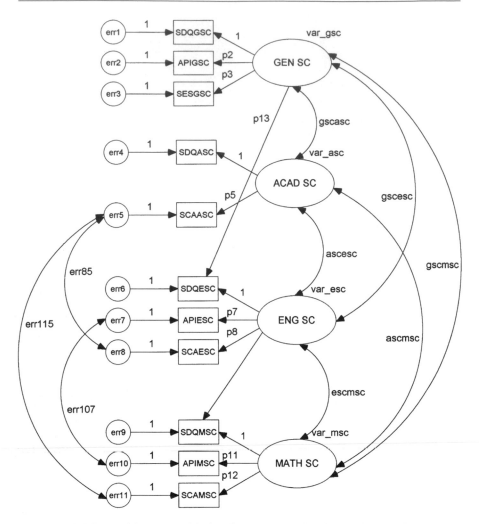

FIG. 8.8.   Model to be tested for invariance across gender with modified labeling.

SDQMSC to the ENG SC factor. On the other hand, if we were to display the model related to the male group, we would observe this path in the diagram.

Testing for the Invariance of Self-Concept Structure: The Specification of Equality Constraints

Once this differential multigroup model has been established, using either of the two strategies just outlined, it can then be tested for its invariance across adolescent males and females. For purposes of this book, I chose to assign a value of zero to

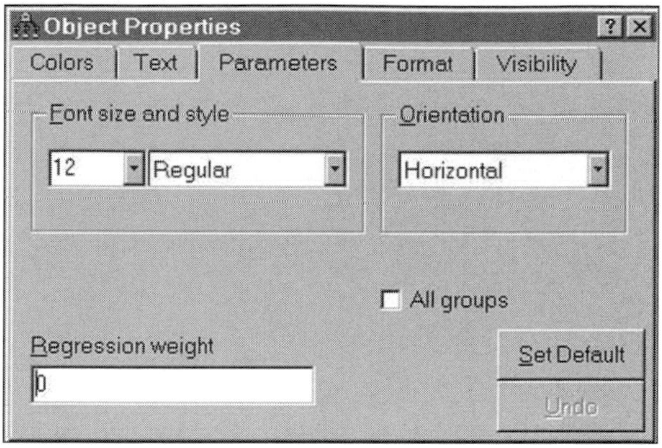

FIG. 8.9. The AMOS Graphics Object Properties dialog box showing assignment of 0 to regression weight.

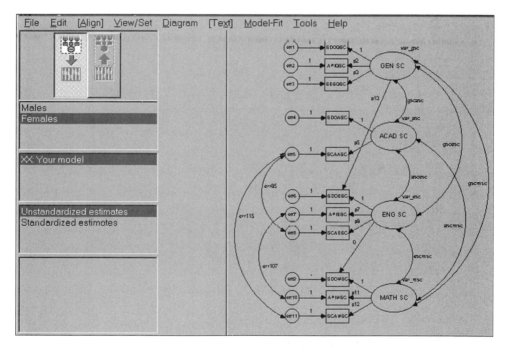

FIG. 8.10. List of group names with the female group selected.

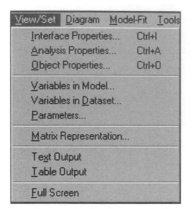

FIG. 8.11. The AMOS Graphics View/Set menu.

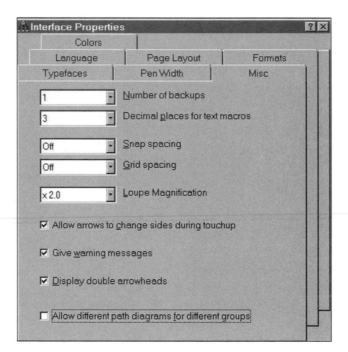

FIG. 8.12. The AMOS Graphics Interface Properties dialog box.

the male-specific cross-loading in specifying the model for females. Because it is always possible (although highly improbable) that all parameters of interest comprising both the measurement and structural models may be invariant across males and females, we can test, first, for the validity of this omnibus test, which is based on the fully constrained model shown in Fig. 8.8. We turn now to the results of this initial test of the constrained model.

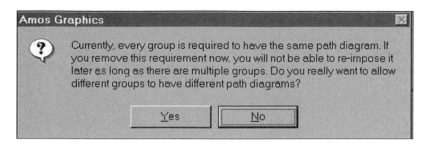

FIG. 8.13.   An AMOS Graphics warning message.

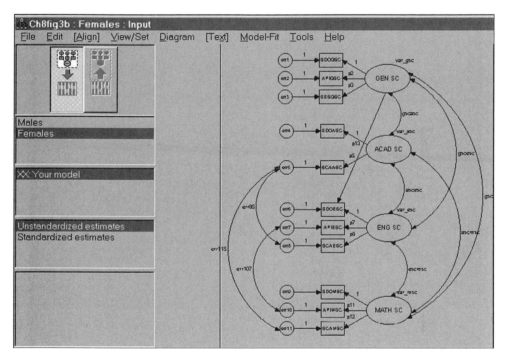

FIG. 8.14.   List of group names with the female group selected.

AMOS Text Output: Two-Group Model
With Equality Constraints Imposed

In reviewing selected portions of the output file related to the initial test of all measurement and structural parameters of interest, I believe it may be helpful if we once again examine the model summary information provided by the program and presented in Table 8.1. First of all, we see that, for both males and females, there are 26

TABLE 8.1

Males

```
          Number of variables in your model:   26
          Number of observed variables:        11
          Number of unobserved variables:      15
          Number of exogenous variables:       15
          Number of endogenous variables:      11
```

Summary of Parameters

	Weights	Covariances	Variances	Means	Intercepts	Total
Fixed:	15	0	0	0	0	15
Labeled:	8	9	4	0	0	21
Unlabeled:	1	0	11	0	0	12
Total:	24	9	15	0	0	48

The model is recursive.

Sample size: 412

Females

```
          Number of variables in your model:   26
          Number of observed variables:        11
          Number of unobserved variables:      15
          Number of exogenous variables:       15
          Number of endogenous variables:      11
```

Summary of Parameters

	Weights	Covariances	Variances	Means	Intercepts	Total
Fixed:	16	0	0	0	0	16
Labeled:	8	9	4	0	0	21
Unlabeled:	0	0	11	0	0	11
Total:	24	9	15	0	0	48

The model is recursive.

Sample size: 420

Computation of Degrees of Freedom

```
          Number of distinct sample moments:          132
Number of distinct parameters to be estimated:         44
                                            ------------------------
                                 Degrees of freedom:     88
```

variables in the model. Eleven of these variables are observed (i.e., the 11 subscale scores) and 15 are unobserved (i.e., the 4 SC factors and the 11 measurement errors).

Let's turn next to the Summary of Parameters section pertinent to both males and females. In the first column, which summarizes the weights (i.e., regression paths), we see that, for males, there are 15 that are fixed (11 measurement error; 4 factor loadings), 8 that are labeled (7 factor loadings; 1 factor cross-loading), and 1 that is unlabeled (the cross-loading specific to only males). The 8 labeled weights, of course, represent parameters that are constrained equal across the two groups. In contrast, although the total number of weights and the number of labeled weights remains the same for females, the number of fixed weights is 16, rather than 15, and the number of unlabeled weights is zero. The additional fixed weight, for females, represents the constraint of 0.0 assigned to the male-specific cross-loading; as a consequence of this constraint, there are no unlabeled regression paths. All remaining entries in this summary table are identical across males and females. As such, there are 9 labeled covariances (6 factor covariances; 3 error covariances), 4 labeled variances (4 factor variances), and 11 unlabeled variances (11 measurement error variances). In total, then, there are 48 parameters in the model for each group.

Finally, we can see from this summary information that the sample size for males is 412, and for females is 420, and that estimation of this multigroup model will yield a χ^2 value having 88 degrees of freedom. Given that the computation of degrees of freedom has been detailed elsewhere in the book prior to this chapter, it is not covered here.

Model Assessment

Goodness-of-Fit Statistics. Table 8.2 presents a summary of the goodness-of-fit statistics associated with this fully constrained multigroup model. As you can note, the model is extremely well-fitting as reflected by the CFI value of .979 and RMSEA value of .043. However, the key statistic of interest in this table is the χ^2 value of 224.551 (88 df), as it provides the basis for determining the extent to which the postulated model is equivalent across adolescent males and females. Accordingly, comparison of this model with the original unconstrained model yields a χ^2 difference value of 61.189 with 21 degrees of freedom, which is statistically significant at the .001 probability level. Presented with these findings, our next task is to locate the nonequivalent parameters in the model. As demonstrated in chapter 7, this process involves a series of logically ordered tests for invariance. However, before reviewing the results of these tests, I wish to point out the difference in maximum-likelihood estimates between males and females with respect to the male-specific cross-loading. We turn now to this portion of the AMOS text output.

Parameter Estimates. Presented in Table 8.3 are the maximum likelihood estimates for both groups of adolescents relative to the fully constrained model shown in Figs. 8.3 and 8.8. Of import here is the fact that the output is consistent

TABLE 8.2

Selected AMOS Text Output for Test of Invariant Self-Concept Structure: Goodness-of-Fit Statistics

Summary of models

- - - - - - - - - - - - - - - - -

Model	NPAR	CMIN	DF	P
Your model	44	224.551	88	0.000
Saturated model	132	0.000	0	
Independence model	22	6465.415	110	0.000

Model	RMR	GFI	AGFI	PGFI
Your model	9.549	0.954	0.932	0.636
Saturated model	0.000	1.000		
Independence model	40.185	0.369	0.243	0.308

Model	DELTA1 NFI	RHO1 RFI	DELTA2 IFI	RHO2 TLI	CFI
Your model	0.965	0.957	0.979	0.973	0.979
Saturated model	1.000		1.000		1.000
Independence model	0.000	0.000	0.000	0.000	0.000

Model	PRATIO	PNFI	PCFI
Your model	0.800	0.772	0.783
Saturated model	0.000	0.000	0.000
Independence model	1.000	0.000	0.000

Model	RMSEA	LO 90	HI 90	PCLOSE
Your model	0.043	0.036	0.050	0.943
Independence model	0.264	0.258	0.269	0.000

Model	ECVI	LO 90	HI 90	MECVI
Your model	0.377	0.328	0.435	0.380
Saturated model	0.318	0.318	0.318	0.328
Independence model	7.843	7.529	8.164	7.844

with model specification whereby the male-specific cross-loading was fixed to zero for females. Thus, in reviewing the boxed areas imposed on the output, you can see that, for males, the regression path from ENG SC to SDQMSC is accompanied by an estimate (−0.138), standard error (0.053), and critical ratio (−2.625); for females, the estimate is 0.0. Note also that, for each group, all parameters to be constrained equal across the groups are accompanied by an associated label.

In contrast to the output shown in Table 8.3, the partial output presented in Table 8.4 resulted from model specification whereby each group was allowed to have a

TABLE 8.3
Selected AMOS Text Output for Test of Invariant Self-Concept Structure:
Maximum Likelihood Estimates (Cross-Loading Fixed to Zero for Females)

Males:

Regression Weights:

	Estimate	S.E.	C.R.	Label
SESGSC <------ GEN SC	0.354	0.012	30.707	p3
APIGSC <------ GEN SC	0.520	0.022	23.917	p2
SDQGSC <------ GEN SC	1.000			
SCAASC <----- ACAD SC	0.414	0.017	24.326	p5
SDQASC <----- ACAD SC	1.000			
SCAESC <------ ENG SC	0.574	0.028	20.722	p8
APIESC <------ ENG SC	1.351	0.061	22.110	p7
SDQESC <------ ENG SC	1.000			
SCAMSC <----- MATH SC	0.429	0.010	41.333	p12
APIMSC <----- MATH SC	0.697	0.014	48.456	p11
SDQMSC <----- MATH SC	1.000			
SDQESC <------ GEN SC	0.110	0.021	5.319	p13
SDQMSC <------ ENG SC	-0.138	0.053	-2.625	

Covariances:

	Estimate	S.E.	C.R.	Label
GEN SC <----> ACAD SC	53.011	5.665	9.358	gscasc
ACAD SC <----> ENG SC	41.697	3.706	11.251	ascesc
ENG SC <----> MATH SC	11.670	4.268	2.734	escmsc
GEN SC <-----> ENG SC	22.666	3.764	6.021	gscesc
ACAD SC <----> MATH SC	101.961	7.419	13.743	ascmsc
GEN SC <----> MATH SC	48.932	7.462	6.557	gscmsc
err7 <--------> err10	10.888	1.347	8.085	err107
err5 <---------> err8	5.715	0.541	10.561	err85
err5 <--------> err11	4.534	0.487	9.302	err115

Variances:

	Estimate	S.E.	C.R.	Label
GEN SC	158.822	10.334	15.369	var_gsc
ACAD SC	104.207	7.589	13.732	var_asc
ENG SC	50.686	4.362	11.620	var_esc
MATH SC	230.350	12.975	17.753	var_msc
err3	5.809	0.752	7.719	
err2	44.827	3.515	12.752	
err1	41.011	5.797	7.074	
err5	10.697	0.919	11.639	
err4	50.290	5.466	9.201	
err8	16.965	1.261	13.453	
err7	22.055	3.760	5.866	
err6	38.383	3.401	11.286	
err11	14.839	1.141	13.002	
err10	19.025	2.046	9.297	
err9	24.789	3.630	6.830	

Females:

Regression Weights:

	Estimate	S.E.	C.R.	Label
SESGSC <------ GEN SC	0.354	0.012	30.707	p3
APIGSC <------ GEN SC	0.520	0.022	23.917	p2
SDQGSC <------ GEN SC	1.000			
SCAASC <----- ACAD SC	0.414	0.017	24.326	p5
SDQASC <----- ACAD SC	1.000			
SCAESC <------ ENG SC	0.574	0.028	20.722	p8
APIESC <------ ENG SC	1.351	0.061	22.110	p7
SDQESC <------ ENG SC	1.000			
SCAMSC <----- MATH SC	0.429	0.010	41.333	p12
APIMSC <----- MATH SC	0.697	0.014	48.456	p11
SDQMSC <----- MATH SC	1.000			
SDQESC <------ GEN SC	0.110	0.021	5.319	p13
SDQMSC <------ ENG SC	0.000			

(Continued)

TABLE 8.3 *(Continued)*

Covariances:	Estimate	S.E.	C.R.	Label
GEN SC <----> ACAD SC	53.011	5.665	9.358	gscasc
ACAD SC <----> ENG SC	41.697	3.706	11.251	ascesc
ENG SC <----> MATH SC	11.670	4.268	2.734	escmsc
GEN SC <----> ENG SC	22.666	3.764	6.021	gscesc
ACAD SC <---> MATH SC	101.961	7.419	13.743	ascmsc
GEN SC <----> MATH SC	48.932	7.462	6.557	gscmsc
err7 <--------> err10	10.888	1.347	8.085	err107
err5 <---------> err8	5.715	0.541	10.561	err85
err5 <--------> err11	4.534	0.487	9.302	err115

Variances:	Estimate	S.E.	C.R.	Label
GEN SC	158.822	10.334	15.369	var_gsc
ACAD SC	104.207	7.589	13.732	var_asc
ENG SC	50.686	4.362	11.620	var_esc
MATH SC	230.350	12.975	17.753	var_msc
err3	3.722	0.600	6.199	
err2	35.882	2.808	12.780	
err1	43.366	5.289	8.199	
err5	9.066	0.801	11.318	
err4	39.312	4.578	8.586	
err8	12.746	1.008	12.650	
err7	26.571	3.808	6.977	
err6	35.898	3.162	11.353	
err11	11.445	0.948	12.074	
err10	18.042	2.011	8.971	
err9	38.176	4.176	9.142	

different path diagram. The only difference between the two outputs is that, although the cross-loading parameter SDQMSC ← ENG SC is specified and accompanied by an estimate, standard error, and critical ratio for males, this parameter is totally absent for females. All other aspects of this portion of the AMOS output remain the same.

Let's return now to the issue of noninvariance relative to the initial model tested. As noted earlier, the difference in χ^2 values between this fully constrained model and the unconstrained multigroup model was statistically significant ($p <$ .001). Proceeding in a logical order that tests first for the equivalence of the measurement model and then for the equivalence of the structural model, we can determine which parameters in the model are noninvariant across adolescent males and females. Results bearing on this series of tests are presented in Table 8.5.

Testing for Invariance of Self-Concept Structure: Pattern of Factor Loadings

The first logical step in the invariance process is to test for the equivalence of the factor loading pattern across the two groups. As indicated in Table 8.5, findings revealed all factor loadings to be equivalent across males and females, as reflected in a χ^2 difference between the model tested and Model 1 that was not statistically significant. Given these findings, we can now feel confident that all measures of

TABLE 8.4

Selected AMOS Text Output for Test of Invariant Self-Concept Structure:
Maximum Likelihood Estimates (Cross-Loading Excluded for Females)

Males:

Regression Weights:

	Estimate	S.E.	C.R.	Label
SESGSC <------ GEN SC	0.354	0.012	30.707	p3
APIGSC <------ GEN SC	0.520	0.022	23.917	p2
SDQGSC <------ GEN SC	1.000			
SCAASC <----- ACAD SC	0.414	0.017	24.326	p5
SDQASC <----- ACAD SC	1.000			
SCAESC <------ ENG SC	0.574	0.028	20.722	p8
APIESC <------ ENG SC	1.351	0.061	22.110	p7
SDQESC <------ ENG SC	1.000			
SCAMSC <----- MATH SC	0.429	0.010	41.333	p12
APIMSC <----- MATH SC	0.697	0.014	48.456	p11
SDQMSC <----- MATH SC	1.000			
SDQESC <------ GEN SC	0.110	0.021	5.319	p13
SDQMSC <------ ENG SC	-0.138	0.053	-2.625	

Females:

Regression Weights:

SESGSC <------ GEN SC	0.354	0.012	30.707	p3
APIGSC <------ GEN SC	0.520	0.022	23.917	p2
SDQGSC <------ GEN SC	1.000			
SCAASC <----- ACAD SC	0.414	0.017	24.326	p5
SDQASC <----- ACAD SC	1.000			
SCAESC <------ ENG SC	0.574	0.028	20.722	p8
APIESC <------ ENG SC	1.351	0.061	22.110	p7
SDQESC <------ ENG SC	1.000			
SCAMSC <----- MATH SC	0.429	0.010	41.333	p12
APIMSC <----- MATH SC	0.697	0.014	48.456	p11
SDQMSC <----- MATH SC	1.000			
SDQESC <------ GEN SC	0.110	0.021	5.319	p13

self-concept are operating in the same way for both groups, and we proceed in testing for the equality of the structural parameters.

Testing for the Invariance of Self-Concept Structure: Variances and Covariances

The next logical step in the process is to test for the invariance of factor variances across groups.[4] Given that all factor loadings were found to be invariant, model

---

[4]Although testing for equivalent factor covariances would seem to be more meaningful than testing for equivalent variances, within the context of the present data, we test for the equality of both for purposes of consistency with the original study.

TABLE 8.5
Goodness-of-Fit Statistics for Tests of Invariance Across Males and Females: A Summary

Model Description	χ^2	df	$\Delta\chi^{2a}$	Δdf	Statistical Significance
1 Combined baseline models (males and females)	163.362	67	—	—	—
2 Factor loadings, variances, and covariances constrained equal	224.551	88	61.189	21	$p < .001$
3 Factor loadings constrained equal	171.173	75	7.811	8	NS
4 Model 3 with all variances constrained equal	190.698	79	27.336	12	$p < .01$
5 Model 3 with variance of GSC constrained equal	172.363	76	9.001	9	NS
6 Model 3 with variances of GSC and ASC constrained equal	190.355	77	26.993	10	$p < .01$
7 Model 3 with variances of GSC and ESC constrained equal	174.426	77	11.064	10	NS
8 Model 3 with variances of GSC, ESC, and MSC constrained equal	175.363	78	12.001	11	NS
9 Model 8 with all covariances constrained equal	219.215	84	55.853	17	$p < .001$
10 Model 8 with covariance between GSC and ASC constrained equal	180.515	79	17.153	12	NS
11 Model 8 with covariances between GSC/ASC and ASC/ESC constrained equal	180.527	80	17.165	13	NS
12 Model 8 with covariances between GSC/ASC, ASC/ESC, and ESC/MSC constrained equal	195.494	81	32.132	14	$p < .01$
13 Model 8 with covariances between GSC/ASC, ASC/ESC, and GSC/ESC constrained equal	181.923	81	18.561	14	NS
14 Model 8 with covariances between GSC/ASC, ASC/ESC, GSC/ESC, and ASC/MSC constrained equal	216.815	82	53.453	15	$p < .001$
15 Model 8 with covariances between GSC/ASC, ASC/ESC, GSC/ESC, and GSC/MSC constrained equal	182.866	82	19.504	15	NS

Note. $\Delta\chi^2$, difference in χ^2 values; Δdf, difference in degrees of freedom.
[a]All models compared with Model 1.

specification will include equality constraints on the factor loadings, as well as on the factor variances.[5] However, let's pause here to ponder the situation where, on the other hand, not all factor loadings had been found to be invariant across groups. Indeed, this was the case with respect to the MBI model illustrated in chapter 7,

---

[5]Of course, in using AMOS Graphics, a revised model that reflects the parameters to be constrained equal must accompany each test for invariance.

although no discussion related to this issue was included there. Essentially, such results would invoke the use of partial measurement invariance in testing for the equality of factor variances and covariances. However, the use of partial measurement invariance is contingent on the number of indicator variables used in measuring each latent construct. Given multiple indicators and at least one invariant measure (other than the one fixed to 1.00 for identification purposes), remaining noninvariant measures can be specified as unconstrained across groups; that is, they can be freely estimated (Byrne et al., 1989; Muthén & Christoffersson, 1981).

In testing for the invariance of factor variances and covariances across gender, the interest focuses on the hypothesized underlying factors of self-concept, as well as on their interrelational structure. As noted in chapter 7, the testing of invariance hypotheses involves increasingly restrictive models. Thus, the model to be tested here (Model 4) is more restrictive than Model 3 because, in addition to equality constraints being imposed on the factor variances, they are also maintained for all factor loadings.

As detailed in Table 8.5, results from the estimation of Model 4 yielded a $\chi^2_{(79)}$ = 190.698. Because the difference in χ^2 value between this model and Model 1 ($\Delta\chi^2_{(12)}$ = 27.336) was statistically significant ($p < .01$), the hypothesis of invariant factor variances must be rejected.[6] Faced with these results, our next task is to determine which variances are contributing to this inequality. Thus, we now proceed in testing, independently, for the invariance of each factor variance parameter, while continuing to hold constrained all parameters found to be cumulatively invariant across adolescent males and females.

For pedagogical purposes, let's briefly review the steps involved in this testing phase. Turning to Table 8.5, we see that the variance of general self-concept was found to be invariant (Model 5). Thus, this parameter was held invariant whilst the variance of academic self-concept was tested for its equivalency across groups (Model 6). Results of this test revealed the latter to be noninvariant across gender; the equality constraint for the variance of the academic self-concept factor was therefore released. As a consequence, the model used in testing for the invariance of English self-concept (Model 7), included two equality constraints: one for the variance of general self-concept, and the other for the variance of English self-concept. Based on this general procedure of cumulatively maintaining equality constraints only for invariant elements, all factor covariances were similarly tested. As indicated in Table 8.5, these tests revealed two covariances to be nonequivalent across gender.

Overall, as indicated by the goodness-of-fit statistics, the results summarized in Table 8.2 reveal self-concept structure to be well described by a four-factor model comprising the facets of general, academic, English and mathematics self-concepts

---

[6]Although the $\Delta\chi^2$ value was based on the difference between Model 4 and Model 3 in the original study, it is equally appropriate to compute the difference between Model 4 and Model 1, along with the accompanying difference in degrees of freedom.

for both adolescent males and females. However, although the observed measures were found to be operating equivalently for both boys and girls, there were some differences in structural relations among the self-concept facets. In particular, significant gender differences were found with respect to the variance of academic self-concept, and with respect to the covariances between academic and mathematics self-concepts and between English and mathematics self-concepts. A final model of self-concept structure, with all invariant parameters labeled, is displayed in Fig. 8.15. (For an extended discussion of these results, readers are referred to Byrne & Shavelson, 1987.)

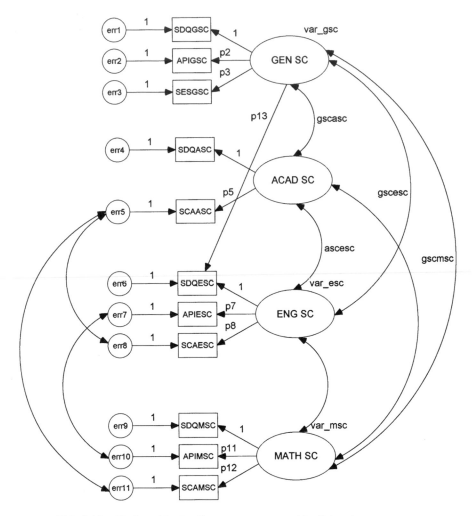

FIG. 8.15.   Final model of self-concept structure with all invariant parameters labeled.

MODELING WITH AMOS BASIC

The AMOS Basic input file illustrated in this chapter is consistent with the multigroup model displayed in Fig. 8.5 in which all parameters to be constrained equal have been labeled; this input file is shown in Table 8.6.

In reviewing this file, you can immediately see that, consistent with the multigroup AMOS Basic file presented in chapter 7, model parameters are specified for each group separately. In the present instance, the analyses involve two groups. As such, the first set of specifications is pertinent to adolescent males, whereas the second set is pertinent to adolescent females.

Also consistent with the AMOS Basic file illustrated in the last chapter is the specification of parameters to be constrained equal across groups. As such, each of

TABLE 8.6
AMOS Basic Input File for Test of Self-Concept Invariance Across Gender

```
Dim Sem As New AmosEngine
'Testing for Invariance of Self-concept Structure Across Gender
(Fig. 8.5)'

SEM.TextOutput

SEM.BeginGroup "ch8males.txt"
    SEM.GroupName "Adolescent Males"

        SEM.Structure " SDQGSC <---GEN SC (1)"
        SEM.Structure " APIGSC <---GEN SC (p2)"
        SEM.Structure " SESGSC <---GEN SC (p3)"
        SEM.Structure " SDQASC <---ACAD SC (1)"
        SEM.Structure " SCAASC <---ACAD SC (P5)"
        SEM.Structure " SDQESC <---ENG SC (1)"
        SEM.Structure " APIESC <---ENG SC (p7)"
        SEM.Structure " SCAESC <---ENG SC (p8)"
        SEM.Structure " SDQMSC <---MATH SC (1)"
        SEM.Structure " APIMSC <---MATH SC (p11)"
        SEM.Structure " SCAMSC <---MATH SC (p12)"
        SEM.Structure " SDQESC <---GEN SC (p13)"
        SEM.Structure " SDQMSC <---ENG SC "

        SEM.Structure " SDQGSC <---err1 (1)"
        SEM.Structure " APIGSC <---err2 (1)"
        SEM.Structure " SESGSC <---err3 (1)"
        SEM.Structure " SDQASC <---err4 (1)"
        SEM.Structure " SCAASC <---err5 (1)"
        SEM.Structure " SDQESC <---err6 (1)"
        SEM.Structure " APIESC <---err7 (1)"
        SEM.Structure " SCAESC <---err8 (1)"
        SEM.Structure " SDQMSC <---err9 (1)"
        SEM.Structure " APIMSC <---err10 (1)"
        SEM.Structure " SCAMSC <---err11 (1)"

        SEM.Structure " GEN SC (v_gsc)"
        SEM.Structure " ACAD SC (v_asc"
        SEM.Structure " ENG SC (v_esc)"
        SEM.Structure " MATH SC (v_msc)"
```

(Continued)

TABLE 8.6 *(Continued)*

```
    SEM.Structure " GEN SC<>ACAD SC (gscasc)"
    SEM.Structure " ACAD SC<>ENG SC (ascesc)"
    SEM.Structure " ENG SC<>MATH SC (escmsc)"
    SEM.Structure " GEN SC<>ENG SC (gscesc)"
    SEM.Structure " ACAD SC<>MATH SC (ascmsc)"
    SEM.Structure " GEN SC<>MATH SC (gscmsc)"

    SEM.Structure " err5<>err8 (err85)"
    SEM.Structure " err7<>err10 (err107)"
    SEM.Structure " err5<>err11 (err115)"

SEM.BeginGroup "ch8females.txt"
    SEM.GroupName "Adolescent Females"

    SEM.Structure " SDQGSC <---GEN SC (1)"
    SEM.Structure " APIGSC <---GEN SC (p2)"
    SEM.Structure " SESGSC <---GEN SC (p3)"
    SEM.Structure " SDQASC <---ACAD SC (1)"
    SEM.Structure " SCAASC <---ACAD SC (P5)"
    SEM.Structure " SDQESC <---ENG SC (1)"
    SEM.Structure " APIESC <---ENG SC (p7)"
    SEM.Structure " SCAESC <---ENG SC (p8)"
    SEM.Structure " SDQMSC <---MATH SC (1)"
    SEM.Structure " APIMSC <---MATH SC (p11)"
    SEM.Structure " SCAMSC <---MATH SC (p12)"
    SEM.Structure " SDQESC <---GEN SC (p13)"
    SEM.Structure " SDQGSC <---err1 (1)"
    SEM.Structure " APIGSC <---err2 (1)"
    SEM.Structure " SESGSC <---err3 (1)"
    SEM.Structure " SDQASC <---err4 (1)"
    SEM.Structure " SCAASC <---err5 (1)"
    SEM.Structure " SDQESC <---err6 (1)"
    SEM.Structure " APIESC <---err7 (1)"
    SEM.Structure " SCAESC <---err8 (1)"
    SEM.Structure " SDQMSC <---err9 (1)"
    SEM.Structure " APIMSC <---err10 (1)"
    SEM.Structure " SCAMSC <---err11 (1)"

    SEM.Structure " GEN SC (v_gsc)"
    SEM.Structure " ACAD SC (v_asc"
    SEM.Structure " ENG SC (v_esc)"
    SEM.Structure " MATH SC (v_msc)"

    SEM.Structure " GEN SC<>ACAD SC (gscasc)"
    SEM.Structure " ACAD SC<>ENG SC (ascesc)"
    SEM.Structure " ENG SC<>MATH SC (escmsc)"
    SEM.Structure " GEN SC<>ENG SC (gscesc)"
    SEM.Structure " ACAD SC<>MATH SC (ascmsc)"
    SEM.Structure " GEN SC<>MATH SC (gscmsc)"

    SEM.Structure " err5<>err8 (err85)"
    SEM.Structure " err7<>err10 (err107)"
    SEM.Structure " err5<>err11 (err115)"

End Sub
```

these parameters is assigned a label which is then parenthesized in the specification statement. Let's turn to the file shown in Table 8.6 and review each section of the file, as specified for Males, the first group. The first section represents the factor loadings. As you can see, all loading specifications, except the last one (SDQMSC ← ENG SC), include either a parenthesized value or a parenthesized label. The parenthesized values [(1)] indicate that the parameter is constrained to a value of 1.00, whereas the parenthesized labels represent factor loadings to be constrained equal across groups; one of these loadings (p13) is actually a cross-loading common to each group. Why, then, is the last factor loading not constrained equal across groups? Recall that this parameter was idiosyncratic for adolescent males, and not for adolescent females, in the establishment of their separate baseline models.

The next set of specifications represent error terms associated with each of the observed variables. Note that these parameters have no parenthesized labels associated with them and, therefore, are not to be constrained equal across groups. The three sections that follow, however, do contain parameter specifications inclusive of labels, thereby indicating their constraints across groups; these parameters represent the factor variances, factor covariances, and correlated error terms, respectively.

Finally, in reviewing model specifications for adolescent females, you can see that, with the exception of the one idiosyncratic cross-loading noted earlier, all factor loadings are identical to those specified for adolescent males.

CHAPTER 9

Application 7: Testing for Invariant Latent Mean Structures

∽

A review of the structural equation modeling literature reveals a dearth of studies involving multigroup comparisons of latent mean structures. This situation likely derives from the many complexities associated with the implementation of these analyses using earlier versions of the various SEM statistical packages. Indeed, it was this very issue that led to the writing of the first paper to explicitly model and demonstrate the necessary specification "tricks" required in testing for differences in mean structures using pre-LISREL 7 (Joreskog & Sorbom, 1988) versions of that program (see Byrne et al., 1989). However, over the past 2 to 3 years, recent versions of SEM programs have addressed these complexities and, as a result, the process is becoming more straightforward. As a consequence of this simplification trend, I fully expect more studies involving latent mean structures to be forthcoming; currently, they are still relatively far and few between. The AMOS program was designed to make mean and intercept modeling easy, and that it has done in spades. Believe me, testing for latent mean differences can't get much simpler than the AMOS approach to these analyses!

The focus of this chapter, then, is to introduce you to basic concepts associated with the analysis of latent mean structures, and to walk you through an application that tests for their invariance across two groups. Specifically, we test for differences in the latent means of general, academic, English, and mathematics self-concepts across high- and low-track secondary school students. The example presented here draws from two published papers: one that focuses on methodological issues related to testing for invariant covariance and mean structures (Byrne et al., 1989), and one oriented toward substantive issues related to social comparison theory (Byrne, 1988b).

BASIC CONCEPTS UNDERLYING TESTS
OF LATENT MEAN STRUCTURES

The General Conceptual Framework

In the usual test of multigroup comparisons based on either univariate or multivariate analyses, interest typically focuses on the extent to which the differences are statistically significant among observed means representing the various groups. Because these values are directly calculable from the raw data, they are considered *observed* values. In contrast, the means of latent variables (i.e., latent constructs) are *unobservable* in the sense that they cannot be observed directly. Rather, they derive structure indirectly from their indicator variables, which are directly observed and therefore measurable. Thus, in testing for the invariance of mean structures, the intent is to test for the equivalence of means related to each underlying construct or factor. In other words, the focus is on testing for differences in the latent means (of factors for each group).

For all examples considered to this point in the book, analyses have been based on covariance structures, and thus only parameters representing regression coefficients, variances, and covariances have been of interest; as such, the covariance structure of the (observed) indicator variables comprised the crucial parametric information. In the analysis of covariance structures, it is implicitly assumed that all observed variables are measured as deviations from their means (i.e., their means are equal to zero). As a consequence, the intercept terms generally associated with regression equations are irrelevant to the analyses.

However, when the observed means take on nonzero values, as is the case in testing for differences in latent mean structures, the intercept parameter must be taken into account. Furthermore, because the observed variable means are functions of the other parameters in the model, the intercept terms must be estimated jointly with all other model parameters (Joreskog & Yang, 1996). In testing for differences in latent variable means, then, the analyses are based on covariance, as well as mean structures.

To help you in understanding the concept of *mean structures*, I draw on the work of Bentler (1995) in demonstrating the difference between covariance and mean structures as it relates to a simple bivariate regression equation. As noted earlier, in covariance structure analysis, the means of x and y are irrelevant to the analysis and presumed to be zero. Furthermore, any correlation between an observed variable (x) and its error term (ε) is also assumed to be zero. As a consequence, the coefficient β and the variances of x and ε are all the parameters that are needed to adequately describe the model. Within the framework of covariance structure analysis, this equation can be presented as follows:

$$y = \beta x + \varepsilon \qquad (1)$$

In mean structure analysis, on the other hand, the mean of y is essential to the analysis and therefore is presumed *not* to be zero. Thus, there needs to be some mechanism whereby the mean of y can be defined; the intercept term is the key element in this necessary process. Within the framework of mean structure analysis, the preceding regression equation is expressed as follows:

$$y = \alpha + \beta x + \varepsilon \qquad (2)$$

where α is an intercept parameter.

It is important to note that although the intercept can assist in defining the mean of y, it does not generally equal the mean (Bentler, 1995). Thus, if we take expectations of both sides of this equation and assume that the mean of ε is zero, the preceding expression yields:

$$\mu_y = \alpha + \beta\mu_x \qquad (3)$$

where μ_y is the mean of y, and μ_x is the mean of x. As such, y and its mean can now be expressed in terms of the model parameters α, β, and μ_x.

It is this decomposition of the mean of y, the dependent variable, that leads to the term *mean structures*. More specifically, it serves to characterize a model in which the means of the dependent variables can be expressed or "structured" in terms of the structural coefficients and the means of the independent variables. Equation (3) serves to illustrate how the incorporation of a mean structure into a model necessarily includes the new parameters α and μ_x, the intercept and observed mean (of x), respectively. Thus, it should now be easy to see how models with structured means merely extend the basic concepts associated with the analysis of covariance structures.

In summary, any model involving mean structures may include the following parameters:

- Regression coefficients.
- Variances and covariances of the independent (i.e., exogenous) variables.
- Intercepts of the dependent (i.e., endogenous) variables.
- Means of the independent variables.

As a consequence, these models typically involve the analysis of both covariance and mean structures.

Estimation of Latent Variable Means

As with the invariance examples presented thus far, applications of structured means models involve testing simultaneously across two or more groups. Typically, the multigroup model illustrated in this chapter is used when one is interested in testing for group differences in the means of particular latent constructs. This approach to the estimation of latent mean structures was first brought to light in Sorbom's (1974) seminal extension of the classic model of factorial invariance. As such, testing for latent mean differences across groups is made possible through the implementation of two important strategies. The first of these addresses the issue of *model identification*. Given the necessary estimation of intercepts associated with the observed variables, in addition to those associated with the unobserved latent constructs, it is evident that the attainment of an overidentified model is possible only with the imposition of several specification constraints. Indeed, it is this very issue that complicates, and ultimately renders impossible, the estimation of latent means in single-group analyses. Multigroup analyses, on the other hand, provide the mechanism for imposing severe restrictions on the model such that the estimation of latent means is possible. More specifically, because two (or more) groups under study are tested simultaneously, evaluation of the identification criterion is considered across groups. As a consequence, although the structured means model may not be identified in one group, it can become so when analyzed within the framework of a multigroup model. This outcome occurs as a function of specified equality constraints across groups. More specifically, these equality constraints derive from the underlying assumption that both the variable intercepts and the factor loadings are invariant across groups.

A second feature of structured means estimation is the necessary additional consideration of *factor identification*. Specifically, this requirement imposes the restriction that the factor intercepts for one group be fixed to zero; this group then operates as a reference group against which latent means for the other group(s) are compared. The reason for this reconceptualization is that when the intercepts of the measured variables are constrained equal across groups, this leads to the latent factor intercepts having no definite origin (i.e., they are undefined in a statistical sense). A standard way of fixing the origin is to set the factor intercepts of one group to zero (see Bentler, 1995; Joreskog & Sorbom, 1996b). As a consequence, factor intercepts are interpretable only in a relative sense. That is to say, one can test whether the latent variable means for one group differ from those of another, but one cannot estimate the mean of each factor in a model for each group. In other words, although it is possible to test for latent mean differences between, say, adolescent boys and girls, it is not possible to estimate, simultaneously, the mean of each factor for both boys and girls; the latent means for one group must be constrained to zero.

Having reviewed the conceptual and statistical underpinning of the mean structures model, let's turn now to AMOS Graphics and work through an actual application of these concepts as they relate to the hypothesized model under study in this chapter.

MODELING WITH AMOS GRAPHICS

The Hypothesized Model

The application to be examined in this chapter bears on the equivalency of the latent means related to four self-concept dimensions (general, academic, English, mathematics) for high ($n = 582$) and low ($n = 248$) academically tracked high school students (Byrne, 1988b). Specifically, the substantive focus of the initial study (Byrne, 1988b) was to test for latent mean differences in multidimensional self-concepts across these two ability groups. Because the originally hypothesized model (see Fig. 9.1) replicates the one portrayed in Fig. 8.1, detailed discussion of this model is not repeated here. Consistent with earlier tests of this model, as explained in the last chapter, the academic self-concept subscale of the Affective Perception Inventory was deleted as one measure of this construct.

The Baseline Models

As with previous examples of multigroup models in this book, goodness of fit related to the hypothesized model (Fig. 9.1) was tested separately for low- and high-track students. Although goodness-of-fit statistics indicated a relatively well-fitting model for both groups (e.g., high track, CFI = .923; low track, CFI = .911), a review of the modification indices revealed substantial evidence of misspecifica-

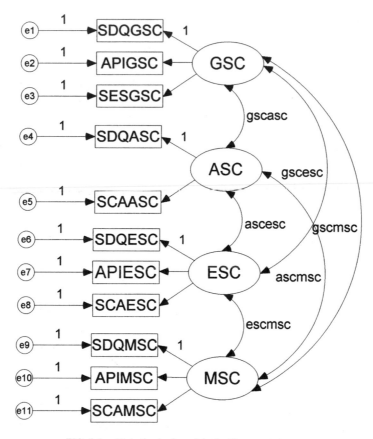

FIG. 9.1.   Hypothesized model of self-concept structure.

tion as a consequence of correlated measurement error among subscales from the same measuring instrument; results varied slightly across the two groups. For both high- and low-track students, testing of the hypothesized model precipitated excessively large modification indices related to two error correlations: (a) between the academic and English self-concept subscales of the Self Concept of Ability Scale (SCA; Brookover, 1962), and (b) between the academic and mathematics subscales of this same scale. For low-track students, however, additional misspecification was noted with respect to a third correlated error between the mathematics and English self-concept subscales of the Affective Perception Inventory (API; Soares & Soares, 1979). Given a psychometrically reasonable rationale for estimating these additional parameters, the originally hypothesized model was respecified and reestimated accordingly for each group. Testing of these respecified models resulted in a substantially better fitting model for both high-track (CFI = .967) and low-track (CFI = .974) students; they serve as the baseline model for each group and are schematically portrayed in Fig. 9.2.

The Structured Means Model

In working with AMOS Graphics, the estimation and testing of structured means models is not that much different from analyzing variance and covariance structures. It does, however, require a few additional steps. As with multigroup applications presented in earlier chapters, the structured means model requires a system of labeling whereby certain parameters are constrained to be equal across groups, whereas others are free to take on any value. In testing for differences in latent means, for example, we would want to know that the measurement model is operating in exactly the same way for both high- and low-track students. For this reason, then, it is essential that all factor loadings (i.e., regression weights) be constrained equal across both groups. We turn now to a more detailed description of this process, as it relates to testing for latent mean differences.

TESTING FOR LATENT MEAN DIFFERENCES

The Input Model

In testing for latent mean differences using AMOS Graphics, the baseline model for each ability group, as shown in Fig. 9.2, must be included in the same file. Of import here, as in chapter 8, is a situation where these two models are not identical across groups. Because we wish to maintain the differential error correlations across the high- and low-track models, this information needs to be conveyed to the program. In chapter 8, I demonstrated two strategies for specifying a multigroup model in which the number of parameters to be estimated was allowed to vary across groups; these were (a) specifying the same model parameters for both groups, but constraining to zero those that were irrelevant to one particular group, and (b)

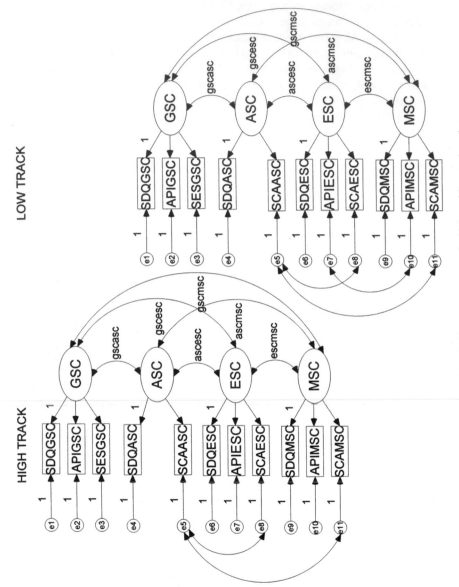

FIG. 9.2. Baseline models of self-concept structure for high- and low-track students.

making use of the Interface Properties dialog box, from which one can request that different path diagrams be allowed for different groups. In the present chapter, I chose the latter option. Given that steps involved in this procedure were detailed in the last chapter (chap. 8), I do not reiterate them here.

Once AMOS has been programmed to allow for a different path diagram for each group, we can proceed in labeling the models in preparation for the analyses. As such, we begin by assigning a label to all factor loading paths, except those that have been constrained to a value of 1.00. Recall that in testing for latent mean differences, it is essential that these regression weights be constrained equal across groups. Thus, working from the Object Properties dialog box, as illustrated in chapters 7 and 8, we first assign a label to a particular factor loading parameter (e.g., p2) and then click on the "all groups" box. This action ensures that the estimated value of these parameters will be held equal to those for the first group, which, in this case, is the high-track group.

Following assignment of labels to the factor loading parameters, the next task is to continue the labeling process, although within the framework of a structured means model. To initiate this process, we need to activate the Analysis Properties dialog box, either by clicking on its related icon 🎛 or by pulling down the View/Set menu. Once the Analysis Properties dialog box is open, we need to click on the Estimation option and then select "Estimate means and intercepts" as shown in Fig. 9.3.

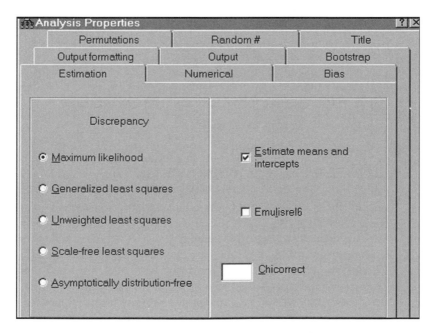

FIG. 9.3.   Programming analyses for a multigroup structured means model using the Analysis Properties dialog box.

Selecting the "Estimate means and intercepts" box triggers a number of changes in the AMOS Graphics analysis strategy. First, the means and intercepts, as well as the variances, covariances, and regression weights, are made visible during input. That is to say, the program automatically attaches a "mean, variance" pair to the exogenous factors comprising each baseline model. Second, constraints may be applied to all intercepts, means, factor loadings, variances, and covariances in all groups. Third, the χ^2 statistics reflects the model fit to sample mean *and* covariance structures (as opposed to all other applications in this book where the χ^2 statistics reflected model fit to only the covariance structure).

Having summarized the global program changes that occur when a structured means model is tested, let me now return to my first point noted earlier, as this aspect of the AMOS Graphics input model is definitely in need of further elaboration. However, to help you in conceptualizing the automated label assignments to be further described, you are referred to Figs. 9.4a and 9.4b, in which the structured means models for high- and low-track students, respectively, are schematically displayed.[1]

Consistent with the pairing pattern noted earlier, as soon as you select the "Estimate means and intercepts" option, you will see, assigned to each model, a set of zero constraints, each of which is accompanied by a comma. In AMOS Graphics, the comma is used to separate specified mean and variance parameters; the first of each pair always represents the mean. The way in which these parameters are labeled in the path diagram is indicative of their estimation status. As such, the assignment of an integer indicates a constraint, a nominal label indicates free estimation (if, and only if, there are no other parameters in the model with the same label, otherwise it will be interpreted by the program as constrained), and the presence of a comma preceded or followed by a blank space implies an unlabeled, but estimated, mean or variance parameter, respectively. To further clarify this pairing system used in AMOS Graphics, let's review the following examples.

1. a,0: Mean (labeled "a") to be freely estimated (provided that there are no other parameters in the model labeled as "a"); variance constrained to zero.

2. 0,1: Mean constrained to zero; variance constrained to 1.0.

3. 0, : Mean constrained to zero; unlabeled variance to be freely estimated.

4. ,1: Unlabeled mean to be freely estimated; variance constrained to 1.0.

Let's turn now to the structured means model shown in Fig. 9.4, a and b. We look first at the exogenous variables in the models; these include the latent factors GSC, ASC, ESC, and MSC, as well as the error terms associated with each observed variable. Assigned automatically to each latent factor is a zero followed by a comma (0,). A space followed by a comma in this pair of integers implies the pres-

---

[1]These models are shown separately for high- and low-track students because when they were included in the same figure the clarity of the imposed text was difficult to read.

HIGH TRACK

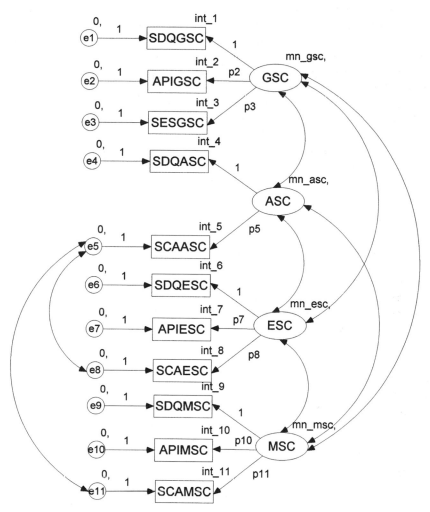

FIG. 9.4.   (a) Structured means model for high-track students.

ence of yet unlabeled variance parameters. In the initial stage of building a mean structures model, this zero constraint is specified for each of the groups, thereby indicating that the latent means of all factors are fixed to zero for both high- and low-track students. However, as described earlier in this chapter, only one group (in the case of two) needs to have these parameters fixed to zero; they are to be freely estimated in the other group. Thus, it is necessary to relabel these factor mean parameters for one of the groups. This relabeling process, as you are now well

LOW TRACK

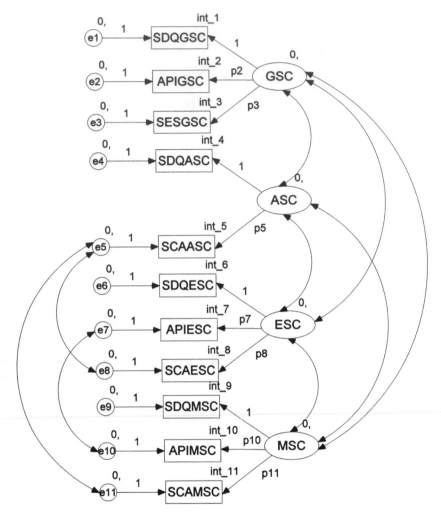

FIG. 9.4.   (b) Structured means model for low-track students.

aware, is easily accomplished by means of the Object Properties dialog box. As such, the parameter assignment of 0 is simply replaced by some label. In reviewing Fig. 9.4a, you can see that I assigned the labels of mn_gsc through mn_msc to these latent factors for the high-track group. The comma and blank space (,) following these latent mean parameters (labeled for the high track; assigned a constraint of zero for the low track [Fig. 9.4b]) represent unlabeled variance parameters.

Let's look now at the other exogenous variables in the models: the error terms. Here, you can note that, for both groups, each of the error means has been constrained to zero, whereas the error variances (unlabeled here) are to be freely estimated.

We turn our attention now to the endogenous variables in the model—the observed subscale scores. Of interest here are the intercept terms associated with each, as they must be constrained equal across the two groups. Once again, their labeling, and specification as equality constraints, are made possible via the Object Properties dialog box. This process involves three steps. First, you need to right-click on a particular observed variable. This action, as illustrated in Fig. 9.5, highlights the selected variable to which the intercept label will be attached.

Once this menu is visible, the next step is to select Object Properties and then, using this dialog box, assign an intercept label. The final step is to click on the "all groups" option. Illustrated in Fig. 9.6, for example, the parameter Int_1 has been selected. Given that the "all groups" box has been checked, this parameter will be constrained equal across high- and low-track students in the test for latent mean differences.

Before turning to the results of this analysis, let's review Fig. 9.4, a and b, once again, this time taking into account all paths and variables as they pertain to the multigroup structured means model. Interpretation of the model can be summarized as follows:

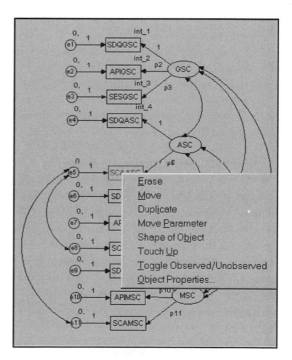

FIG. 9.5. Selecting an observed variable for placement of an intercept label.

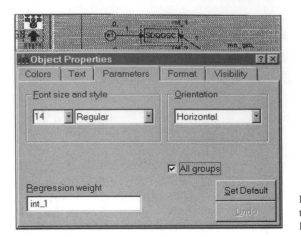

FIG. 9.6. Assigning intercept labels to observed variables using the Object Properties dialog box.

- Variances of the four self-concept factors are freely estimated in each group (implied here by an unlabeled space following the comma), as are the covariances among them.
- Means of the error terms are not estimated and remain constrained to zero. Variances of the error terms are freely estimated in each group (unlabeled space following the comma), as are the error covariances.[2]
- Except for those fixed to 1.00, all factor loadings are constrained equal across groups (the "p" labels).
- All intercepts for the observed measures are constrained equal across groups (the intercept labels).
- The four factor means are freely estimated for the high-track group (mean labels preceding the comma), but constrained equal to zero for the low-track group (zero preceding the comma). The latter group is therefore regarded as the "reference" group.[3]

One additional point regarding the intercepts may be helpful to your understanding of means structure analyses. Bentler (1995) noted that the number of estimated intercepts should be less than the number of measured variables. This caveat addresses the model identification issue. In a multigroup model, this requirement is controlled by the imposition of equality constraints across the groups. In the present case, a review of the structured means portion of the models in Fig. 9.4, a and b, reveals that there are 22 measured variables (11 for each group); there are 17 intercepts to be estimated (11 equated across groups, and 4

---

[2]Because specification of equality constraints related to the error terms is considered to be excessively stringent, these constraints were not imposed.

[3]Determination of which group to serve as the reference group is purely arbitrary. Regardless of which group is chosen, the results will be identical.

freely estimated in one group, but constrained to zero in the other group), thereby leaving 5 degrees of freedom (pertinent to means and intercepts only).

AMOS Text Output: Two-Group Structured Means Model

Of primary interest in analyses related to structured means models are (a) the latent mean estimates and (b) the goodness of fit between the hypothesized model and the multigroup data. Before turning to these results for our analysis of high- and low-track students, let's once again take a few minutes to review the model and sample summary information reported in the output file. Selected portions of this summary are presented in Table 9.1.

Reviewing the number of variables, we are told that there are 11 observed variables (the subscale scores), 15 unobserved variables (4 factors; 11 error terms), 15 exogenous variables (11 error terms; 4 factors), and 11 endogenous variables (the subscale scores). Presented next is the Summary of Parameters for the high-track group, followed by the summary for the low-track group. For both groups, we see that there are 7 labeled weights (factor loadings having a "p" label attached), 15 variances (4 factor variances; 11 error variances), and 11 intercepts associated with the observed variables. The groups differ, however, in (a) the number of covariances to be estimated and (b) the number of means to be estimated. For the high-track group, the number of covariances to be estimated is 8 (6 factor covariances; 2 error covariances); for the low-track group, this number is 9 as a consequence of the additional error covariance. Finally, the number of means to be estimated for the high-track group is 4; these parameters, for the low-track group, were fixed to zero.

Let's now dissect the program's computation of degrees of freedom as summarized at the bottom of Table 9.1. The number of distinct sample moments reported is 154. If you had calculated the number of moments, in the same manner by which we have with all other applications in this book, you would have arrived at the number "132" [(11 × 12/2) = 66; times 2 groups = 132]. Why this discrepancy? The answer lies in the analysis of covariance versus means structures. All applications, prior to the present chapter, were based on covariance structures, and thus the only pieces of information needed for the analysis were the covariances among the observed variables. However, in the analysis of structured means models, information related to both the covariance matrix and the sample means is required. With 11 observed variables in the model, there will be 11 means: 22 means for the two groups. The resulting number of moments is 132 + 22 = 154.

It may be helpful if we also examine a breakdown of the 69 distinct parameters to be estimated as reported by the program. Let's turn first to the number of parameters being estimated for the high-track group. As such, we have 7 factor loadings, 8 covariances, 15 variances, 11 intercepts, and 4 latent means, thereby yielding a total of 45 parameters to be estimated. For the low-track group, on the other hand, we have 9 covariances and 15 variances, resulting in a total of 24 parameters to be

Group 1: High Track

Number of variables in your model: 26

Number of observed variables:	11
Number of unobserved variables:	15
Number of exogenous variables:	15
Number of endogenous variables:	11

Summary of Parameters

	Weights	Covariances	Variances	Means	Intercepts	Total
Fixed:	15	0	0	0	0	15
Labeled:	7	0	0	4	11	22
Unlabeled:	0	8	15	0	0	23
Total:	22	8	15	4	11	60

Group 2: Low Track

Summary of Parameters

	Weights	Covariances	Variances	Means	Intercepts	Total
Fixed:	15	0	0	0	0	15
Labeled:	7	0	0	0	11	18
Unlabeled:	0	9	15	0	0	24
Total:	22	9	15	0	11	57

For Group: High Track

Sample size: 582

For group: Low Track

Sample size: 248

Computation of Degrees of Freedom

Number of distinct sample moments:	154
Number of distinct parameters to be estimated:	69
Degrees of freedom:	85

estimated; all other parameters have been constrained equal to those of the high track group. Across the two groups, then, there are 69 (45 + 24) parameters to be estimated. With 154 sample moments, and 69 estimable parameters, we know that the number of degrees of freedom will be 85.

Parameter Estimates.   We turn now to Table 9.2, in which selected estimates are reported; in the interest of space, the factor and error variances are not reported here. Reported first are the estimates for the high-track group. A brief perusal of the critical ratios (CRs) associated with these estimates reveals all except the covariance between the factors ESC and MSC to be statistically significant. However, this finding is quite consistent with self-concept theory, as it relates to these academic dimensions, and therefore is no cause for concern.

Of major interest here are the latent mean estimates reported for high-track students, as they provide the key to the question of whether the latent factor means for this group are significantly different from those of low-track students. Given that the low-track group was designated as the reference group and, as such, their factor means were fixed to zero, the values reported here represent latent mean differences between the two groups. Reviewing these values, we see that although the latent factor means related to the more specific facets of academic, English, and mathematics self-concepts were statistically significant (as indicated by the critical ratio values >1.96), this was not the case for general self-concept (C.R. = .304).

Given that the latent mean parameters were estimated for the high-track group, and that they represent positive values, we interpret these findings as indicating that high-track students in secondary school appear to have significantly higher perceptions of self with respect to their mathematics and English capabilities, as well as to school in general, than do their low-track peers. On the other hand, when it comes to a global perception of self, there appears to be little difference between the two groups of students. Readers interested in a more detailed discussion of these results from a substantive perspective are referred to the original article (Byrne, 1988b).

Model Assessment

Goodness-of-Fit Statistics.   Finally, let's turn to the goodness-of-fit statistics resulting from this analysis, which are reported in Table 9.3. A review of the information reported here indicates that, despite the equality constraints imposed on both the factor loadings and the observed variable intercepts across the two groups, the model fitted the data exceptionally well (e.g., CFI = .993) and demonstrated an adequate approximation to the two adolescent ability track populations (RMSEA = .061). Given these findings, then, we can feel confident in interpreting the estimates associated with the current solution. I draw your attention to the fact that no statistics bearing on the RMR, GFI, and AGFI are reported here. These values are not reported in the AMOS output because they do not generalize to the case where means and intercepts are model parameters (Arbuckle, personal communication, November 13, 1999).

TABLE 9.2
Selected AMOS Text Output for Test of Latent Mean Differences: Maximum Likelihood Estimates

High Track:

Regression Weights:	Estimate	S.E.	C.R.	Label
APIGSC <------- GSC	0.535	0.022	24.122	p2
SDQGSC <------- GSC	1.000			
SESGSC <------- GSC	0.357	0.012	30.460	p3
SDQASC <------- ASC	1.000			
SCAASC <------- ASC	0.447	0.018	25.022	p5
APIESC <------- ESC	1.312	0.055	24.044	p7
SDQESC <------- ESC	1.000			
SCAESC <------- ESC	0.581	0.026	22.082	p8
APIMSC <------- MSC	0.690	0.014	48.694	p10
SDQMSC <------- MSC	1.000			
SCAMSC <------- MSC	0.426	0.010	41.440	p11

Means:	Estimate	S.E.	C.R.	Label
GSC	0.297	0.977	0.304	mn_gsc
ASC	10.371	0.788	13.326	mn_asc
ESC	3.437	0.574	5.992	mn_esc
MSC	7.644	1.067	7.161	mn_msc

Intercepts:	Estimate	S.E.	C.R.	Label
APIGSC	76.652	0.474	161.794	int_2
SDQGSC	75.638	0.812	93.123	int_1
SESGSC	31.317	0.292	107.398	int_3
SDQASC	47.918	0.673	71.238	int_4
SCAASC	25.419	0.283	89.816	int_5
APIESC	57.416	0.607	94.648	int_7
SDQESC	54.369	0.493	110.322	int_6
SCAESC	26.466	0.288	92.049	int_8
APIMSC	41.852	0.581	72.066	int_10
SDQMSC	41.438	0.833	49.749	int_9
SCAMSC	22.968	0.364	63.074	int_11

Covariances:	Estimate	S.E.	C.R.	Label
GSC <---------> ASC	52.904	6.223	8.502	
ASC <---------> ESC	37.923	4.047	9.371	
GSC <---------> ESC	25.297	4.836	5.231	
ASC <---------> MSC	90.402	8.144	11.100	
GSC <---------> MSC	53.411	9.583	5.573	
ESC <---------> MSC	1.599	5.605	0.285	
e5 <---------> e11	4.649	0.562	8.279	
e5 <---------> e8	5.142	0.594	8.656	

(Continued)

TABLE 9.2 *(Continued)*

Low Track:

Regression Weights:

	Estimate	S.E.	C.R.	Label
APIGSC <------- GSC	0.535	0.022	24.122	p2
SDQGSC <------- GSC	1.000			
SESGSC <------- GSC	0.357	0.012	30.460	p3
SDQASC <------- ASC	1.000			
SCAASC <------- ASC	0.447	0.018	25.022	p5
APIESC <------- ESC	1.312	0.055	24.044	p7
SDQESC <------- ESC	1.000			
SCAESC <------- ESC	0.581	0.026	22.082	p8
APIMSC <------- MSC	0.690	0.014	48.694	p10
SDQMSC <------- MSC	1.000			
SCAMSC <------- MSC	0.426	0.010	41.440	p11

Intercepts:

	Estimate	S.E.	C.R.	Label
APIGSC	76.652	0.474	161.794	int_2
SDQGSC	75.638	0.812	93.123	int_1
SESGSC	31.317	0.292	107.398	int_3
SDQASC	47.918	0.673	71.238	int_4
SCAASC	25.419	0.283	89.816	int_5
APIESC	57.416	0.607	94.648	int_7
SDQESC	54.369	0.493	110.322	int_6
SCAESC	26.466	0.288	92.049	int_8
APIMSC	41.852	0.581	72.066	int_10
SDQMSC	41.438	0.833	49.749	int_9
SCAMSC	22.968	0.364	63.074	int_11

Covariances:

	Estimate	S.E.	C.R.	Label
GSC <---------> ASC	40.809	8.094	5.042	
ASC <---------> ESC	31.612	4.980	6.347	
GSC <---------> ESC	23.240	5.860	3.966	
MSC <---------> ASC	49.282	8.601	5.730	
MSC <---------> GSC	50.161	10.765	4.660	
MSC <---------> ESC	2.908	5.797	0.502	
e5 <---------> e11	3.910	0.864	4.523	
e7 <---------> e10	17.390	3.275	5.310	
e5 <---------> e8	5.050	1.048	4.821	

MODELING WITH AMOS BASIC

Let's turn now to the same input file for testing mean structures, albeit structured within the framework of AMOS Basic. This file is shown in Table 9.4.

This file, consistent with the other multigroup AMOS Basic input files, presents the model specifications for each group separately. Shown first in Table 9.4 are specifications for the high-track group, followed by those for the low-track group. Although the structure of this file is fairly straightforward, I consider it worthwhile

TABLE 9.3

Selected AMOS Text Output for Test of Latent Mean Differences: Goodness-of-Fit Statistics

Summary of models

Model	NPAR	CMIN	DF	P	CMIN/DF
Default model	69	348.976	85	0.000	4.106
Saturated model	154	0.000	0		
Independence model	22	36047.722	132	0.000	273.089

Model	DELTA1 NFI	RHO1 RFI	DELTA2 IFI	RHO2 TLI	CFI
Default model	0.990	0.985	0.993	0.989	0.993
Saturated model	1.000		1.000		1.000
Independence model	0.000	0.000	0.000	0.000	0.000

Model	PRATIO	PNFI	PCFI
Default model	0.644	0.638	0.639
Saturated model	0.000	0.000	0.000
Independence model	1.000	0.000	0.000

Model	RMSEA	LO 90	HI 90	PCLOSE
Default model	0.061	0.055	0.068	0.003
Independence model	0.573	0.568	0.578	0.000

Model	AIC	BCC	BIC	CAIC
Default model	486.976	492.024		
Saturated model	308.000	319.266		
Independence model	36091.722	36093.331		

Model	ECVI	LO 90	HI 90	MECVI
Default model	0.588	0.523	0.662	0.594
Saturated model	0.372	0.372	0.372	0.386
Independence model	43.589	42.839	44.346	43.591

to highlight a few of its characteristics. One of the first things to note is the second command statement appearing at the top of the file: "**SEM.MeansandIntercepts**." This command identifies the specification input as being pertinent to a structured means model. Failure to include this statement triggers an error message and the analyses do not proceed.

The first set of specifications for each group relates to the intercepts, the factor loading weights, and the error terms. As is customary in multigroup models, the parenthesized labels represent parameters that are estimated for the first group, but constrained equal to these to estimates for the second group; the parenthesized 1's, of course, indicate that those parameters are constrained to a value of 1.00. Look-

TABLE 9.4
AMOS Basic Input File for Test of Latent Mean Differences

```
Dim Sem As New AmosEngine
'Testing for Latent mean Differences Across Academic Track (Fig. 9.4)'

SEM.TextOutput
SEM.ModelMeansandIntercepts

SEM.BeginGroup "HighTrack.csv"
    SEM.GroupName "High Track Ability Group"

    SEM.Structure "SDQGSC = (int_1)  + (1) GSC + (1) e1"
    SEM.Structure " APIGSC  =  (int_2)  + (p2) GSC + (1) e2"
    SEM.Structure " SESGSC  = (int_3) + (p3) GSC + (1) e3"
    SEM.Structure " SDQASC  = (int_4) + (1) ASC + (1) e4"
    SEM.Structure " SCAASC  = (int_5) + (p5) ASC + (1) e5"
    SEM.Structure " SDQESC = (int_6) + (1) ESC + (1) e6"
    SEM.Structure " APIESC  =  (int_7) + (p7) ESC + (1) e7"
    SEM.Structure " SCAESC = (int_8) + (p8) ESC + (1) e8"
    SEM.Structure "SDQMSC  = (int_9) + (1) MSC + (1) e9"
    SEM.Structure " APIMSC  = (int_10) + (p10) MSC + (1) e10"
    SEM.Structure " SCAMSC  = (int_11) + (p11) MSC + (1) e11"

    SEM.Mean " GSC", "mn_gsc"
    SEM.Mean " ASC", "mn_asc"
    SEM.Mean " ESC", "mn_esc"
    SEM.Mean " MSC", "mn_msc"

    SEM.Structure " e5 <> e8 "
    SEM.Structure " e5 <> e11"

SEM.BeginGroup "LowTrack.csv"
    SEM.GroupName "Low Track Ability Group"

    SEM.Structure "SDQGSC = (int_1)  + (1) GSC + (1) e1"
    SEM.Structure " APIGSC  =  (int_2)  + (p2) GSC + (1) e2"
    SEM.Structure " SESGSC  = (int_3) + (p3) GSC + (1) e3"
    SEM.Structure " SDQASC  = (int_4) + (1) ASC + (1) e4"
    SEM.Structure " SCAASC  = (int_5) + (p5) ASC + (1) e5"
    SEM.Structure " SDQESC = (int_6) + (1) ESC + (1) e6"
    SEM.Structure " APIESC  =  (int_7) + (p7) ESC + (1) e7"
    SEM.Structure " SCAESC = (int_8) + (p8) ESC + (1) e8"
    SEM.Structure "SDQMSC  = (int_9) + (1) MSC + (1) e9"
    SEM.Structure " APIMSC  = (int_10) + (p10) MSC + (1) e10"
    SEM.Structure " SCAMSC  = (int_11) + (p11) MSC + (1) e11"

    SEM.Mean " GSC", "0"
    SEM.Mean " ASC", "0"
    SEM.Mean " ESC", "0"
    SEM.Mean " MSC", "0"

    SEM.Structure " e5 <> e8"
    SEM.Structure " e5 <> e11"
    SEM.Structure " e7 <> e10"

End Sub
```

ing at the first specification, for example, we see that the observed variable "SDQGSC" derives from the sum of three parameters: its intercept term (int_1), its factor loading weight (which in this case is fixed to 1.00), and its error term.

The second set of specifications relates to the latent means for the high-track group. Given that these parameters are to be freely estimated for high-track students only, the parameter labels (mn_gsc–mn_msc) have not been parenthesized. The last set of specifications for this group relates to the two error covariances, which are to be freely estimated.

Turning to specifications relative to the second group, low-track students, you can quickly see only two differences from Group 1. First, in the specification of latent factor means, we see a zero value in lieu of a nominally labeled variable. Second, consistent with the model for the low-track group, three error covariances have been specified, rather than two.

As I noted earlier in the chapter, testing for latent mean differences using AMOS 4.0 is the easiest approach that I have yet encountered. Indeed, this holds true whether one works within the Graphics or the Basic interface. One reason for this simplicity may lie with not having to specify and otherwise deal with a constant dummy variable, which to date, has been necessary within the framework of other SEM statistical packages. Within the AMOS framework, however, this fabrication is not necessary as the means of exogenous variables can be explicitly estimated (Arbuckle, personal communication, November 13, 1999).

CHAPTER

10

Application 8:
Testing for Invariant
Pattern of Causal Structure

I n chapter 4, I highlighted several problematic aspects of post hoc model fitting in structural equation modeling. Indeed, so common is this practice, and so frequently is it conducted with little to no regard for the substantive meaningfulness of the respecified models, that concerned researchers have provided a variety of different means by which such models can be tested more stringently (see Anderson & Gerbing, 1988; Cudeck & Henly, 1991; MacCallum, 1995; MacCallum et al., 1992, 1993). In chapter 4, I noted that one approach to addressing problems associated with post hoc model fitting is to apply some mode of cross-validation analysis; this is the focus of the present chapter. Before walking through this procedure, however, let's first review some of the issues related to cross-validation.

CROSS-VALIDATION IN COVARIANCE
STRUCTURE MODELING

Typically, in applications of covariance structure modeling, the researcher tests an hypothesized model and then, from an assessment of various goodness-of-fit criteria, concludes that a statistically better fitting model could be attained by respecifying the model such that particular parameters previously constrained to zero are freely estimated (Breckler, 1990; MacCallum, et al., 1992, 1993; MacCallum et al., 1994). Possibly, as a consequence of considerable criticism of covariance structure modeling procedures over the past decade (e.g., Biddle & Marlin, 1987; Breckler, 1990; Cliff, 1983), most researchers who proceed with this respecification process are now generally familiar with the issues. In particular, they are cognizant of the exploratory nature of these follow-up procedures, as well as the fact that additionally specified parameters in the model must be theoretically substantiated.

Indeed, the pros and cons of post hoc model fitting have been rigorously debated in the literature. Although some have severely criticized the practice (e.g., Cliff, 1983; Cudeck & Browne, 1983), others have argued that as long as the researcher is fully cognizant of the exploratory nature of his or her analyses, the process can be substantively meaningful because practical as well as statistical significance can be taken into account (Byrne et al., 1989; Tanaka & Huba, 1984). However, Joreskog (1993, p. 298) was very clear in stating that "If the model is rejected by the data, the problem is to determine what is wrong with the model and how the model should be modified to fit the data better." The purists would argue that once a hypothesized model is rejected, that's the end of the story. More realistically, however, other researchers in this area recognize the obvious impracticality in the termination of all subsequent model analyses. Clearly, in the interest of future research, it behooves the investigator to probe more deeply into the question of why the model is malfitting (see Tanaka, 1993). As a consequence of the concerted efforts of statistical experts in covariance structure modeling in addressing this issue, there are now several different approaches that can be used to increase the soundness of findings derived from these post hoc analyses.

Undoubtedly, post hoc model fitting in the analysis of covariance structures is problematic. With multiple model specifications, there is the risk of capitalization on chance factors because model modification may be driven by characteristics of the particular sample on which the model was tested (e.g., sample size, sample heterogeneity) (MacCallum et al., 1992). As a consequence of this sequential testing procedure, then, there is increased risk of making either a Type I or Type II error and, at this point in time, there is no direct way to adjust for the probability of such error. Because hypothesized covariance structure models represent only approximations of reality and thus are not expected to fit real-world phenomena exactly (Cudeck & Browne, 1983; MacCallum et al., 1992), most research applications are likely to require the specification of alternative models in the quest for one that fits the data well (Anderson & Gerbing, 1988; MacCallum, 1986). Indeed, this aspect of covariance structure modeling represents a serious limitation, and, to date, several alternative strategies for model testing have been proposed (see Anderson & Gerbing, 1988; Cudeck & Henly, 1991; MacCallum, 1995; MacCallum et al., 1992, 1993).

One approach to addressing problems associated with post hoc model fitting is to employ a cross-validation strategy whereby the final model derived from the post hoc analyses is tested on a second (or more) independent sample(s) from the same population. Barring the availability of separate data samples, but with a sufficiently large sample, one may wish to randomly split the data into two (or more) parts, thereby making it possible to cross-validate the findings (see Cudeck & Browne, 1983). As such, Sample A serves as the calibration sample on which the initially hypothesized model is tested, and on which any post hoc analyses are conducted in the process of attaining a well-fitting model. Once this final model is determined, the validity of its structure can then be tested based on Sample B (the validation sample). In other words, the final best fitting model for the calibration sample becomes the hypothesized model under test for the validation sample.

There are several ways by which the similarity of model structure can be tested (see MacCallum et al., 1994). For example, Cudeck and Browne suggested the computation of a cross-validation index (CVI), which measures the distance between the restricted (i.e., model-imposed) variance–covariance matrix for the calibration sample and the unrestricted variance–covariance matrix for the validation sample. Because the estimated predictive validity of the model is gauged by the smallness of the CVI value, evaluation is facilitated by their comparison based on a series of alternative models. It is important to note, however, that the CVI estimate reflects overall discrepancy between "the actual population covariance matrix, Σ, and the estimated population covariance matrix reconstructed from the parameter estimates obtained from fitting the model to the sample" (MacCallum et al., 1994, p. 4). More specifically, this global index of discrepancy represents combined effects arising from the discrepancy of approximation (e.g., nonlinear influences among variables) and the discrepancy of estimation (e.g., representative sample; sample size). (For a more extended discussion of these aspects of discrepancy, see Browne & Cudeck, 1989; Cudeck & Henly, 1991; MacCallum et al., 1994.)

In the present chapter, we examine another approach to cross-validation. Specifically, we use an invariance-testing strategy to test for the replicability of structural paths across groups. Although there are numerous approaches to cross-validation in structural equation modeling, depending on the focus of one's study (see Anderson & Gerbing, 1988; Browne & Cudeck, 1989; Cudeck & Browne, 1983), the application described here is straightforward in addressing the question of whether a model that has been respecified in one sample replicates over a second independent sample from the same population (for another approach, see Byrne & Baron, 1994).

TESTING FOR INVARIANCE ACROSS CALIBRATION/VALIDATION SAMPLES

The present example comes from the same study briefly described in chapter 6 (Byrne, 1994b). The intent of this study was (a) to validate a causal structure involving the impact of organizational and personality factors on three facets of burnout for elementary, intermediate, and secondary teachers, (b) to cross-validate this model across a second independent sample within each teaching panel, and (c) to test for the invariance of common structural paths across teaching panels. In this chapter, we focus on (b) in testing for model replication across calibration and validation samples of secondary teachers. (For an in-depth examination of invariance-testing procedures within and between the three teacher groups, see Byrne, 1994b.)

It is perhaps important to note that although the present example of cross-validation is based on a full structural equation model, the practice is in no way limited to such applications. Indeed, cross-validation is equally as important for CFA models, and examples of such applications can be found across a variety of disciplines; for those relevant to psychology, see Byrne et al. (Byrne, 1993, 1994a; Byrne & Baron, 1994; Byrne et al., 1993, 1994, 1995; Byrne, Baron, Melin, & Larsson, 1996; Byrne, Baron, & Balev, 1996; Byrne et al., 1998); to education, see Benson and Bandalos (1992); and to medicine, see Francis, Fletcher, and Rourke (1988). We turn now to the model under study.

The original study from which the present example is taken comprised a sample of 1,431 high school teachers. For purposes of cross-validation, this sample was randomly split into two; Sample A ($n = 716$) was used as the calibration group, and Sample B ($n = 715$) as the validation group. Preliminary analyses conducted for the original study determined 2 outlying cases, which were deleted from all subsequent analyses, thereby rendering final sample sizes of 715 (Sample A) and 714 (Sample B).

The Hypothesized and Baseline Models

The originally hypothesized model (as shown in chap. 6) was tested and modified based on data from the calibration sample (Sample A) of high school teachers. The final best-fitting model for this sample is shown schematically in Fig. 10.1. It is important to note that, for purposes of clarity, not all factor intercorrelations, error terms, and cross-loadings have been incorporated into the figure; only the structural parameters are shown here, as they are the parameters of interest in the present chapter. (For a review of the measurement model, readers are referred to chap. 6, Fig. 6.2.)

In the original study, testing of the initially hypothesized model was conducted using the EQS program. As such, all model modifications and tests of equality constraints were based on the Lagrange multiplier test statistics, which are derived multivariately. It is important that I draw your attention to this fact because, in this chapter, these same tests for invariance are based on a univariate approach using AMOS 4.0. As a result, findings from the current set of analyses can deviate slightly from those reported for the original study. This final model of burnout structure for high school teachers, as determined in the original study, yielded $\chi^2_{(441)} = 1514.09$, and CFI = .91. The task before us now is to determine if this final model replicates over Sample B, the validation group of high school teachers.

MODELING WITH AMOS GRAPHICS

Testing for the Validity of Causal Structure

Following the procedure that was illustrated in chapters 7 and 8, we begin by first establishing a multigroup baseline model against which we can compare a subsequent model in which equality constraints are specified. However, unlike the previous two multigroup models in which each group had its own specific baseline

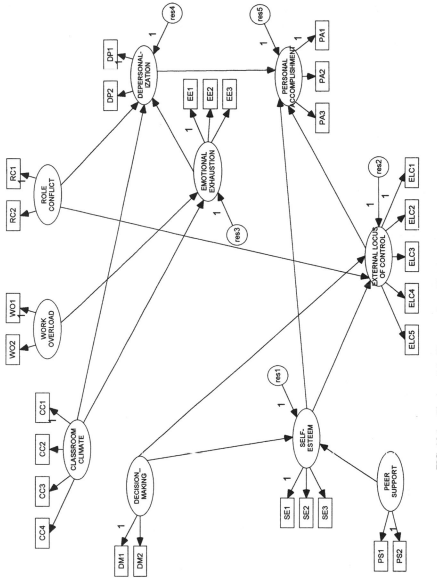

FIG. 10.1.   Final model of burnout for calibration sample of high school teachers.

251

model, the one presented here is specific only to the calibration group. In other words, specifications describing the final model for the calibration sample are similarly specified for the validation sample. Selected information from this initial test of causal structure is summarized in Table 10.1, and the goodness-of fit results in Table 10.2.

Information of primary interest in Table 10.1 is the number of parameters to be estimated (158; 79 in each group), the number of degrees of freedom (654), and the sample sizes (715; 714). From Table 10.2, we can determine that goodness of fit of the model for the two groups in combination and with no equality constraints imposed is excellent (CFI = .942; RMSEA = .034). The χ^2 value, with 654 degrees of freedom, is 1733.181; this value serves as our comparison point in determining the extent to which causal structure is the same across calibration and validation

TABLE 10.1
Selected AMOS Text Output for Simultaneous Test
of Burnout Structure: Model and Sample Summary

Number of variables in model: 71

```
              Number of observed variables:      28
              Number of unobserved variables:    43
              Number of exogenous variables:     38
              Number of endogenous variables:    33
```

Summary of Parameters

	Weights	Covariances	Variances	Means	Intercepts	Total
Fixed:	43	0	0	0	0	43
Labeled:	0	0	0	0	0	0
Unlabeled:	31	10	38	0	0	79
Total:	74	10	38	0	0	122

Calibration Sample

Sample size: 715

Validation Sample

Sample size: 714

Computation of Degrees of Freedom

```
                  Number of distinct sample moments:    812
      Number of distinct parameters to be estimated:    158
                  ---------------------------
                           Degrees of freedom:    654
```

TABLE 10.2
Selected AMOS Text Output for Simultaneous Multigroup
Test of Hypothesized Model: Goodness-of-Fit Statistics

Summary of models

- - - - - - - - - - - - - - - - - -

Model	NPAR	CMIN	DF	P
Default model	158	1733.181	654	0.000
Saturated model	812	0.000	0	
Independence model	56	19246.192	756	0.000

Model	RMR	GFI	AGFI	PGFI
Default model	0.050	0.918	0.899	0.740
Saturated model	0.000	1.000		
Independence model	0.278	0.312	0.261	0.291

Model	DELTA1 NFI	RHO1 RFI	DELTA2 IFI	RHO2 TLI	CFI
Default model	0.910	0.896	0.942	0.933	0.942
Saturated model	1.000		1.000		1.000
Independence model	0.000	0.000	0.000	0.000	0.000

Model	PRATIO	PNFI	PCFI
Default model	0.865	0.787	0.815
Saturated model	0.000	0.000	0.000
Independence model	1.000	0.000	0.000

Model	RMSEA	LO 90	HI 90	PCLOSE
Default model	0.034	0.032	0.036	1.000
Independence model	0.131	0.129	0.133	0.000

Model	ECVI	LO 90	HI 90	MECVI
Default model	1.436	1.352	1.525	1.445
Saturated model	1.138	1.138	1.138	1.186
Independence model	13.566	13.251	13.885	13.569

groups. We now turn to the next step in testing for invariance: the specification of equality constraints.

Testing for the Invariance of Causal Structure: The Specification of Equality Constraints

From working through the applications presented in the two previous chapters, you are familiar with the manner by which equality constraints are specified using AMOS Graphics. Specifically, this process involves first selecting the group for which the labels apply, and second, labeling all parameters to be constrained equal across groups. In the present case, the group selected is the calibration group. Figure 10.2 illustrates the labeling of the first parameter to be constrained (P1), which represents the structural path flowing from role conflict (RC) to depersonalization (DP). Shown in Fig. 10.2 is the opened Object Properties dialog box that resulted from having either (a) clicked on its related icon ![icon], (b) selected from the View/Set pull-down menu, or (c) right-clicked on the mouse. Note that the model under study is also open, and therefore visible (although only a portion of it is visible in the figure). As noted in the three previous chapters, given that one must first select the parameter to be labeled (see broken-line rectangle surrounding the path from RC to DP) and then enter the label (P1) in the Object Properties box, both the dialog box and the model must be opened at the same time. This procedure is repeated until all desired paths in the model have been labeled (and therefore constrained equal across groups). Note that the "All groups" option has been check-marked, thereby indicating that the model, as labeled, pertains to all groups involved in the test for invariance. In the present case, of course, this means that the estimated values of the structural paths for the calibration group will be held constrained at those values for the validation group. The model with all structural paths labeled is shown in Fig. 10.3.

In this chapter, I would like to show you another means of specifying equality constraints using a matrix approach. With the calibration group once again selected, pull down the View/Set menu and select Matrix Representation, as shown in Fig. 10.4, to display the parameter labels in a spreadsheet format as presented in Fig. 10.5.

On the left side of the spreadsheet, you see a column of miniature SEM models, each with a different set of ellipses and/or rectangles highlighted. In Fig. 10.6, the mouse has been clicked on the exogenous variable icon, which simultaneously triggers the message shown. What we want to do here is to display the exogenous variables on

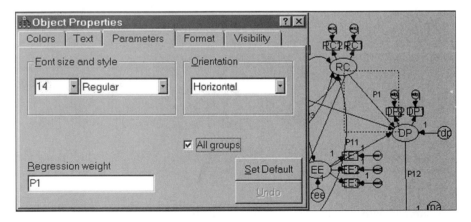

FIG. 10.2.   Labeling parameters using the Object Properties dialog box.

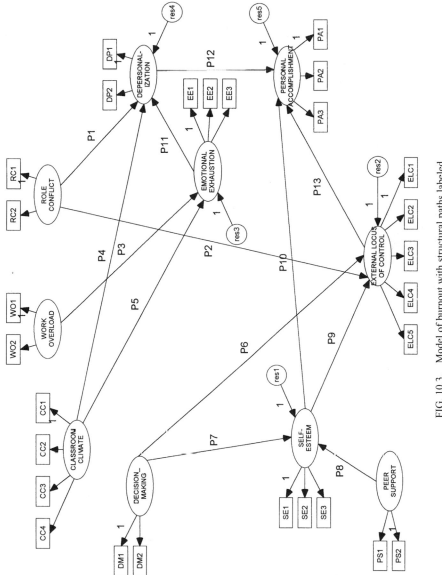

FIG. 10.3.   Model of burnout with structural paths labeled.

255

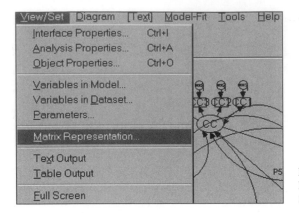

FIG. 10.4. Selecting the Matrix Representation option from the View/Set menu.

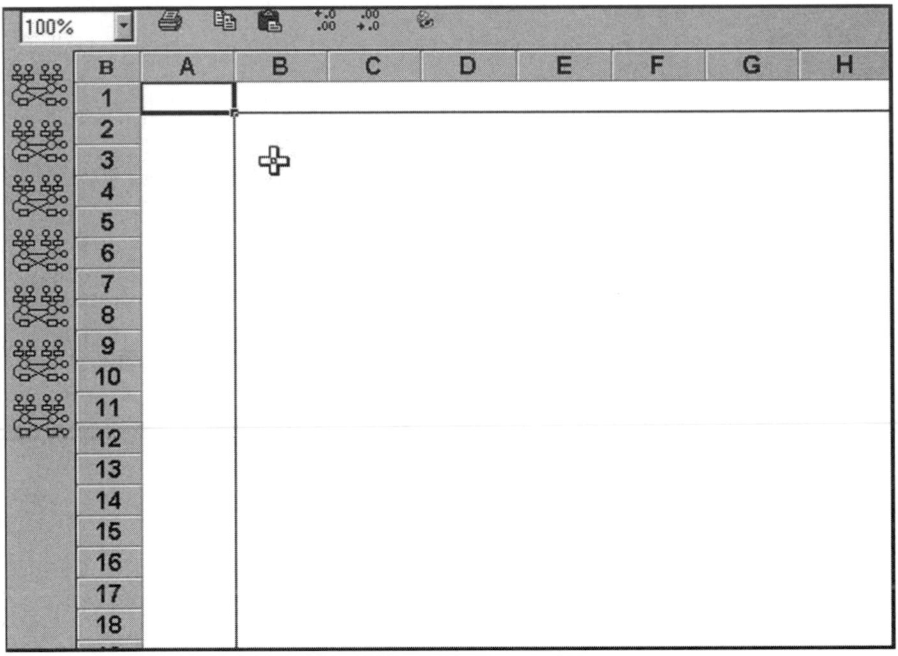

FIG. 10.5.   Parameter spreadsheet with cell "A1" selected.

the top row of the matrix. To accomplish this, we hold the right mouse button down and then drag the exogenous icon to the "B" cell of Row 1, as shown in Fig. 10.7. Release of the right mouse button subsequently yields the name of each exogenous variable in the model and prints it on the top row of the matrix, as seen in Fig. 10.8.

To further complete the matrix, we now need to enter the endogenous variables in the model. To do so, we click on the endogenous icon and then drag it to the sec-

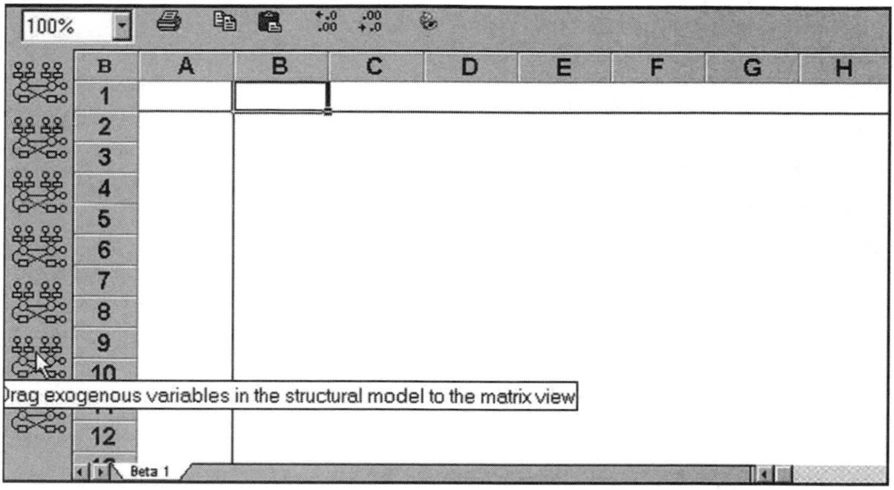

FIG. 10.6. Parameter spreadsheet with exogenous variable icon selected.

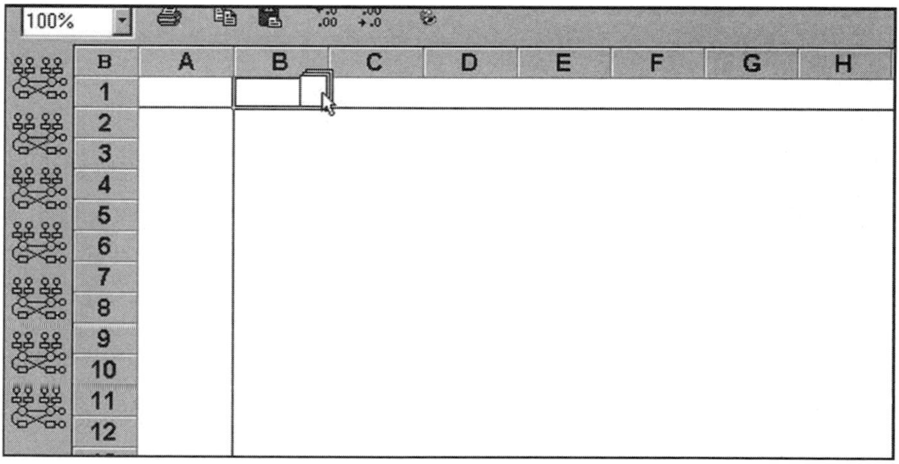

FIG. 10.7. Parameter spreadsheet showing targeted location for placement of exogenous variables.

ond cell in Column A, as shown in Fig. 10.9. Once both the exogenous and endogenous variables have been entered into the matrix, the program displays labels consistent with the parameters to be estimated. From a review of the matrix in Fig. 10.10, we see that eight structural paths are to be estimated (P1–P8). Identification of these paths is consistent with matrix presentations associated with LISREL program output files. As such, you simply read down from the top row (which displays

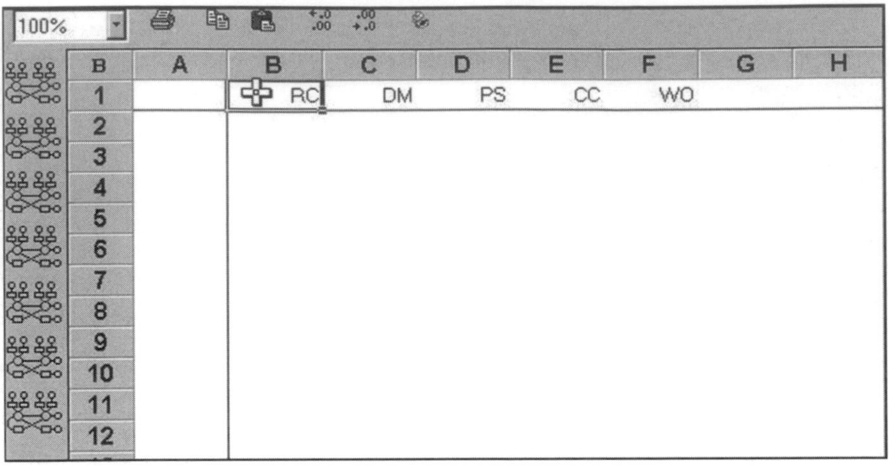

FIG. 10.8.   Parameter spreadsheet with exogenous variables placed in row 1.

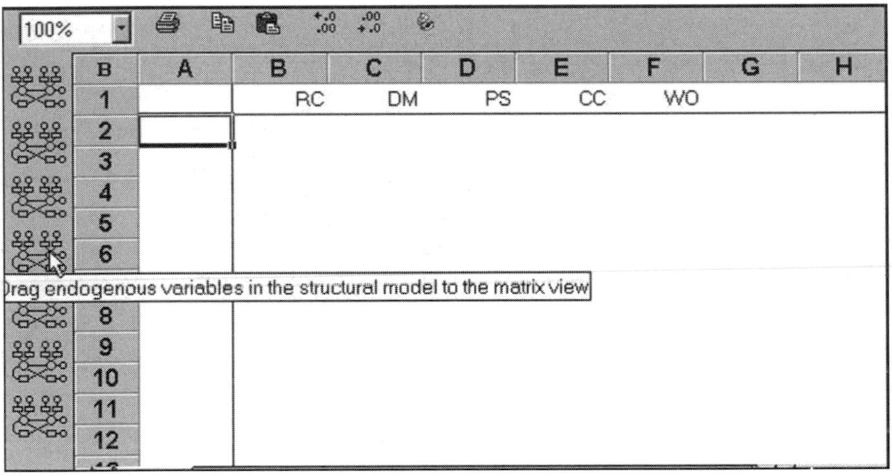

FIG. 10.9.   Parameter spreadsheet with endogenous variable icon selected.

the exogenous variables) and then left, over to the "A" column (which displays the endogenous variables). For example, reading down from CC and across to DP, we see the parameter label "P4"; this parameter represents the structural path flowing from classroom climate to depersonalization.

The eight labeled parameters shown in Fig. 10.10, however, represent only relations between exogenous and endogenous (i.e., independent and dependent) variables in the model; yet to be included in the matrix are structural paths flowing

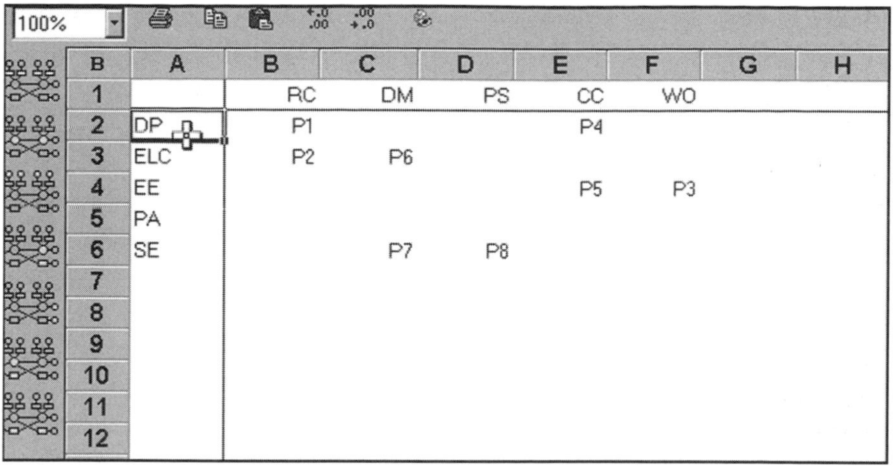

FIG. 10.10.   Parameter spreadsheet showing labeled structural paths between exogenous and endogenous variables.

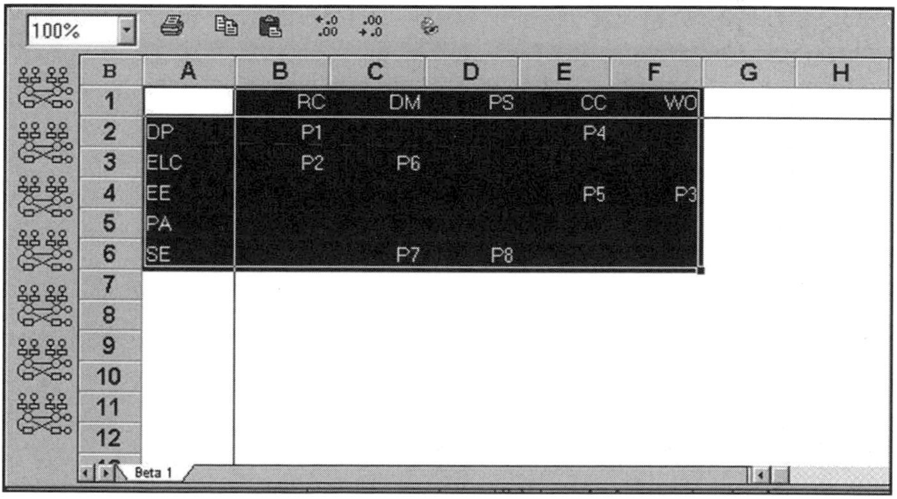

FIG. 10.11.   Parameter spreadsheet with structural paths selected.

from one endogenous variable to another endogenous variable. However, because the inclusion of these parameters necessarily extends the matrix beyond page view, I address this issue after demonstrating, first, the specification of equality constraints when using the matrix approach. This task simply involves five simple steps. First, as shown in Fig. 10.11, select the entire parameter matrix, which, at the present time, includes fields A1 through F6 (the two diagonal points of the rectangle). Second, using the Edit pull-down menu, copy the matrix to the Window's clip-board (see Fig. 10.12). Third, select "Validation Sample"—either via the left panel of the AMOS working screen as illustrated in Fig. 10.13, or by selecting the Man-age Groups option from the Model-Fit pull-down menu. Fourth, with "Validation Sample" highlighted, open the View/Set pull-down menu and select Matrix Repre-sentation to display the parameter labels in spreadsheet form. Finally, click on the "A1" cell and paste the parameter into it (select Edit → Paste).

Undo	Alt+Bksp
Redo	
Copy (to clipboard)	Ctrl+C
Select	F2
Select All	
Deselect All	F11
Link	
Move	Ctrl+M
Duplicate	
Erase	Del
Move Parameter	
Reflect	
Rotate	
Shape of Object	
Space Horizontally	
Space Vertically	
Drag Properties...	Ctrl+G
Fit to Page	Ctrl+F
Touch Up	Ctrl+H

FIG. 10.12.   Selecting the Copy op-tion from the Edit menu.

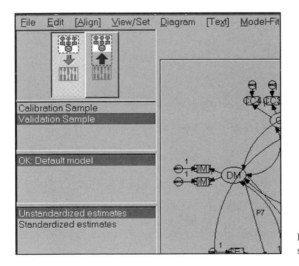

FIG. 10.13.   Selecting the validation sample.

Recall that the matrix just described incorporated only paths flowing from exogenous to endogenous variables. Thus, it is important to note that, under normal circumstances, you would have also included the endogenous–endogenous paths before copying over the matrix for the validation group. However, as I explained earlier, my reason for not doing so was purely for the sake of visual clarity in demonstrating these procedures. Although I am still restricted in my ability to display the complete matrix, I can, at least, show in Fig. 10.14 the labeled parameters involving structural paths from one endogenous variable to another (P9–P13). The portion of the matrix that is missing is the list of exogenous variables in column A.

AMOS Text Output: Two-Group Model With Equality Constraints Imposed

Model Assessment

Goodness-of-Fit Statistics. Having constrained the structural paths to be equal across groups, of course, we are now interested in viewing the goodness-of-fit results, and these are summarized in Table 10.3. Of primary interest is the χ^2 value, as it provides the basis for comparison with the initial multigroup model in which no equality constraints were imposed. From Table 10.3, we see this value to be 1747.818, with 667 degrees of freedom. The difference in χ^2 values between this test and the omnibus test is 14.637, with 13 degrees of freedom, which is not statistically significant.

In sum, based on these findings, we can conclude that causal structure related to the model of burnout presented in Fig. 10.1 is equivalent across the calibration and validation samples of teachers. From the perspective of cross-validation, this

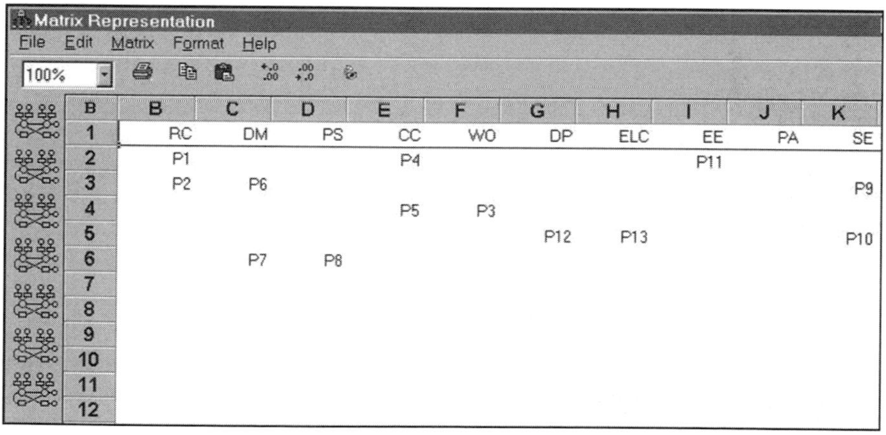

FIG. 10.14.   Parameter spreadsheet with all structural paths labeled.

TABLE 10.3
Selected AMOS Text Output for Test of Invariant Structural Paths: Goodness-of-Fit Statistics

```
Summary of models
------------------
```

Model	NPAR	CMIN	DF	P
Default model	145	1747.818	667	0.000
Saturated model	812	0.000	0	
Independence model	56	19246.192	756	0.000

Model	RMR	GFI	AGFI	PGFI
Default model	0.052	0.918	0.900	0.754
Saturated model	0.000	1.000		
Independence model	0.278	0.312	0.261	0.291

Model	DELTA1 NFI	RHO1 RFI	DELTA2 IFI	RHO2 TLI	CFI
Default model	0.909	0.897	0.942	0.934	0.942
Saturated model	1.000		1.000		1.000
Independence model	0.000	0.000	0.000	0.000	0.000

Model	PRATIO	PNFI	PCFI
Default model	0.882	0.802	0.831
Saturated model	0.000	0.000	0.000
Independence model	1.000	0.000	0.000

Model	RMSEA	LO 90	HI 90	PCLOSE
Default model	0.034	0.032	0.036	1.000
Independence model	0.131	0.129	0.133	0.000

Model	ECVI	LO 90	HI 90	MECVI
Default model	1.428	1.344	1.517	1.437
Saturated model	1.138	1.138	1.138	1.186
Independence model	13.566	13.251	13.885	13.569

illustrated equality serves as strong support for the final model of burnout derived from post hoc model fitting for the calibration sample of high school teachers.

MODELING WITH AMOS BASIC

The AMOS Basic input file illustrated in this chapter reflects the multigroup model displayed in Fig. 10.3. All causal paths have been labeled, thereby indicating that these parameters are to be constrained equal across calibration and validation samples; the input file is presented in Table 10.4.

TABLE 10.4
AMOS Basic Input File: Testing for Invariance
of Causal Structure Across Calibration/Validation Samples

Dim Sem As New Amosengine
'Testing for Invariance of Causal Structure Across Calibration/Calibration Samples (Fig. 10.3)
SEM.TextOutput

SEM.BeginGroup "secind1l.txt"
  SEM.GroupName "Calibration Group"

SEM.Structure "RC1	=	(1)	ROLE CONFLICT + (1) erc1"
SEM.Structure "RC2	=		ROLE CONFLICT + (1) erc2"
SEM.Structure "WO1	=	(1)	WORK OVERLOAD + (1) erwo1"
SEM.Structure "WO2	=		WORK OVERLOAD + (1) erwo2"
SEM.Structure "CC1	=	(1)	CLASSROOM CLIMATE + (1) ecc1"
SEM.Structure "CC2	=		CLASSROOM CLIMATE + (1) ecc2"
SEM.Structure "CC3	=		CLASSROOM CLIMATE + (1) ecc3"
SEM.Structure "CC4	=		CLASSROOM CLIMATE + (1) ecc4"
SEM.Structure "DM1	=	(1)	DECISIONMAKING + (1) edm1"
SEM.Structure "DM2	=		DECISIONMAKING + (1) edm2"
SEM.Structure "SE1	=	(1)	SELF-ESTEEM + (1) ese1"
SEM.Structure "SE2	=		SELF-ESTEEM + (1) ese2"
SEM.Structure "SE3	=		SELF-ESTEEM + (1) ese3"
SEM.Structure "PS1	=		PEER SUPPORT + (1) eps1"
SEM.Structure "PS2	=	(1)	PEER SUPPORT + (1) eps2"
SEM.Structure "ELC1	=	(1)	EXTERNAL LOCUS OF CONTROL + (1) eel1"
SEM.Structure "ELC2	=		EXTERNAL LOCUS OF CONTROL + (1) eel2"
SEM.Structure "ELC3	=		EXTERNAL LOCUS OF CONTROL + (1) eel3"
SEM.Structure "ELC4	=		EXTERNAL LOCUS OF CONTROL + (1) eel4"
SEM.Structure "ELC5	=		EXTERNAL LOCUS OF CONTROL + (1) eel5"
SEM.Structure "EE1	=	(1)	EMOTIONAL EXHAUSTION + (1) eee1"
SEM.Structure "EE2	=		EMOTIONAL EXHAUSTION + (1) eee2"
SEM.Structure "EE3	=		EMOTIONAL EXHAUSTION + (1) eee3"
SEM.Structure "DP1	=	(1)	DEPERSONALIZATION + (1) edp1"
SEM.Structure "DP2	=		DEPERSONALIZATION + (1) edp2"
SEM.Structure "PA1	=	(1)	PERSONAL ACCOMPLISHMENT + (1) epa1"
SEM.Structure "PA2	=		PERSONAL ACCOMPLISHMENT + (1) epa2"
SEM.Structure "PA3	=		PERSONAL ACCOMPLISHMENT + (1) epa3"

  SEM.Structure "SELF-ESTEEM = DECISIONMAKING (P7) + PEER SUPPORT (P8) + (1) res1"
  SEM.Structure "EXTERNAL LOCUS OF CONTROL = ROLE CONFLICT (P2) +
      DECISION MAKING (P6) + SELF-ESTEEM (P9) + (1) res2"
  SEM.Structure "EMOTIONAL EXHAUSTION = WORK OVERLOAD (P3) + CLASSROOM
      CLIMATE (P5) + (1) res3"
  SEM.Structure "DEPERSONALIZATION = ROLE CONFLICT (P1) + CLASSROOM CLIMATE
      (P4) + EMOTIONAL EXHAUSTION (P11) + (1) res4"
  SEM.Structure "PERSONAL ACCOMPLISHMENT= DEPERSONALIZATION (P12) + SELF-
      ESTEEM (P10) + EXTERNAL LOCUS OF CONTROL (P13) + (1) res5"

SEM.BeginGroup "secind2l.txt"
  SEM.GroupName "Validation Group"

File Input repeated as above

End Sub

As with the multigroup files illustrated in earlier chapters, model parameters are specified for each group separately. In the present instance, the analyses again involve only two groups; the first set of specifications is pertinent to a calibration sample, while the second set is pertinent to its validation sample. Given that the present application provides an example of cross-validation, specifications related to the model, as determined for the calibration sample, remain identical for the validation group. In the interest of space, these specifications are not repeated in Table 10.4. However, in the actual execution of this input file, it would be necessary to repeat the model specifications for the validation sample.

Consistent with previous AMOS Basic files illustrated for multigroup analyses, is the specification of parameters to be constrained equal across groups. As you can see in the table, only specifications related to the structural paths include parenthesized labels (P1-P13) as the equality of these parameters are of primary interest. In the interest of completeness, however, let us review the AMOS Basic file shown in Table 10.4.

Presented first are parameter specifications bearing on the measurement model. As such, each statement represents a factor regression path plus an error term. Factor regression paths that were fixed to a value of 1.00 for identification purposes are shown with a parenthesized 1 [(1)] preceding the name of the observed variable; regression paths related to the error terms, of course, are all constrained to a value of 1.00.

These measurement model specifications are followed by those related to the structural model. In comparing this latter set of specifications with the model shown in Fig. 10.4, it is easy to see that all structural paths are constrained to be equal across the two samples. The parenthesized values of 1, as was the case for the measurement error terms, indicate that the regression path associated with the residual error term is to be fixed to a value of 1.00; in both cases, only error variance is of interest.

IV

OTHER IMPORTANT TOPICS

Chapter

Application 9:
Bootstrapping as an Aid
to Nonnormal Data

Two critically important assumptions associated with structural equation modeling (SEM), in the analysis of covariance and mean structures, are the requirements that the data be of a continuous scale and have a multivariate normal distribution. These underlying assumptions are linked to large-sample (i.e., asymptotic) theory, within which SEM is embedded. More specifically, they derive from the approach taken in the estimation of parameters using the SEM methodology. Typically, either maximum likelihood (ML) or normal theory generalized least squares (GLS) estimation is used; both demand that the data be continuous and multivariate normal. This chapter focuses on the issue of multivariate nonnormality; readers interested in the issue of noncontinuous variables are referred to Bollen (1989a), Byrne (1998), Coenders, Satorra, and Saris (1997), and West et al. (1995).

Despite its import for all parametric statistical analyses, a review of the literature provides ample evidence of empirical research wherein the issue of distributional normality has been blatantly ignored. For example, in an analysis of 440 achievement and psychometric data sets, all of which exceeded a sample size of 400, Micceri (1989) reported that the majority of these data failed to follow either a univariate or a multivariate normal distribution. Furthermore, he found that most researchers seemed to be totally oblivious to the fact that they had even violated this statistical assumption (see also Zhu, 1997). Within the more limited context of the SEM literature, it is easy to find evidence of the same phenomenon. As a case in point, we can turn to Breckler (1990), who identified 72 articles appearing in personality and social psychology journals, between the years 1977 and 1987, that employed the SEM methodology. His review of these published studies revealed that only 19% actually acknowledged the normal theory assumptions, and fewer than 10% explicitly tested for their possible violation.

Following a review of empirical studies of nonnormality in SEM, West et al. (1995) summarized four important findings. First, as data become increasingly nonnormal, the χ^2 value derived from both ML and GLS estimation becomes excessively large. This situation encourages researchers to seek further modification of their hypothesized model in an effort to attain adequate fit to the data. However, given the spuriously high value of the χ^2 value, these efforts can lead to inappropriate and nonreplicable modifications to otherwise theoretically adequate models (see also MacCallum et al., 1992). Second, when sample sizes are small (even in the event of multivariate normality), both the ML and GLS estimators yield χ^2 values that are somewhat inflated. Furthermore, as sample size decreases, and nonnormality increases, researchers are faced with a growing proportion of analyses that fail to converge, or that result in an improper solution (see Anderson & Gerbing, 1984; Boomsma, 1982). Third, when data are nonnormal, fit indexes such as the Tucker–Lewis index (TLI; Tucker & Lewis, 1973) and the comparative fit index (CFI; Bentler, 1990), yield values that are modestly underestimated (see also Marsh et al., 1988). Finally, nonnormality can lead to spuriously low standard errors, with degrees of underestimation ranging from moderate to severe. The consequences here are that, because the standard errors are underestimated, the regression paths and factor/error covariances will be statistically significant, although they may not be so in the population.

Given that, in practice, most data fail to meet the assumption of multivariate normality, West et al. (1995) noted increasing interest among SEM researchers in (a) establishing the robustness of SEM to violations of the normality assumption, and (b) developing alternative reparatory strategies when this assumption is violated. Particularly troublesome in SEM analyses is the presence of excessive kurtosis (see Bollen & Stine, 1993; West et al., 1995). In a very clearly presented review of both the problems encountered in working with multivariate nonnormal data in SEM, and the diverse remedial options proposed for their resolution, West and colleagues provided a solid framework within which to comprehend the difficulties that arise. I highly recommend their book chapter to all SEM researchers, with double emphasis for those who may be new to this methodology.

One approach to handling the presence of multivariate nonnormal data is to use a procedure known as "the bootstrap" (West et al., 1995; Yung & Bentler, 1996; Zhu, 1997). This technique was first brought to light by Efron (1979, 1982) and was subsequently highlighted by Kotz and Johnson (1992) as having had a significant impact on the field of statistics. The term *bootstrap* derives from the expression "to pull oneself up by the bootstraps," thereby reflecting the notion that the original sample gives rise to multiple additional ones. As such, bootstrapping serves as a resampling procedure by which the original sample is considered to represent the population. Multiple subsamples of the same size as the parent sample are then drawn randomly, *with replacement*, from this population and provide the data for empirical investigation of the variability of parameter estimates and indexes of fit. For very comprehensible introductions to the underlying rationale and operation of bootstrapping, readers are referred to Diaconis and Efron (1983), Stine (1990), and Zhu (1997).

Prior to the advent of high-speed computers, the technique of bootstrapping could not have existed (Efron, 1979). In fact, it is for this very reason that bootstrapping has been categorized as a computer-intensive statistical procedure in the literature (see Diaconis & Efron, 1983; Noreen, 1989). Computer-intensive techniques share the appealing feature of being free from two constraining statistical assumptions generally associated with the analysis of data: (a) that the data are normally distributed, and (b) that the researcher is able to explore more complicated problems, using a wider array of statistical tools than was previously possible (Diaconis & Efron, 1983). Before turning to our example application in this chapter, let's review, first, the basic principles associated with the bootstrap technique, its major benefits and limitations, and finally, some caveats bearing on its use in SEM.

BASIC PRINCIPLES UNDERLYING THE BOOTSTRAP PROCEDURE

The key idea underlying the bootstrap technique is that it enables the researcher to create multiple subsamples from an original data base. The importance of this action is that one can then examine parameter distributions relative to each of these spawned samples. Considered cumulatively, these distributions serve as a bootstrap sampling distribution, which technically operates in the same way as does the sampling distribution generally associated with parametric inferential statistics. In contrast to traditional statistical methods, however, the bootstrapping sampling distribution is concrete and allows for comparison of parametric values over repeated samples that have been drawn (with replacement) from the original sample. With traditional inferential procedures, on the other hand, comparison is based on an infinite number of samples drawn hypothetically from the population of interest. Of import here is the fact that the sampling distribution of the inferential approach is based on available analytic formulas that are linked to assumptions of normality, whereas the bootstrap sampling distribution is rendered free from such restrictions (Zhu, 1997).

To give you a general flavor of how the bootstrapping strategy operates in practice, let's examine a very simple example. Suppose that we have an original sample of 350 cases; the computed mean on variable X is found to be 8.0, with a standard error of 2.5. Then, suppose that we have the computer generate 200 samples consisting of 350 cases each by randomly selecting cases *with replacement* from the original sample. For each of these subsamples, the computer will record a mean value, compute the average mean value across the 200 samples, and calculate the standard error.

Within the framework of SEM, the same procedure holds, although one can evaluate the stability of model parameters, and a wide variety of other estimated quantities (Kline, 1998; Stine, 1990; Yung & Bentler, 1996). Furthermore, depending on the bootstrapping capabilities of the particular computer program in use, one may also test for the stability of goodness-of-fit indexes relative to the model as a whole (Bollen & Stine, 1993; Kline, 1998); AMOS 4.0 can provide this information. (For an evaluative review of the application and results of bootstrapping to SEM models, readers are referred to Yung and Bentler, 1996.)

Benefits and Limitations of the Bootstrap Procedure

The primary advantage of bootstrapping, in general, is that it allows researchers to assess the stability of parameter estimates and thereby report their values with a greater degree of accuracy. As Zhu (1997, p. 50) noted, in implied reference to the traditional parametric approach, "it may be better to draw conclusions about the parameters of a population strictly from the sample at hand . . . , than to make perhaps unrealistic assumptions about the population." Within the more specific context of SEM, the bootstrap procedure provides a mechanism for addressing situations where the ponderous statistical assumptions of large sample size and multivariate normality may not hold (Yung & Bentler, 1996). Perhaps the strongest advantage of bootstrapping in SEM is "its 'automatic' refinement on standard asymptotic theories (e.g., higher-order accuracy) so that the bootstrap can be applied even for samples with moderate (but not extremely small) sizes" (Yung & Bentler, 1996, p. 223).

These benefits notwithstanding, the bootstrap procedure is not without its limitations and difficulties. Of primary interest are four such limitations. First, the bootstrap sampling distribution is generated from one "original" sample, which is assumed to be representative of the population. In the event that such representation is not forthcoming, the bootstrap procedure will lead to misleading results (Zhu, 1997). Second, Yung and Bentler (1996) noted that in order for the bootstrap to work within the framework of covariance structure analysis, the assumption of independence and identical distribution of observations must be met. They contend that such an assumption is intrinsic to any justification of replacement sampling from the reproduced correlation matrix of the bootstrap. Third, the success of a bootstrap analysis depends on the degree to which the sampling behavior of the statistic of interest is consistent when the samples are drawn from the empirical distribution, and when they are drawn from the original population (Bollen & Stine, 1993). Finally, when data are multivariate normal, the bootstrap standard error estimates have been found to be more biased than those derived from the standard ML method (Ichikawa & Konishi, 1995). In contrast, when the underlying distribution is nonnormal, the bootstrap estimates are less biased than they are for the standard ML estimates.

Caveats Regarding the Use of Bootstrapping in SEM

Although the bootstrap procedure is recommended for SEM as an approach to dealing with data that are multivariate nonnormal, it is important that researchers be cognizant of its limitations (as noted earlier), as well as of important caveats related to its use. Foremost among such caveats is Yung and Bentler's (1996) admonition that bootstrapping is *definitely not* a panacea for small samples. Because the bootstrap sample distributions depend heavily on the accuracy of estimates based on the parent distribution, it seems evident that such precision can only derive from a sample that is at least moderately large (see Ichikawa & Konishi, 1995; Yung & Bentler, 1994).

A second caveat addresses the adequacy of standard errors derived from bootstrapping. Yung and Bentler (1996) exhorted that although the bootstrap procedure is helpful in estimating standard errors in the face of nonnormal data, it should not be regarded as the absolutely *only* and *best* method. They noted that researchers may wish to achieve particular statistical properties such as efficiency, robustness, and the like, and thus may prefer using an alternate estimation procedure.

As a third caveat, Yung and Bentler (1996) cautioned researchers against using the bootstrap procedure with the naive belief that the results will be accurate and trustworthy. They pointed to the studies of Bollen and Stine (1988, 1993) in noting that, indeed, there are situations where bootstrapping simply will not work. The primary difficulty here, however, is that there is yet no way of pinpointing when and how the bootstrap procedure will fail. In the interim, we must await further developments in this area of SEM research.

Finally, Arbuckle and Wothke (1999) admonished that when bootstrapping is used to generate empirical standard errors for parameters of interest in SEM, it is critical that the researcher constrain to some nonzero value, one factor loading path per factor, rather than the factor variance in the process of establishing model identification. The constraint of factor variances, in lieu of the factor regression weights, leads to bootstrap standard errors that are highly inflated (Hancock & Nevitt, 1999).

At this point, you should have a fairly good idea of the ins and outs of bootstrapping as it relates to SEM. With this background information in place, let's move on to an actual application of the bootstrap procedure using AMOS 4.0.

MODELING WITH AMOS GRAPHICS

When using the bootstrap procedure with AMOS 4.0, the researcher is provided with one set of parameter estimates, but two sets of their related standard errors. The first set of estimates is part of the regular AMOS output when ML or GLS estimation is requested. The calculation of these standard errors is based on formulas that assume a multivariate normal distribution of the data. The second set of estimates derives from the bootstrap samples and thus is empirically determined. The advantage of bootstrapping, as discussed earlier, is that it can be used to generate an approximate standard error for many statistics that AMOS computes, without having to satisfy the assumption of multivariate normality. It is with this beneficial feature in mind that we review the present application.

The Hypothesized Model

The model to be used in demonstrating the bootstrap procedure represents a second-order CFA model akin to the one presented in chapter 5. As in chapter 5, the hypothesized model in the present chapter postulates that the Beck Depression Inventory (BDI; Beck et al., 1961) can be represented as a higher order factorial structure for high school adolescents. In contrast to the sample used in chapter 5, however, the data here represent BDI item scores for 1,096 Swedish adolescents. The purpose of the original study from which this application is taken was to demonstrate, paradigmatically, the extent to which item score data can vary across culture, despite measurements from an instrument for which the factorial structure is equivalently specified in each group (Byrne & Campbell, 1999). Although data pertinent to Canadian ($n = 658$) and Bulgarian ($n = 691$) high school adolescents were also included in the original study, we focus our attention on only the Swedish group in the present chapter. In particular, we focus on bootstrap samples related to the final baseline model for Swedish adolescents, which is displayed in Fig. 11.1.

Characteristics of the Sample

Of import in this bootstrapping example is that, despite the adequately large size of the Swedish sample, the data are severely nonnormally distributed. Univariate skewness (SK) values range from 0.78 to 5.38, with a mean SK of 2.60; univariate kurtosis (KU) values range from 0.79 to 32.97, with a mean KU of 8.54. From a multivariate perspective, Mardia's (1970) normalized estimate of multivariate kurtosis was found to be 292.84. Based on a very large sample from a multivariate normal population, this estimate is distributed as a unit normal variate (Bentler, 1995). Thus, when estimated values are large, they indicate significant positive kurtosis. With a normalized Mardia value of this magnitude, it seems evident that the data are definitely multivariate nonnormal.

Applying the Bootstrap Procedure

Application of the bootstrap procedure, using AMOS 4.0, is very easy and straightforward. With the model shown in Fig. 11.1 open, all that is needed is to access the Analysis Properties dialog box, either from the pull-down menu or by clicking on its related icon ▦. Once this dialog box has been opened, you then simply select the Bootstrap tab, which is shown in Fig. 11.2. Noting the checked boxes, you can see that I have requested AMOS to perform a bootstrap on 500 samples using the ML estimator, and to provide bias-corrected confidence intervals for each of the bootstrap estimates; the 90% level is default. As you can readily see from the figure, the program provides the researcher with several choices regarding estimators, in addition to the options of (a) Monte Carlo bootstrapping, (b) obtaining details related to each of the bootstrap samples, (c) use of the Bollen–Stine bootstrap (to

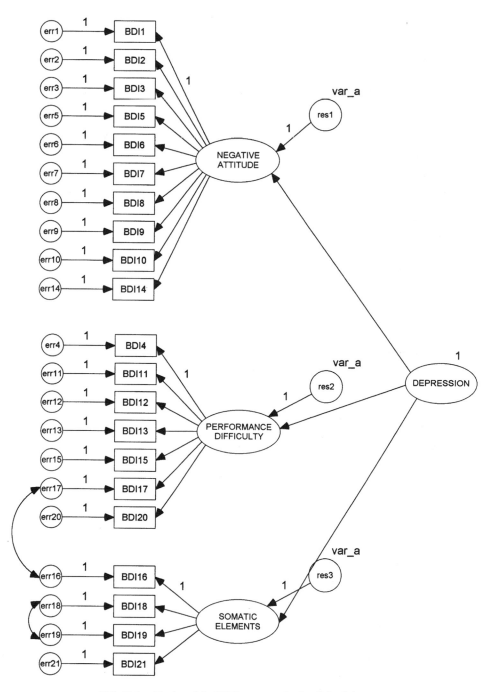

FIG. 11.1.   Final model of BDI structure for Swedish adolescents.

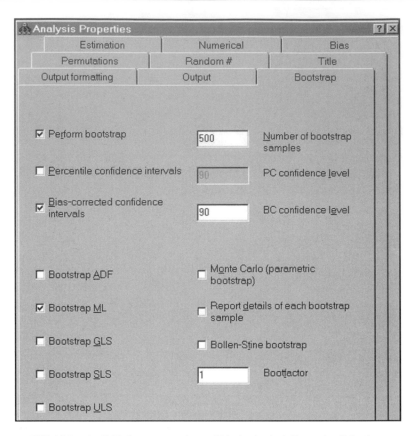

FIG. 11.2.   Available bootstrap options within the Analysis Properties dialog box.

be discussed later), and (d) adjusting the speed of the bootstrap algorithm via the Bootfactor.

Before leaving the Bootstrap tab from the Analysis Properties dialog box, let's take a closer look at two of its entries. To receive a description of a particular option offered on this tab (likewise for all tabs), just select the option for which you wish more information and then right-click on the mouse. This action will yield the "What's This?" box, as shown in Fig. 11.3 for my selected option of Bootstrap ML. After right-clicking a second time on "What's This?" you are presented with the related explanatory comments, as illustrated in Fig. 11.4 for the Bootstrap ML. For a second descriptive bootstrap example, see Fig. 11.5, in which an explanation of the Bootfactor is provided. Clicking on "Help" yields assistance of a more general nature pertinent to the entire window that was originally right-clicked.

Once you have made your selections on the Bootstrap tab, you are ready to execute the job. Selecting "Calculate Estimates," either by clicking on the icon ▦ or

Output formatting
Output
Bootstrap
Perform bootstrap
500
Number of bootstrap samples
Percentile confidence intervals
90
PC confidence level
Bias-corrected confidence intervals
90
BC confidence level
Bootstrap ADF
Monte Carlo (parametric bootstrap)
What's This?
Help
Report details of each bootstrap sample
Bollen-Stine bootstrap
Bootstrap SLS
1
Bootfactor
Bootstrap ULS

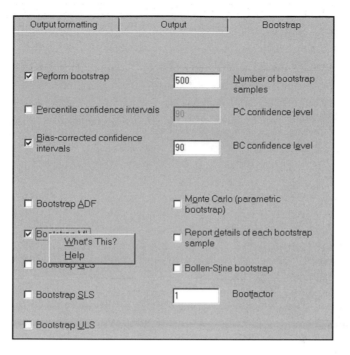

FIG. 11.3. Application of the "What's This?" help box.

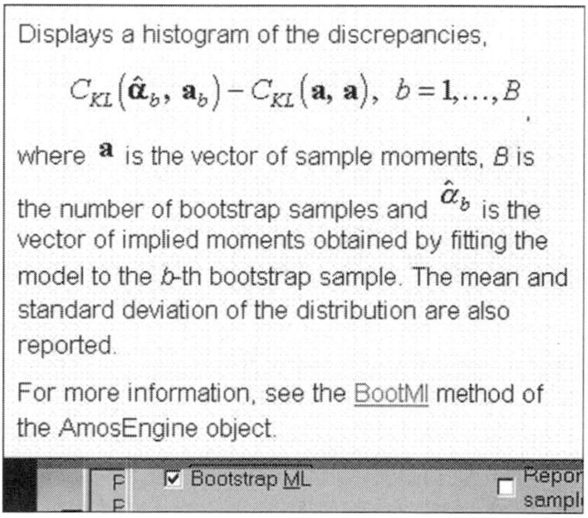

Displays a histogram of the discrepancies,
$C_{KL}(\hat{\boldsymbol{\alpha}}_b, \mathbf{a}_b) - C_{KL}(\mathbf{a}, \mathbf{a}),\ b = 1, \ldots, B$
where $\mathbf{a}$ is the vector of sample moments, B is the number of bootstrap samples and $\hat{\alpha}_b$ is the vector of implied moments obtained by fitting the model to the b-th bootstrap sample. The mean and standard deviation of the distribution are also reported.
For more information, see the BootMl method of the AmosEngine object.
Bootstrap ML

FIG. 11.4. Explanation of the Bootstrap ML option via the "What's This?" help box.

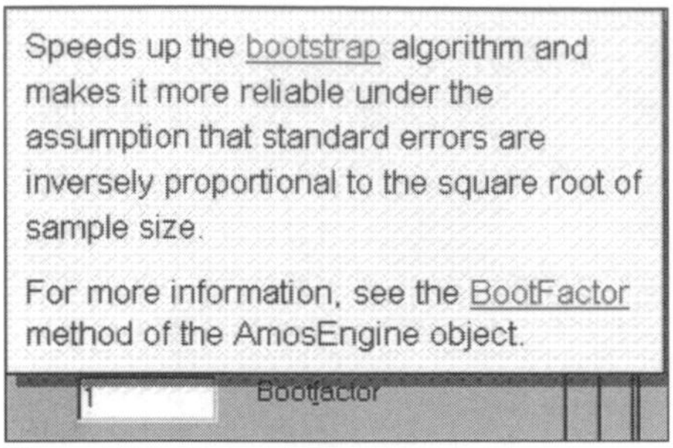

Speeds up the <u>bootstrap</u> algorithm and makes it more reliable under the assumption that standard errors are inversely proportional to the square root of sample size.

For more information, see the <u>BootFactor</u> method of the AmosEngine object.

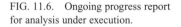

FIG. 11.5.   Explanation of the Boot-factor option via the "What's This?" help box.

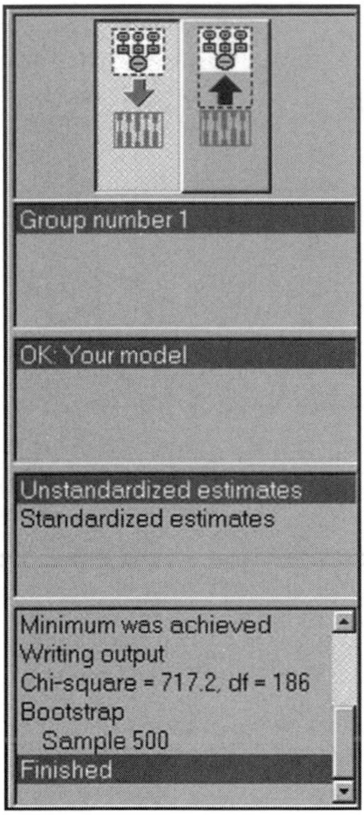

Group number 1

OK: Your model

Unstandardized estimates
Standardized estimates

Minimum was achieved
Writing output
Chi-square = 717.2, df = 186
Bootstrap
    Sample 500
Finished

FIG. 11.6.   Ongoing progress report for analysis under execution.

by selecting from the Model-Fit pull-down menu, will set the bootstrapping activity in motion. Figure 11.6 shows the information provided by the program once the execution has been completed. As you can readily see in Fig. 11.6, there were no estimation problems (minimum was achieved), the χ^2 value is reported as 717.2, with 186 degrees of freedom, and 500 bootstrap samples were generated. Considering the work involved in estimating model parameters for these 500 samples, it's amazing how fast the job is accomplished. In the present case, it took all of 39.32 seconds!

AMOS Text Output: The Bootstrap Samples

Let's turn now to the AMOS text output. Consistent with other applications in this book, Table 11.1 summarizes information related to both the model and the original sample. Although, by now, you have no difficulty interpreting the Summary of Parameters, I would like to draw your attention to the three labeled parameters listed in the "Variances" column; these variances relate to the three residual errors, which, as in chapter 5, were constrained to be equal.

Assessment of Normality.   Because I considered it to be of interest for you to see the extent to which these data for Swedish adolescents were nonnormal, I requested that this information be included in the output by checking off the "Normality/Outliers" box on the Estimation tab of the Analysis Properties dialog box. Although this information was summarized earlier, the output presented in Table 11.2 enables you

TABLE 11.1

Selected AMOS Text Output for Bootstrapped Samples: Model and Sample

```
           Number of variables in your model:    49
           Number of observed variables:         21
           Number of unobserved variables:       28
           Number of exogenous variables:        25
           Number of endogenous variables:       24
```

Summary of Parameters

	Weights	Covariances	Variances	Means	Intercepts	Total
Fixed:	27	0	1	0	0	28
Labeled:	0	0	3	0	0	3
Unlabeled:	21	2	21	0	0	44
Total:	48	2	25	0	0	75

The model is recursive.

Sample size: 1096

Computation of Degrees of Freedom

```
                 Number of distinct sample moments:   231
      Number of distinct parameters to be estimated:   45
                                  -------------------------
                          Degrees of freedom:   186
```

Minimum was achieved

```
Chi-square =    717.169
Degrees of freedom =   186
Probability level =      0.000
```

TABLE 11.2
Selected AMOS Text Output for Bootstrapped Samples: Test for Normality and Outliers

Assessment of normality

	min	max	skew	c.r.	kurtosis	c.r.
BDI16	1.000	4.000	1.177	15.903	1.898	12.823
BDI18	1.000	4.000	2.737	36.990	7.876	53.223
BDI19	1.000	4.000	4.139	55.940	19.876	134.313
BDI21	1.000	4.000	5.381	72.722	32.971	222.807
BDI4	1.000	4.000	2.081	28.128	4.939	33.379
BDI11	1.000	4.000	1.708	23.080	2.869	19.385
BDI12	1.000	4.000	4.270	57.710	20.302	137.193
BDI13	1.000	4.000	1.822	24.630	2.652	17.920
BDI15	1.000	4.000	0.943	12.749	0.794	5.363
BDI17	1.000	4.000	1.464	19.781	2.403	16.238
BDI20	1.000	4.000	3.921	52.989	16.567	111.956
BDI1	1.000	4.000	2.328	31.468	5.196	35.116
BDI2	1.000	4.000	2.597	35.099	6.003	40.569
BDI3	1.000	4.000	2.023	27.348	2.815	19.021
BDI5	1.000	4.000	3.340	45.137	11.620	78.527
BDI6	1.000	4.000	2.716	36.712	8.429	56.959
BDI7	1.000	4.000	2.209	29.861	6.238	42.152
BDI8	1.000	4.000	0.784	10.590	-0.838	-5.666
BDI9	1.000	4.000	3.240	43.785	11.504	77.744
BDI10	1.000	4.000	3.219	43.509	10.040	67.849
BDI14	1.000	4.000	2.569	34.722	5.127	34.646
Multivariate					549.848	292.839

Observations farthest from the centroid (Mahalanobis distance)

Observation number	Mahalanobis d-squared	p1	p2
886	220.485	0.000	0.000
389	160.701	0.000	0.000
369	155.071	0.000	0.000
464	139.782	0.000	0.000
392	130.636	0.000	0.000
391	130.636	0.000	0.000
415	129.104	0.000	0.000
956	127.226	0.000	0.000
664	124.657	0.000	0.000
825	124.656	0.000	0.000
390	123.972	0.000	0.000
.			
.			
.			
.			
250	52.352	0.000	0.000
197	52.211	0.000	0.000
603	52.101	0.000	0.000

to review the individual values. The multivariate value of 549.848 represents Mardia's (1970) coefficient of multivariate kurtosis, the critical ratio of which is 292.839 (see normalized multivariate estimate noted earlier).

In addition to the skewness and kurtosis information, AMOS provides further evidence bearing on the question of normality by focusing on possible outliers in the data. As such, the program identifies any case for which the observed scores differ markedly from the centroid of scores for all 1,096 cases; Mahalanobis d-squared values are used as the measure of distance, and they are reported in decreasing rank order. Thus, turning to the second section of Table 11.2, we see that Case 886 is the furthest from the centroid with a Mahalanobis d^2 value of 220.485; this value is then followed by two columns, p1 and p2. The p1 column indicates that, assuming normality, the probability of d^2 (for Case 886) exceeding a value of 220.485 is <.000. The p2 column, also assuming normality, reveals that the probability is still <.000 that the largest d^2 value for any individual case would exceed 220.485. Arbuckle (1997, p. 240) noted that although small numbers appearing in the first column (p1) are to be expected, small numbers in the second column (p2) "indicate observations that are improbably far from the centroid under the hypothesis of normality." Given the wide gap in Mahalanobis d^2 values between Case 886 and the second case (389), relative to all other cases, I would judge Case 886 to be an outlier and would consider deleting this case from further analyses. Indeed, based on the same rationale of comparison, I would probably delete the next three cases as well. Overall, then, I think that we can clearly consider these data to be multivariate nonnormal!

Regular ML Estimates.   The portion of the output presented in Table 11.3 represents the regular ML estimates of only the regression weights (i.e., first- and second-order factor loadings). Although the program provides ML estimates for all parameters, in the interest of space, only the regression weights are presented here. As you will realize in perusing this table, the output presented represents the usual parameter estimation report. I include these values here because they provide a basis of comparison with the bootstrap standard error estimates to which we turn next.

Bootstrap ML Estimates.   Once the ML parameter estimates have been reported for the original sample of cases, the program turns to results bearing on the bootstrap samples. Prior to reporting the bootstrap standard errors, however, AMOS provides a summary of the extent to which the process was successful. This information, relative to our Swedish sample, appeared as follows:

```
Bootstrap Results
-------------------------
    0 bootstrap samples were unused because of a sin-
    gular covariance matrix.
    0 bootstrap samples were unused because a solu-
    tion was not found.
  500 usable bootstrap samples were obtained.
```

TABLE 11.3
Selected AMOS Text Output for Bootstrapped Samples: Maximum Likelihood Estimates

Regression Weights:	Estimate	S.E.	C.R.	Label
PERFORMANCE_DIFFICULTY <- DEPRESSION	0.288	0.014	20.338	
NEGATIVE_ATTITUDE <------ DEPRESSION	0.303	0.015	20.465	
SOMATIC_ELEMENTS <------- DEPRESSION	0.293	0.021	14.017	
BDI14 <----------- NEGATIVE_ATTITUDE	1.228	0.084	14.701	
BDI10 <----------- NEGATIVE_ATTITUDE	0.928	0.067	13.880	
BDI9 <----------- NEGATIVE_ATTITUDE	1.110	0.057	19.573	
BDI8 <----------- NEGATIVE_ATTITUDE	1.389	0.090	15.406	
BDI7 <----------- NEGATIVE_ATTITUDE	1.115	0.057	19.440	
BDI6 <----------- NEGATIVE_ATTITUDE	0.913	0.056	16.329	
BDI5 <----------- NEGATIVE_ATTITUDE	1.104	0.056	19.674	
BDI3 <----------- NEGATIVE_ATTITUDE	1.390	0.073	18.958	
BDI2 <----------- NEGATIVE_ATTITUDE	1.101	0.064	17.077	
BDI1 <----------- NEGATIVE_ATTITUDE	1.000			
BDI20 <------ PERFORMANCE_DIFFICULTY	0.695	0.054	12.975	
BDI17 <------ PERFORMANCE_DIFFICULTY	1.269	0.079	16.087	
BDI15 <------ PERFORMANCE_DIFFICULTY	1.019	0.068	14.995	
BDI13 <------ PERFORMANCE_DIFFICULTY	0.942	0.068	13.898	
BDI12 <------ PERFORMANCE_DIFFICULTY	0.700	0.049	14.277	
BDI11 <------ PERFORMANCE_DIFFICULTY	0.839	0.084	10.008	
BDI4 <------- PERFORMANCE_DIFFICULTY	1.000			
BDI21 <------------ SOMATIC_ELEMENTS	0.426	0.046	9.355	
BDI19 <------------ SOMATIC_ELEMENTS	0.358	0.047	7.551	
BDI18 <------------ SOMATIC_ELEMENTS	0.690	0.073	9.479	
BDI16 <------------ SOMATIC_ELEMENTS	1.000			

Standardized Regression Weights:	Estimate
PERFORMANCE_DIFFICULTY <- DEPRESSION	0.918
NEGATIVE_ATTITUDE <------ DEPRESSION	0.925
SOMATIC_ELEMENTS <------- DEPRESSION	0.921
BDI14 <----------- NEGATIVE_ATTITUDE	0.497
BDI10 <----------- NEGATIVE_ATTITUDE	0.467
BDI9 <----------- NEGATIVE_ATTITUDE	0.692
BDI8 <----------- NEGATIVE_ATTITUDE	0.524
BDI7 <----------- NEGATIVE_ATTITUDE	0.687
BDI6 <----------- NEGATIVE_ATTITUDE	0.559
BDI5 <----------- NEGATIVE_ATTITUDE	0.697
BDI3 <----------- NEGATIVE_ATTITUDE	0.666
BDI2 <----------- NEGATIVE_ATTITUDE	0.589
BDI1 <----------- NEGATIVE_ATTITUDE	0.646
BDI20 <------ PERFORMANCE_DIFFICULTY	0.454
BDI17 <------ PERFORMANCE_DIFFICULTY	0.576
BDI15 <------ PERFORMANCE_DIFFICULTY	0.533
BDI13 <------ PERFORMANCE_DIFFICULTY	0.490
BDI12 <------ PERFORMANCE_DIFFICULTY	0.505
BDI11 <------ PERFORMANCE_DIFFICULTY	0.343
BDI4 <------- PERFORMANCE_DIFFICULTY	0.660
BDI21 <------------ SOMATIC_ELEMENTS	0.385
BDI19 <------------ SOMATIC_ELEMENTS	0.294
BDI18 <------------ SOMATIC_ELEMENTS	0.394
BDI16 <------------ SOMATIC_ELEMENTS	0.480

It is important to note that, in the case of an original sample that is either small or is not continuously distributed (or both), it would be quite conceivable that one or more of the bootstrap samples would have nonpositive definite covariance matrices. Arbuckle and Wothke (1999) noted that in such instances, AMOS may not be able to find a solution for some of the bootstrap samples, at least within the limits of the minimization algorithm. Given such an event, the program reports these failed bootstrap samples here. These samples, however, are not used in either the calculation of bootstrap standard errors or in the distribution graphs. Arbuckle and Wothke further noted that if such a message reports several problematic samples, it is likely that bootstrapping should not be performed in relation to the problem at hand.

We turn now to the bootstrap information presented in Table 11.4 where you will note that only the regression weights have been included. The first column (S.E.) lists the bootstrap estimate of the standard error for each factor loading parameter in the model. This value represents the standard deviation of the parameter estimates computed across the 500 bootstrap samples. These values should be compared with the approximate ML standard error estimates presented in Table 11.3. In doing so, you can note several large discrepancies between the two sets of standard error estimates. For example, in a comparison of the regression weight for BDI Item 9 (BDI9) across the original and bootstrap samples, we see a differential of 0.06, which represents a 95% increase in the bootstrap standard error over that of the ML approximate standard error. Likewise, the bootstrap standard error for Item 3 (BDI3) is 98% larger than the ML estimate. These findings suggest that the distribution of these parameter estimates appear to be wider than would be expected under normal theory assumptions. No doubt, these results reflect the presence of outliers, as well as the extremely kurtotic nature of these data.

Bootstrap Standard Errors. The second column, labeled S.E. S.E., provides the approximate standard error of the bootstrap standard error itself. As you can see, these values are all very small, and so they should be. Column 3, labeled Mean, lists the mean parameter estimate computed across the 500 bootstrap samples. Arbuckle and Wothke (1999) pointed out that this bootstrap mean is not necessarily identical to the original estimate, and they cautioned that, in fact, it can often be quite different. The information provided in column 4 (Bias) represents the difference between the bootstrap mean estimate and the original estimate. In the event that the mean estimate of the bootstrap samples is higher than the original estimate, the resulting bias will be positive. Finally, the last column, labeled S.E. Bias, reports the approximate standard error of the bias estimate.

In addition to the bootstrap information reported in Table 11.4, AMOS 4.0 can provide additional documentation that can be helpful to the researcher in assessing the bootstrap results. For our purposes here, however, we focus on information related only to the bias-corrected confidence intervals, which are presented in Table 11.5.

TABLE 11.4

Selected AMOS Text Output for Bootstrapped Samples: Bootstrap Standard Errors

Regression Weights:	S.E.	S.E. S.E.	Mean	Bias	S.E. Bias
PERFORMANCE_DI <- DEPRESSION	0.019	0.001	0.289	0.001	0.001
NEGATIVE_ATTIT <- DEPRESSION	0.032	0.001	0.303	0.001	0.001
SOMATIC_ELEMEN <- DEPRESSION	0.023	0.001	0.291	-0.002	0.001
BDI14 <--- NEGATIVE_ATTITUDE	0.150	0.005	1.237	0.009	0.007
BDI10 <--- NEGATIVE_ATTITUDE	0.102	0.003	0.915	-0.013	0.005
BDI9 <---- NEGATIVE_ATTITUDE	0.111	0.004	1.108	-0.002	0.005
BDI8 <---- NEGATIVE_ATTITUDE	0.164	0.005	1.398	0.009	0.007
BDI7 <---- NEGATIVE_ATTITUDE	0.117	0.004	1.118	0.003	0.005
BDI6 <---- NEGATIVE_ATTITUDE	0.088	0.003	0.913	-0.001	0.004
BDI5 <---- NEGATIVE_ATTITUDE	0.103	0.003	1.101	-0.003	0.005
BDI3 <---- NEGATIVE_ATTITUDE	0.145	0.005	1.392	0.002	0.006
BDI2 <---- NEGATIVE_ATTITUDE	0.105	0.003	1.106	0.005	0.005
BDI1 <---- NEGATIVE_ATTITUDE	0.000	0.000	1.000	0.000	0.000
BDI20 <- PERFORMANCE_DIFFICU	0.099	0.003	0.690	-0.005	0.004
BDI17 <- PERFORMANCE_DIFFICU	0.103	0.003	1.273	0.004	0.005
BDI15 <- PERFORMANCE_DIFFICU	0.120	0.004	1.027	0.008	0.005
BDI13 <- PERFORMANCE_DIFFICU	0.106	0.003	0.943	0.001	0.005
BDI12 <- PERFORMANCE_DIFFICU	0.097	0.003	0.707	0.007	0.004
BDI11 <- PERFORMANCE_DIFFICU	0.088	0.003	0.832	-0.007	0.004
BDI4 <- PERFORMANCE_DIFFICUL	0.000	0.000	1.000	0.000	0.000
BDI21 <---- SOMATIC_ELEMENTS	0.094	0.003	0.422	-0.004	0.004
BDI19 <---- SOMATIC_ELEMENTS	0.095	0.003	0.362	0.003	0.004
BDI18 <---- SOMATIC_ELEMENTS	0.110	0.003	0.681	-0.008	0.005
BDI16 <---- SOMATIC_ELEMENTS	0.000	0.000	1.000	0.000	0.000

Standardized (Beta) Weights:	S.E.	S.E. S.E.	Mean	Bias	S.E. Bias
PERFORMANCE_DI <- DEPRESSION	0.013	0.000	0.919	0.000	0.001
NEGATIVE_ATTIT <- DEPRESSION	0.019	0.001	0.924	-0.001	0.001
SOMATIC_ELEMEN <- DEPRESSION	0.016	0.000	0.919	-0.001	0.001
BDI14 <--- NEGATIVE_ATTITUDE	0.036	0.001	0.498	0.001	0.002
BDI10 <--- NEGATIVE_ATTITUDE	0.043	0.001	0.461	-0.006	0.002
BDI9 <---- NEGATIVE_ATTITUDE	0.033	0.001	0.691	-0.001	0.001
BDI8 <---- NEGATIVE_ATTITUDE	0.029	0.001	0.524	0.000	0.001
BDI7 <---- NEGATIVE_ATTITUDE	0.032	0.001	0.687	0.000	0.001
BDI6 <---- NEGATIVE_ATTITUDE	0.039	0.001	0.558	-0.001	0.002
BDI5 <---- NEGATIVE_ATTITUDE	0.029	0.001	0.695	0.002	0.001
BDI3 <---- NEGATIVE_ATTITUDE	0.027	0.001	0.663	-0.003	0.001
BDI2 <---- NEGATIVE_ATTITUDE	0.034	0.001	0.589	0.000	0.002
BDI1 <---- NEGATIVE_ATTITUDE	0.039	0.001	0.647	0.001	0.002
BDI20 <- PERFORMANCE_DIFFICU	0.047	0.001	0.451	-0.003	0.002
BDI17 <- PERFORMANCE_DIFFICU	0.030	0.001	0.576	0.000	0.001
BDI15 <- PERFORMANCE_DIFFICU	0.042	0.001	0.534	0.001	0.002
BDI13 <- PERFORMANCE_DIFFICU	0.035	0.001	0.490	0.000	0.002
BDI12 <- PERFORMANCE_DIFFICU	0.050	0.002	0.508	0.003	0.002
BDI11 <- PERFORMANCE_DIFFICU	0.036	0.001	0.340	-0.003	0.002
BDI4 <- PERFORMANCE_DIFFICUL	0.029	0.001	0.659	-0.000	0.001
BDI21 <---- SOMATIC_ELEMENTS	0.065	0.002	0.378	-0.007	0.003
BDI19 <---- SOMATIC_ELEMENTS	0.068	0.002	0.292	-0.002	0.003
BDI18 <---- SOMATIC_ELEMENTS	0.054	0.002	0.387	-0.007	0.002
BDI16 <---- SOMATIC_ELEMENTS	0.029	0.001	0.478	-0.002	0.001

Bootstrap Confidence Intervals. Shown here are the 90% (default) bias-corrected confidence intervals for both the unstandardized and standardized regression weight parameter estimates. AMOS 4.0 has the capability to produce percentile as well as bias-corrected confidence intervals. However, the latter are considered to yield the more accurate values (Efron & Tibshirani, 1993). Values for BDI items 1, 4, and 16 are replaced with dots (. . .) because these parameters were constrained to

TABLE 11.5

Selected AMOS Text Output for Bootstrapped Samples: Confidence Intervals

Regression Weights:	Lower Bound	Upper Bound	p
PERFORMANCE_DI <- DEPRESSION	0.259	0.323	0.004
NEGATIVE_ATTIT <- DEPRESSION	0.251	0.352	0.004
SOMATIC_ELEMEN <- DEPRESSION	0.260	0.333	0.002
BDI14 <--- NEGATIVE_ATTITUDE	1.021	1.494	0.003
BDI10 <--- NEGATIVE_ATTITUDE	0.778	1.132	0.002
BDI9 <---- NEGATIVE_ATTITUDE	0.940	1.303	0.003
BDI8 <---- NEGATIVE_ATTITUDE	1.168	1.697	0.003
BDI7 <---- NEGATIVE_ATTITUDE	0.944	1.315	0.004
BDI6 <---- NEGATIVE_ATTITUDE	0.770	1.081	0.003
BDI5 <---- NEGATIVE_ATTITUDE	0.957	1.304	0.002
BDI3 <---- NEGATIVE_ATTITUDE	1.200	1.733	0.002
BDI2 <---- NEGATIVE_ATTITUDE	0.947	1.295	0.003
BDI1 <---- NEGATIVE_ATTITUDE	...	...	...
BDI20 <- PERFORMANCE_DIFFICU	0.542	0.864	0.003
BDI17 <- PERFORMANCE_DIFFICU	1.107	1.445	0.005
BDI15 <- PERFORMANCE_DIFFICU	0.814	1.215	0.006
BDI13 <- PERFORMANCE_DIFFICU	0.765	1.119	0.004
BDI12 <- PERFORMANCE_DIFFICU	0.541	0.865	0.004
BDI11 <- PERFORMANCE_DIFFICU	0.703	0.994	0.002
BDI4 <- PERFORMANCE_DIFFICUL	...	...	...
BDI21 <---- SOMATIC_ELEMENTS	0.283	0.600	0.003
BDI19 <---- SOMATIC_ELEMENTS	0.213	0.508	0.005
BDI18 <---- SOMATIC_ELEMENTS	0.524	0.899	0.002
BDI16 <---- SOMATIC_ELEMENTS	...	...	...

Standardized (Beta) Weights:	Lower Bound	Upper Bound	p
PERFORMANCE_DI <- DEPRESSION	0.894	0.939	0.006
NEGATIVE_ATTIT <- DEPRESSION	0.885	0.950	0.005
SOMATIC_ELEMEN <- DEPRESSION	0.894	0.943	0.004
BDI14 <--- NEGATIVE_ATTITUDE	0.442	0.555	0.005
BDI10 <--- NEGATIVE_ATTITUDE	0.390	0.538	0.003
BDI9 <---- NEGATIVE_ATTITUDE	0.633	0.744	0.004
BDI8 <---- NEGATIVE_ATTITUDE	0.478	0.574	0.004
BDI7 <---- NEGATIVE_ATTITUDE	0.634	0.737	0.004
BDI6 <---- NEGATIVE_ATTITUDE	0.493	0.618	0.004
BDI5 <---- NEGATIVE_ATTITUDE	0.648	0.743	0.003
BDI3 <---- NEGATIVE_ATTITUDE	0.620	0.710	0.003
BDI2 <---- NEGATIVE_ATTITUDE	0.531	0.639	0.005
BDI1 <---- NEGATIVE_ATTITUDE	0.571	0.700	0.008
BDI20 <- PERFORMANCE_DIFFICU	0.370	0.536	0.003
BDI17 <- PERFORMANCE_DIFFICU	0.519	0.622	0.005
BDI15 <- PERFORMANCE_DIFFICU	0.448	0.596	0.007
BDI13 <- PERFORMANCE_DIFFICU	0.423	0.542	0.006
BDI12 <- PERFORMANCE_DIFFICU	0.404	0.575	0.008
BDI11 <- PERFORMANCE_DIFFICU	0.286	0.404	0.003
BDI4 <- PERFORMANCE_DIFFICUL	0.607	0.703	0.006
BDI21 <---- SOMATIC_ELEMENTS	0.287	0.498	0.002
BDI19 <---- SOMATIC_ELEMENTS	0.186	0.406	0.003
BDI18 <---- SOMATIC_ELEMENTS	0.310	0.493	0.002
BDI16 <---- SOMATIC_ELEMENTS	0.433	0.530	0.003

a nonzero value for purposes of model identification. Bias-corrected confidence intervals are interpreted in the usual manner. For example, the loading of BDI14 on the factor of Negative Attitude has a confidence interval ranging from 1.021 to 1.494. Because this range does not include zero, the hypothesis that the BDI14 regression weight is equal to zero in the population can be rejected. This information can also be derived from the *p* values, which indicate how small the confidence level must be to yield a confidence interval that would include zero. Turning again to the BDI14 parameter, a p value of .003 implies that the confidence interval would have to be at the 99.7% level before the lower bound value would be zero.

The Bollen–Stine Bootstrap

In addition to a comparison of the original ML and the bootstrap ML parameter estimates, it is also of interest to evaluate the appropriateness of the hypothesized model itself. Indeed, Bollen and Stine (1993) provided a means to testing the null hypothesis that the specified model is correct. The Bollen–Stine option represents a modified bootstrap method for the χ^2 goodness-of-fit statistic. More specifically, the Bollen–Stine approach to testing the adequacy of the hypothesized model is based on a transformation of the sample data such that the model is made to fit the data perfectly. Bootstrap samples are then drawn, with replacement, from this transformed sample. The distribution of the discrepancy function across bootstrap samples is then taken as an estimate of its distribution under the hypothesis that the model is correct (Arbuckle, 1997). To obtain this information using AMOS 4.0, simply access the Analysis Properties dialog box, check off the box accompanying the Bollen–Stine bootstrap option, and rerun the job. The portion of the output related to this test is shown in Table 11.6.

AMOS Text Output: Bollen–Stine Bootstrap Samples

Model Assessment.   Presented first in Table 11.6 is the ML-estimated likelihood ratio χ^2 value of 717.169 with 186 degrees of freedom ($p = 0.000$). Shown below it, however, is the Bollen–Stine bootstrap p value, which is .002. In other words, consistent with the ML results for the original sample, the Bollen–Stine corrected p value indicates that the hypothesized model should be rejected. However, as is now well known, the χ^2 is highly sensitive to sample size and thus should not be used as an indicator of goodness of fit between the model and the data. Indeed, given a sample size of 1,096, it is not surprising that the probability value associated with the χ^2 statistic is less than .05. As noted and described elsewhere in this book, evaluation of model fit should be more appropriately based on alternatively realistic indices of fit. Nonetheless, the Bollen–Stine probability results are presented here in the interest of completeness.

Finally, the program presents the bootstrap distribution bearing on the Bollen–Stine procedure. Presented in the form of a histogram, this distribution represents the discrepancy between the unrestricted sample covariance S and the restricted (or fitted) covariance matrix Σ. (For a review of these matrices, see chap. 1.) However, in contrast to the usual ML and standard bootstrap estimations, this

TABLE 11.6

Selected AMOS Text Output for Bootstrapped Samples: The Bollen–Stine Test

```
Chi-square = 717.169
Degrees of freedom = 186
Probability level = 0.000


Bootstrap Results
-----------------

    0 bootstrap samples were unused because of a singular covariance matrix.
    0 bootstrap samples were unused because a solution was not found.
  500 usable bootstrap samples were obtained.


Testing the null hypothesis that the specified model is correct:

        Bollen-Stine bootstrapped p = 0.002


Bootstrap Distributions
-----------------------

                            --------+--------------------
                            218.842 |*
                            247.344 |****
                            275.847 |********
        ML discrepancy      304.350 |***************
      (implied vs sample)   332.852 |*****************
                            361.355 |****************
                            389.857 |**********
        N = 500             418.360 |********
      Mean = 350.575        446.862 |****
      S. e. = 2.656         475.365 |**
                            503.867 |*
                            532.370 |*
                            560.872 |*
                            589.375 |
                            617.878 |*
                            --------+--------------------
```

comparison of sample and fitted covariance matrices is based on the Bollen–Stine transformed sample matrix.

MODELING WITH AMOS BASIC

In closing this chapter on bootstrapping, I present you with the AMOS Basic input file (Table 11.7). If you compare this input with the AMOS Basic file presented in chapter 5, you can note that the only difference (other than specification of error covariances) is the inclusion of the bootstrap command: **SEM.Bootstrap 500**. Given that explanations related to model were detailed in chapter 5, they are not repeated here.

TABLE 11.7
AMOS Basic Input File for Final Model of BDI Structure for Swedish Adolescents

---

Sub Main
Dim sem As New AmosEngine

SEM.Bootstrap 500
SEM.TextOutput
SEM.Standardized

SEM.BeginGroup "bdiswed.txt"

```
SEM.Structure "BDI1 =    (1)  NEGATIVE_ATTITUDE + (1) err1"
SEM.Structure "BDI2 =         NEGATIVE_ATTITUDE + (1) err2"
SEM.Structure "BDI3 =         NEGATIVE_ATTITUDE + (1) err3"
SEM.Structure "BDI5 =         NEGATIVE_ATTITUDE + (1) err5"
SEM.Structure "BDI6 =         NEGATIVE_ATTITUDE + (1) err6"
SEM.Structure "BDI7 =         NEGATIVE_ATTITUDE + (1) err7"
SEM.Structure "BDI8 =         NEGATIVE_ATTITUDE + (1) err8"
SEM.Structure "BDI9 =         NEGATIVE_ATTITUDE + (1) err9"
SEM.Structure "BDI10 =        NEGATIVE_ATTITUDE + (1) err10"
SEM.Structure "BDI14 =        NEGATIVE_ATTITUDE + (1) err14"

SEM.Structure "BDI4 =   (1)  PERFORMANCE_DIFFICULTY + (1) err4"
SEM.Structure "BDI11 =       PERFORMANCE_DIFFICULTY + (1) err11"
SEM.Structure "BDI12 =       PERFORMANCE_DIFFICULTY + (1) err12"
SEM.Structure "BDI13 =       PERFORMANCE_DIFFICULTY + (1) err13"
SEM.Structure "BDI15 =       PERFORMANCE_DIFFICULTY + (1) err15"
SEM.Structure "BDI17 =       PERFORMANCE_DIFFICULTY + (1) err17"
SEM.Structure "BDI20 =       PERFORMANCE_DIFFICULTY + (1) err20"

SEM.Structure "BDI16 = (1)   SOMATIC_ELEMENTS + (1) err16"
SEM.Structure "BDI18 =       SOMATIC_ELEMENTS + (1) err18"
SEM.Structure "BDI19 =       SOMATIC_ELEMENTS + (1) err19"
SEM.Structure "BDI21 =       SOMATIC_ELEMENTS + (1) err21"

SEM.Structure "NEGATIVE_ATTITUDE = DEPRESSION + (1) res1"
SEM.Structure "PERFORMANCE_DIFFICULTY = DEPRESSION + (1) res2"
SEM.Structure "SOMATIC_ELEMENTS = DEPRESSION + (1) res3"

SEM.Structure "DEPRESSION (1)"

SEM.Structure "res1 (var_a)"
SEM.Structure "res2 (var_a)"
SEM.Structure "res3 (var_a)"

SEM.Structure "err16 ↔ err17"
SEM.Structure "err18 ↔ err19"
```

End Sub

CHAPTER 12

Application 10: Dealing With Incomplete Data

❧

Incomplete (or missing) data, an almost inevitable occurrence in social science research, may be viewed either as a curse, or as a gold mine of untapped resources. As with other life events, the extent to which they are viewed either positively or negatively is a matter of perspective. For example, McArdle (1994) noted that although the term *missing data*, typically conjures up images of negative consequences and problems, such missingness can provide a wealth of information in its own right and, indeed, often serves as a useful part of experimental analyses. (For an interesting example in support of this statement, see Rosén, 1998.) In reality, of course, the issue of terminology is moot. Of import is the extent to which, and pattern by which, data are incomplete, missing, or otherwise unobserved, and the steps taken in addressing the situation.

The presence of incomplete data can occur for a wide variety of reasons that are usually beyond the researcher's control. Some examples are: absence on the day of data collection, failure to answer certain items in the questionnaire, refusal to answer sensitive items related to one's age and/or income, equipment failure or malfunction, attrition of subjects (e.g., family moved away, individual no longer wishes to participate, subject dies), and so on. In contrast, data may be incomplete by design, a situation in which the researcher is in total control. Two examples suggested by Kline (1998) include the cases where (a) a questionnaire is excessively long and the researcher decides to administer only a subset of items to each of several different subsamples, and (b) a relatively inexpensive measure is administered to the entire sample, whereas another more expensive test is administered to a smaller set of randomly selected subjects. Needless to say, there may be many more examples that are not cited here.

Because incomplete data can seriously bias conclusions drawn from an empirical study, they must be addressed, regardless of the reason for their missingness. The extent to which such conclusions can be biased depends on both the amount and pattern of missing values. Unfortunately, to the best of my knowledge, there are currently no clear guidelines regarding what constitutes a "large" amount of incomplete data, although Kline (1998, p. 75) suggested that they should probably constitute less than 10% of the data. On the other hand, guidelines related to the pattern of incomplete data are now widely cited and derive from the seminal works of Rubin (1976), Allison (1987), and Little and Rubin (1987). In order for you to more fully comprehend the AMOS 4.0 approach to handling incomplete data, it behooves us to review, first, the differential patterns of missingness proposed by Rubin and by Little and Rubin.

BASIC PATTERNS OF INCOMPLETE DATA

Rubin (1976) and Little and Rubin (1987) distinguished between three primary patterns of missing data: those missing *completely* at random (MCAR), those missing at random (MAR), and those considered to be nonignorable. Each of these conditions is now described.

- MCAR represents the most restrictive assumption and argues that the missingness is independent of both the unobserved values and the observed values of all other variables in the data. Indeed, Muthén, Kaplan, and Hollis (1987) noted that MCAR is usually what is meant when researchers use, although imprecisely, the expression "missing at random".
- MAR is somewhat less restrictive than MCAR and argues that the missingness is independent only of the missing values and *not* of the observed values of other variables in the data. That is to say, although the occurrence of the missing values themselves may be random, their missingness can be linked to the observed values of other variables in the data.
- Nonignorable is the least restrictive condition and refers to missingness that is nonrandom, or of a systematic nature. In other words, there is an existing dependency between the variables for which the values are missing and those for which the values are present. This condition is particularly serious because (a) there is no known statistical means to alleviation of the problem, and (b) it can seriously impede the generalizability of findings.

Before reviewing various approaches to the handling of incomplete data, I consider it worthwhile to detour momentarily, in order to provide a simple fictitious example that can help in distinguishing between the two major patterns of missingness—MCAR and MAR. Indeed, Muthén et al. (1987) noted that most researchers when confronted with incomplete data typically assume that the missingness is MCAR when, in fact, it is often MAR. Drawing on the works of Allison (1987) and Little and Rubin (1987), and paraphrasing Arbuckle (1996), suppose a questionnaire is composed of two items. One item taps into years of schooling; the other taps into income. Suppose, further, that although all respondents answer the educaton question, not everyone answers the income question. Within the framework of the missingness issue, the question is whether the incomplete data on the income variable are MCAR or MAR. Rubin reasons that if a respondent's answer to the income question is independent of both income and education, then the missing data can be regarded as MCAR. If, on the other hand, those with higher education are either more or less likely than others to reveal their income, but among those with the same level of education the probability of reporting income is unrelated to income, then the missing data are MAR. Finally, given that, even among people with the same level of education, high-income individuals are either more or less likely to report their income, then the missing data are not even MAR; the systematic pattern of this type of missingness make them *nonignorable*, or NMAR (see Jamshidian & Bentler, 1999).

Once again, to give you a more complete understanding of the AMOS approach to the treatment of incomplete data, we turn first to a review and evaluation of the most commonly applied strategies; these include listwise deletion, pairwise deletion, and imputation. These methods are categorized as *indirect* approaches to the resolution of missing data. Although other suggested methods can be found in the literature, they are rarely applied in practice (see McArdle, 1994; Muthén et al., 1987; Raaijmakers, 1999; Schafer & Olsen, 1998).

COMMON APPROACHES
TO HANDLING INCOMPLETE DATA

Listwise Deletion

By far, the most popular method for dealing with incomplete data is that of listwise deletion. Such popularity likely got its jumpstart in the 1980s when numerous articles appeared in the SEM literature detailing various problems that can occur when the analysis of covariance structures is based on incomplete data (see Bentler & Chou, 1987; Boomsma, 1985). Because SEM models are based on the premise that the covariance matrix follows a Wishart distribution (Brown, 1994; Joreskog, 1969), complete data are required for the probability density. In meeting this requirement, researchers have therefore sought to modify incomplete data sets, through either removal of cases or the substitution of values for those that are unobserved. The fact that listwise deletion of missing data is by far the fastest and simplest answer to the problem likely has led to the popularity of its use.

Implementation of listwise deletion simply means that all cases having a missing value for any of the variables in the data are excluded from all computations.

As a consequence, the final sample to be used in the analyses includes only cases with complete records. The obvious disadvantage of the listwise deletion approach, then, is the loss of information resulting from the reduced sample size. As a result, two related problems subsequently emerge: (a) the decrease in statistical power (Raaijmakers, 1999), and (b) the risk of nonconvergent solutions, incorrect standard errors, and other difficulties encountered in SEM when sample sizes are small (see e.g., Boomsma, 1982; Marsh & Balla, 1994; Marsh et al., 1988). Of course, the extent to which these problems manifest themselves is a function of both the size of the original sample and the amount of incomplete data. For example, if only a few cases have missing values, and the sample size is adequately large, then the deletion of these cases is likely a good choice. Finally, use of listwise deletion assumes that the incomplete data are MCAR (Arbuckle, 1996; Brown, 1994). Given the validity of this assumption, there will be consistent estimation of model parameters (Bollen, 1989a; Brown, 1994); failing such validity, the estimates will be severely biased, regardless of sample size (Arbuckle & Wothke, 1999) .

Pairwise Deletion

In the application of pairwise deletion, only cases having missing values on variables tagged for a particular computation are excluded from the analysis. In contrast to listwise deletion, then, a case is not totally deleted from the entire set of analyses, but rather only from particular analyses involving variables for which there are unobserved scores. The critical result of this approach is that the sample size necessarily varies across variables in the data set. This phenomenon subsequently leads to at least four major problems. First, the sample covariance matrix can fail to be nonpositive definite, thereby impeding the attainment of a convergent solution (Arbuckle, 1996; Bollen, 1989a; Brown, 1994; Wothke, 1993; but see Marsh, 1998). Second, the choice of which sample size to use in obtaining appropriate parameter estimates is equivocal (Bollen, 1989a; Brown, 1994). Given the presence of multiple sample sizes, the assumption that the sample covariance matrix follows a Wishart distribution is clearly violated (Brown, 1994). Third, goodness-of fit indices, based on the χ^2 statistic, can be substantially biased as a result of interaction between the percentage of missing data and the sample size (Marsh, 1998). Finally, consistent with listwise deletion of missing data, pairwise deletion assumes all missing values to be MCAR.

Imputation

A third indirect method for dealing with incomplete data is to simply impute or, in other words, replace the unobserved score with some estimated value. Typically, one of three strategies is used to provide these estimates. Probably the most common of these is *mean imputation* whereby the arithmetic mean is substituted for a missing value. Despite the relative simplicity of this procedure, however, it can be problematic in at least two ways. First, because the arithmetic mean represents the most likely score value for any variable, the variance of the variable will necessarily shrink; as a consequence, the correlation between the variable in question and other variables in the model will also be reduced (Brown, 1994). The overall net effect is that the standard errors will be biased, as will the other reported statistics. Second, if the mean imputation of missing values is substantial, the frequency distribution of the imputed variable may be misleading because too many centrally located values will invoke a leptokurtic distribution (Rovine & Delaney, 1990). In summary, Arbuckle and Wothke (1999) cautioned that, because structural equation modeling is based on variance and covariance information, "means imputation is not a recommended approach" (see also Brown, 1994).

A second type of imputation is based on multiple regression procedures. With *regression imputation*, the incomplete data serve as the dependent variables, whereas the complete data serve as the predictors. In other words, cases having complete data are used to generate the regression equation that is subsequently used to postulate missing values for the cases having incomplete data. At least three difficulties have been linked to regression imputation. First, although this approach provides for greater variability than is the case with mean imputation, it nevertheless suffers from the same limitation of inappropriately restricting variance. Second, substitution of the regression-predicted scores will spuriously inflate the covariances (Schafer & Olsen, 1998). Finally, Kline (1998) cautioned that this procedure may not be feasible in the case where the variable having the missing value does not covary, at least moderately, with other variables in the data.

The third procedure for imputing values may be termed *pattern-matching imputation*. Although application of this approach is less common than the others noted already, it is included here because the SEM statistical package, within which it is embedded, is so widely used (LISREL 8; Joreskog & Sorbom, 1996b).[1] With pattern-matching imputation, a missing value is replaced with an observed score from another case in the data for which the response pattern across all variables is similar (Byrne, 1998). One limitation of this procedure is that in the event that no matching case is determined, no imputation is performed. As a consequence, the researcher is still left with a proportion of the data that is incomplete. To date, however, I am not aware of any scholarly articles that have evaluated pattern-matching imputation. As a consequence, little is yet known about the strengths and/or weaknesses associated with this approach within the context of SEM (Brown, 1994).

Having reviewed the most commonly used methods of dealing with incomplete data in covariance structure modeling, let's now examine the approach taken in the AMOS 4.0 program, as it differs substantially from those just described.

---

[1]The imputation is actually performed using the companion preprocessing package, PRELIS 2 (Joreskog & Sorbom, 1996c).

THE AMOS APPROACH
TO HANDLING INCOMPLETE DATA

AMOS 4.0 does not provide for the application of any of the above missing data treatments, each of which represent an indirect approach to resolution of the difficulty. In contrast, the method used in AMOS represents a direct approach that is based on maximum likelihood (ML) estimation and, thus, is theoretically based (Arbuckle, 1996).[2] In contrast, the previously described methods lack any kind of theoretical rationale and must therefore be considered ad hoc procedures. Arbuckle (1996) noted that although the ML estimation of parameters from incomplete data has long been recognized, it has not caught on as a possible approach. He further conjectured that such underestimation of this direct approach likely derives from its unavailability as an option in most SEM programs.[3] Although Allison (1987) and Muthén et al. (1987) proposed strategies for using ML estimation with incomplete data for the LISREL program, their techniques are limited in that (a) they are only applicable to situations where the number of distinct missing patterns is small, and (b) they require the user to have an exceptionally high level of expertise (Arbuckle, 1996). Recently, however, Bentler and colleagues actively pursued important information bearing on ML estimation in the presence of incomplete data (see Jamshidian & Bentler, 1999; Tang & Bentler, 1998; Yuan & Bentler, 1996, in press). Given the largely mathematical nature of this research, and because it focuses on a restricted version of the ML procedure used in AMOS 4.0, it is not reviewed here.

Arbuckle (1996; Arbuckle & Wothke, 1999) described the extent to which ML estimation, in the presence of incomplete data, offers several important advantages over both the listwise and pairwise deletion approaches. First, where the unobserved values are MCAR, listwise and pairwise estimates are consistent, but *not* efficient (in the statistical sense); ML estimates are *both* consistent and efficient. Second, where the unobserved values are only MAR, both listwise and pairwise estimates can be biased; ML estimates are asymptotically unbiased. In fact, it has been suggested that ML estimation will reduce bias even when the MAR condition is not completely satisfied (Little & Rubin, 1989; Muthén et al. 1987). Third, pairwise estimation, in contrast to ML estimation, is unable to yield standard error estimates or to provide a method for testing hypotheses. Finally, when missing values are NMAR (i.e., nonignorable), all procedures can yield biased results. However, compared with the other options, ML estimates will exhibit the least bias (Little & Rubin, 1989; Muthén et al., 1987; Schafer, 1997). (For more extensive discussion and illustration of the comparative advantages/disadvantages across the listwise, pairwise, and ML approaches to incomplete data, see Arbuckle, 1996.)

---

[2]ML estimation is sometimes referred to as *full information maximum likelihood* (FIML) estimation (see Arbuckle & Wothke, 1999).

[3]In addition to AMOS 4.0, ML estimation based on incomplete data is currently an option in the Mplus (Muthén & Muthén, 1998) and Mx (Neale, Boker, Xie, & Maes, 1999) programs.

With this background on issues related to incomplete data, let's move on to an actual application of ML estimation of data that are incomplete.

MODELING WITH AMOS GRAPHICS

The basic strategy used by AMOS in fitting structural equation models with incomplete data differs in at least two ways from the procedure followed when data are complete (Arbuckle & Wothke, 1999). First, in addition to fitting a hypothesized model, the program also needs to fit the completely saturated model in order to compute the χ^2 value, as well as derived statistics such as the AIC and RMSEA; the independence model, as for complete data, must also be computed. Second, because substantially more computations are required in the determination of parameter estimates when data are missing, the execution time can be more extensive (although my experience with the present application revealed this additional time to be minimal). In contrast to analyses based on AMOS Basic, for which the hypothesized and saturated models must be estimated separately (to be discussed later), in AMOS Graphics these models are computed simultaneously.

The Hypothesized Model

Because the primary interest in this application focuses on the extent to which estimates and goodness-of-fit indexes vary between an analysis based on complete data and one for which the data are incomplete, I have chosen to use the hypothesized CFA model presented in chapter 3. Thus, rather than reproduce the schematic representation of this model again here, readers are referred to Fig. 3.1.

Although the same sample of 265 Grade 7 adolescents provides the base for both chapters, the data used in testing the hypothesized model in chapter 3 were complete, whereas the data to be used in this chapter have 25% of the data points missing. These artificially derived missing data points were deleted randomly. AMOS automatically recognizes missing data designations from many different formats. In the case of the current data, which are in ASCII format with comma delimiters, two adjacent delimiters indicate missing data. In this case, then, two adjacent commas (, ,) are indicative of missing data. For illustrative purposes, the first five lines of the incomplete data set used in the current chapter are shown here.

```
SDQ2N01,SDQ2N13,SDQ2N25,SDQ2N37,SDQ2N04,
SDQ2N16,SDQ2N28,SDQ2N40,SDQ2N10,SDQ2N22,
SDQ2N34,SDQ2N46,SDQ2N07,SDQ2N19,SDQ2N31,SDQ2N43
6,,4,,3,4,,6,2,6,,5,,,,6
6,6,6,,6,6,6,6,5,,6,6,6,6,6,6
4,6,6,2,6,4,6,3,6,5,4,5,6,6,3,1
5,5,5,6,5,6,5,,5,6,3,5,6,6,6,5
6,5,,4,3,4,4,4,4,6,5,6,3,4,4,5
```

ML estimation of the hypothesized model incurs only one basic difference when data are incomplete from when they are complete. That is, in specifying the model (for analysis based on incomplete data), it is imperative that "means and intercepts" be checked off on the Estimation tab. This marked tab is illustrated in Fig. 12.1.

Once this input information has been specified, the originally hypothesized model shown in Fig. 3.1 becomes transformed into the one shown in Fig. 12.2. Of course, you will quickly recognize similarities in constrained parameters between this model and the one representing the low track in chapter 9 (Fig. 9.4b) in which we tested for latent mean differences between high and low academically tracked high school students. In both Figs. 9.4 and 12.2, the means of the factors, as well as those for the error terms, were constrained to zero. Although the intercept terms were estimated for both the latent means model and the missing data model, their related labels do not appear in Fig. 12.2. The reason for this important difference is twofold: (a) In test-

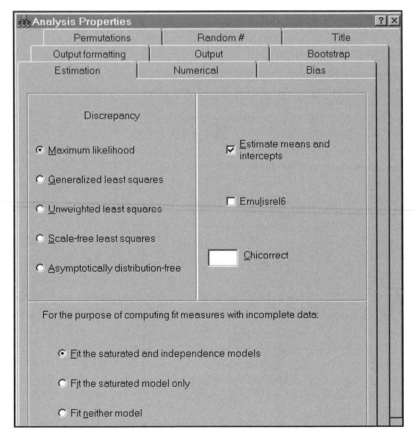

FIG. 12.1.   Selection of the "Estimate means and intercepts" option on the Estimation tab of the Analysis Properties dialog box.

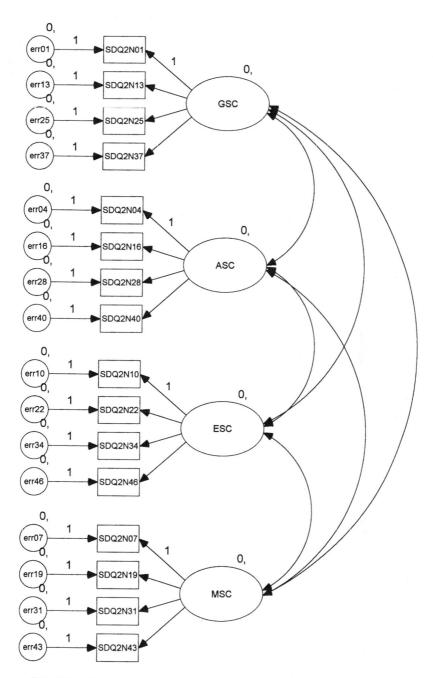

FIG. 12.2.　Hypothesized model of self-concept structure to be tested for a sample with incomplete data.

ing for latent mean differences, the intercepts must be constrained equal across groups, and (b) in order to specify these constraints in AMOS Graphics, it is necessary to attach matching labels to the constrained parameters. Because we are working with only a single group in this chapter, the intercept labels are not necessary.

AMOS Graphics Text Output: The Incomplete Data Model

Let's turn now to the output text for our incomplete data sample presented in Table 12.1, and then make some comparisons of the same portion of the file for the complete data sample (see Table 3.3). Three such comparisons are of primary interest. First, notice that, although the number of fixed parameters in the model is the same for both groups, the number of unlabeled parameters (the estimated parameters) varies, with the incomplete data group having 54, and the complete data sample having 38. The explanation of this discrepancy lies with the estimation of 16 intercepts for the incomplete data sample. Second, observe that, although the number of degrees of freedom (98) remains the same across the two samples, it derives from a different number of sample moments (152 vs. 136), as well as from the different number of

TABLE 12.1
Selected AMOS Text Output for Incomplete Data Sample: Model and Sample

Summary of Parameters

	Weights	Covariances	Variances	Means	Intercepts	Total
Fixed:	20	0	0	0	0	20
Labeled:	0	0	0	0	0	0
Unlabeled:	12	6	20	0	16	54
Total:	32	6	20	0	16	74

Sample size: 265

Computation of Degrees of Freedom

```
              Number of distinct sample moments:    152
      Number of distinct parameters to be estimated:    54
                                          -------------------------
                          Degrees of freedom:    98
```

Minimum was achieved

```
Chi-square =    159.650
Degrees of freedom =    98
Probability level =       0.000
```

estimated parameters (54 vs. 38). Finally, note that, despite the loss of 25% of the data for the one sample, the overall χ^2 value is relatively close (159.65 vs. 158.51).

Parameter Estimates.   Let's turn our attention now to a comparison of parameter estimates between the incomplete and complete data samples. In reviewing these estimates for the incomplete data sample (Table 12.2) and for the complete data sample (Table 3.4), you can see that the values are relatively close. Although the estimates for the incomplete data sample are sometimes a little higher and sometimes a little lower than those for the complete data sample, overall they are not very much different. Indeed, considering the substantial depletion of data for the sample used in this chapter, it seems quite amazing that the estimates are as close as they are!

Implied Covariances and Means.   Summarized in Table 12.3 are the implied covariances and means for the incomplete data sample. These values, of course, were not present in the output for the complete data sample. However, it is important to emphasize that the presence of implied covariances and means in the output file is *not* a function of whether or not the data are complete, but rather, because "means and intercepts" were checked off on the Estimation tab.

Goodness-of-Fit Statistics.   In comparing the goodness-of-fit statistics, in Table 12.4 for the incomplete data sample and in Table 3.5 for the complete data sample, you can note some values that are almost the same (e.g., RMSEA: .049 vs. .048), whereas others vary slightly at the second or third decimal point (e.g., CFI: .993 vs. .962). Generally speaking, however, the goodness-of-fit statistics are very similar across the two samples. Given the extent to which both the parameter estimates and the goodness-of-fit statistics are similar, despite the 25% data loss for one sample, these findings provide strong supportive evidence for the effectiveness of the direct ML approach to addressing the problem of missing data values.

One final comparison of interest is the difference in execution time for data that are complete, versus data that are incomplete. This comparison is summarized in Table 12.5. Although the total time required by AMOS to yield ML estimates for the complete data sample was 5 seconds, it was 33 seconds for the incomplete data sample. Although the execution time is slightly longer when the data are incomplete, the speed with which the final solution is reached is quite remarkable!

MODELING WITH AMOS BASIC

Although the testing of a model with incomplete data using AMOS Graphics is relatively straightforward and only requires one job run, the procedure using AMOS Basic involves three separate steps. First, in specifying and estimating the hypothesized model, it is essential to request the means and intercepts. Second, it is necessary to specify and estimate a separate second model, the saturated model, again

TABLE 12.2
Selected AMOS Output Text for Incomplete Data Sample: Maximum Likelihood Estimates

Regression Weights:			Estimate	S.E.	C.R.	Label
SDQ2N37	<--------	GSC	0.843	0.152	5.549	
SDQ2N25	<--------	GSC	0.950	0.171	5.565	
SDQ2N13	<--------	GSC	1.103	0.192	5.741	
SDQ2N01	<--------	GSC	1.000			
SDQ2N40	<--------	ASC	1.218	0.197	6.191	
SDQ2N28	<--------	ASC	1.439	0.212	6.774	
SDQ2N16	<--------	ASC	1.340	0.195	6.883	
SDQ2N04	<--------	ASC	1.000			
SDQ2N46	<--------	ESC	0.837	0.149	5.632	
SDQ2N34	<--------	ESC	0.609	0.180	3.381	
SDQ2N22	<--------	ESC	0.817	0.127	6.440	
SDQ2N10	<--------	ESC	1.000			
SDQ2N43	<--------	MSC	0.728	0.064	11.358	
SDQ2N31	<--------	MSC	1.037	0.071	14.513	
SDQ2N19	<--------	MSC	0.795	0.079	10.104	
SDQ2N07	<--------	MSC	1.000			

Intercepts:	Estimate	S.E.	C.R.	Label
SDQ2N37	4.776	0.077	61.660	
SDQ2N25	5.021	0.087	57.661	
SDQ2N13	4.993	0.095	52.543	
SDQ2N01	4.385	0.091	48.426	
SDQ2N40	5.003	0.093	53.905	
SDQ2N28	4.626	0.091	50.855	
SDQ2N16	4.634	0.081	57.216	
SDQ2N04	4.571	0.094	48.776	
SDQ2N46	5.257	0.092	56.855	
SDQ2N34	3.917	0.120	32.650	
SDQ2N22	5.406	0.075	71.886	
SDQ2N10	4.626	0.079	58.496	
SDQ2N43	5.014	0.091	55.277	
SDQ2N31	4.735	0.098	48.214	
SDQ2N19	4.560	0.111	41.223	
SDQ2N07	4.318	0.119	36.415	

Covariances:			Estimate	S.E.	C.R.	Label
ASC	<----------->	ESC	0.463	0.089	5.182	
GSC	<----------->	ESC	0.373	0.084	4.418	
MSC	<----------->	ASC	0.789	0.140	5.638	
MSC	<----------->	GSC	0.633	0.127	4.975	
GSC	<----------->	ASC	0.352	0.080	4.406	
MSC	<----------->	ESC	0.403	0.108	3.732	

(Continued)

TABLE 12.2 *(Continued)*

Variances:		Estimate	S.E.	C.R.	Label
	GSC	0.612	0.161	3.802	
	ASC	0.497	0.135	3.679	
	ESC	0.664	0.143	4.640	
	MSC	2.035	0.300	6.786	
	err37	0.825	0.106	7.762	
	err25	1.016	0.133	7.641	
	err13	1.159	0.159	7.288	
	err01	1.147	0.147	7.814	
	err40	1.081	0.125	8.614	
	err28	0.823	0.106	7.748	
	err16	0.628	0.083	7.555	
	err04	1.299	0.142	9.120	
	err46	1.303	0.152	8.575	
	err34	2.611	0.274	9.515	
	err22	0.700	0.095	7.348	
	err10	0.694	0.109	6.363	
	err43	0.866	0.097	8.926	
	err31	0.161	0.077	2.097	
	err19	1.412	0.158	8.960	
	err07	1.177	0.146	8.066	

requesting the estimation of the means and intercepts. Finally, because these two models do not yield a χ^2 statistic, this value must be computed manually. The reason for this step is because when model fit is based on incomplete data, the "function of the log likelihood" value is reported, rather than the χ^2 statistic. Thus, to obtain a χ^2 value, its degrees of freedom, and its probability value, one must resort to other means. One such possibility is to determine the log likelihood discrepancy value between the hypothesized and saturated models.

Let's turn now to the AMOS Basic input files pertinent to (a) the hypothesized model shown in Fig. 12.2 and (b) its related saturated model.

The Hypothesized Model

Model input related to the hypothesized model is shown in Table 12.6. Because it is important to recognize differences in the input file setup when the data are incomplete as opposed to when they are complete, it may be helpful to turn to Table 3.2 in order to compare the two AMOS Basic files. Although, at first blush, the input file shown in Table 12.6 (for incomplete data) might appear to be quite different from its companion file in Table 3.2, this is really not the case. Most of the difference stems from the more parsimonious way in which the file has been structured in Table 12.6. More specifically, in lieu of specifying the impact of the latent factors and error terms on each of the observed measures in separate sections of the file (as in Table 3.2), the observed measures, as dependent variables in the model, are each specified as being equal to their related factor and error terms.

Implied (for all variables) Covariances

	ESC	ASC	GSC	MSC	SDQ2N07	SDQ2N19	SDQ2N31
ESC	0.664						
ASC	0.463	0.497					
GSC	0.373	0.352	0.612				
MSC	0.403	0.789	0.633	2.035			
SDQ2N07	0.403	0.789	0.633	2.035	3.212		
SDQ2N19	0.320	0.627	0.503	1.617	1.617	2.697	
SDQ2N31	0.418	0.818	0.657	2.110	2.110	1.676	2.348
SDQ2N43	0.293	0.574	0.461	1.481	1.481	1.177	1.535
SDQ2N10	0.664	0.463	0.373	0.403	0.403	0.320	0.418
SDQ2N22	0.542	0.378	0.305	0.329	0.329	0.262	0.341
SDQ2N34	0.404	0.282	0.227	0.245	0.245	0.195	0.254
SDQ2N46	0.556	0.388	0.313	0.337	0.337	0.268	0.350
SDQ2N04	0.463	0.497	0.352	0.789	0.789	0.627	0.818
SDQ2N16	0.620	0.666	0.471	1.056	1.056	0.839	1.095
SDQ2N28	0.666	0.715	0.506	1.135	1.135	0.902	1.177
SDQ2N40	0.564	0.605	0.428	0.960	0.960	0.763	0.996
SDQ2N01	0.373	0.352	0.612	0.633	0.633	0.503	0.657
SDQ2N13	0.412	0.388	0.675	0.699	0.699	0.555	0.725
SDQ2N25	0.355	0.334	0.582	0.602	0.602	0.478	0.624
SDQ2N37	0.315	0.297	0.516	0.534	0.534	0.424	0.554

	SDQ2N43	SDQ2N10	SDQ2N22	SDQ2N34	SDQ2N46	SDQ2N04	SDQ2N16
SDQ2N43	1.944						
SDQ2N10	0.293	1.357					
SDQ2N22	0.240	0.542	1.143				
SDQ2N34	0.179	0.404	0.330	2.857			
SDQ2N46	0.246	0.556	0.454	0.338	1.769		
SDQ2N04	0.574	0.463	0.378	0.282	0.388	1.796	
SDQ2N16	0.769	0.620	0.507	0.377	0.519	0.666	1.520
SDQ2N28	0.826	0.666	0.544	0.405	0.558	0.715	0.958
SDQ2N40	0.699	0.564	0.461	0.343	0.472	0.605	0.811
SDQ2N01	0.461	0.373	0.305	0.227	0.313	0.352	0.471
SDQ2N13	0.508	0.412	0.336	0.251	0.345	0.388	0.520
SDQ2N25	0.438	0.355	0.290	0.216	0.297	0.334	0.448
SDQ2N37	0.389	0.315	0.257	0.192	0.264	0.297	0.397

	SDQ2N28	SDQ2N40	SDQ2N01	SDQ2N13	SDQ2N25	SDQ2N37
SDQ2N28	1.853					
SDQ2N40	0.871	1.818				
SDQ2N01	0.506	0.428	1.759			
SDQ2N13	0.558	0.473	0.675	1.904		
SDQ2N25	0.481	0.407	0.582	0.642	1.569	
SDQ2N37	0.427	0.361	0.516	0.569	0.490	1.261

Implied (for all variables) Means

ESC	ASC	GSC	MSC	SDQ2N07	SDQ2N19	SDQ2N31
0.000	0.000	0.000	0.000	4.318	4.560	4.735

SDQ2N43	SDQ2N10	SDQ2N22	SDQ2N34	SDQ2N46	SDQ2N04	SDQ2N16
5.014	4.626	5.406	3.917	5.257	4.571	4.634

SDQ2N28	SDQ2N40	SDQ2N01	SDQ2N13	SDQ2N25	SDQ2N37
4.626	5.003	4.385	4.993	5.021	4.776

TABLE 12.4

Selected AMOS Text Output for Incomplete Data Sample: Goodness-of-Fit Statistics

Summary of models

Model	NPAR	CMIN	DF	P
Your model	54	159.650	98	0.000
Saturated model	152	0.000	0	
Independence model	16	9314.466	136	0.000

Model	DELTA1 NFI	RHO1 RFI	DELTA2 IFI	RHO2 TLI	CFI
Your model	0.983	0.976	0.993	0.991	0.993
Saturated model	1.000		1.000		1.000
Independence model	0.000	0.000	0.000	0.000	0.000

Model	PRATIO	PNFI	PCFI
Your model	0.721	0.708	0.716
Saturated model	0.000	0.000	0.000
Independence model	1.000	0.000	0.000

Model	RMSEA	LO 90	HI 90	PCLOSE
Your model	0.049	0.035	0.062	0.541
Independence model	0.506	0.497	0.514	0.000

Model	ECVI	LO 90	HI 90	MECVI
Your model	1.014	0.898	1.160	1.042
Saturated model	1.152	1.152	1.152	1.231
Independence model	35.403	34.217	36.613	35.412

TABLE 12.5

Selected AMOS Text Output for Complete and Incomplete
Data Samples: Execution Time Summary

Complete Data Sample

Execution time summary:

Minimization:	0.220
Miscellaneous:	5.110
Bootstrap:	0.000
Total:	5.330

Incomplete Data Sample

Execution time summary:

Minimization:	31.090
Miscellaneous:	2.470
Bootstrap:	0.000
Total:	33.560

TABLE 12.6
AMOS BASIC Input for Hypothesized Four-Factor CFA Model

Sub Main

Dim Sem as New AmosEngine
'Testing for Multidimensionality of SC for Grade 7 Sample with Incomplete Data'

With SEM
.TextOutput
.Standardized
.AllimpliedMoments
.ModelMeansandIntercepts

.BeginGroup "asc7miss25.txt"

   .Structure "SDQ2N01 = ( ) + GSC (1) + err01 (1)"
   .Structure "SDQ2N13 = ( ) + GSC   + err13 (1)"
   .Structure "SDQ2N25 = ( ) + GSC   + err25 (1)"
   .Structure "SDQ2N37 = ( ) + GSC   + err37 (1)"

   .Structure "SDQ2N04 = ( ) + ASC (1)   + err04 (1)"
   .Structure "SDQ2N16 = ( ) + ASC   + err16 (1)"
   .Structure "SDQ2N28 = ( ) + ASC   + err28 (1)"
   .Structure "SDQ2N40 = ( ) + ASC   + err40 (1)"

   .Structure "SDQ2N10 = ( ) + ESC (1) + err10 (1)"
   .Structure "SDQ2N22 = ( ) + ESC   + err22 (1)"
   .Structure "SDQ2N34 = ( ) + ESC   + err34 (1)"
   .Structure "SDQ2N46 = ( ) + ESC   + err46 (1)"

   .Structure "SDQ2N07 = ( ) + MSC (1)   + err 07 (1)"
   .Structure "SDQ2N19 = ( ) + MSC   + err19 (1)"
   .Structure "SDQ2N31 = ( ) + MSC   + err31 (1)"
   .Structure "SDQ2N43 = ( ) + MSC   + err43 (1)"

End With
End Sub

The truly important difference between the two input files, however, is the inclusion of empty parentheses in Table 12.6; these relate to the intercept terms. When analyzing data with missing values, it is imperative that estimation of all additive constants (except those assumed to be zero) be requested. This requirement varies from analyses involving complete data where the additive constants are not necessary unless the model specifies constraints among the intercepts.

The Saturated Model

The saturated model has as many free parameters as there are first and second moments (i.e., means and variances). When analyses are based on complete data, the saturated model will always fit the sample data perfectly; as a result, $\chi^2 = 0.0$, with zero degrees of freedom. Because the saturated model can fit the sample data no worse than the more restricted hypothesized model, its "function of log likelihood" value will necessarily be smaller. The AMOS Basic input file for the saturated model related to Fig. 12.2 is presented in Table 12.7.

As you can see, the top section of the input file for the saturated model replicates exactly with that for the hypothesized model with one exception—the term *Saturated* replaces the term *SEM* accompanying the "With" command. Subsequent to the ".BeginGroup" statement, however, the input is different. First of all, notice that there are 16 .Mean commands requesting mean estimates for each of the observed variables. Arbuckle and Wothke (1999) noted that a useful property of the .Mean command is that it automatically adds variance and covariance terms for the observed indicator variables to the set of free model parameters. As a consequence, the saturated model will have 152 freely estimated parameters: 16 means, 16 variances, and 120 $(16 \times 15/2)$ covariances.

TABLE 12.7
AMOS BASIC Input for Saturated Four-Factor CFA Model

Sub Main

Dim Saturated as New AmosEngine
'Testing for Multidimensionality of SC for Grade 7 Sample with Incomplete Data'

With Saturated
.TextOutput
.AllimpliedMoments
.ModelMeansandIntercepts

.BeginGroup "asc7miss25.txt"

   .Mean "SDQ2N01"
   .Mean "SDQ2N13"
   .Mean "SDQ2N25"
   .Mean "SDQ2N37"
   .Mean "SDQ2N04"
   .Mean "SDQ2N16"
   .Mean "SDQ2N28"
   .Mean "SDQ2N40"
   .Mean "SDQ2N10"
   .Mean "SDQ2N22"
   .Mean "SDQ2N34"
   .Mean "SDQ2N46"
   .Mean "SDQ2N07"
   .Mean "SDQ2N19"
   .Mean "SDQ2N31"
   .Mean "SDQ2N43"

End With
End Sub

As noted earlier, when using AMOS Basic to fit a model to a sample having incomplete data, it is necessary to manually compute the χ^2 statistic. Thus, as a final look at the AMOS Basic procedure, I wish to show you how this is accomplished. Turning to Table 12.8, you can see a value related to the "function of log likelihood" for each of the hypothesized and saturated models. As noted earlier, also, this value for the saturated model is typically lower than it is for the hypothesized model. Indeed, the values shown in Table 12.8 are consistent with this common finding. Taking the difference between these two log likelihood values (4381.951 − 4222.301) yields the value 159.65, which is the χ^2 value reported in the AMOS Graphics output file (see Table 12.1). Relatedly, taking the difference between the number of parameters for each model (152 − 54) yields the number of degrees of freedom (98).

TABLE 12.8
Selected AMOS Basic Output Text:
Determination of Chi-Square Statistics

Hypothesized Model

Minimum was achieved

Function of log likelihood =   4381.951
Number of parameters =   54

Saturated Model

Minimum was achieved

Function of log likelihood =   4222.301
Number of parameters =   152

References

Aish, A. M., & Joreskog, K. G. (1990). A panel model for political efficacy and responsiveness: An application of LISREL 7 with weighted least squares. *Quality and Quantity, 19*, 716–723.

Akaike, H. (1987). Factor Analysis and AIC. *Psychometrika, 52*, 317–332.

Allison, P. D. (1987). Estimation of linear models with incomplete data. In C. Clogg (Ed.), *Sociological methodology 1987* (pp. 71–103). San Francisco: Jossey-Bass.

Anderson, J. C., & Gerbing, D. W. (1984). The effect of sampling error on convergence, improper solutions, and goodness-of- fit indices for maximum likelihood confirmatory factor analysis. *Psychometrika, 49*, 155–173.

Anderson, J. C., & Gerbing, D. W. (1988). Structural equation modeling in practice: A review and recommended two-step approach. *Psychological Bulletin, 103*, 411–423.

Arbuckle, J. L. (1996). Full information estimation in the presence of incomplete data. In G. A. Marcoulides & R. E. Schumacker (Eds.), *Advanced structural equation modeling: Issues and techniques* (pp. 243–277). Mahwah, NJ: Lawrence Erlbaum Associates.

Arbuckle, J. L. (1997). *Amos user's guide version 3.6.* Chicago: Smallwaters.

Arbuckle, J. L. (1999). Amos 4.0 [Computer software]. Chicago: Smallwaters.

Arbuckle, J. L., & Wothke, W. (1999). *AMOS 4.0 user's guide.* Chicago: Smallwaters.

Atkinson, L. (1988). The measurement-statistics controversy: Factor analysis and subinterval data. *Bulletin of the Psychonomic Society, 26*, 361–364.

Austin, J. T., & Calderón, R. F. (1996). Theoretical and technical contributions to structural equation modeling: An updated bibliography. *Structural Equation Modeling: A Multidisciplinary Journal, 3*, 105–175.

Babakus, E., Ferguson, C. E., Jr., & Joreskog, K. G. (1987). The sensitivity of confirmatory maximum likelihood factor analysis to violations of measurement scale and distributional assumptions. *Journal of Marketing Research, 24*, 222–228.

Bacharac, S. B., Bauer, S. C., & Conley, S. (1986). Organizational analysis of stress: The case of elementary and secondary schools. *Work and Occupations, 13*, 7–32.

Bandalos, D. L. (1993). Factors influencing cross-validation of confirmatory factor analysis models. *Multivariate Behavioral Research, 28*, 351–374.

Beck, A. T., Ward, C. H., Mendelson, M., Mock, J., & Erbaugh, J. (1961). An inventory for measuring depression. *Archives of General Psychiatry, 4*, 561–571.

Benson, J., & Bandalos, D. L. (1992). Second-order confirmatory factor analysis of the Reactions to Tests Scale with cross-validation. *Multivariate Behavioral Research, 27*, 459–487.

Bentler, P. M. (1980). Multivariate analysis with latent variables: Causal modeling. *Annual Review of Psychology, 31*, 419–456.

Bentler, P. M. (1988). Causal modeling via structural equation systems. In J. R. Nesselroade & R. B. Cattell (Eds.), *Handbook of multivariate experimental psychology* (2nd edition, pp. 317–335). New York: Plenum.

Bentler, P. M. (1990). Comparative fit indexes in structural models. *Psychological Bulletin, 107*, 238–246.

Bentler, P. M. (1992). On the fit of models to covariances and methodology to the Bulletin. *Psychological Bulletin, 112*, 400–404.

Bentler, P. M. (1995). *EQS: Structural equations program manual.* Encino, CA: Multivariate Software, Inc.

Bentler, P. M. (2000). *EQS6 structural equations program manual.* Encino, CA: Multivariate Software, Inc.

Bentler, P. M., & Bonett, D. G. (1980). Significance tests and goodness of fit in the analysis of covariance structures. *Psychological Bulletin, 88*, 588–606.

Bentler, P. M., & Bonett, D. G. (1987). This week's citation classic. *Current Contents, Social & Behavioral Sciences, 19*, 16.

Bentler, P. M., & Chou, C.-P. (1987). Practical issues in structural modeling. *Sociological Methods & Research, 16*, 78–117.

Bentler, P. M., & Wu, E. J. C. (1995). *EQS for Windows: User's guide.* Encino CA: Multivariate Software, Inc.

Bentler, P. M., & Yuan, K.-H. (1999). Structural equation modeling with small samples: Test statistics. *Multivariate Behavioral Research, 34*, 181–197.

Biddle, B. J., & Marlin, M. M. (1987). Causality, confirmation, credulity, and structural equation modeling. *Child Development, 58*, 4–17.

Bollen, K. A. (1986). Sample size and Bentler and Bonett's nonnormed fit index. *Psychometrika, 51*, 375–377.

Bollen, K. A. (1989a). *Structural equations with latent variables.* New York: Wiley.

Bollen, K. A. (1989b). A new incremental fit index for general structural models. *Sociological Methods & Research, 17*, 303–316.

Bollen, K. A., & Barb, K. H. (1981). Pearson's *r* and coursely categorized measures. *American Sociological Review, 46*, 232–239.

Bollen, K. A., & Long, J. S. (Eds.). (1993). *Testing structural equation models.* Newbury Park, CA: Sage.

Bollen, K. A., & Stine, R. A. (1988, August). *Bootstrapping structural equation models: Variability of indirect effects and goodness-of-fit measures.* Paper presented at the American Sociological Association Annual Meeting, Atlanta, GA.

Bollen, K. A., & Stine, R. A. (1993). Bootstrapping goodness-of-fit measures in structural equation modeling (pp. 111–135). In K. A. Bollen, & J. S. Long (Eds.), *Testing structural equation models.* Newbury Park, CA: Sage.

Boomsma, A. (1982). The robustness of LISREL against small sample sizes in factor analysis models. In H. Wold & K. Joreskog (Eds.), *Systems under indirect observation* (pp. 149–173). New York: Elsevier-North-Holland.

Boomsma, A. (1985). Nonconvergence, improper solutions, and starting values in LISREL maximum likelihood estimation. *Psychometrika, 50*, 229–242.

Bozdogan, H. (1987). Model selection and Akaike's information criteria (AIC): The general theory and its analytical extensions. *Psychometrika, 52*, 345–370.

Breckler, S. J. (1990). Applications of covariance structure modeling in Psychology: Cause for concern? *Psychological Bulletin, 52*, 260–271.

Brookover, W. B. (1962). *Self-concept of Ability Scale.* East Lansing, MI: Educational Publication Services.

Brown, R. L. (1994). Efficacy of the indirect approach for estimating structural equation models with missing data: A comparison of five methods. *Structural Equation Modeling: A Multidisciplinary Journal, 1*, 287–316.

Browne, M. W. (1984). Asymptotically distribution-free methods for the analysis of covariance structures. *British Journal of Mathematical and Statistical Psychology, 37*, 62–83.

Browne, M. W., & Cudeck, R. (1989). Single sample cross-validation indices for covariance structures. *Multivariate Behavioral Research, 24*, 445–455.

Browne, M. W., & Cudeck, R. (1993). Alternative ways of assessing model fit. In K. A. Bollen & J. S. Long (Eds.), *Testing structural equation models* (pp. 445–455). Newbury Park, CA: Sage.

Byrne, B. M. (1988a). The Self Description Questionnaire III: Testing for equivalent factorial validity across ability. *Educational and Psychological Measurement, 48*, 397–406.

Byrne, B. M. (1988b). Adolescent self-concept, ability grouping, and social comparison: Reexamining academic track differences in high school. *Youth and Society, 20*, 46–67.

Byrne, B. M. (1989). *A primer of LISREL: Basic applications and programming for confirmatory factor analytic models.* New York: Springer-Verlag.

Byrne, B. M. (1991). The Maslach Inventory: Validating factorial structure and invariance across intermediate, secondary, and university educators. *Multivariate Behavioral Research, 26*, 583–605.

Byrne, B. M. (1993). The Maslach Inventory: Testing for factorial validity and invariance across elementary, intermediate, and secondary teachers. *Journal of Occupational and Organizational Psychology, 66*, 197–212.

Byrne, B. M. (1994a). Testing for the factorial validity, replication, and invariance of a measuring instrument: A paradigmatic application based on the Maslach Burnout Inventory. *Multivariate Behavioral Research, 29*, 289–311.

Byrne, B. M. (1994b). Burnout: Testing for the validity, replication, and invariance of causal structure across elementary, intermediate, and secondary teachers. *American Educational Research Journal, 31*, 645–673.

Byrne, B. M. (1994c). *Structural equation modeling with EQS and EQS/Windows: Basic concepts, applications, and programming.* Thousand Oaks, CA: Sage.

Byrne, B. M. (1996). *Measuring self-concept across the lifespan: Issues and instrumentation.* Washington DC: American Psychological Association.

Byrne, B. M. (1998). *Structural equation modeling with LISREL, PRELIS, and SIMPLIS: Basic concepts, applications, and programming.* Mahwah, NJ: Lawrence Erlbaum Associates.

Byrne, B. M. (1999). The nomological network of teacher burnout: A literature review and empirically validated model. In M. Huberman & R. Vandenberghe (Eds.), *Understanding and preventing teacher burnout: A sourcebook of international research and practice* (pp. 15–37). London: Cambridge Press.

Byrne, B. M., & Baron P. (1993). The Beck Depression Inventory: Testing and cross-validating an hierarchical factor structure for nonclinical adolescents. *Measurement and Evaluation in Counseling and Development, 26*, 164–178.

Byrne, B. M., & Baron, P. (1994). Measuring adolescent depression: Tests of equivalent factorial structure for English and French versions of the Beck Depression Inventory. *Applied Psychology: An International Review, 44*, 33–47.

Byrne, B. M., Baron, P., & Balev, J. (1996). The Beck Depression Inventory: Testing for its factorial validity and invariance across gender for Bulgarian adolescents. *Personality and Individual Differences, 21*, 641–651.

Byrne, B. M., Baron, P., & Balev, J. (1998). The Beck Depression Inventory: A cross-validated test of second-order structure for Bulgarian adolescents. *Educational and Psychological Measurement, 58*, 241–251.

Byrne, B. M., Baron, P., & Campbell, T. L. (1993). Measuring adolescent depression: Factorial validity and invariance of the Beck Depression Inventory across gender. *Journal of Research on Adolescence, 3*, 127–143.

Byrne, B. M., Baron, P., & Campbell, T. L. (1994). The Beck Depression Inventory (French Version): Testing for gender-invariant factorial structure for nonclinical adolescents). *Journal of Adolescent Research, 9*, 166–179.

Byrne, B. M., & Baron, P., Larsson, B., & Melin, L. (1995). The Beck Depression Inventory: Testing and cross-validating a second-order factorial structure for Swedish nonclinical adolescents. *Behaviour Research and Therapy, 33*, 345–356.

Byrne, B. M., & Baron, P. Larsson, B., & Melin, L. (1996). Measuring depression for Swedish nonclinical adolescents: Factorial validity and equivalence of the Beck Depression Inventory. *Scandinavian Journal of Psychology, 37*, 37–45.

Byrne, B. M., & Campbell, T. L. (1999). Cross-cultural comparisons and the presumption of equivalent measurement and theoretical structure: A look beneath the surface. *Journal of Cross-cultural Psychology, 30*, 557–576.

Byrne, B. M., & Shavelson, R. J. (1986). On the structure of adolescent self-concept. *Journal of Educational Psychology, 78*, 474–481.

Byrne, B. M., & Shavelson, R. J. (1987). Adolescent self-concept: Testing the assumption of equivalent structure across gender. *American Educational Research Journal, 24*, 365–385.

Byrne, B. M., & Shavelson, R. J. (1996). On the structure of social self-concept for pre-, early, and late adolescents. *Journal of Personality and Social Psychology, 70*, 599–613.

Byrne, B. M., Shavelson, R. J., & Muthén, B. (1989). Testing for the equivalence of factor covariance and mean structures: The issue of partial measurement invariance. *Psychological Bulletin, 88*, 456–466.

Byrne, B. M., & Worth Gavin, D. A. (1996). The Shavelson model revisited: Testing for the structure of academic self-concept across pre-, early, and late adolescents. *Journal of Educational Psychology, 88*, 215–228.

Carlson, M., & Mulaik, S. A. (1993). Trait ratings from descriptions of behavior as mediated by components of meaning. *Multivariate Behavioral Research, 28*, 111–159.

Chou, C.-P., Bentler, P. M., & Satorra, A. (1991). Scaled test statistics and robust standard errors for non-normal data in covariance structure analysis: A Monte Carlo study. *British Journal of Mathematical and Statistical Psychology, 44*, 347–357.

Cliff, N. (1983). Some cautions concerning the application of causal modeling methods. *Multivariate Behavioral Research, 18*, 115–126.

Coenders, G., Satorra, A., & Saris, W. E. (1997). Alternative approaches to structural modeling of ordinal data: A Monte Carlo study. *Structural Equation Modeling: A Multidisciplinary Journal, 4*, 261–282.

Cohen, J. (1994). The earth is round ($p < .05$). *American Psychologist, 49*, 997–1003.

Comrey, A. L. (1992). *A first course in factor analysis.* Hillsdale, NJ: Lawrence Erlbaum Associates.

Cudeck, R., & Browne, M. W. (1983). Cross-validation of covariance structures. *Multivariate Behavioral Research, 18*, 147–167.

Cudeck, R., & Henly, S. J. (1991). Model selection in covariance structures analysis and the "problem" of sample size: A clarification. *Psychological Bulletin, 109*, 512–519.

Curran, P. J., West, S. G., & Finch, J. F. (1996). The robustness of test statistics to nonnormality and specification error in confirmatory factor analysis. *Psychological Methods, 1*, 16–29.

Diaconis, P., & Efron, B. (1983). Computer-intensive methods in statistics. *Scientific American, 248*, 116–130.

Efron, B. (1979). Bootstrap methods: Another look at the jackknife. *Annals of Statistics, 7*, 1–26.

Efron, B. (1982). *The jackknife, the bootstrap and other resampling plans.* Philadelphia, PA: SIAM.

Efron, B., & Tibshirani, R. J. (1993). *An introduction to the bootstrap.* New York: Chapman and Hall.

Fabrigar, L. R., Wegener, D. T., MacCallum, R. C., & Strahan, E. J. (1999). Evaluating the use of exploratory factor analysis in psychological research. *Psychological Methods, 4*, 272–299.

Fan, X., Thompson, B., & Wang, L. (1999). Effects of sample size, estimation methods, and model specification on structural equation modeling fit indexes. *Structural Equation Modeling: A Multidisciplinary Journal, 6*, 56–83.

Finch, J. F., West, S. G., & MacKinnon, D. P. (1997). Effects of sample size and nonnormality on the estimation of mediated effects in latent variable models. *Structural Equation Modeling: A Multidisciplinary Journal, 4*, 87–107.

Fornell, C. (1982). *A second generation of multivariate analysis. Vol. 1: Methods.* New York: Praeger.

Francis, D. J., Fletcher, J. M., & Rourke, B. P. (1988). Discriminant validity of lateral sensorimotor tests in children. *Journal of Clinical and Experimental Neuropsychology, 10,* 779–799.

Gerbing, D. W., & Anderson, J. C. (1984). On the meaning of within-factor correlated measurement errors. *Journal of Consumer Research, 11,* 572–580.

Gerbing, D. W., & Anderson, J. C. (1993). Monte Carlo evaluations of goodness-of-fit indices for structural equation models. In K. A. Bollen & J. S. Long (Eds.), *Testing structural equation models* (pp. 40–65). Newbury Park, CA: Sage.

Gorsuch, R. L. (1983). *Factor Analysis.* Hillsdale, NJ: Lawrence Erlbaum Associates.

Green, S. B., Akey, T. M., Fleming, K. K., Hershberger, S. L., & Marquis, J. G. (1997). *Structural Equation Modeling: A Multidisciplinary Journal, 4,* 108–120.

Hancock, G. R., & Nevitt, J. (1999). Bootstrapping and the identification of exogenous latent variables within structural equation models. *Structural Equation Modeling: A Multidisciplinary Journal, 6,* 394–99.

Harter, S. (1990). Causes, correlates, and the functional role of global self-worth; A lifespan perspective. In R. J. Sternberg & J. Kolligian (Eds.), *Competence considered* (pp. 67–97). New Haven, CT: Yale University Press.

Hayduk, L. A. (1987). *Structural equation modeling with LISREL: Essentials and advances.* Baltimore, MD: Johns Hopkins University Press.

Hoelter, J. W. (1983). The analysis of covariance structures: Goodness-of-fit indices. *Sociological Methods & Research, 11,* 325–344.

Hoyle, R. H. (Ed.). (1995a). *Structural equation modeling: Concepts, issues, and applications.* Thousand Oaks, CA: Sage.

Hoyle, R. H. (1995b). The structural equation modeling approach: Basic concepts and fundamental issues. In R. H. Hoyle (Ed.), *Structural equation modeling: Concepts, issues, and applications* (pp. 1–15). Thousand Oaks, CA: Sage.

Hu, L.-T., & Bentler, P. M. (1995). Evaluating model fit. In R. H. Hoyle (Ed.), *Structural equation modeling: Concepts, issues, and applications* (pp. 76–99). Thousand Oaks, CA: Sage.

Hu, L.-T., & Bentler, P. M. (1998). Fit indices in covariance structure modeling: Sensitivity to underparameterized model misspecification. *Psychological Methods, 3,* 424–453.

Hu, L.-T., & Bentler, P. M. (1999). Cutoff criteria for fit indexes in covariance structure analysis: Conventional criteria versus new alternatives. *Structural Equation Modeling: A Multidisciplinary Journal, 6,* 1–55.

Hu, L.-T., Bentler, P. M., & Kano, Y. (1992). Can test statistics in covariance structure analysis be trusted? *Psychological Bulletin, 112,* 351–362.

Ichikawa, M., & Konishi, S. (1995). Application of the bootstrap methods in factor analysis. *Psychometrika, 60,* 77–93.

James, L. R., Mulaik, S. A., & Brett, J. M. (1982). *Causal analysis: Assumptions. models, and data.* Beverly Hills, CA: Sage.

Jamshidian, M., & Bentler, P. M. (1999). ML estimation of mean and covariance structures with missing data using complete data routines. *Journal of Educational and Behavioral Statistics, 24,* 21–41.

Joreskog, K. G. (1969). A general approach to confirmatory maximum likelihood factor analysis. *Psychometrika, 34,* 183–202.

Joreskog, K. G. (1971a). Statistical analysis of sets of congeneric tests. *Psychometrika, 36,* 109–133.

Joreskog, K. G. (1971b). Simultaneous factor analysis in several populations. *Psychometrika, 36,* 409–426.

Joreskog, K. G. (1990). New developments in LISREL: Analysis of ordinal variables using polychoric correlations and weighted least squares. *Quality and Quantity, 24,* 387–404.

Joreskog, K. G. (1993). Testing structural equation models. In K. A. Bollen & J. S. Long (Eds.), *Testing structural equation models* (pp. 294–316). Newbury Park, CA: Sage.

Joreskog, K. G., & Sorbom, D. (1988). *LISREL 7: A guide to the program and applications.* Chicago: SPSS, Inc.

Joreskog, K. G., & Sorbom, D. (1989). *LISREL 7 User's reference guide.* Chicago: Scientific Software, Inc.

Joreskog, K. G., & Sorbom, D. (1993). *LISREL 8: Structural equation modeling with the SIMPLIS command language.* Chicago: Scientific Software International.

Joreskog, K. G., & Sorbom, D. (1996a, April). *Structural equation modeling.* Workshop presented for the NORC Social Science Research Professional Development Training Sessions, Chicago.

Joreskog, K. G., & Sorbom, D. (1996b). *LISREL 8: User's reference guide.* Chicago: Scientific Software International.

Joreskog, K. G., & Sorbom, D. (1996c). *PRELIS: User's reference guide.* Chicago: Scientific Software International.

Joreskog, K. G., & Yang, F. (1996). Nonlinear structural equation models: The Kenny–Judd model with interaction effects. In G. A. Marcoulides & R. E. Schumacker (Eds.), *Advanced structural equation modeling: Issues and techniques* (pp. 57–88). Mahwah, NJ: Lawrence Erlbaum Associates.

Kerlinger, F. N. (1984). *Liberalism and conservatism: The nature and structure of social attitudes.* Hillsdale, NJ: Lawrence Erlbaum Associates.

Kirk, R. E. (1996). Practical significance: A concept whose time has come. *Educational and Psychological Measurement, 56,* 746–759.

Kline, R. B. (1998). *Principles and practice of structural equation modeling.* New York: Guildford Press.

Kotz, S., & Johnson, N. I. (1992). *Breakthrough in Statistics* (Vols. 1 and 2). New York: Springer-Verlag.

La Du, T. J., & Tanaka, J. S. (1989). Influence of sample size, estimation method, and model specification on goodness-of-fit assessments in structural equation modeling. *Journal of Applied Psychology, 74,* 625–636.

Leiter, M. P. (1991). Coping patterns as predictors of burnout: The function of control and escapist coping patterns. *Journal of Organizational Behavior, 12,* 123–144.

Little, R. J. A., & Rubin, D. B. (1987). *Statistical analysis with missing data.* New York: Wiley.

Little, R. J. A., & Rubin, D. B. (1989). The analysis of social science data with missing values. *Sociological Methods and Research, 18,* 292–326.

Little, T. D., Lindenberger, U., & Nesselroade, J. R. (1999). On selecting indicators for multivariate measurement and modeling with latent variables: When "good" indicators are bad and "bad" indicators are good. *Psychological Methods, 4,* 192–211.

Loehlin, J. C. (1992). *Latent variable models: An introduction to factor, path, & structural analyses.* Hillsdale, NJ: Lawrence Erlbaum Associates.

Long, J. S. (1983a). *Confirmatory factor analysis.* Beverly Hills, CA: Sage.

Long, J. S. (1983b). *Covariance structure models: An introduction to LISREL.* Beverly Hills, CA: Sage.

MacCallum, R. C. (1986). Specification searches in covariance structure modeling. *Psychological Bulletin, 100,* 107–120.

MacCallum, R. C. (1995; Model specification: Procedures, strategies, and related issues. In R. H. Hoyle (Ed.), *Structural equation modeling: Concepts, issues, and applications* (pp. 76–99). Newbury Park, CA: Sage.

MacCallum, R. C., Browne, M. W., & Sugawara, H. M. (1996). Power analysis and determination of sample size for covariance structure modeling. *Psychological Methods, 1,* 130–149.

MacCallum, R. C., Roznowski, M., Mar, M., & Reith, J. V. (1994). Alternative strategies for cross-validation of covariance structure models. *Multivariate Behavioral Research, 29,* 1–32.

MacCallum, R. C., Roznowski, M., & Necowitz, L. B. (1992). Model modifications in covariance structure analysis: The problem of capitalization on chance. *Psychological Bulletin, 111,* 490–504.

MacCallum, R. C., Wegener, D. T., Uchino, B. N., & Fabrigar, L. R. (1993). The problem of equivalent models in applications of covariance structure analysis. *Psychological Bulletin, 114,* 185–199.

MacCallum, R. C., Widaman, K. F., Zhang, S., & Hong, S. (1999). Sample size in factor analysis. *Psychological Methods, 4,* 84–99.

Marcoulides, G. A., & Schumacker, R. E. (Eds.). (1996). *Advanced structural equation modeling: Issues and techniques.* Mahwah, NJ: Lawrence Erlbaum Associates.

Mardia, K. V. (1970). Measures of multivariate skewness and kurtosis with applications. *Biometrika, 57*, 519–530.

Marsh, H. W. (1992a). *Self Description Questionnaire (SDQ) II: A theoretical and empirical basis for the measurement of multiple dimensions of adolescent self-concept: An interim test manual and research monograph.* Macarthur, NSW, Australia: Faculty of Education, University of Western Sydney.

Marsh, H. W. (1992b). *Self Description Questionnaire (SDQ) III: A theoretical and empirical basis for the measurement of multiple dimensions of late adolescent self-concept: An interim test manual and research monograph.* Macarthur, NSW, Australia: Faculty of Education, University of Western Sydney.

Marsh, H. W. (1998). Pairwise deletion for missing data in structural equation models: Nonpositive definite matrices, parameter estimates, goodness of fit, and adjusted sample sizes. *Structural Equation Modeling: A Multidisciplinary Journal, 5*, 22–36.

Marsh, H. W., & Balla, J. R. (1994). Goodness-of-fit indices in confirmatory factor analysis: The effect of sample size and model complexity. *Quality and Quantity, 28*, 185–217.

Marsh, H. W., Balla, J. R., & McDonald, R. P. (1988). Goodness-of-fit indexes in confirmatory factor analysis: The effect of sample size. *Psychological Bulletin, 103*, 391–410.

Marsh, H. W., Hau, K.-T., Balla, J. R., & Grayson, D. (1998). Is more ever too much? The number of indicators per factor in confirmatory factor analysis. *Multivariate Behavioral Research, 33*, 181–220.

Maslach, C., & Jackson, S. E. (1981). *Maslach Burnout Inventory manual.* Palo Alto, CA: Consulting Psychologists Press.

Maslach, C., & Jackson, S. E. (1986). *Maslach Burnout Inventory manual* (2nd ed.). Palo Alto, CA: Consulting Psychologists Press.

McArdle, J. J. (1994). Structural factor analysis experiments with incomplete data. *Multivariate Behavioral Research, 29*, 409–454.

McDonald, R. P. (1985). *Factor analysis and related methods.* Hillsdale, NJ: Lawrence Erlbaum Associates.

Micceri, T. (1989). The unicorn, the normal curve, and other improbable creatures. *Psychological Bulletin, 105*, 156–166.

Mislevy, R. J. (1986). Recent developments in the factor analysis of categorical variables. *Journal of Educational Statistics, 11*, 3–31.

Mulaik, S. A. (1972). *The foundations of factor analysis.* New York: McGraw-Hill.

Mulaik, S. A., James, L. R., Van Altine, J., Bennett, N., Lind, S., and Stilwell, C. D. (1989). Evaluation of goodness-of-fit indices for structural equation models. *Psychological Bulletin, 105*, 430–445.

Muthén, B. O. (1984). A general structural equation model with dichotomous, ordered categorical, and continuous latent variable indicators. *Psychometrika, 49*, 115–132.

Muthén, B., & Christoffersson, A. (1981). Simultaneous factor analysis of dichotomous variables in several groups. *Psychometrika, 46*, 407–419.

Muthén, B., & Kaplan, D. (1985). A comparison of some methodologies for the factor analysis of nonnormal Likert variables. *British Journal of Mathematical and Statistical Psychology, 38*, 171–189.

Muthén, B., Kaplan, D., & Hollis, M. (1987). On structural equation modeling with data that are not missing completely at random. *Psychometrika, 52*, 431–462.

Muthén, L. K., & Muthén, B. O. (1998). *Mplus user's guide.* Los Angeles: Authors.

Neale, M. C., Boker, S. M., Xie, G., & Maes, H. H. (1999). *Mx: Statistical modeling* (5th ed.) Richmond, VA: Department of Psychiatry, Virginia Commonwealth University.

Neale, M. C. (1994). *Mx: Statistical modeling* (2nd ed.). Richmond, VA: Department of Psychology, Medical College of Virginia.

Noreen, E. W. (1989). *Computer-intensive methods for testing hypotheses.* New York: Wiley.

Pettegrew, L. S., & Wolf, G. E. (1982). Validating measures of teacher stress. *American Educational Research Journal, 19*, 373–396.

Raaijmakers, Q. A. (1999). Effectiveness of different missing data treatments in surveys with Likert-type data: Introducing the relative mean substitution approach. *Educational and Psychological Measurement, 59*, 725–748.

Raftery, A. E. (1993). Baysian model selection in structural equation models. In K. A. Bollen & J. S. Long (Eds.), *Testing structural equation models* (pp. 163–180). Newbury Park, CA: Sage.

Raykov, T., & Widaman, K. F. (1995). Issues in structural equation modeling research. *Structural Equation Modeling: A Multidisciplinary Journal, 2,* 289–318.

Rindskopf, D., & Rose, T. (1988). Some theory and applications of confirmatory second-order factor analysis. *Multivariate Behavioral Research, 23,* 51–67.

Rosén, M. (1998). Gender differences in hierarchically ordered ability dimensions: The impact of missing data. *Structural Equation Modeling: A Multidisciplinary Journal, 5,* 37–62.

Rovine, M. J., & Delaney, M. (1990). Missing data estimation in developmental research. In A. Von Eye (Ed.), *Statistical methods in longitudinal research: Vol. I. Principles and structuring change* (pp. 35–79). New York: Academic Press.

Rozeboom, W. W. (1960). The fallacy of the null hypothesis significance test. *Psychological Bulletin, 57,* 416–428.

Rubin, D. B. (1976). Inference and missing data. *Biometrika, 63,* 581–592.

Saris, W., & Stronkhorst, H. (1984). *Causal modeling: nonexperimental research: An introduction to the LISREL approach.* Amsterdam: Sociometric Research Foundation.

Saris, W. E., Satorra, A., & Sorbom, D. (1987). The detection and correction of specification errors in structural equation models. In C. Clogg (Ed.), *Sociological Methodology 1987* (pp. 105–130). San Francisco: Jossey-Bass.

Satorra, A., & Bentler, P. M. (1988). Scaling corrections for chi-square statistics in covariance structure analysis. *American Statistical Association 1988 proceedings of the business and economics section* (pp. 308–313). Alexandria VA: American Statistical Association.

Satorra, A., & Saris, W. E. (1985). Power of the likelihood ratio test in covariance structure analysis. *Psychometrika, 50,* 83–90.

Schafer, J. L. (1997). *Analysis of incomplete multivariate data.* London: Chapman & Hall.

Schafer, J. L., & Olsen, M. K. (1998). Multiple imputation for multivariate missing-data problems: A data analyst's perspective. *Multivariate Behavioral Research, 33,* 545–571.

Schmidt, F. L. (1996). Statistical significance testing and cumulative knowledge in psychology: Implications for training of researchers. *Psychological Methods, 1,* 115–129.

Schumacker, R. E., & Lomax, R. G. (1996). *A beginner's guide to structural equation modeling.* Mahwah, NJ: Lawrence Erlbaum Associates.

Schwarz, G. (1978). Estimating the dimension of a model. *Annals of Statistics, 6,* 461–464.

Shavelson, R. J., Hubner, J. J., & Stanton, G. C. (1976). Self-concept: Validation of construct interpretations. *Review of Educational Research, 46,* 407–441.

Soares, A. T., & Soares, L. M. (1979). *The Affective Perception Inventory: Advanced level.* Trumbell, CT: ALSO.

Sobel, M. F., & Bohrnstedt, G. W. (1985). Use of null models in evaluating the fit of covariance structure models. In N. B. Tuma (Ed.), *Sociological Methodology 1985* (pp. 152–178). San Francisco: Jossey-Bass.

Sorbom, D. (1974). A general method for studying differences in factor means and factor structures between groups. *British Journal of Mathematical and Statistical Psychology, 27,* 229–239.

Steiger, J. H. (1990). Structural model evaluation and modification: An interval estimation approach. *Multivariate Behavioral Research, 25,* 173–180.

Steiger, J. H. (1998). A note on multiple sample extensions of the RMSEA fit index. *Structural Equation Modeling: A Multidisciplinary Journal, 5,* 411–419.

Steiger, J. H., & Lind, J. C. (1980, June). *Statistically based tests for the number of common factors.* Paper presented at the Psychometric Society Annual Meeting, Iowa City, IA.

Stine, R. A. (1990). An introduction to bootstrap methods: Examples and ideas. *Sociological Methods and Research, 8,* 243–291.

Sugawara, H. M., & MacCallum, R. C. (1993). Effect of estimation method on incremental fit indexes for covariance structure models. *Applied Psychological Measurement, 17,* 365–377.

Tanaka, J. S. (1993). Multifaceted conceptions of fit in structural equation models. In J. A. Bollen & J. S. Long (Eds.), *Testing structural equation models* (pp. 10–39). Newbury Park, CA: Sage.

Tanaka, J. S., & Huba, G. J. (1984). Confirmatory hierarchical factor analyses of psychological distress measures. *Journal of Personality and Social Psychology, 46*, 621–635.

Tang, M.-L., & Bentler, P. M. (1998). Theory and method for constrained estimation in structural equation models with incomplete data. *Computational Statistics & Data Analysis, 27*, 257–270.

Thompson, B. (1996). AERA editorial policies regarding statistical significance testing: Three suggested reforms. *Educational Researcher, 25*, 26–30.

Tucker, L. R., & Lewis, C. (1973). A reliability coefficient for maximum likelihood factor analysis. *Psychometrika, 38*, 1–10.

Weng, L.-J., & Cheng, C.-P. (1997). Why might relative fit indices differ between estimators? *Structural Equation Modeling: A Multidisciplinary Journal, 4*, 121–128.

Werts, C. E., Rock, D. A., Linn, R. L., & Joreskog, K. G. (1976). Comparison of correlations, variances, covariances, and regression weights with or without measurement error. *Psychological Bulletin, 83*, 1007–1013.

West, S. G., Finch, J. F., & Curran, P. J. (1995). Structural equation models with nonnormal variables: Problems and remedies. In R. H. Hoyle (Ed.), *Structural equation modeling: Concepts, issues, and applications* (pp. 56–75). Thousand Oaks, CA: Sage.

Wheaton, B. (1987). Assessment of fit in overidentified models with latent variables. *Sociological Methods & Research, 16*, 118–154.

Wheaton, B., Muthén, B., Alwin, D. F., & Summers, G. F. (1977). Assessing reliability and stability in panel models. In D. R. Heise (Ed.), *Sociological methodology 1977* (pp. 84–136). San Francisco: Jossey-Bass.

Williams, L. J., & Holahan, P. J. (1994). Parsimony-based fit indices for multiple-indicator models: Do they work? *Structural Equation Modeling, 1*, 161–189.

Wood, J. M., Tataryn, D. J., & Gorsuch, R. L. (1996). Effects of under- and overextraction on principal axis factor analysis with varimax rotation. *Psychological Methods, 1*, 354–365.

Wothke, W. (1993). Nonpositive definite matrices in structural modeling. In K. A. Bollen & J. S. Long (Eds.), *Testing structural equation models* (pp. 256–293). Newbury Park, CA: Sage.

Yuan, K.-H., & Bentler, P. M. (1996). Mean and covariance structure analysis with missing data. In A. Gupta & V. Girko (Eds.), *Multivariate statistical analysis and theory of random matrices: Proceedings of the Sixth Eugene Lukacs Symposium* (pp. 307–326). Utrecht, The Netherlands: VSP.

Yuan, K.-H., & Bentler, P. M. (in press). Three likelihood-based methods for mean and covariance structure analysis with nonnormal missing data. Sociological Methodology 2000. Washington, DC: American Sociological Association.

Yung, Y.-F., & Bentler, P. M. (1994). Bootstrap-corrected ADF test statistics in covariance structure analysis. *British Journal of Mathematical and Statistical Psychology, 47*, 63–84.

Yung, Y.-F., & Bentler, P. M. (1996). Bootstrapping techniques in analysis of mean and covariance structures. In G. A. Marcoulides & R. F. Schumacker (Eds.), *Advanced structural equation modeling: Issues and techniques* (pp. 195–226). Mahwah, NJ: Lawrence Erlbaum Associates.

Zhu, W. (1997). Making bootstrap statistical inferences: A tutorial. *Research Quarterly for Exercise and Sport, 68*, 44–55.

Sample Covariance Data for Chapter 3: Application 1

	SDQ2N07	SDQ2N19	SDQ2N31	SDQ2N43	SDQ2N10	SDQ2N22	SDQ2N34
SDQ2N07	3.161						
SDQ2N19	1.996	2.859					
SDQ2N31	2.238	1.757	2.457				
SDQ2N43	1.430	1.439	1.428	1.954			
SDQ2N10	0.246	0.348	0.339	0.225	1.322		
SDQ2N22	0.245	0.365	0.370	0.186	0.584	1.186	
SDQ2N34	-0.327	-0.080	-0.123	-0.067	0.510	0.347	2.890
SDQ2N46	0.212	0.160	0.330	0.346	0.543	0.525	0.452
SDQ2N04	0.882	0.725	0.879	0.491	0.593	0.370	0.231
SDQ2N16	1.018	0.998	1.071	0.743	0.581	0.578	0.188
SDQ2N28	0.975	1.059	1.119	0.744	0.517	0.505	0.079
SDQ2N40	0.887	1.035	1.013	0.833	0.637	0.575	0.326
SDQ2N01	0.560	0.496	0.574	0.273	0.350	0.265	0.362
SDQ2N13	0.512	0.564	0.650	0.472	0.409	0.342	0.461
SDQ2N25	0.542	0.347	0.576	0.331	0.252	0.257	0.282
SDQ2N37	0.580	0.475	0.713	0.343	0.323	0.299	0.313

	SDQ2N46	SDQ2N04	SDQ2N16	SDQ2N28	SDQ2N40	SDQ2N01	SDQ2N13
SDQ2N46	1.675						
SDQ2N04	0.347	1.955					
SDQ2N16	0.471	0.749	1.533				
SDQ2N28	0.449	0.689	0.944	1.768			
SDQ2N40	0.602	0.514	0.875	0.925	1.841		
SDQ2N01	0.378	0.418	0.464	0.375	0.451	1.811	
SDQ2N13	0.373	0.662	0.552	0.477	0.540	0.681	1.838
SDQ2N25	0.174	0.300	0.393	0.347	0.432	0.749	0.502
SDQ2N37	0.224	0.468	0.577	0.539	0.660	0.475	0.653

	SDQ2N25	SDQ2N37
SDQ2N25	1.500	
SDQ2N37	0.428	1.306

Sample Covariance Data for Chapter 4: Application 2

	Item4	Item7	Item9	Item17	Item18	Item19	Item21
Item4	0.870						
Item7	0.345	0.765					
Item9	0.270	0.333	1.775				
Item17	0.312	0.279	0.446	0.781			
Item18	0.269	0.288	0.521	0.480	1.476		
Item19	0.240	0.310	0.657	0.404	0.737	1.283	
Item21	0.310	0.352	0.520	0.287	0.328	0.329	1.661
Item5	-0.210	-0.301	-0.386	-0.364	-0.342	-0.380	-0.348
Item10	-0.223	-0.200	-0.371	-0.451	-0.469	-0.380	-0.324
Item11	-0.235	-0.234	-0.369	-0.347	-0.348	-0.313	-0.344
Item15	-0.207	-0.236	-0.220	-0.240	-0.250	-0.223	-0.215
Item22	-0.106	-0.199	-0.126	-0.288	-0.139	-0.259	-0.045
Item1	-0.065	-0.095	-0.325	-0.309	-0.247	-0.198	-0.211
Item2	-0.078	-0.085	-0.253	-0.318	-0.175	-0.212	-0.231
Item3	-0.136	-0.226	-0.518	-0.376	-0.443	-0.400	-0.354
Item6	-0.106	-0.253	-0.295	-0.415	-0.388	-0.427	-0.410
Item8	-0.195	-0.280	-0.592	-0.534	-0.503	-0.331	-0.431
Item13	-0.212	-0.270	-0.646	-0.421	-0.505	-0.421	-0.361
Item14	-0.042	-0.128	-0.188	-0.228	-0.110	-0.068	-0.172
Item20	-0.171	-0.198	-0.455	-0.393	-0.360	-0.288	-0.283

	Item5	Item10	Item11	Item15	Item22	Item1	Item2
Item5	2.182						
Item10	0.936	2.178					
Item11	0.876	1.520	2.283				
Item15	0.704	0.595	0.601	1.255			
Item22	0.682	0.536	0.581	0.339	2.379		
Item1	0.625	0.749	0.850	0.462	0.606	2.752	
Item2	0.512	0.640	0.741	0.379	0.506	1.915	2.472
Item3	0.854	0.746	0.930	0.512	0.542	1.709	1.545
Item6	1.016	0.869	0.867	0.589	0.553	1.198	1.097
Item8	0.802	0.972	1.202	0.620	0.531	2.004	1.851
Item13	0.855	1.027	1.142	0.529	0.662	1.614	1.429
Item14	0.564	0.627	0.838	0.363	0.444	1.593	1.613
Item20	0.654	0.816	0.872	0.456	0.487	1.216	1.096

	Item3	Item6	Item8	Item13	Item14	Item20
Item3	2.924					
Item6	1.349	2.747				
Item8	2.003	1.529	3.288			
Item13	1.553	1.305	1.964	2.968		
Item14	1.523	1.064	1.758	1.766	3.321	
Item20	1.281	1.036	1.750	1.532	1.236	2.068

	BDI16	BDI18	BDI19	BDI21	BDI4	BDI11	BDI12
BDI16	0.687						
BDI18	0.230	0.816					
BDI19	0.034	0.018	0.362				
BDI21	0.039	0.070	0.019	0.342			
BDI4	0.197	0.125	-0.027	0.054	0.791		
BDI11	0.087	0.152	-0.044	0.052	0.146	0.875	
BDI12	0.094	0.104	-0.018	0.032	0.127	0.011	0.266
BDI13	0.210	0.166	-0.037	0.080	0.336	0.166	0.098
BDI15	0.103	0.114	-0.016	0.042	0.214	0.141	0.067
BDI17	0.144	0.128	-0.022	0.084	0.236	0.084	0.117
BDI20	0.087	0.131	-0.032	0.145	0.082	0.066	0.063
BDI1	0.118	0.151	-0.020	0.052	0.204	0.149	0.106
BDI2	0.126	0.140	-0.051	0.021	0.158	-0.002	0.093
BDI3	0.160	0.185	-0.044	0.073	0.155	0.136	0.111
BDI5	0.095	0.138	-0.016	0.054	0.116	0.119	0.060
BDI6	0.123	0.170	-0.019	0.054	0.235	0.112	0.099
BDI7	0.136	0.189	-0.040	0.051	0.213	0.060	0.089
BDI8	0.150	0.184	0.036	0.033	0.200	0.109	0.055
BDI9	0.079	0.199	-0.018	0.016	0.162	0.064	0.082
BDI10	0.142	0.286	-0.023	0.106	0.185	0.291	0.137
BDI14	0.201	0.208	-0.075	0.073	0.200	0.188	0.063

	BDI13	BDI15	BDI17	BDI20	BDI1	BDI2	BDI3
BDI13	0.850						
BDI15	0.240	0.552					
BDI17	0.183	0.178	0.524				
BDI20	0.164	0.082	0.125	0.542			
BDI1	0.194	0.160	0.210	0.136	0.579		
BDI2	0.213	0.083	0.082	0.142	0.168	0.580	
BDI3	0.222	0.097	0.125	0.174	0.211	0.202	0.528
BDI5	0.155	0.093	0.060	0.104	0.112	0.126	0.150
BDI6	0.253	0.092	0.144	0.260	0.265	0.247	0.238
BDI7	0.230	0.130	0.155	0.181	0.216	0.231	0.263
BDI8	0.303	0.179	0.139	0.111	0.172	0.155	0.166
BDI9	0.159	0.117	0.105	0.074	0.183	0.141	0.121
BDI10	0.279	0.195	0.210	0.226	0.309	0.145	0.281
BDI14	0.274	0.085	0.100	0.178	0.180	0.274	0.196

	BDI5	BDI6	BDI7	BDI8	BDI9	BDI10	BDI14
BDI5	0.381						
BDI6	0.204	1.044					
BDI7	0.146	0.292	0.553				
BDI8	0.132	0.147	0.198	0.666			
BDI9	0.068	0.214	0.206	0.141	0.381		
BDI10	0.148	0.357	0.224	0.139	0.177	1.178	
BDI14	0.107	0.192	0.290	0.195	0.182	0.192	1.153

	PA1	EE3	ELC5	ELC4	ELC3	CC1	CC2
PA1	0.653						
EE3	-0.489	1.845					
ELC5	-0.095	0.289	0.466				
ELC4	-0.105	0.190	0.237	0.427			
ELC3	-0.081	0.205	0.243	0.190	0.348		
CC1	0.107	-0.256	-0.036	-0.056	-0.033	0.308	
CC2	0.106	-0.256	-0.019	-0.057	-0.039	0.156	0.360
CC3	0.102	-0.139	-0.042	-0.073	-0.054	0.105	0.169
CC4	0.116	-0.281	-0.041	-0.082	-0.031	0.171	0.223
SE3	0.152	-0.306	-0.120	-0.090	-0.070	0.043	0.048
SE1	0.121	-0.225	-0.079	-0.068	-0.044	0.041	0.041
SE2	0.103	-0.234	-0.119	-0.094	-0.072	0.031	0.041
PA3	0.423	-0.424	-0.125	-0.139	-0.120	0.082	0.087
PA2	0.425	-0.336	-0.074	-0.069	-0.054	0.056	0.107
EE2	-0.422	1.447	0.278	0.176	0.181	-0.209	-0.204
EE1	-0.355	1.406	0.203	0.128	0.132	-0.224	-0.183
ELC2	-0.040	0.169	0.181	0.142	0.152	-0.027	-0.030
ELC1	-0.087	0.222	0.216	0.182	0.173	-0.032	-0.035
PS1	0.188	-0.419	-0.137	-0.157	-0.105	0.083	0.064
PS2	0.203	-0.353	-0.149	-0.152	-0.116	0.091	0.061
SS1	0.200	-0.614	-0.193	-0.192	-0.156	0.153	0.116
SS2	0.255	-0.549	-0.212	-0.201	-0.196	0.125	0.109
DM1	0.231	-0.579	-0.214	-0.184	-0.169	0.170	0.136
DM2	0.256	-0.598	-0.198	-0.168	-0.172	0.155	0.133
WO1	-0.213	0.829	0.238	0.156	0.174	-0.202	-0.178
WO2	-0.224	0.610	0.245	0.222	0.156	-0.128	-0.117
RC1	-0.191	0.494	0.242	0.215	0.223	-0.110	-0.111
RC2	-0.294	0.772	0.313	0.222	0.236	-0.187	-0.176
RA1	-0.214	0.450	0.199	0.178	0.144	-0.102	-0.113
RA2	-0.235	0.585	0.214	0.187	0.165	-0.141	-0.123
DP1	-0.301	0.764	0.138	0.157	0.138	-0.202	-0.227
DP2	-0.302	0.666	0.112	0.136	0.094	-0.138	-0.136

	CC3	CC4	SE3	SE1	SE2	PA3	PA2
CC3	0.277						
CC4	0.173	0.495					
SE3	0.040	0.042	0.315				
SE1	0.026	0.042	0.180	0.219			
SE2	0.029	0.040	0.223	0.162	0.292		
PA3	0.064	0.102	0.145	0.107	0.106	0.752	
PA2	0.085	0.086	0.103	0.078	0.060	0.393	0.735
EE2	-0.127	-0.214	-0.277	-0.201	-0.211	-0.365	-0.257
EE1	-0.108	-0.199	-0.230	-0.154	-0.177	-0.294	-0.212
ELC2	-0.046	-0.029	-0.053	-0.011	-0.038	-0.066	-0.050
ELC1	-0.033	-0.031	-0.085	-0.040	-0.072	-0.112	-0.088
PS1	0.065	0.099	0.154	0.131	0.143	0.179	0.121
PS2	0.087	0.119	0.146	0.129	0.119	0.203	0.161
SS1	0.101	0.183	0.162	0.106	0.138	0.175	0.132
SS2	0.121	0.194	0.188	0.127	0.148	0.256	0.168
DM1	0.120	0.176	0.149	0.121	0.128	0.215	0.152
DM2	0.126	0.203	0.171	0.137	0.152	0.271	0.161
WO1	-0.116	-0.218	-0.183	-0.118	-0.154	-0.149	-0.086
WO2	-0.115	-0.123	-0.156	-0.122	-0.175	-0.137	-0.191
RC1	-0.103	-0.158	-0.158	-0.105	-0.146	-0.136	-0.083
RC2	-0.121	-0.175	-0.217	-0.150	-0.189	-0.253	-0.211
RA1	-0.105	-0.112	-0.141	-0.126	-0.124	-0.163	-0.149
RA2	-0.104	-0.135	-0.155	-0.123	-0.136	-0.191	-0.159
DP1	-0.161	-0.232	-0.209	-0.143	-0.141	-0.272	-0.265
DP2	-0.122	-0.154	-0.187	-0.130	-0.142	-0.295	-0.295

(Continued)

	EE2	EE1	ELC2	ELC1	PS1	PS2	SS1
EE2	1.833						
EE1	1.524	1.841					
ELC2	0.121	0.101	0.369				
ELC1	0.212	0.181	0.179	0.358			
PS1	-0.405	-0.391	-0.067	-0.104	0.937		
PS2	-0.338	-0.303	-0.080	-0.115	0.649	0.841	
SS1	-0.542	-0.527	-0.105	-0.163	0.443	0.415	1.518
SS2	-0.524	-0.469	-0.104	-0.194	0.447	0.504	1.282
DM1	-0.564	-0.509	-0.120	-0.161	0.442	0.443	0.798
DM2	-0.604	-0.528	-0.112	-0.175	0.457	0.526	1.032
WO1	0.765	0.846	0.136	0.184	-0.297	-0.268	-0.607
WO2	0.532	0.649	0.127	0.165	-0.321	-0.254	-0.469
RC1	0.402	0.434	0.171	0.184	-0.345	-0.253	-0.639
RC2	0.764	0.735	0.180	0.253	-0.345	-0.306	-0.604
RA1	0.408	0.392	0.094	0.118	-0.276	-0.301	-0.517
RA2	0.514	0.456	0.097	0.127	-0.375	-0.318	-0.633
DP1	0.734	0.704	0.083	0.101	-0.273	-0.247	-0.346
DP2	0.646	0.578	0.076	0.104	-0.257	-0.210	-0.236

	SS2	DM1	DM2	WO1	WO2	RC1	RC2
SS2	1.509						
DM1	0.803	1.160					
DM2	1.160	0.818	1.544				
WO1	-0.567	-0.497	-0.507	1.305			
WO2	-0.435	-0.412	-0.410	0.649	1.470		
RC1	-0.620	-0.494	-0.508	0.677	0.531	1.243	
RC2	-0.590	-0.526	-0.548	0.881	0.855	0.767	1.672
RA1	-0.525	-0.442	-0.521	0.408	0.482	0.444	0.561
RA2	-0.614	-0.534	-0.589	0.509	0.504	0.559	0.663
DP1	-0.330	-0.284	-0.284	0.403	0.341	0.323	0.466
DP2	-0.273	-0.233	-0.226	0.266	0.280	0.215	0.315

	RA1	RA2	DP1	DP2
RA1	0.913			
RA2	0.557	0.971		
DP1	0.283	0.328	1.235	
DP2	0.258	0.242	0.752	1.148

Group 1: Elementary Teachers

	ITEM4	ITEM7	ITEM9	ITEM17	ITEM18	ITEM19	ITEM21
ITEM4	0.855						
ITEM7	0.302	0.748					
ITEM9	0.302	0.405	1.709				
ITEM17	0.271	0.278	0.437	0.786			
ITEM18	0.280	0.341	0.539	0.478	1.416		
ITEM19	0.235	0.353	0.696	0.384	0.715	1.254	
ITEM21	0.222	0.342	0.504	0.291	0.328	0.321	1.596
ITEM5	-0.297	-0.361	-0.386	-0.332	-0.418	-0.390	-0.236
ITEM10	-0.229	-0.245	-0.360	-0.361	-0.506	-0.408	-0.283
ITEM11	-0.250	-0.273	-0.393	-0.330	-0.427	-0.400	-0.286
ITEM15	-0.249	-0.254	-0.288	-0.230	-0.377	-0.289	-0.152
ITEM22	-0.146	-0.241	-0.150	-0.310	-0.251	-0.315	-0.071
ITEM1	-0.064	-0.143	-0.259	-0.315	-0.286	-0.235	-0.184
ITEM2	-0.081	-0.117	-0.232	-0.287	-0.256	-0.215	-0.239
ITEM3	-0.201	-0.272	-0.489	-0.360	-0.547	-0.435	-0.357
ITEM6	-0.120	-0.282	-0.251	-0.347	-0.435	-0.357	-0.315
ITEM8	-0.226	-0.316	-0.514	-0.493	-0.623	-0.430	-0.408
ITEM13	-0.211	-0.309	-0.553	-0.387	-0.540	-0.461	-0.313
ITEM14	-0.041	-0.114	-0.091	-0.219	-0.175	-0.097	-0.197
ITEM20	-0.179	-0.234	-0.417	-0.381	-0.434	-0.328	-0.349

	ITEM5	ITEM10	ITEM11	ITEM15	ITEM22	ITEM1	ITEM2
ITEM5	2.243						
ITEM10	0.852	2.210					
ITEM11	0.797	1.582	2.373				
ITEM15	0.704	0.610	0.624	1.235			
ITEM22	0.709	0.627	0.720	0.473	2.491		
ITEM1	0.566	0.722	0.851	0.361	0.627	2.659	
ITEM2	0.505	0.634	0.712	0.293	0.497	1.899	2.456
ITEM3	0.753	0.836	0.983	0.479	0.587	1.645	1.590
ITEM6	0.962	0.832	0.847	0.522	0.642	1.153	1.082
ITEM8	0.813	0.997	1.150	0.575	0.679	1.852	1.720
ITEM13	0.773	1.055	1.159	0.518	0.860	1.567	1.359
ITEM14	0.474	0.672	0.858	0.295	0.577	1.594	1.529
ITEM20	0.628	0.819	0.903	0.489	0.695	1.247	1.120

	ITEM3	ITEM6	ITEM8	ITEM13	ITEM14	ITEM20
ITEM3	2.874					
ITEM6	1.286	2.690				
ITEM8	1.965	1.534	3.163			
ITEM13	1.520	1.304	1.804	2.924		
ITEM14	1.472	1.081	1.626	1.714	3.255	
ITEM20	1.327	1.089	1.751	1.494	1.194	2.163

(Continued)

Group 2: Intermediate Teachers

	ITEM4	ITEM7	ITEM9	ITEM17	ITEM18	ITEM19	ITEM21
ITEM4	1.102						
ITEM7	0.311	1.038					
ITEM9	0.251	0.542	2.111				
ITEM17	0.325	0.450	0.455	1.084			
ITEM18	0.270	0.417	0.894	0.640	1.627		
ITEM19	0.169	0.500	1.071	0.462	0.859	1.743	
ITEM21	0.431	0.693	0.533	0.517	0.480	0.401	1.776
ITEM5	-0.250	-0.393	-0.452	-0.304	-0.293	-0.359	-0.357
ITEM10	-0.127	-0.309	-0.493	-0.341	-0.486	-0.364	-0.500
ITEM11	-0.195	-0.418	-0.648	-0.547	-0.498	-0.535	-0.543
ITEM15	-0.193	-0.431	-0.582	-0.355	-0.423	-0.536	-0.307
ITEM22	-0.022	-0.121	-0.284	-0.237	-0.355	-0.279	-0.164
ITEM1	-0.021	-0.228	-0.192	-0.280	-0.190	-0.210	-0.119
ITEM2	0.094	-0.238	-0.164	-0.227	-0.182	-0.209	-0.225
ITEM3	-0.092	-0.236	-0.377	-0.289	-0.381	-0.527	-0.199
ITEM6	-0.103	-0.306	-0.402	-0.321	-0.389	-0.391	-0.160
ITEM8	0.008	-0.346	-0.637	-0.311	-0.529	-0.565	-0.328
ITEM13	-0.063	-0.381	-0.740	-0.512	-0.690	-0.809	-0.348
ITEM14	0.114	-0.173	-0.330	-0.189	-0.317	-0.292	-0.222
ITEM20	-0.001	-0.261	-0.392	-0.348	-0.433	-0.565	-0.176

	ITEM5	ITEM10	ITEM11	ITEM15	ITEM22	ITEM1	ITEM2
ITEM5	2.175						
ITEM10	0.653	2.615					
ITEM11	0.835	1.742	2.936				
ITEM15	1.069	0.634	0.817	1.881			
ITEM22	0.653	0.570	0.900	0.654	2.960		
ITEM1	0.516	0.694	1.067	0.344	0.580	2.650	
ITEM2	0.440	0.664	0.852	0.255	0.563	1.966	2.389
ITEM3	0.557	0.937	1.203	0.500	0.699	1.756	1.564
ITEM6	0.547	0.710	0.902	0.568	0.697	1.115	1.066
ITEM8	0.711	1.201	1.402	0.741	0.763	1.800	1.659
ITEM13	0.638	0.994	1.390	0.808	0.974	1.571	1.312
ITEM14	0.384	0.574	0.972	0.457	0.593	1.581	1.525
ITEM20	0.423	0.906	1.139	0.659	0.665	1.238	1.123

	ITEM3	ITEM6	ITEM8	ITEM13	ITEM14	ITEM20
ITEM3	2.953					
ITEM6	1.181	2.761				
ITEM8	2.066	1.521	3.110			
ITEM13	1.759	1.353	1.988	3.151		
ITEM14	1.432	0.792	1.685	1.586	2.920	
ITEM20	1.419	0.980	1.730	1.629	1.132	2.171

(Continued)

Group 3: Secondary Teachers

	ITEM4	ITEM7	ITEM9	ITEM17	ITEM18	ITEM19	ITEM21
ITEM4	1.297						
ITEM7	0.441	1.310					
ITEM9	0.389	0.717	2.075				
ITEM17	0.330	0.443	0.500	0.934			
ITEM18	0.381	0.441	0.817	0.551	1.480		
ITEM19	0.337	0.587	1.115	0.442	0.875	1.765	
ITEM21	0.412	0.640	0.646	0.402	0.386	0.514	2.350
ITEM5	-0.260	-0.373	-0.427	-0.319	-0.410	-0.452	-0.223
ITEM10	-0.216	-0.245	-0.395	-0.311	-0.378	-0.331	-0.198
ITEM11	-0.214	-0.292	-0.425	-0.329	-0.460	-0.385	-0.255
ITEM15	-0.255	-0.364	-0.393	-0.256	-0.436	-0.414	-0.232
ITEM22	-0.156	-0.244	-0.277	-0.290	-0.342	-0.362	-0.080
ITEM1	0.025	-0.120	-0.286	-0.206	-0.217	-0.234	-0.053
ITEM2	0.014	-0.134	-0.280	-0.208	-0.243	-0.260	-0.091
ITEM3	-0.103	-0.250	-0.489	-0.271	-0.466	-0.468	-0.191
ITEM6	-0.173	-0.338	-0.556	-0.393	-0.500	-0.522	-0.111
ITEM8	-0.187	-0.283	-0.515	-0.315	-0.546	-0.480	-0.251
ITEM13	-0.165	-0.251	-0.529	-0.315	-0.442	-0.501	-0.129
ITEM14	0.031	-0.070	-0.161	-0.169	-0.198	-0.149	-0.142
ITEM20	-0.138	-0.235	-0.440	-0.314	-0.428	-0.376	-0.189

	ITEM5	ITEM10	ITEM11	ITEM15	ITEM22	ITEM1	ITEM2
ITEM5	2.044						
ITEM10	0.784	2.271					
ITEM11	0.638	1.564	2.230				
ITEM15	0.815	0.771	0.603	1.782			
ITEM22	0.722	0.723	0.707	0.573	2.426		
ITEM1	0.316	0.574	0.686	0.225	0.571	2.532	
ITEM2	0.307	0.491	0.586	0.259	0.504	1.825	2.371
ITEM3	0.455	0.625	0.848	0.395	0.571	1.555	1.499
ITEM6	0.684	0.722	0.831	0.539	0.632	1.175	1.069
ITEM8	0.500	0.835	1.022	0.531	0.700	1.645	1.544
ITEM13	0.638	0.878	0.931	0.583	0.933	1.397	1.262
ITEM14	0.236	0.535	0.637	0.288	0.565	1.479	1.462
ITEM20	0.404	0.718	0.847	0.497	0.625	1.053	0.930

	ITEM3	ITEM6	ITEM8	ITEM13	ITEM14	ITEM20
ITEM3	2.778					
ITEM6	1.175	2.699				
ITEM8	1.007	1.432	2.833			
ITEM13	1.379	1.178	1.701	2.730		
ITEM14	1.334	0.992	1.578	1.541	3.173	
ITEM20	1.241	0.929	1.589	1.271	1.099	1.950

Group 1: Adolescent Males

	SDQMSC	APIMSC	SCAMSC	SDQESC	APIESC	SCAESC	SDQASC
SDQMSC	254.645						
APIMSC	164.970	138.009					
SCAMSC	103.773	74.641	61.834				
SDQESC	18.200	23.742	9.991	100.097			
APIESC	25.296	37.767	13.511	80.298	122.889		
SCAESC	13.419	13.844	10.896	29.979	41.357	35.068	
SDQASC	123.501	94.374	55.287	50.417	63.568	32.533	178.670
SCAASC	55.980	43.304	31.553	20.013	23.952	19.368	55.778
SDQGSC	55.652	40.157	22.635	39.738	25.467	8.523	63.820
APIGSC	38.375	31.907	18.762	23.871	27.599	11.113	42.229
SESGSC	21.662	17.726	8.870	14.754	11.692	4.713	22.127

	SCAASC	SDQGSC	APIGSC	SESGSC
SCAASC	35.234			
SDQGSC	20.865	191.523		
APIGSC	17.465	83.135	88.935	
SESGSC	9.072	51.900	27.630	23.844

Group 2: Adolescent Females

	SDQMSC	APIMSC	SCAMSC	SDQESC	APIESC	SCAESC	SDQASC
SDQMSC	266.588						
APIMSC	154.757	122.319					
SCAMSC	95.003	63.100	50.106				
SDQESC	-10.512	-2.722	-2.614	89.638			
APIESC	-7.330	8.393	-1.967	68.508	114.239		
SCAESC	2.255	2.879	3.008	27.866	37.306	28.224	
SDQASC	68.075	49.397	28.189	39.266	47.032	27.702	121.019
SCAASC	30.039	21.963	17.536	15.483	21.277	16.187	35.285
SDQGSC	25.818	19.734	8.112	38.182	22.637	12.948	46.759
APIGSC	18.624	18.190	5.133	17.664	17.484	6.577	29.182
SESGSC	13.096	10.257	4.400	14.761	11.305	6.205	18.254

	SCAASC	SDQGSC	APIGSC	SESGSC
SCAASC	23.690			
SDQGSC	13.486	210.444		
APIGSC	5.896	84.148	78.189	
SESGSC	6.417	59.996	30.010	25.130

APPENDIX G
Sample Covariance Data for Chapter 9: Application 7

Group 1: High Track Students

	SCAMSC	SDQMSC	APIMSC	SCAESC	SDQESC	APIESC	SCAASC
SCAMSC	63.667						
SDQMSC	113.921	286.843					
APIMSC	76.242	175.185	134.468				
SCAESC	3.927	-0.678	2.720	32.742			
SDQESC	1.180	-1.837	4.687	31.534	97.190		
APIESC	-1.427	-7.575	8.558	44.403	79.698	125.023	
SCAASC	24.000	41.619	29.408	15.074	16.571	18.739	24.155
SDQASC	37.477	84.706	61.800	27.814	45.842	53.958	37.994
SESGSC	7.629	19.363	16.132	4.052	14.463	11.369	7.757
SDQGSC	15.441	42.633	30.371	8.326	38.300	24.567	17.878
APIGSC	14.454	31.793	29.604	5.747	19.617	19.730	12.270

	SDQASC	SESGSC	SDQGSC	APIGSC
SDQASC	137.193			
SESGSC	19.257	25.590		
SDQGSC	56.241	59.768	211.717	
APIGSC	35.510	31.717	89.863	88.096

Group 2: Low Track Students

	SCAMSC	SDQMSC	APIMSC	SCAESC	SDQESC	APIESC	SCAASC
SCAMSC	33.782						
SDQMSC	55.952	179.263					
APIMSC	45.476	109.981	111.190				
SCAESC	2.170	0.260	1.380	23.505			
SDQESC	-0.659	-6.958	6.277	19.836	89.282		
APIESC	4.655	4.290	26.126	25.784	62.866	114.050	
SCAASC	11.486	13.529	16.265	11.033	11.195	17.810	19.989
SDQASC	25.012	58.776	50.593	22.602	34.820	56.786	32.067
SESGSC	6.051	16.611	12.005	5.779	12.688	5.611	5.873
SDQGSC	18.245	43.825	35.364	15.024	38.914	20.487	16.194
APIGSC	10.421	32.209	23.276	11.576	18.218	17.416	8.822

	SDQASC	SESGSC	SDQGSC	APIGSC
SDQASC	152.918			
SESGSC	15.702	23.670		
SDQGSC	53.084	49.275	179.959	
APIGSC	26.405	25.774	74.211	81.176

Group 1: Calibration Sample

	WO1	WO2	PA1	EE3	ELC5	ELC4	ELC3
WO1	1.472						
WO2	0.679	1.176					
PA1	-0.229	-0.211	0.787				
EE3	0.783	0.529	-0.499	1.741			
ELC5	0.211	0.208	-0.153	0.234	0.427		
ELC4	0.143	0.181	-0.088	0.128	0.209	0.388	
ELC3	0.146	0.145	-0.096	0.153	0.223	0.166	0.313
CC1	-0.192	-0.119	0.111	-0.232	-0.022	-0.034	-0.019
CC2	-0.073	-0.076	0.124	-0.236	-0.037	-0.033	-0.042
CC3	-0.022	-0.041	0.079	-0.125	-0.022	-0.024	-0.030
CC4	-0.055	-0.087	0.105	-0.185	-0.067	-0.052	-0.053
SE3	-0.177	-0.160	0.200	-0.322	-0.104	-0.071	-0.074
SE1	-0.118	-0.129	0.153	-0.215	-0.071	-0.053	-0.045
SE2	-0.154	-0.137	0.161	-0.271	-0.103	-0.064	-0.072
PA3	-0.180	-0.142	0.487	-0.301	-0.133	-0.091	-0.085
PA2	-0.134	-0.155	0.512	-0.313	-0.124	-0.087	-0.079
EE2	0.727	0.449	-0.431	1.324	0.201	0.105	0.125
EE1	0.878	0.541	-0.342	1.247	0.166	0.092	0.107
ELC2	0.043	0.081	-0.097	0.115	0.172	0.153	0.158
ELC1	0.133	0.074	-0.116	0.173	0.198	0.144	0.178
PS1	-0.324	-0.200	0.230	-0.370	-0.111	-0.085	-0.104
PS2	-0.306	-0.219	0.237	-0.355	-0.150	-0.112	-0.128
DM1	-0.563	-0.310	0.281	-0.521	-0.174	-0.109	-0.120
DM2	-0.531	-0.374	0.379	-0.648	-0.207	-0.118	-0.166
RC1	0.719	0.483	-0.208	0.632	0.259	0.195	0.201
RC2	0.923	0.731	-0.315	0.793	0.251	0.214	0.199
DP1	0.368	0.301	-0.363	0.784	0.146	0.133	0.133
DP2	0.336	0.167	-0.346	0.678	0.127	0.056	0.107

	CC1	CC2	CC3	CC4	SE3	SE1	SE2
CC1	0.281						
CC2	0.156	0.404					
CC3	0.094	0.165	0.242				
CC4	0.134	0.228	0.131	0.507			
SE3	0.047	0.040	0.032	0.035	0.305		
SE1	0.034	0.046	0.025	0.035	0.167	0.197	
SE2	0.046	0.048	0.034	0.031	0.209	0.153	0.257
PA3	0.082	0.085	0.049	0.095	0.158	0.125	0.132
PA2	0.093	0.134	0.075	0.146	0.127	0.113	0.089
EE2	-0.203	-0.145	-0.085	-0.141	-0.273	-0.200	-0.241
EE1	-0.243	-0.138	-0.084	-0.108	-0.236	-0.162	-0.208
ELC2	-0.020	-0.069	-0.061	-0.066	-0.054	-0.034	-0.054
ELC1	-0.024	-0.036	-0.034	-0.046	-0.076	-0.049	-0.068
PS1	0.101	0.085	0.035	0.069	0.120	0.102	0.108
PS2	0.101	0.075	0.053	0.050	0.145	0.122	0.126
DM1	0.151	0.125	0.042	0.086	0.136	0.115	0.139
DM2	0.197	0.201	0.093	0.153	0.183	0.140	0.146
RC1	-0.143	-0.097	-0.041	-0.041	-0.180	-0.111	-0.171
RC2	-0.193	-0.159	-0.045	-0.103	-0.197	-0.122	-0.178
DP1	-0.208	-0.268	-0.147	-0.211	-0.220	-0.145	-0.182
DP2	-0.168	-0.207	-0.133	-0.182	-0.180	-0.102	-0.156

(Continued)

	PA3	PA2	EE2	EE1	ELC2	ELC1	PS1
PA3	0.914						
PA2	0.560	0.893					
EE2	-0.292	-0.290	1.563				
EE1	-0.237	-0.201	1.336	1.705			
ELC2	-0.077	-0.088	0.093	0.053	0.412		
ELC1	-0.099	-0.093	0.139	0.106	0.183	0.375	
PS1	0.183	0.191	-0.354	-0.351	-0.065	-0.080	0.976
PS2	0.194	0.202	-0.306	-0.288	-0.086	-0.130	0.686
DM1	0.193	0.185	-0.456	-0.465	-0.074	-0.145	0.453
DM2	0.290	0.288	-0.562	-0.461	-0.135	-0.200	0.439
RC1	-0.111	-0.094	0.502	0.475	0.129	0.191	-0.302
RC2	-0.223	-0.217	0.671	0.684	0.150	0.163	-0.335
DP1	-0.313	-0.349	0.679	0.593	0.102	0.118	-0.256
DP2	-0.317	-0.387	0.598	0.474	0.115	0.129	-0.220

	PS2	DM1	DM2	RC1	RC2	DP1	DP2
PS2	0.882						
DM1	0.447	1.064					
DM2	0.510	0.777	1.776				
RC1	-0.319	-0.542	-0.575	1.298			
RC2	-0.318	-0.562	-0.694	0.851	1.610		
DP1	-0.238	-0.285	-0.448	0.438	0.495	1.267	
DP2	-0.196	-0.323	-0.406	0.351	0.379	0.927	1.529

Group 2: Validation Sample

	WO1	WO2	PA1	EE3	ELC5	ELC4	ELC3
WO1	1.413						
WO2	0.643	1.198					
PA1	-0.223	-0.259	0.859				
EE3	0.757	0.542	-0.511	1.622			
ELC5	0.201	0.209	-0.142	0.211	0.403		
ELC4	0.125	0.146	-0.102	0.111	0.188	0.344	
ELC3	0.170	0.115	-0.094	0.158	0.176	0.150	0.286
CC1	-0.185	-0.132	0.133	-0.219	-0.064	-0.044	-0.053
CC2	-0.154	-0.115	0.154	-0.243	-0.060	-0.061	-0.059
CC3	-0.100	-0.081	0.109	-0.136	-0.043	-0.037	-0.045
CC4	-0.174	-0.160	0.172	-0.289	-0.058	-0.065	-0.049
SE3	-0.137	-0.122	0.161	-0.261	-0.097	-0.067	-0.069
SE1	-0.083	-0.100	0.135	-0.191	-0.065	-0.053	-0.035
SE2	-0.132	-0.118	0.144	-0.228	-0.080	-0.065	-0.035
PA3	-0.159	-0.210	0.563	-0.364	-0.109	0.101	-0.077
PA2	-0.150	-0.218	0.647	-0.399	-0.103	-0.078	-0.050
EE2	0.728	0.487	-0.466	1.249	0.233	0.131	0.166
EE1	0.857	0.514	-0.348	1.203	0.215	0.106	0.157
ELC2	0.168	0.100	-0.107	0.136	0.138	0.131	0.134
ELC1	0.213	0.122	-0.150	0.200	0.194	0.162	0.168
PS1	-0.264	-0.171	0.162	-0.273	-0.086	-0.095	-0.060
PS2	-0.217	-0.210	0.210	-0.254	-0.101	-0.112	-0.068
DM1	-0.449	-0.263	0.296	-0.473	-0.125	-0.100	-0.116
DM2	-0.381	-0.319	0.466	-0.478	-0.148	-0.123	-0.119
RC1	0.607	0.422	-0.152	0.470	0.156	0.145	0.135
RC2	0.803	0.649	-0.263	0.673	0.220	0.146	0.170
DP1	0.368	0.383	-0.308	0.579	0.109	0.085	0.090
DP2	0.323	0.298	-0.332	0.551	0.112	0.055	0.061

(Continued)

	CC1	CC2	CC3	CC4	SE3	SE1	SE2
CC1	0.303						
CC2	0.160	0.385					
CC3	0.116	0.165	0.240				
CC4	0.155	0.220	0.145	0.563			
SE3	0.032	0.056	0.030	0.055	0.288		
SE1	0.033	0.038	0.028	0.041	0.143	0.197	
SE2	0.035	0.043	0.026	0.048	0.194	0.143	0.250
PA3	0.108	0.117	0.077	0.138	0.121	0.106	0.137
PA2	0.121	0.144	0.107	0.176	0.138	0.110	0.112
EE2	-0.196	-0.189	-0.108	-0.262	-0.254	-0.193	-0.217
EE1	-0.184	-0.156	-0.097	-0.240	-0.232	-0.169	-0.203
ELC2	-0.064	-0.055	-0.046	-0.084	-0.042	-0.024	-0.051
ELC1	-0.073	-0.059	-0.057	-0.091	-0.069	-0.043	-0.071
PS1	0.075	0.068	0.048	0.049	0.094	0.075	0.100
PS2	0.081	0.077	0.046	0.087	0.090	0.083	0.091
DM1	0.125	0.107	0.073	0.125	0.093	0.069	0.105
DM2	0.181	0.157	0.103	0.222	0.140	0.076	0.144
RC1	-0.111	-0.095	-0.040	-0.146	-0.112	-0.073	-0.112
RC2	-0.174	-0.138	-0.076	-0.172	-0.184	-0.104	-0.149
DP1	-0.182	-0.209	-0.130	-0.188	-0.174	-0.125	-0.149
DP2	-0.138	-0.151	-0.116	-0.159	-0.143	-0.100	-0.137

	PA3	PA2	EE2	EE1	ELC2	ELC1	PS1
PA3	0.945						
PA2	0.623	0.962					
EE2	-0.303	-0.380	1.591				
EE1	-0.234	-0.279	1.361	1.712			
ELC2	-0.108	-0.071	0.118	0.118	0.373		
ELC1	-0.124	-0.109	0.228	0.220	0.195	0.401	
PS1	0.159	0.113	-0.182	-0.246	-0.073	-0.100	0.886
PS2	0.211	0.174	-0.182	-0.205	-0.104	-0.107	0.599
DM1	0.239	0.197	-0.403	-0.424	-0.120	-0.157	0.382
DM2	0.373	0.348	-0.439	-0.354	-0.151	-0.191	0.324
RC1	-0.106	-0.064	0.350	0.420	0.130	0.156	-0.285
RC2	-0.170	-0.190	0.638	0.642	0.140	0.190	-0.300
DP1	-0.263	-0.345	0.519	0.522	0.125	0.142	-0.166
DP2	-0.293	-0.334	0.514	0.475	0.096	0.133	-0.181

	PS2	DM1	DM2	RC1	RC2	DP1	DP2
PS2	0.833						
DM1	0.390	0.970					
DM2	0.443	0.678	1.734				
RC1	-0.275	-0.401	-0.405	1.122			
RC2	-0.272	-0.500	-0.445	0.614	1.435		
DP1	-0.168	-0.233	-0.243	0.253	0.406	1.097	
DP2	-0.154	-0.202	-0.209	0.243	0.343	0.730	1.237

APPENDIX I
Sample Covariance Data for Chapter 11: Application 9

	BDI16	BDI18	BDI19	BDI21	BDI4	BDI11	BDI12
BDI16	0.439						
BDI18	0.094	0.311					
BDI19	0.040	0.074	0.150				
BDI21	0.035	0.030	0.008	0.124			
BDI4	0.087	0.049	0.037	0.038	0.222		
BDI11	0.087	0.089	0.042	0.053	0.076	0.589	
BDI12	0.040	0.038	0.037	0.041	0.073	0.052	0.189
BDI13	0.112	0.059	0.018	0.021	0.074	0.082	0.054
BDI15	0.113	0.041	0.014	0.039	0.090	0.075	0.061
BDI17	0.193	0.086	0.031	0.043	0.126	0.145	0.077
BDI20	0.066	0.062	0.028	0.056	0.058	0.059	0.045
BDI1	0.095	0.051	0.036	0.049	0.114	0.064	0.081
BDI2	0.084	0.057	0.038	0.036	0.123	0.059	0.064
BDI3	0.131	0.061	0.042	0.045	0.128	0.095	0.076
BDI5	0.078	0.059	0.038	0.038	0.079	0.056	0.065
BDI6	0.065	0.048	0.023	0.037	0.077	0.053	0.078
BDI7	0.081	0.062	0.036	0.030	0.096	0.063	0.065
BDI8	0.130	0.085	0.031	0.019	0.120	0.117	0.045
BDI9	0.092	0.080	0.037	0.049	0.098	0.073	0.093
BDI10	0.086	0.081	0.036	0.041	0.077	0.086	0.052
BDI14	0.108	0.061	0.027	0.034	0.098	0.082	0.066

	BDI13	BDI15	BDI17	BDI20	BDI1	BDI2	BDI3
BDI13	0.365						
BDI15	0.115	0.359					
BDI17	0.117	0.148	0.480				
BDI20	0.065	0.066	0.101	0.231			
BDI1	0.083	0.107	0.122	0.063	0.261		
BDI2	0.093	0.096	0.103	0.059	0.127	0.375	
BDI3	0.125	0.132	0.146	0.059	0.129	0.175	0.468
BDI5	0.086	0.085	0.101	0.070	0.122	0.127	0.165
BDI6	0.088	0.084	0.102	0.059	0.108	0.110	0.132
BDI7	0.101	0.097	0.104	0.059	0.113	0.137	0.183
BDI8	0.150	0.139	0.158	0.082	0.116	0.151	0.234
BDI9	0.097	0.094	0.107	0.062	0.121	0.132	0.162
BDI10	0.098	0.066	0.108	0.077	0.121	0.094	0.129
BDI14	0.100	0.119	0.129	0.072	0.126	0.125	0.197

	BDI5	BDI6	BDI7	BDI8	BDI9	BDI10	BDI14
BDI5	0.269						
BDI6	0.119	0.286					
BDI7	0.140	0.097	0.283				
BDI8	0.166	0.130	0.202	0.754			
BDI9	0.137	0.101	0.133	0.145	0.276		
BDI10	0.113	0.106	0.091	0.121	0.114	0.424	
BDI14	0.152	0.104	0.155	0.256	0.146	0.109	0.654

APPENDIX J
Implied Covariance and Mean Data for Chapter 12: Application 10

Implied (for All Variables) Covariances

	ESC	ASC	GSC	MSC	SDQ2N07	SDQ2N19	SDQ2N31
ESC	0.664						
ASC	0.463	0.497					
GSC	0.373	0.352	0.612				
MSC	0.403	0.789	0.633	2.035			
SDQ2N07	0.403	0.789	0.633	2.035	3.212		
SDQ2N19	0.320	0.627	0.503	1.617	1.617	2.697	
SDQ2N31	0.418	0.818	0.657	2.110	2.110	1.676	2.348
SDQ2N43	0.293	0.574	0.461	1.481	1.481	1.177	1.535
SDQ2N10	0.664	0.463	0.373	0.403	0.403	0.320	0.418
SDQ2N22	0.542	0.378	0.305	0.329	0.329	0.262	0.341
SDQ2N34	0.404	0.282	0.227	0.245	0.245	0.195	0.254
SDQ2N46	0.556	0.388	0.313	0.337	0.337	0.268	0.350
SDQ2N04	0.463	0.497	0.352	0.789	0.789	0.627	0.818
SDQ2N16	0.620	0.666	0.471	1.056	1.056	0.839	1.095
SDQ2N28	0.666	0.715	0.506	1.135	1.135	0.902	1.177
SDQ2N40	0.564	0.605	0.428	0.960	0.960	0.763	0.996
SDQ2N01	0.373	0.352	0.612	0.633	0.633	0.503	0.657
SDQ2N13	0.412	0.388	0.675	0.699	0.699	0.555	0.725
SDQ2N25	0.355	0.334	0.582	0.602	0.602	0.478	0.624
SDQ2N37	0.315	0.297	0.516	0.534	0.534	0.424	0.554

	SDQ2N43	SDQ2N10	SDQ2N22	SDQ2N34	SDQ2N46	SDQ2N04	SDQ2N16
SDQ2N43	1.944						
SDQ2N10	0.293	1.357					
SDQ2N22	0.240	0.542	1.143				
SDQ2N34	0.179	0.404	0.330	2.857			
SDQ2N46	0.246	0.556	0.454	0.338	1.769		
SDQ2N04	0.574	0.463	0.378	0.282	0.388	1.796	
SDQ2N16	0.769	0.620	0.507	0.377	0.519	0.666	1.520
SDQ2N28	0.826	0.666	0.544	0.405	0.558	0.715	0.958
SDQ2N40	0.699	0.564	0.461	0.343	0.472	0.605	0.811
SDQ2N01	0.461	0.373	0.305	0.227	0.313	0.352	0.471
SDQ2N13	0.508	0.412	0.336	0.251	0.345	0.388	0.520
SDQ2N25	0.438	0.355	0.290	0.216	0.297	0.334	0.448
SDQ2N37	0.389	0.315	0.257	0.192	0.264	0.297	0.397

	SDQ2N28	SDQ2N40	SDQ2N01	SDQ2N13	SDQ2N25	SDQ2N37
SDQ2N28	1.853					
SDQ2N40	0.871	1.818				
SDQ2N01	0.506	0.428	1.759			
SDQ2N13	0.558	0.473	0.675	1.904		
SDQ2N25	0.481	0.407	0.582	0.642	1.569	
SDQ2N37	0.427	0.361	0.516	0.569	0.490	1.261

Implied (for All Variables) Means

ESC	ASC	GSC	MSC	SDQ2N07	SDQ2N19	SDQ2N31
0.000	0.000	0.000	0.000	4.318	4.560	4.735

SDQ2N43	SDQ2N10	SDQ2N22	SDQ2N34	SDQ2N46	SDQ2N04	SDQ2N16
5.014	4.626	5.406	3.917	5.257	4.571	4.634

SDQ2N28	SDQ2N40	SDQ2N01	SDQ2N13	SDQ2N25	SDQ2N37
4.626	5.003	4.385	4.993	5.021	4.776

Author Index

W

X

Y

Z

Subject Index